Colonialism and Landscape

Postcolonial Theory and Applications

ANDREW SLUYTER

ROWMAN & LITTLEFIELD PUBLISHERS, INC.
Lanham • Boulder • New York • Oxford

ROWMAN & LITTLEFIELD PUBLISHERS, INC.

Published in the United States of America
by Rowman & Littlefield Publishers, Inc.
4720 Boston Way, Lanham, Maryland 20706
www.rowmanlittlefield.com

12 Hid's Copse Road, Cumnor Hill, Oxford OX2 9JJ, England

British Library Cataloguing in Publication Information Available

Library of Congress Cataloging-in-Publication Data Available

ISBN 0-7425-1559-1 (cloth : alk. paper)
ISBN 0-7425-1560-5 (paper : alk. paper)

Printed in the United States of America

♾™ The paper used in this publication meets the minimum requirements of American National Standard for Information Sciences—Permanence of Paper for Printed Library Materials, ANSI/NISO Z39.48-1992.

For
Nicolaas Sluijter

11 December 1916 to 28 September 2000

Contents

Preface

I first saw the well-known Diego Rivera murals in the National Palace in Mexico City in 1988, just before visiting the Veracruz lowlands for the first time. I last saw the murals in 1999, just as I was beginning to write this book. Rivera clearly understood landscape's power. The murals cover the walls of the symbolic center of Mexican sovereign power in a sprawl of precolonial, colonial, and postcolonial landscapes. My effort is to understand the processes, both social and biophysical, involved in the colonial transformation as well as their continuing consequences for current development and conservation efforts.

The Veracruz lowlands hold particular relevance for understanding European colonization of the Americas. The region formed the beachhead for the invasion and became the Atlantic entrepôt for the colony of New Spain, bearing the first brunt of the war, the disease, and the livestock. But more than that, this case study of those lowlands provides the basis for beginning to conceptualize and test a comprehensive geographical theory of colonialism and landscape for the Americas. That task is as urgent as it is neglected. The scope and magnitude of colonial landscape transformations have ensured their continuing consequences for some of our greatest postcolonial challenges, such as achieving global social and environmental well-being. Since as a general rule inadequate theorization of process results in misformulation of policy, a theory that facilitates understanding colonial landscape transformations and their continuing consequences remains one of geography's most significant obligations.

One of the joys of writing a book is being able to elaborate on journal articles, to increase the ratio of exposition to explanation, to provide fuller supporting evidence, and to repair the damages to prose and logic that journal editors sometimes inflict. In writing this book, then, I have drawn on a series of articles published over the past decade. While none of them directly corresponds to any particular chapter, I do thank the copyright holders for permission to use previously published text and figures. More specifically, parts of chapters 1 and 7 are based on "Colonialism and Landscape in the Americas," published in the *Annals of the Association of American Geographers* in 2001. Chapter 2 incorporates sections from "Regional, Holocene Records of the Human Dimension of Global Change: Sea-Level and Land-Use Change in Prehistoric Mexico," published in *Global and Planetary Change* in 1997, "Intensive Wetland Agriculture in Mesoamerica," published in the *Annals of the Association of American Geographers* in 1994, and material written by me deriving from an article jointly published with Alfred H. Siemens: "Vestiges of Prehispanic, Sloping-Field Terraces on the Piedmont of Central Veracruz," which appeared in *Latin American Antiquity* in 1992. Chapter 3 is an elaboration of "The Ecological Origins and Consequences of Cattle Ranching in Sixteenth-Century New Spain," published in *The Geographical Review* in 1996. Chapter 4 merges "Landscape Change and Livestock in Sixteenth-Century New Spain," published in the *Conference of Latin Americanist Geographers Yearbook, 1997*, with "From Archive to Map to Pastoral Landscape," published in *Environmental History* in 1998. Part of chapter 5 elaborates on "The Making of the Myth in Postcolonial Development," published in the *Annals of the Association of American Geographers* in 1999.

I thank those colleagues who have assisted the research in various ways, including commenting on manuscripts and oral presentations: Griselda Avendaño, Elizabeth Butzer, Karl Butzer, Roger Byrne, Diane Cargill, Judy Carney, Bill Denevan, Bill Doolittle, Carlos Gay, Steve Hall, Cole Harris, Richard Hebda, Ted Killian, Greg Knapp, Dean Lambert, Peirce Lewis, Mike Meyers, Lorenzo Noyola, Francisco Pérez, Adam Rome, Alf Siemens, Paul Starrs, Billie Turner, Lucky Yapa, and Karl Zimmerer. In addition, I have learned much from many anonymous journal reviewers over the years. In doing so, I have been more fortunate than Gore Vidal, who when asked if he had learned anything from critics reputedly replied, "Are you crazy? They should be learning from me, but they're too dumb." Brenda Hadenfeldt, Renee Jardine and the rest of the folks at Rowman & Littlefield got behind the project early and never stinted advice and encouragement. None of the archival research would have been possible without the dedication of the staffs of the Archivo General de la Nación, the Archivo Notorial de Jalapa, and the archive of Benson Latin American Collection. More generally, I have been fortunate to be associated with intellectually dynamic and supportive academic departments for much of the effort leading up to the publication of this book, namely at The University of British Columbia in Vancouver and The University of Texas at Austin. Veracruzanos—from *vaqueros* to *músicos*—have made research as pleasant as it is intellectually rewarding.

Over the years, various organizations have funded the research. My thanks to the Social Sciences and Humanities Research Council of Canada, University of British Columbia, University of Texas at Austin, National Aeronautics and Space Administration, National Science Foundation, and National Geographic Society.

The final chapters have been the toughest to write, and making it through to publication has only been possible with much support. I thank the wonderful people of Penn State's Cancer Institute at the Hershey Medical Center, Centre Medical and Surgical Associates, and the Vancouver Cancer Centre. I especially thank friends old and new, Carina, and my family for helping me through such a difficult period.

Materials from *Annals of the Association of American Geographers*, vol. 84, A. Sluyter, Intensive Wetland Agriculture in Mesoamerica: Space, Time, and Form, pp. 557-84, Copyright 1994; vol. 89, A. Sluyter, The Making of the Myth in Postcolonial Development: Material-Conceptual Landscape Transformation in Sixteenth-Century Veracruz, pp. 377-401, Copyright 1999; and vol. 91, A. Sluyter, Colonialism and Landscape in the Americas: Material/Conceptual Transformations and Continuing Consequences, pp. 410-28, Copyright 2001, are used with permission from Blackwell Publishers. Materials from *Conference of Latin Americanist Geographers Yearbook, 1997*, vol. 23, A. Sluyter, Landscape Change and Livestock in Sixteenth-Century New Spain: The Archival Data Base, pp. 27-39, Copyright 1997, are used with permission from the Conference of Latin Americanist Geographers. Materials from *Environmental History*, vol. 3, A. Sluyter, From Archive to Map to Pastoral Landscape: A Spatial Perspective on the Livestock Ecology of Sixteenth-Century New Spain, pp. 508-28, Copyright 1998, are used with permission from the American Society for Environmental History and the Forest History Society. Materials from *Global and Planetary Change*, vol. 14, A. Sluyter, Regional, Holocene Records of the Human Dimension of Global Change: Sea-Level and Land-Use Change in Prehistoric Mexico, pp. 127-46, Copyright 1997, are used with permission from Elsevier Science. Materials from *Geographical Review*, vol. 86, A. Sluyter, The Ecological Origins and Consequences of Cattle Ranching in Sixteenth-Century New Spain, pp. 161-77, Copyright 1996, are used with permission from the American Geographical Society. Materials from *Latin American Antiquity*, vol. 3, A. Sluyter and A. H. Siemens, Vestiges of Prehispanic, Sloping-Field Terraces on the Piedmont of Central Veracruz, Mexico, pp. 148-60, Copyright 1992, are used with permission from the Society for American Archaeology.

—Vancouver, October 2001

1

Colonialism and Landscape

In 1519, while writing a dispatch to his sovereign a few months after landing at Chalchicueyecan, Hernando Cortés outlined a prospectus for colonization. In doing so, he described the tropical lowlands along the Gulf of Mexico with a possessive eye: "beautiful bottomlands and river banks," "very apt and agreeable for traveling through" and, prospectively, "for pasturing all kinds of livestock" (Cortés 1988, 20).[1] Within a century, the Spaniards had indeed colonized much of the Americas. The mainland beachhead at Chalchicueyecan had become the port of Veracruz, the designated destination of the Seville fleet and thus the entrepôt for the entire colony of New Spain (figure 1.1). Beyond that dramatic reconfiguration of political geography, the focus of so many repetitious monographs by historians, colonization had transformed the landscape to fulfill Cortés's prospectus. Even as early as 1580, the district governor of Veracruz could report a landscape "so fertile and full of pastures that more than 150,000 head of livestock, between the cows and the mares, ordinarily graze within little more than seven leagues [twenty-nine kilometers] all around, even without counting the innumerable sheep that descend from the highlands to over-winter" (JGI, ms. xxv-8, f. 5).[2] Yet by 1850, in the first comprehensive description of the region's vegetation, Carl Christian Sartorius reported that much of it was "dreary wilderness, overgrown with low thorny mimosas" (Sartorius 1961, 9). Somehow, over little more than three centuries, as a series of smallpox and typhus epidemics ravaged the native population and the Spaniards introduced vast herds of livestock, the "beautiful bottomlands and river banks" of Cortés seemingly became the "dreary wilderness" of Sartorius.

Those three glimpses into the past—courtesy of a conquistador at the inception of the colonial project, a bureaucrat of the established colony of New Spain, and an expatriate scientist-entrepreneur at the dawn of Mexico's postcolonial period—signpost a dramatic landscape transformation associated with European

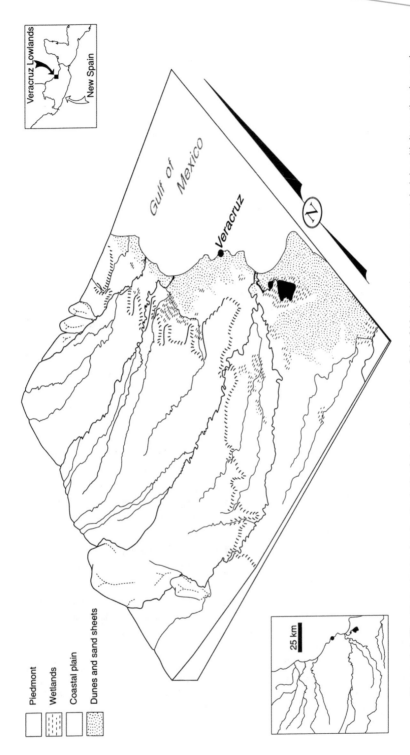

Figure 1.1. The Veracruz lowlands: the belt of dunes fronting the Gulf of Mexico, the narrow coastal plain with its wetlands, and the piedmont dissected by the ravines of the streams draining the escarpment of the Sierra Madre Oriental to the west.

colonization. Throughout the Americas, one of the major realms of European imperialism, colonization transformed landscapes on a scale and to a degree unprecedented since retreat of the continental ice sheets. The European invasion rejoined two ecosystems that had for the most part been diverging since the Pangean supercontinent fragmented some 200 million years previous. At the regional scale of analysis much remains unclear, particularly concerning the initial ecological effects and processes of the Columbian exchange (Sauer 1966; Crosby 1972; Cronon 1983; Merchant 1989). At the continental scale, however, the effects have become well known. Exotic pathogens exploded through native populations (Crosby 1972). Old World biologies and institutions filled empty niches to bursting (Crosby 1986). And capitalists commodified landscapes, accumulating space and extinguishing species (Wolf 1982).

Yet despite the magnitude and continuing consequences of that transformation, geographers have not produced a meaningful conceptual framework for understanding the relationships between colonization and landscape transformation. A comprehensive theory of colonialism and landscape that would help explain the processes involved simply does not exist, neither for the Americas generally nor for particular places like the Veracruz lowlands. That lack of disciplinary accomplishment remains just as glaring for those assessments of the literature that proceed from a direct concern with landscape as for those focused on imperialism or ecology (Duncan 1993, 1994, 1995; Smith 1994; Mathewson 1998, 1999). If even a preliminary plan for such a project existed, some progress might be apparent under the rubrics of cultural or political geography, of cultural or political ecology. But none is apparent, neither progress nor even preliminary plan.

In academic terms, the lack of anything that even approximates a comprehensive geographic theory of colonialism and landscape seems somewhat astounding at first. Landscape, after all, is a key unit of geographic analysis and its transformation through social/biophysical processes a primary phenomenon of geographic inquiry. At the same time, the establishment of the discipline has been congruent with and inseparable from European colonization, a congenital relationship that presumably should have catalyzed a thorough theorization of the relationship between colonialism and landscape. Beginning in the fifteenth century, as the landscapes of the world successively became geographic objects of European power, landscape became an object of increasingly professionalized geographic knowledge (Stoddart 1986; Livingstone 1992; Godlewska and Smith 1994; Bell et al. 1995). The explorer who textually or cartographically represented landscapes generated an increment of geographic knowledge at the same time as producing a prospectus and resource for the extension of European power through space (Cormack 1997). Similarly, the colonial bureaucrat who developed techniques to inventory and analyze landscapes refined geographic method at the same time as consolidating European surveillance and control (Butzer 1992).

Given the conjunction of knowledge and power involved in disciplinary genesis, suppression of a thorough theorization of colonialism and landscape is, in hindsight, perhaps not so astounding after all (Foucault 1970). Rather than foster theorization of processes of colonial landscape transformation, the congenital relationship between geography and colonialism seems to have stifled such a project in favor of environmentalistic and teleological justifications for imperialism (Keller 1908; Bowman 1931). In fact, as settler geographers have continued to labor under and perpetuate colonial fusions of knowledge and power even while rebelling against them, that suppression has persisted well into the postcolonial period, well beyond the waning of sovereign European control of colonies (Harris 1997, 194-95). Only relatively recently, stimulated by the blossoming of self-critical western intellectual movements such as postcolonial studies, has a comprehensive effort to theorize the relationship between colonialism and landscape even begun to seem possible.

Practical imperatives certainly demand filling of that theoretical vacuum at, what should be, the intellectual core of the discipline. The scope and magnitude of colonialism have ensured its continuing consequences for some of our greatest postcolonial challenges, such as global poverty and environmental degradation (Porter and Sheppard 1998). And since as a general rule inadequate theorization of process results in misformulation of policy, a theory that facilitates understanding colonial landscape transformations and their continuing consequences for social and environmental well-being would seem to remain one of geography's most significant obligations.

With a sometimes subtle but nonetheless powerful inertia, material landscape transformations have continued to affect postcolonial land uses that relate to, for example, food production and biodiversity. In the Valle de Mezquital, to take one well-known case, overgrazing might have so eroded soils that current agricultural options remain severely limited (Melville 1994). Just to the south, in the Basin of Mexico, drainage of the lakes that ringed the Aztec city of Tenochtitlán has had even more dire continuing consequences, not the least being near complete destruction of the highly productive *chinampa* agroecosystem (Sluyter 1994). In other cases, colonization enhanced particular resources, forest expansion upon the destruction of native agriculture being one example (Sauer 1966).

Conceptual landscape transformations (ideological, discursive, symbolic, and so on)[3] equally continue to affect postcolonial land uses. Planners now categorize regions that had dense precolonial populations, such as Valle de Mezquital, as having a naturally impoverished resource base that limits agricultural productivity. Entire categories of landscape that were agriculturally productive before colonization have become reconceived as wastelands (Sluyter 1999). Thus natives from Mexico to Bolivia long favored tropical wetlands as foci of highly productive agricultural systems and dense settlement, but westerners now think of the same environments as nasty tropical swamps that need to be claimed (or rather strangely, *re*claimed, as if having been lost) through

drainage projects (Denevan 1992a; Siemens 1998). Such conceptual transformations have persisted despite the vast reduction of European sovereign power in
the nineteenth century (Blaut 1993). Far from being an academic issue, of no
more than historic or moralistic interest, that persistent colonizer's model of the
world continues to diminish our ability to address effectively the global challenges we face in the postcolonial present. The assumption that the West is advanced and the non-West backward invariably leads to a monolithic postcolonial
solution to global poverty and environmental degradation—namely, continued
diffusion of institutional, technological, and intellectual innovations from the so-
called developed West to the so-called developing or underdeveloped non-West
(Yapa 1996). Arguably, that deductive logic perpetuates the very processes that
have precipitated global poverty and environmental degradation (Sachs 1992;
Peet and Watts 1993). At the same time, westernization destroys a plurality of
dynamic alternatives to orthodox development, alternatives that are highly productive and might well be sustainable because they are based on intimate
knowledge of the changing, complex realities of particular places (Clay 1988;
Browder 1989; Gliessman 1990; Netting 1993; Jackson 1994).

The lack of even a preliminary outline for a comprehensive theory relating
landscape transformation to colonization, despite those academic and practical
imperatives, dictates that what follows must constitute but a rough prototype for
such a theory—a beginning. In that spirit, the following first seeks some basic
perspective on the scope appropriate to such a theory by outlining how the goals
of scholarship on colonial landscape transformation have changed in relation to
social and environmental context. That historical sketch focuses on the Americas in order to maintain rigor by staying close to places and literatures most familiar to me. It focuses on the development and conservation literature in order
to maintain connection with the practical imperative of achieving so-
cial/environmental well-being. And it therefore focuses on the non-urban landscapes such literature has tended to emphasize in geography, not necessarily so
but as a function of intellectual and institutional genealogy (Butzer 1989). With
the project's scope thus specified and historically contextualized, the subsequent
analysis compares and contrasts prior and existing conceptualizations of colonialism and landscape. Each such theoretical framework has emphasized particular
elements and relationships at the expense of others, and they thus jointly yield
insights into what a more comprehensive framework must include. That analysis
then provides the basis for elaborating a comprehensive geographic theory that
relates colonization to landscape in the Americas, or at least a preliminary plan
for working toward such a theory. In order to test and elaborate that conceptual
framework, subsequent chapters apply it to the Veracruz lowlands. The conclud-
ing chapter returns more directly to broader considerations in the effort to develop a comprehensive geographical theory of colonialism and landscape in
relation to conservation and development applications.

Historical Sketch of Changing Goals

With the vast reduction of European sovereign power in the Americas in the nineteenth century, mainstream geographers studied the process of colonization as an environmentally determined teleological progression, as one stage in a sequence leading to naturally dominant, western landscapes (Keller 1908; Bowman 1931; Godlewska and Smith 1994). *The Western Invasions of the Pacific and Its Continents, a Study of Moving Frontiers and Changing Landscapes* provides a prominent illustration of the mature version of that genre by one of its leading scholars (Price 1963). In that monograph and elsewhere, Sir A. Grenfell Price naturalized colonial landscapes with the goal of justifying and perpetuating associated power relationships (Powell 1982). For such geographers, the benefits of colonization far outweighed the costs, and the greatest benefits of all clearly accrued to the colonized, with the colonizers bearing the burden of westernizing the world. An ethnocentric axiom underpins such complicity with dominant social structures, clear enough in hindsight: colonization westernized non-European peoples and their landscapes, thereby improving them—a bias encapsulated by the phrase "West is best." From that axiom, deductive logic invariably leads to the conclusion that continued westernization will further improve former colonies, even if implemented by politically independent settler colonists or westernized natives rather than through continued European sovereignty. The effective result, and often the explicit goal, has been to perpetuate colonial power relations into the postcolonial period, therefore termed (post)colonial by some (Gregory 1994, 168-95; Wolfe 1997; King 1999).

Those who criticized such teleological study of colonization-as-natural-progression remained on the intellectual periphery. A romanticist critique, of course, has long paired disapproval of everything western with approval of everything else, particularly of an idealized precolonial landscape (Sale 1990). Yet that romanticist, anti-modern belief in a precolonial unspoiled wilderness is as Eurocentric as the complementary pro-modern belief in unexploited resources (Willems-Braun 1997). Both beliefs draw on and reaffirm the western myth of emptiness, termed the pristine myth in relation to the Americas, that erroneously characterizes precolonial landscapes as having lacked dense populations and productive land uses (Denevan 1992a; Blaut 1993). In contrast, Carl Sauer early and persistently attempted to demonstrate just how profoundly native peoples had modified the precolonial landscapes of the Americas and that westernization itself had caused any so-called backwardness. The Eurocentricism of such ostensibly objective categories as "underprivileged" and "backward"—"think of the gall of these almost official designations"—clearly irked him (Sauer 1956, 1133). Yet that early and much needed "corrective to our romantic self-approval as to the process of European colonization" went largely unheeded (Sauer 1938a, 495; also Sauer 1938b). As an advisor to the Rockefeller Foundation during the 1940s, Sauer argued for the importance of respecting local ecological knowledge, yet such international development organizations and host governments nonetheless attempted to industrialize agricultural practice and homogenize crop biodiversity (Jennings 1988, 50-56).

The mainstream began to become more critical of westernization only as incontrovertible demonstrations of the global *Limits to Growth* (Meadows et al. 1972) undermined the long-standing belief that environmental constraints would fade away as development progressed towards a western telos, whether defined according to ideologies complicit with or critical of capitalism (Spengler 1961; Rosenberg 1982; Lowenthal 1990; Porter and Sheppard 1998). As evidence has mounted of the negative social/environmental consequences of westernization, due to its seemingly inescapable contradictions, several generations of geographers and allied scholars have built a case to demonstrate that the non-West was not and is not inferior to the West. One major goal of that effort has been to test the hypothesis that the precolonial landscapes of the Americas were densely populated, intensively cultivated, and profoundly modified rather than pristine wilderness/untrammeled resources and thereby to infer the productivity and sustainability of native land uses (Denevan 1992a; McCann 1999a, 1999b). A complementary goal has been to understand the dynamism, sophistication, and productivity of the ecologies, typically but not exclusively agroecologies, of living natives (Wilken 1987; Berkes 1999). "Native," in this context, does not so much designate any particular ethnicity as an intimate familiarity with a system of production and consumption rooted in the dynamic realities of a particular place—a folk ecology or vernacular ecology, then, that people create over many generations of local tenure or come to share in by learning from those with such tenure (Hecht and Cockburn 1989; Jackson 1994; Atran et al. 1999). Such research on both past and present landscapes has stimulated alternatives to western development models, and consequently a third goal has been to redeploy, perpetuate, and test native ecologies (Smith 1987; Browder 1989; Warren et al. 1995). The same scholars have often been involved in all three efforts (perhaps least problematically termed historical ecology, ethnoecology, and applied ecology), many influenced by Sauer's insight that westernization precipitates the very social/environmental problems that its agents claim to be solving.

Yet despite those efforts steadily advancing understanding of native landscapes and ecologies, both historical and contemporary, the overall goal of downgrading the diffusion of western technologies, measures of success, and institutions to but one option among many has been no more than minimally achieved. What some term traditional ecological knowledge (TEK) has indeed achieved acceptance and even inclusion in such key documents as the *Rio Declaration* and *Agenda 21* (Carruthers 1997, 260-62). Yet for the mainstream, nonwestern knowledges remain in the realm of so-called ethnoscience, subsumed by rather than equal to the putatively transcultural and therefore objective real science of the West (Latour 1993). As the "traditional" that leads the acronym suggests, TEK projects view the West as dynamic and advanced, the non-West as static and traditional, and typically co-opt specific non-western knowledges and

practices (often related to plants), decontextualize them, eliminate their dynamism, and negotiate the terms of their commodification (Sachs 1992; Redclift
and Benton 1994; Escobar 1995). So while the institutional changes seem re-
markably radical relative to just a generation ago, western goals and ways of
achieving them remain dominant over native ones—although arguably at a more
basic, and therefore more subtle, epistemological level.

Better understanding of the reasons for that continued dominance has
emerged only relatively recently, together with self-critical western intellectual
movements that have emphasized the importance of culture, demonstrated the
indivisibility of knowledge/power, decoded (post)colonial scientific and other
discourses, and thereby revealed deeply taken-for-granted epistemological assumptions (Said 1979, 1993; Spivak 1988; Klor de Alva 1995; Wolfe 1997;
King 1999). Clearly, in part, westernization continues to dominate because diffusion remains materially profitable for the diffusors—for westerners (Peet and
Watts 1993). Yet, just as significantly, the western myth of emptiness validates
that very economic profitability and its political and legal corollaries by privileging diffusion from the West into the supposed vacuum of the non-West. That
key element of what Blaut (1993) has termed the colonizer's model of the world
emerged as the colonial redistribution of global resources, labor, and capital
became naturalized and justified through a concomitant conceptual redistribution of categories. The West became categorized as advanced and dynamic in
contrast to a backward and static non-West, Europe thus becoming the source of
everything good and non-Europe becoming empty, pristine, puerile (Said 1979;
Wolf 1982; Adas 1989). The myth of emptiness thus became a foundational
categorization in the definition of the West as distinct from and superior to the
non-West, an opposition intrinsic to the existence of the West *qua* West. The
economics, politics, and culture of westernization became mutually reinforcing.
And myths of emptiness, such as the pristine myth, became so indurated as to
resist erosion even by the accumulation of much contrary evidence (Turner and
Butzer 1992; Blaut 1993; Perry 1996). The foundational myths of other cultures
display similar persistence, of course, the critical difference being the global
extent over which the West's mythology has come to have such an enormous
impact (Latour 1993).

That global significance, intractability, and insights derived from postcolonial studies, have combined to stimulate research on the colonial landscape
transformations through which the categories that constitute myths of emptiness
have emerged and persisted, categories such as wilderness and forest primeval
(Sluyter 1999). The methods of textual analysis used in the field of postcolonial
studies to explicate the emergence of other Eurocentric categories such as the
Orient would seem to apply equally to understanding the emergence of landscape categories (Said 1979). Moreover, commonalties between the geographic
effort and postcolonial studies would seem to facilitate such methodological
borrowing. Both are critical of Eurocentricism and rampant westernization. Both
are entangled but far from synonymous with ongoing critiques of capitalism

from economic, ecological, and ideological angles (O'Connor 1994; Peet and Watts 1993; Wolfe 1997). And both have gained credence as the negative social/environmental consequences of westernization have mounted. Nonetheless, transfers of method remain far from straightforward because postcolonial studies has tended to ignore material processes and landscapes while ecological geographers, even those explicitly concerned with culture and despite some notable exceptions, have tended to emphasize material aspects of landscape (Sauer 1966; Hecht and Cockburn 1989; Butzer 1989). While ignoring material process might be appropriate in literary criticism, such ethereal analysis certainly falls flat when ingenuously transferred to the analysis of landscape transformations involving processes as clearly biophysical as growing food and clearing forests, no matter how indubitably they also involve social processes, including conceptual ones (Sluyter 1997a). Nonetheless, the work of cultural geographers provides much direction for adapting textual analysis to bricks and mortar through demonstrating how landscape patterns are both material and conceptual, constitute both physical infrastructure and symbolic communication, and simultaneously result from and influence transformative processes such as human labor and categorization (Duncan 1990; Cosgrove 1993; Mitchell 1996; King 1999). While the focus of such human geography has been on thoroughly architectonic landscapes that de-emphasize biophysical processes, the theoretical framework nonetheless provides a basis for studying linked material and conceptual landscape transformations that involve social/biophysical processes as non-urban as terracing mountain slopes and herding livestock. The landscape ecology framework that has emerged among biological ecologists, in which landscape patterning both results from so-called disturbances and mediates further transformations, somewhat parallels cultural landscape theory but does not encompass conceptual processes (Zimmerer 1994; Pickett and Cadenasso 1995).

Thus sketching out the changing goals of pertinent research over the last century provides some perspective on the present intellectual juncture, its relationship to social and environmental context, and thus the appropriate scope and goals of a comprehensive geographic theory of colonialism and landscape. Clearly it must address colonial landscape transformations as seminal to current social/environmental challenges rather than as esoteric history. It must treat material/conceptual transformation as a unified process to understand how landscape acts as a "visual vehicle of subtle and gradual inculcation . . . to make what is patently cultural appear as if it were natural" (Duncan 1990, 19). And it must encompass the social/biophysical processes, particularly those involved in human-vegetation interactions, that seem to be so critical to the material-conceptual feedbacks that naturalize and obscure non-urban landscape transformations. For New England, for example, Cronon (1983) has suggested that human-vegetation interactions played a key role in the material/conceptual transformation of that landscape, with recategorization as forest primeval stimulated by native depopulation, cessation of the regular burning of forests by natives, and consequent vegetation succession to later successional species and a denser, darker forest that appeared to be primordial to Euro-Americans.

A theoretical framework that might encompass such goals remains far less clear than the goals themselves. I have previously suggested that a slight modification of what Hulme (1992) calls the colonial triangle might provide an appropriate conceptualization of the relationship between colonialism and landscape (Sluyter 1999). On the basis of research on the colonial Caribbean, Hulme observed that the essence of the colonization process consists of a three-way, or triangular, relationship among three elements: European, native, and land. He did not elaborate on, systematically apply, test, or even sketch out that colonial triangle, but it does in fact seem to encompass the three elements essential to any colonial transformation of landscape. With slight modification, namely the replacement of Hulme's land element with landscape, the colonial triangle might provide a basis for conceptualizing a comprehensive geographic theory of colonial landscape transformation (figure 1.2). Land is certainly an appropriate and adequate category to signify the environment that natives and Europeans struggle over: the resources such as soil, vegetation, animals, minerals, and water. Yet more than simply control over environment, the struggle revolves around control over space, over territories—over landscapes. In some cases that struggle is for control over a contiguous area of resources, as in the agricultural colony of New England. In other cases that struggle is for control over commercial nodes and transport corridors, as with the Hudson's Bay Company, whose objective was to extract a dispersed resource, furs, through trading posts, waterways, and portages. And in still other cases that struggle is for control over resource nodes and labor distribution, as on Hispaniola, where the objective was to extract a nucleated resource, gold, by congregating natives at placers. At the same time as being an object of control, however, space is a medium through which the struggle for control takes place, the spatial strategies of domination and resistance that ultimately resulted in a landscape of Indian reservations in the United States

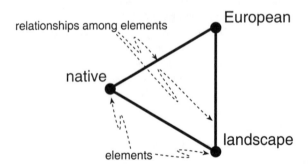

Figure 1.2. Modified colonial triangle proposed as encompassing the essential elements and relationships involved in colonial landscape transformation (Sluyter 1999).

being one relevant example (Hannah 1993). The redefinition of Hulme's land element as landscape thus is doubly essential, to indicate both conflict over space and conflict through space.

Analysis of Prior and Existing Conceptualizations

That modified colonial triangle provides a preliminary framework that permits consistent comparison among conceptualizations of colonialism and landscape—some actively held, some now largely considered passé. Each such theoretical framework emphasizes particular elements and relationships at the expense of others, thus revealing each other's strengths and weaknesses. At the same time, they jointly yield insights into what a comprehensive framework must include and thereby test how robust the colonial triangle actually might be. The goal is theory rather than history; in order to achieve the breadth and balance necessary to formulate comprehensive theory, the imperative throughout is to select across the range of conceptualizations and to analyze rather than to provide a descriptive literature review. Moreover, the focus on landscape, on non-urban contexts, and on the Americas continues to dominate. The somewhat chronological order of analysis does not necessarily imply continuous progress in understanding or that new conceptualizations completely replace previous ones. Differing emphases provide different insights or lessons, and although ideally the overall tendency of scholarship should be cumulative, some understandings become obscured as others are gained or, in many cases, regained but disguised by new jargon (Sluyter 1997a; Turner 1997).

Environmental Determinism

As academic geography became established a century ago, the analytic framework consisted of classifying colonialism according to economic criteria and correlating the resulting categories with environmental categories. The most basic studies correlated the farm colony, or settler colonization, with temperate latitudes and the plantation colony with tropical latitudes (Keller 1908). Attempts at greater sophistication introduced more categories: colonies of permanent settlement, or *colonies de peuplement* or *d'enracinement*; economic colonization, or *colonies d'exploitation* or *d'encadrement*; and strategic colonies, or *colonies de position* (Church 1951, 26-27). Presumed natural variation in resources and, particularly, in climate determined variation among the political-economies of colonizers, differentiated the overall teleological processes of westernization, and thus created variation among the morphologies of colonial landscapes.

The colonial triangle encompasses that conceptualization (figure 1.3). Environmental determinism clearly dominated such putative explanations but went hand-in-hand with a racism that included natives in the environment. Settler colonization characterized the Americas because "the whites encountered in those lands large areas which possessed suitable climates for their settlements— weak, divided, and, in most regions, sparsely settled native peoples, and adequate natural resources for future development" (Price 1963, 62). Sojourner colonization, in contrast, occurred when "climatic conditions in lands such as Burma, the immense weight of vast indigenous populations as in Japan, or a combination of both factors as in India and Indonesia, kept the white exotic, and still more his wife and children, as visitors rather than as the settlers which they became in temperate and sparsely populated lands" (Price 1963, 105). By lumping the native and landscape elements under the label of environment, the framework made native peoples into non-humans. It emphasized the environment as determinative of human-environment interactions. And it subordinated the reciprocal processes through which Europeans modified environment (natives and landscapes) to environmental determination, as the relative line-weights of the arrows in the figure indicate.

The resulting generalizations were long on justifying colonialism as a natural condition and short on explaining colonization as a process of conflict between natives and Europeans over and through landscape. Settler colonization of temperate lands, whether in the mid latitudes or at elevation in the tropics, became a natural process, unquestionably proper and progressive (Bowman 1931). The establishment of plantations in the tropics was a natural consequence of their climate just as the dispossession and suffering of natives was a natural consequence of their being native, a categorical condition rather than a relationship. Since natives were lumped with landscape under the rubric of environment, by definition the precolonial landscape had to be pristine, natural—a wilderness empty of human modification.

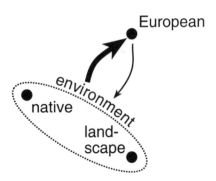

Figure 1.3. Conceptual structure that assumes environment is determinative. In this and subsequent figures, relative line-weights of arrows indicate relative conceptual importance given to processes.

Cultural Determinism

The overt racism that underpinned that environmentalistic framework has not endured as broadly as has the faith in progress through westernization and the associated attempt to correlate categories of colonization with categories of landscape morphology. As part of the backlash against environmental determinism, human geographers turned towards analysis that focused on the cultures of the European colonizers rather than on the environments of the colonies. Subordination of the study of social/biophysical processes to environmental determinism metamorphosed into subordination to cultural determinism (Duncan 1980). Turner's frontier thesis and Hartz's simplification thesis, in particular, influenced that new way of discerning general patterns in types of colonization and resulting landscape morphologies (Meinig 1993, 258-64; Harris 1997, 254-56). Turner emphasized the transformation of European social structure through adaptation to economic conditions radically different from those of Europe. In the case of the United States, the relatively low cost of land and high cost of labor along the frontier proved inimical to feudal relations and transformed colonial society (exclusive of natives) into a democracy of independent farmers. Hartz also emphasized the transformation of European social structure, but due to selective migration of social elements rather than due to adaptation to new conditions. Because of the conditions in Spain and England during colonization and the social groups that in each case dominated the process, a feudal fragment dominated New Spain and a liberal bourgeois one New England. The Turnerian and Hartzian models being as complimentary as their biological analogs, namely adaptation and the founder effect, geographers employed varying admixtures of the two to conceptualize the relationship between colonialism and landscape.

No matter the theoretical basis for the rejection of environmental determinism, however—whether Turnerian, Hartzian, or both—categorical and teleological thinking persisted. The focus on the internal dynamics of European cultures continued to lump natives and landscape together under the category of environment just as surely as had environmental determinism. But that environment now became a stage for the unfolding drama of the emergence of colonial and national cultures rather than a determining variable. Landscape morphologies became the imprints of a process of social transformation intrinsic to categories of European culture—French, English, and Spanish destinies made manifest. Thus the attenuated networks characteristic of the French and English so-called Boreal Riverine Empires eventually transformed into Settler Empires as the frontier of cheap land and dear labor moved westward and left behind a progression of social structures and their landscape corollaries (Meinig 1969). In contrast, the general landscape morphology of Spain's Continental Empire supposedly emerged in the wake of a moving political frontier that left behind contiguous economic, settlement, and transportation systems—presumed to be similar in process and pattern to the Iberian Reconquista (Meinig 1969). Turnerian social adaptation dominated explanations applied north of the Rio Grande and

Hartzian social simplification to the south, but in both cases the status of independent variable was transferred from the lumped native and landscape elements to the European element. Environmentalism had become culturism.

The colonial triangle again encompasses that theoretical framework (figure 1.4). The conceptual configuration remains unchanged from environmental determinism except that the determinative arrow is reversed—in hindsight, really more of a volte-face than a metamorphosis. By emphasizing the internal dynamics of European culture as the transformative force, the lack of epistemological separation between the native and landscape elements continued. In what became the United States, European society supposedly progressed and "in the process" transformed the environment, including natives and landscapes. The reciprocal processes through which natives and landscapes transformed Europeans became conceptually subordinate. For example, the abundant land of the frontier merely released the democratic social structure intrinsic to human nature that until then had been suppressed by feudalism. The resulting progression of landscape morphologies left in the wake of the frontier became identifiably more western with time as well as with decreasing distance from Europe: from the "traditional system" of "palisaded villages," "seasonal camps," and "tribal societies" to eventual integration with the "modern world system" of "central place infilling," "complete occupance," and "civic leadership" (Meinig 1986, 258-66; 1993, 262-63). Thus European landscapes were "endogenic," and U.S. landscapes were "exogenic" (Vance 1970). Despite such countries as Mexico, Brazil, and Argentina all having had colonial frontiers, the same logic did not apply to Latin America—apparently. Instead, the Hartzian model justified preconceptions of landscapes south of the Río Bravo del Norte as being the result of a static, feudal implant rather than of a progressive adaptation.

Characteristic of the congenital relationship between geography and colonialism, such a conceptualization integrates with the pristine myth just as effortlessly as does environmental determinism. No part of the political spectrum has held a monopoly on such Eurocentrism and modernist teleology. If some could argue that through Westernization "traditional societies" would "take off" and eventually "catch up" to the West's "high mass consumption," then others could

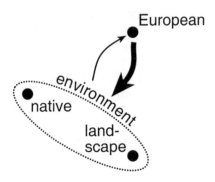

Figure 1.4. Conceptual structure that assumes European culture is determinative.

argue for a similar progression through "primitive accumulation" and "advanced capitalism," albeit with a somewhat different telos in mind (Denoon 1983; Adas 1989, 411-16). In both cases the transformation of natives and landscapes remains viewed as determined by non-natives—assumed to arrive in North America, for example, with "capitalism in their bones" (Baran 1973, 273). In both cases the eighteenth-century Linnaean typology of *Homo sapiens* remains evident, European superiority naturalized, codified, and axiomatic: European—fair, sanguine, and governed by consciously formulated laws that rise above brute nature; Native American—copper-colored, choleric, and regulated by mere customs and myths.[4] Noble savages thus blend into a primordial wilderness that, in the case of the United States, formed a blank page for an egalitarian nation of rugged individualists to inscribe a homegrown progression of landscape morphologies, taking them through the stages of social evolution so rapidly as to be exceptional. In going from pristine nature to civilization in two centuries flat, that "Midas culture" (Sluyter 1999, 381) became not only a part of the West but, many argue, the best of the West. In that view the precolonial native landscape had barely existed—a pristine, static stage that only became dynamic and progressive with European colonization. Particular categories of landscape morphologies simply correlated with their respective categories of colonizers—English, Spanish, bourgeois, feudal, and so on—the social/biophysical processes involved seemingly not of interest (Pollock 1980).

Ethnohistoricism

Only with the emergence of ethnohistory does analysis of natives as agents in the colonization process even begin to become possible. The proximate origin of such ethnohistorical approaches in the United States dates to the Great Depression and New Deal. In order to allow the emerging welfare state to assimilate natives into its social engineering model, the Social Science Research Council of the 1930s began to promote so-called acculturation studies that combined oral history and archival research (Meyer and Klein 1998, 184-85).

That research, through integrating diverse types of field and archival data, began to dispel the representation of the precolonial Americas as a primordial wilderness, sparsely inhabited and little altered by native peoples. While George Catlin, who himself had helped to forge the image of the noble savage in the nineteenth century, conjectured sixteen million as the contact-period population of North America, that figure had come to seem unreasonably high to most scholars of the first half of the twentieth century—high even for North, Middle, and South America combined (Catlin 1973, 1:6). Then, with a controversially high estimate of half a million for northwestern Mexico alone, Carl Sauer initiated a continuing tradition of scholarship that now places the late-precolonial hemispheric population at some fifty million (Sauer 1935; Denevan 1992b). Neither a Lost Tribe of Israel nor Nabataens had built the pyramids among the savages of the American wilderness, as had seemed axiomatic for so long. The

archival records, the architectural vestiges, the less discernible agricultural vestiges, and the vegetation itself have all increasingly confirmed that the landscapes of the Americas before Europe were not pristine at all. They had long
been densely inhabited and profoundly modified by native peoples (Denevan
1992a).

When natives escalated their claims for access to resources after World War
II, demand for ethnohistorical research greatly increased, but for studies related
to land tenure and ethnogenesis rather than acculturation. The founding of the
American Society for Ethnohistory and its journal *Ethnohistory* in the early
1950s in combination with the civil rights movements of the 1960s consolidated
that trend. The multidisciplinary field of ethnohistory became institutionalized in
the United States and more broadly throughout the Americas. The essential applied rationale became to reconstruct ethnogenesis, population, settlement and
resource-use patterns, cosmologies, treaty boundaries, and other factors that bear
on claims to territory, resources, and knowledge (Aschmann 1974; Hecht and
Cockburn 1989; Escobar 1998; Berkes 1999). The essential academic rationale
became to recover the histories of native peoples and thereby redefine them as
active agents (Leon-Portilla 1959; Gibson 1964; Nash 1974).

Some recent (and prominent) analyses of colonialism and landscape, however, though clearly influenced by ethnohistory, only hint at native agency, even
regarding social let alone biophysical processes. Thus while Meinig (1986, 65-
76) models landscape morphologies that resulted from different types of interactions between natives and Europeans, he simply correlates each type of interaction with a particular category of Europeans: English, French, or Iberian. So-
called Expulsion, as in early Virginia, resulted in a frontier that excluded natives
from European territory. Articulation, exemplified by New France, resulted in a
permeable frontier and benign interaction between natives and Europeans at
trading centers. Stratification, as in New Spain, resulted in relatively thorough
"racial and cultural mixture and fusion" (Meinig 1986, 72). That framework
applies equally to studies of conceptual landscape transformation. Bowden
(1992), for example, in the most comprehensive study of the emergence of the
pristine myth in the United States, greatly emphasizes the imposition of ideology
on landscape and natives by European and Euro-American elites.

In terms of the colonial triangle, such conceptualizations no longer blend
natives and landscape together into a necessarily pristine environment (figure
1.5). Natives and landscape become distinct elements related through transformative processes. Yet environmental determinism resurfaces, selectively applied
to the relationship between natives and landscape. In this framework, the landscape's biophysical characteristics determine native social structures; the reciprocal processes through which natives modify vegetation and hydrology are
subordinate and environmentally determined. Moreover, by continuing to emphasize the transformation of European cultures through their own internal dynamics released by the colonization process, Europeans continue to be credited
with determining the transformation of both natives and landscapes. The recip-

rocal processes through which the native and landscape elements transform the European element remain subordinate. The ultimate determinant remains the intrinsic nature of the colonizer. Under ethnohistoricism, the precolonial landscape thus remains largely pristine, a wild nature that determined the characteristics of natives and only became ordered when Europeans arrived to tame it. Ethnohistory's very prefix signals a lesser type of history, merely a minor subfield and peripheral to real history, to (Euro)history.

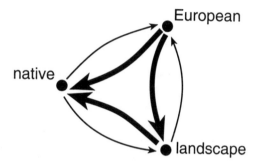

Figure 1.5. Conceptual structure that achieves epistemological separation of native and landscape elements, even while assuming native agency is inconsequential relative to European agency, that environment is determinative along the native-landscape side of the triangle, and therefore that the result of colonization is largely immanent to Europeans.

Postcolonialism

Harris, influenced by postcolonial studies, has recently reconceptualized the relationship between colonization and landscape and thereby substantially altered the ethnohistoricist framework (Harris 1991, 1997). Even in a lengthy collection of linked essays on *The Resettlement of British Columbia*, however, he fails to make his conceptual framework explicit, self-critically consider the elements and relationships involved, or systematically apply and test their rigor. Yet his implicit framework structures an empirical effort that does uncover much evidence for potentially equal, reciprocal interactions among the native, landscape, and European elements of the colonial triangle—substantially increasing the agency typically attributed to native peoples in the colonization process as well as the "agency" through which landscape patterns mediate the processes that transform those patterns.

To illustrate, Harris begins with smallpox. Similarly to elsewhere in the Americas, epidemic disease caused a native depopulation of some ninety percent in colonial British Columbia (BC). Being basic to any understanding, he therefore reconstructs precolonial population, native depopulation and desettlement, and European resettlement (Harris 1994, 1997). The epidemics, at their most essential, consisted of a relationship between European and native elements in which the former introduced smallpox and other exotic pathogens and the latter died due to a lack of antibodies—an inexorable and unidirectional impact by Europeans on natives.

But he soon begins to elaborate on that basic understanding, on that overly simplistic focus on the biophysical, on the epidemiological and the demographic. Harris draws in relationships with landscape and social processes, and therefore with social responsibilities. At higher resolutions, both temporal and spatial, the process of native desettlement and European resettlement begins to appear more complex and interactive among all three elements. And it begins to appear to involve both material and conceptual processes.

The Fraser Canyon, where the Fraser River slices through the mountains some hundred kilometers up country from its delta near Vancouver, has been the focus of much of Harris's recent research and provides the evidence for more complex interactions among natives, Europeans, and landscape (Harris 1997, 103-36). When Simon Fraser descended the river on his way to the Pacific in 1808, thousands of natives lived in a series of towns along the canyon, one of the most densely settled regions of precolonial BC. Introduced diseases devastated the native population in repeated epidemics. With the Cariboo Gold Rush of 1858, Europeans (and Euro-Americans) swarmed up the canyon to establish placer operations on bars and terraces where the surviving native population remained settled. As the firepower of the miners overwhelmed the natives, colonial bureaucrats began to regulate the gold rush; and processes other than reciprocal physical violence became dominant. Through processes such as the application of property law, Europeans rapidly reconceptualized native spaces into parcels of private property, made material on the landscape through surveying and fencing. That dramatic material/conceptual transformation, as represented on paper by cadastral maps and as lived by people in a landscape of Trespassers Shot signs, impacted native practices by limiting daily and seasonal access to a spatially and temporally dispersed suite of resources. The establishment of Indian Reservations epitomized that transformation, making possible the control of natives by Europeans through a process of spatial congregation, fixation, and enumeration. The transcripts of the inquiries of the Royal Commission on Indian Affairs reveal native conceptual resistance to such control. Natives met imposition of exotic spatial categories such as acres with claims, real or feigned, of not understanding such rigid areal measures, appropriate as fixed categories in the machinery of state control but not for living with the fluid ecology of the canyon. When bureaucrats irrationally "enjoined Natives 'to help themselves and obey the instructions of the Indian agent,' self-reliance and submission apparently going hand in hand" (Harris 1997, 132), natives used irony to try to shift and expand the terms of reference. Thus "Patrick," a native of Boston Bar, seeing that rational argument had no chance given the myths that Europeans labored under, tried hyperbole to shock the commissioners out of their self-congratulatory categories.

> It is as though Christ himself has come, when the Duke of Connaught sent you here to investigate our conditions. . . . I shall now endeavour to speak to you, just as if I were speaking to God Almighty. So that now, my conditions will be improved, and I will never have any cause to be sorry in the future (quoted in Harris 1997, 133).

Irony invariably being wasted on bureaucrats, natives would have much more cause for regret.

The conceptual framework implicit in Harris's analysis more closely conforms to a comprehensive and balanced colonial triangle than do environmental determinism, cultural determinism, or ethnohistoricism (figure 1.6).[5] He reveals potentially equal, reciprocal, material/conceptual processes interrelating all three elements. Materially, Europeans introduced disease; natives died and desettled the landscape; Europeans resettled and built fences. Conceptually, Europeans divided the landscape into enumerated parcels of private property plotted on cadastral maps, and natives employed irony to struggle against the cartographic terms of reference that the material fences and Trespassers Shot signs validated.

Harris (1997, xiv-xv) himself notes a methodological limitation to his analysis. While in conceptual terms natives might have had potentially equal, reciprocal relations with Europeans, much of that native agency goes unrecorded in the archives. That archival lacuna exists for two main reasons. First, such agency was by definition subversive and therefore consisted of surreptitious practices, potentially recorded only when apprehended. Second, the terms of reference of such agency might be so foreign to Europeans as to escape recognition as being subversive—such as irony being mistaken for ingratiating flattery—and therefore not be recorded or, if recorded, perhaps not subsequently recognized as subversive by western or westernized scholars. "Can the Subaltern

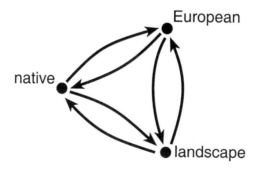

Figure 1.6. Conceptual structure that assumes reciprocal and potentially equal interactions among all three elements.

Speak?" from between the lines of colonial documents has therefore been a persistent epistemological question in postcolonial studies (Spivak 1988; Mallon 1994). The most daunting answer has been that, indeed, the "subaltern cannot speak"—at least not very much (Spivak 1988, 308). Limiting analysis to colonial documents certainly exacerbates that issue. Recovering precolonial categories and practices clearly demands study of relict landscape morphologies and artifacts in addition to documents, the recent discovery of precolonial agricultural fields in BC being a prime example of that necessity and one that has profound implications for understanding of precolonial land use in that region (Deur 1997). And such methods, in conjunction with study of archival materials and oral history, are equally applicable and necessary to the recovery of colonial, particularly native colonial, categories and practices.

That methodological issue raises a deeper epistemological one, however, in that except at broad scales of analysis and in general terms, Harris tends to minimize the biophysical aspects of material/conceptual processes and the agency of landscape. He certainly recognizes that native depopulation due to epidemics, beginning with a devastating smallpox epidemic around 1782, resulted in a landscape that seemed to be untrammeled wilderness to Europeans by the time resettlement began in earnest in the late nineteenth century. The landscape itself thus visually validated the regional expression of the myth of emptiness. Representations of precolonial natives and their landscapes emerged out of late nineteenth-century ethnographies based on native informants who had already undergone a dramatic transformation due to a devastating series of epidemics and who were anything but representative of eighteenth-century natives (Harris 1997, 28-29). The ethnographers' eldest informants related childhoods that postdated major depopulation, and that conveyed the impression that native population had always been low. Those more directly concerned with landscape than ethnographers, such as the geologist George Dawson (Willems-Braun 1997), recorded a moribund landscape. Its vestigial patterns of settlement and resource use could have been no more than a shadow of the past and directly influenced representations of native villages as isolated patches in a matrix of pristine resources. That process entailed much more than a simplistic, unilateral imposition of exotic categories on the landscape, predetermined by the intrinsic nature of Europeans (Willems-Braun 1997, 16-18). It was instead part of an ongoing, complex, reciprocal interaction among natives, Europeans, and landscape.

Despite Harris's recognition of the ways in which landscape reciprocally impacted concepts, categories, and habits of thought through social/biophysical processes at the provincial scale of analysis, at the scale of the Fraser Canyon, such reciprocity disappears except for hints, and he lapses into the ethnohistoricist framework. The miners who came in 1858 used high-pressure jets of water to blast the soil, the so-called overburden, from the terraces. That hydraulicing left behind wasted land, obliterating much of the native cultural landscape and perhaps visually validating its reconceptualization as a sparsely populated wilderness and its redistribution as private property. Whether such a material-conceptual feedback process operated in the canyon and ultimately helped to relegate natives to a few small reservations remains an issue for further empirical research—but clearly research that includes biophysical aspects, in this case geomorphologic aspects, of material/conceptual processes.

Toward a Comprehensive Geographic Theory

Each theoretical framework has emphasized particular elements and relationships at the expense of others. They thus jointly yield insight into what a more comprehensive geographic theory of colonialism and landscape must include, particularly in terms of conceptual structure and scale of analysis.

Conceptual Structure

Comparing and contrasting the two hyper-deterministic frameworks reiterates a basic lesson: defining a conceptual structure by naming and distinguishing among elements is an epistemological necessity rather than an ontological assertion that the elements can somehow exist independently of their relations to each other. Clearly the native, European, and landscape elements come into being through processes of colonization that relate those elements to each other, and those elements change by virtue of those processes rather than by virtue of some sort of autonomous, internal dynamic—by what some would call their intrinsic natures. For example, an environmental determinist would characterize the establishment of plantations in the tropics as a natural consequence of their climate just as the dispossession and suffering of natives would be a natural consequence of being native, a categorical condition rather than a relationship. Ontologically, therefore, the dynamic processes relating the three elements to each other constitute, together, the process of colonization. The elements themselves constitute the changing manifestation of that process as reflected in the three primary faces of colonialism, each being internally heterogeneous, of course. And the changing heterogeneity of the elements constitutes the changing parameters that enable and constrain ongoing processes of transformation. For example, on racial criteria, the European and native elements might both become transformed through miscegenation, a biological process that transfers matter and information between the gene pools of the two elements and thereby transforms both of them. As both elements become predominantly mestizo, that biological process becomes less and less consequential relative to social processes of transformation such as syncretism or acculturation. Epistemologically, however, in order to discern and understand such transformative processes and their dynamics, analysis must distinguish elements from each other as well as from their relations. The process of miscegenation, for example, remains impos-

sible to analyze without first conceiving of at least two gene pools and their propinquity in a landscape.

Significantly, the colonial triangle does seem to exhaust the elements and
relationships intrinsic to the colonization process. Indeed, two of the frameworks
analyzed failed to distinguish the native from the landscape element, treating the
two as a lumped environment element (figures 1.3 and 1.4). The ethnohistoricist
framework does satiate the colonial triangle in terms of elements but applies
different a priori assumptions to each side of the triangle (figure 1.5). Environmental determinism applies to the native-landscape side, cultural determinism to
the two others. In contrast, the conceptual structure stimulated by postcolonial
studies, which I exemplify through Harris's recent BC research, treats all three
elements as epistemologically distinct and, potentially at least, related to each
other through reciprocal processes that are equal in both directions (figure 1.6).

While none of the comparisons suggest that any necessary elements or relationships are missing from the colonial triangle, adding more of both to any
model is always possible. The issue, however, is whether three elements are
sufficient. More narrowly defining or closely specifying elements by splitting
and multiplying them would certainly permit more complex analyses—but only
if appropriate data were available and perhaps only at the cost of an incompre-
hensible welter of interrelationships. In an effort to more closely approach the
complexity of reality, a triangle that becomes a square and then a pentagon soon
becomes a hyperpolygon that through reductionism obscures integrative understanding. The use of "native" instead of making the heterogeneity of that element explicit through the naming of hundreds of ethic groups, for example, facilitates rather than obscures understanding of the fluid, contested, and ambiguous relationships involved in such namings (Klor de Alva 1995). Ultimately,
whether more elements become necessary remains to be worked out through
research that applies the colonial triangle to particular cases. For the time being,
since only one of the prior and existing frameworks even begins to satiate the
conceptual structure of the colonial triangle, its three essential elements and their
interrelations seem sufficient as well as necessary.

In terms of the relationships among elements, applying the same epistemological standards to each side of the triangle permits, by definition, unbiased
analysis. Conceiving of reciprocal processes as potentially equal in both directions certainly recognizes case-to-case empirical variation in the relative impact
of one element on another but also recognizes that a priori privileging of one
element or relationship over others can result in specious determinisms. In the
case of the first century of colonialism in the Caribbean, for example, the European element had the ultimate unidirectional impact on the native element, the
native peoples of the Antilles being extirpated through processes of labor exploitation and introduced disease (Cook 1998). Yet what seems so obviously a unidirectional process cannot be universalized and therefore the dominance of
Europeans cannot be privileged in any theory purporting to be comprehensive.
After all, even in the case of the Caribbean, by the time Columbus returned on

his second voyage, the Taino had extirpated the three dozen Spaniards he had left behind in 1493 to garrison Navidad (Sauer 1966, 33, 72). Such case-to-case variation in the relative impact of one element on another thus remains an empirical issue and in no way justifies a priori bias that assumes native agency to be relatively inconsequential (figure 1.5) or that assumes the results of the colonization process to be immanent to Europeans (figure 1.4).

The conceptual structure that Harris's BC research exemplifies only weakly begins to demonstrate that all three sides of the triangle encompass both material and conceptual processes. For example, along the native-European side, as introduced epidemic disease materially reduces native population, Europeans might conceptually transform the surviving natives into a "dying race." The processes relating the landscape element to the native and to the European elements are also both material and conceptual because people transform landscape through processes of labor *and* categorization, and the resulting landscape patterns influence the habits of practice *and* thought that structure such processes as well as the conflicts of practice *and* thought that change structures, either catastrophically or secularly. For example, as Europeans accumulate space at the expense of natives, native land-use practices such as annual burning might contract and vegetation succession processes create a more closed forest. Material transformations thus create a landscape morphology that catalyze Europeans to transform that landscape conceptually into a so-called pristine wilderness and the natives into so-called pre-agricultural savages, thus facilitating the further material accumulation of space by non-natives. The material/conceptual character of those processes and of the three elements requires explicit stipulation (figure 1.7).

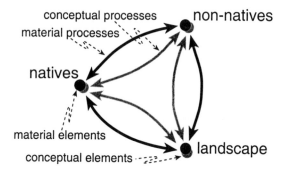

Figure 1.7. Conceptual structure with epistemological separation among all three material-conceptual elements and with potentially equal, reciprocal, material/conceptual processes relating those elements. The diagrammatic distinction between the material and the conceptual realms does not signal ontological separation.

The BC case also, partially because colonization occurred so recently, with sovereign British power ending upon Confederation with Canada only in 1871, stimulates further terminological consideration beyond the original modification of Hulme's land element into a landscape element. The term European hardly applies, for example, to the many U.S. citizens (Euro-Americans) who participated in the Cariboo Gold Rush of 1858. Replacing Hulme's other two apical terms with non-natives and natives thus immediately achieves a more inclusive framework than his more restricted purpose required. Non-natives subsumes greater heterogeneity in that element by potentially including European colonizers as well as their associates, voluntary or not: for example, indentured servants or slaves. Appropriate assignment of any individual or group to that element versus the native element seems relatively clear for periods immediately following the encounter between non-natives and natives in any particular region but becomes increasingly problematic with protracted miscegenation, acculturation, syncretism, maroonism, resettlement, indirect rule through westernized, native elites, and other processes that blur the distinction between native and non-native. Making the distinction between natives and non-natives, however, is as necessary as it is difficult because natives and non-natives played generally opposing roles in the colonization process, with one element's gain in power and space typically being the other's loss. Despite that oppositional relationship being so basic to colonialism, some analyses of colonialism have tended either to ignore ethnicity and its manifestation as a suite of cultural variables or elevate culture to the level of an independent variable, explaining everything and nothing at the same time. Thus economism subjugates ethnicity and culture, as well as gender and sexuality, to class (Wolfe 1997). And culturism invents a culture of poverty—a race of poverty darkly lurking in the conceptual shadows (Lewis 1966).

Precursors for such a comprehensive understanding of material/conceptual landscape transformation certainly exist in the literature on the Americas but none that explicitly theorize colonialism and landscape. Sauer's 1966 study of *The Early Spanish Main* remains a prominent example that explicates how Caribbean peoples and landscapes became remade and reconceptualized, from initial idiosyncrasies to final codification (Sluyter 1997a). Loot became the rubric inscribed over the landscape element, puerile labor the rubric over the natives. In the gold placers, those categories intersected in the destructive logic that consumed thousands of native lives. The colonization process materially and conceptually erased the highly productive precolonial cultural landscape and created a naturalized landscape of reforested native fields that "appears primeval" (Sauer 1966, 68). The ecological traditions that derive to greater or lesser degree from Sauer's stimulus have tended only partially to build on that foundation, stimulated more in terms of general topic than of approach (Blaikie and Brookfield 1987, 25-26). Both cultural and political ecologists have tended to emphasize material over conceptual processes, as already noted. At the same time, cultural ecologists have emphasized analysis of the relationship between natives and landscapes at local-to-regional scales while sacrificing analysis of the relationship between natives and non-natives, particularly at the global scale (Butzer 1989). In contrast, political ecologists have emphasized the relationship between natives and non-natives at local-to-global scales as well as the heterogeneity of each element (especially along class and gender lines) but with landscape all too typically becoming reduced to Hulme's aspatial land element (Bryant 1992). As one example of those intellectual tendencies, much of the effort to reconstruct native demography has focused on the pattern of precolonial population rather than the process of colonial depopulation, perhaps because first reconstructing precolonial patterns is basic to subsequent study of colonial processes (Denevan 1992b). Moreover, significant exceptions to those tendencies certainly exist, such as research on native demography during the colonial period (Lovell 1992) and integration of analysis of conceptual process (Hecht and Cockburn 1989). Yet only relatively recently has the intellectual space for a more integrated, comprehensive perspective and balanced conceptual framework emerged, one that can draw on the range of geography's complementary traditions while drawing on and contributing to cutting-edge biophysical and social theory (Zimmerer 1996).

Scale of Analysis

The analysis of contrasting conceptualizations also uncovers the significance of analytic scale in terms of the relative impact of one element on another, as illustrated through the example of the extirpation of Spaniard by Taino versus the extirpation of Taino by Spaniard in the Caribbean. Clearly, as well as being an empirical issue, apparent variation in relative impact of one element on another relates to the scale of analysis. In the one case, Taino extirpated Spaniard at the temporal scale of months and the spatial scale of a locality (although extirpation in that single locality at that time happened to equate with extirpation of all Europeans in the Caribbean). In the other case, Spaniard extirpated Taino at the temporal scale of decades and the spatial scale of the Caribbean. More systematically applying the colonial triangle across the scale continuum provides perspective on the scale of analysis appropriate to meeting the objective of a comprehensive theory of colonialism and landscape.

Toward the global-to-continental end of the scale continuum, the process that operated most dramatically and pervasively was epidemic disease (figure 1.8). Introduced diseases such as smallpox ultimately did more to materially and conceptually transform the landscape of the Americas than any other single process. As disease vastly reduced native population, desettlement resulted in changes in land use and vegetation patterning. Non-natives eventually recategorized the moribund cultural landscape that they had resettled, believing it to be a pristine wilderness. Several generations of scholars have conducted the regional-to-local scale studies and continental-to-hemispheric syntheses that, despite

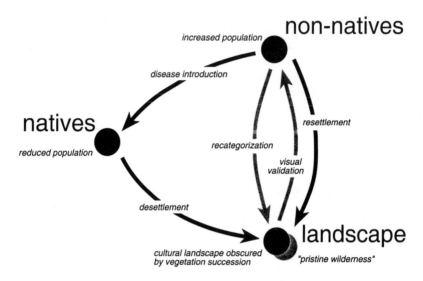

Figure 1.8. The colonial triangle applied at the global-to-continental end of the scale continuum, to the Americas as a whole, with selected material/conceptual processes and characteristics of elements indicated. See figure 1.7 for symbolization.

ongoing controversies over data and interpretations, have established that general model for the Americas (Denevan 1992a; Turner and Butzer 1992). Application at that scale, however, obscures much regional variation, specific processes, and their continuing consequences.

A suite of regional case studies that apply the colonial triangle to span the range of colonial contexts might generate such understanding as well as address specific social and environmental challenges. The BC study, among others, already begins to illustrate the potential of such analyses (Harris 1997). Much remains conjectural and subject to continued research, but in contrast to application of the colonial triangle at the global-to-continental scale, application at the regional-to-local scale can actually generate testable hypotheses, such as that hydraulicing played a major material/conceptual role in the colonization of the Fraser Canyon and continues to affect the way it is conceptualized and used at present. Others have likewise noted that geographers can make their greatest contributions by focusing research towards the regional-to-local end of the scale continuum without ignoring the need to integrate understanding across scales of analysis (Meyer et al. 1992, 266). In that effort, processes analyzed at coarser resolutions, at global-to-continental scales, provide context for models of landscape transformation at the regional-to-local scale. For example, the global process of smallpox virus evolution and diffusion that began thousands of years before that disease reached the Americas does not directly bear on processes of colonial landscape transformation in BC. That process does explain why small-pox proved so virulent among natives, however, and thus provides important context. At the same time, processes analyzed at finer resolutions become ab-stracted into models of landscape transformation at the regional-to-local scale. The process through which the smallpox virus enters the respiratory tract, multi-plies in the cells of the internal organs, and within days causes a rash of pustules and then death does not directly bear on understanding the process of colonial landscape transformation in BC either. That process is, however, the horrible way in which thousands upon thousands of people died.

The Tropical Lowlands of Veracruz

Application of the colonial triangle to a study of the colonial transformation of the environs of the port of Veracruz begins to explicitly test and build on the theoretical structure of the colonial triangle at the regional scale of analysis for a region that played an early and significant role in the colonization of the Ameri-cas. As the beachhead for the invasion of Mesoamerica and subsequently the entrepôt for the colony of New Spain, these tropical lowlands bore the first brunt of the war, the disease, and the livestock (Sluyter 1996, 1997b, 1998). By the end of the sixteenth century, they had become the quintessential cattle range of New Spain and winter pasture for flocks of sheep from the Central Highlands. Few regions, therefore, have more relevance for understanding prototypical colonization processes in the Americas, particularly those related to the intro-duction of livestock into the Neotropics.

Yet the record of scholarly research pertaining to the colonial transforma-tion of the Veracruz lowlands remains inordinately brief and theoretically irrele-vant—a situation in good part fostered by the region's climate and the persis-tence of environmental determinism (figure 1.9). The region extends from the shore, through the dunes, across the coastal plain, and up the piedmont to the 500-meter contour, an elevation that the inhabitants associate with the transition to the more temperate climate of the escarpment of the Sierra Madre Oriental. As one nineteenth-century traveler observed, heat defines the lowlands: "Cerro Gordo guards the passage from the hot low lands to the salubrious temperate region" (Ober 1887, 189). While the hot weather lasts throughout the year, pre-cipitation is seasonal. A mountain spur that reaches the coast at Villa Rica blocks the winter northers and casts a rain shadow that falls deepest in the north of the region. The upper piedmont and the escarpment rising inland receive rain-fall throughout the year, the trade winds condensing as they sweep upslope, but the rain shadow parches the lowlands from November through April, particu-larly in the north and on the lower piedmont. The seasonality is so extreme that approximately ninety percent of the total of some 1,200 millimeters falls from

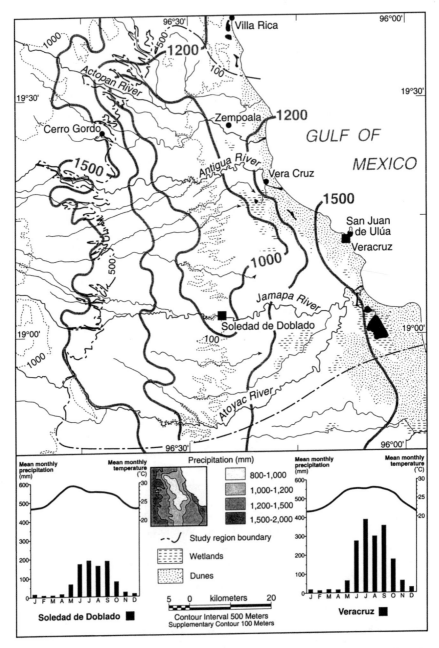

Figure 1.9. The Veracruz lowlands: the 500-meter contour and the coast define the study region on the west, east, and north; the drainage of the Atoyac River marks the southern limit. Average annual precipitation after García (1970).

late May to early October (García 1970; Lauer 1978). The hot temperatures result in high potential evapotranspiration that in combination with the low winter precipitation yields an average annual soil moisture deficit of 715 millimeters (Thornthwaite 1964). In addition, the annual two-week drought in August, or *canícula*, coincides with maize's pollination period, and insufficient moisture at that point in the growth cycle can drastically reduce the yield (Claassen and Shaw 1970; Melgarejo Vivanco 1980, 22). The region thus forms a subhumid enclave along the Gulf Coast, with hot humid lowlands to the north and south, and the temperate humid escarpment inland (Gómez-Pompa 1973; Rzedowski 1978, fig. 179).

That subhumid lowland climate, according to some prominent archaeologists, would have precluded intensive, productive agriculture and dense population, at least until the Totonac constructed an irrigation system at Zempoala shortly before Cortés arrived (Sanders 1953, 41-42; Palerm 1955, 33; Wolf 1959, 13; Sanders 1971, 552-54).

> Farming for one annual crop, the restricted size of the [riverine] gallery forest and its longitudinal form of growth did not favor high population densities or large population centers. The grasslands which surrounded these forests and could not be used agriculturally tended to isolate them. Political units were fragmented; their axes were always formed by the rivers. . . . Lands [at Zempoala] came into use later when application of small-scale irrigation allowed . . . urban centers like those of the Highlands [to emerge]. . . . No case of autochthonous self-generated political development is known, however; all seem to be secondary formations with centers of origins in the Highlands (Palerm and Wolf 1957, 15-16).

Generally, the streams rising in the Sierra Madre Oriental to the west are deeply incised into a piedmont that gently slopes down to a narrow coastal plain. They cannot supply irrigation agriculture on the extensive interfluvial uplands without the use of pumps or substantial, cross-channel dams. The narrow flood plains themselves, difficult to access and small in area, cannot have supported much agriculture. Near Zempoala, however, an arm of the Actopan River supposedly is untypical in this regard and on the basis of small diversion weirs and canals supplied an irrigation system.

> Most of the area is true savannah, the most difficult vegetation for the primitive farmer to cope with, and also the rains in general are undependable. . . . The only incentive for heavy settlement would be on the basis of irrigation agriculture, and . . . [at Zempoala] this incentive was presented (Sanders 1953, 76).

Seemingly then, intensive agriculture and dense settlement, with all their social corollaries such as urbanism and social stratification, could only have occurred at Zempoala and did not emerge until the late precolonial period, during what archaeologists have termed the Middle Postclassic (A.D. 1200 to 1400).

More recent research has begun to overturn that orthodoxy by uncovering evidence of dense populations and intensive agriculture. Within the last two decades, the Instituto Nacional de Antropología e Historia (INAH) has surveyed extensive areas of the lowlands, mapping settlement patterns and excavating selected sites (Ruiz Gordillo 1985, 1989; Navarrete Hernández 1988; Brügge-mann 1989, 1991; Casimir 1990, 1991; Daneels 1990, 1991, 1992; León Pérez 1991). That effort builds on earlier work, of course, much of it carried out or directed by García Payón and Medellín Zenil during the 1940s through 1960s (García Payón 1949a, 1949b, 1950, 1963, 1966, 1971; Medellín Zenil 1952, 1953, 1955, 1960; Bernal and Dávalos Hurtado 1953). That first generation of archaeologists, accomplishing so much with so few resources, themselves built on the work of the antiquarians of the nineteenth and early twentieth centuries (Esteva 1843; Sartorius 1861, 1869; Fink 1871; Strebel 1883, 1889; Paso y Troncoso 1892-1893, 2:7-30, 275-377; Fewkes 1907, 1919; Nuttal 1910; Galindo y Villa 1912). Geographers, also within the last two decades, have in-vestigated the traces of intensive agriculture, some of them first noted by those same antiquarians (Sartorius 1861; Fink 1871). The first indications came from the wetlands of the coastal plain, where the relict planting platforms and canals of intensive wetland agriculture pattern several thousand hectares (Siemens 1980, 1983a, 1983b, 1983c, 1985, 1989; Siemens et al. 1988; Sluyter 1994). Inland, relict sloping-field terraces occur throughout some thousand square kilometers of piedmont (Sluyter and Siemens 1992). Much still remains unclear, particularly the timings and relationships of the various settlement and agricul-tural systems, the precolonial chronology of these lowlands remaining one of the "softest," or most relative, in all of Mesoamerica (Tolstoy 1978, 269-72). That lack of an absolute chronology relates, of course, to the lack of research re-sources applied to these lowlands, which in turn relates to the perception that the subhumid climate precluded intensive agriculture and dense population. That situation led García Payón to lament that the cost of one radiocarbon assay ex-ceeded his entire budget for excavating Chalahuite and Mata Verde, two mound groups near, and quite likely older than, Zempoala (García Payón 1966, 187n).

By the early postcolonial period, according to Sartorius, much of the region had become overgrown with thickets of thorny, deciduous shrubs and low trees. A belt of woodlands—fragmented by wetlands harboring mosquitoes, vectors for the yellow fever that gave Veracruz its macabre reputation (Arreola 1980; Siemens 1990a)—hugged the coast just inland of the jumble of sand dunes. But the traveler bound for Mexico City from the port quickly confronted the long climb through the "dreary wilderness" of the savanna country. The only respite before reaching the more temperate elevations of the Sierra Madre Oriental came when the road dipped into verdant river gorges. In general, except for the port itself, the lowlands remained the domain of vast herds of cattle through the colonial and into the early postcolonial periods, but sparsely populated and little cultivated (Siemens 1990a). Only with the fall of Porfirio Díaz and the ensuing land reform of the twentieth century did the reign of the cattle barons wane and rural population begin to rise appreciably from its colonial nadir (Skerritt Gardner 1989). Mestizo immigrants from the highlands claimed *ejido* lands, expropriated from the haciendas and held communally. The state coffers funded the irrigation canals that allowed ejido sugar cane to challenge cattle, drawing the lowlands ever more tightly into the net of the global economy (Siemens 1998). While the irrigation and drainage projects of the twentieth century have obliterated much of the landscape Sartorius once rode through, especially on the coastal plain, his savanna "overgrown with low thorny mimosas" still dominates the piedmont.

Yet the colonial transformation that intervenes between those precolonial and postcolonial landscapes remains largely unknown and unexplored—the scholarly literature, as already noted, being inordinately brief. A string of standard regional histories recount deeds and dates (Ramirez Cabañas 1943; Melgarejo Vivanco 1943, 1949, 1975; Trens 1947, 1955; Pasquel 1958; Blazquez Dominguez 1988). Several more incisive studies treat aspects of the regions just to the north, south, and west (Kelly and Palerm 1952; Winfield Capitaine 1984; Carroll 1991). Others deal with the lowlands of central Veracruz, but focus on the port of Veracruz, sharply circumscribed family or community histories, or transportation routes (González 1943; Gold 1965, 1970; Arreola 1980, 1982; Bermúdez Gorrochotegui 1987; Booker 1993; Driever 1995). Two analyses of colonial maps, however, do begin to provide a more comprehensive regional perspective, as do some tentative studies of colonial population, ranching, and agriculture (Cline 1961; Chavez Orozco and Florescano 1965; Siemens and Brinckmann 1976; González Jácome 1988; Melgarejo Vivanco n.d.).

Beginning to understand the processes involved in the colonial landscape transformation of these tropical lowlands thus occupies the bulk of the following chapters. Chapter 2 first demonstrates that precolonial population was dense rather than sparse and that land use was intensive rather than extensive. Chapters 3, 4, and 5 then explicate the material/conceptual transformation of the colonial landscape, focusing on the decisive first century of colonization and on interactions among natives, non-natives and their livestock, vegetation, and categories of land use, land cover, and land tenure. Chapter 6 sketches the postcolonial landscape and its transformations, from the "dreary wilderness" Sartorius describes to canal irrigation projects and efforts to redeploy the intensive wetland agriculture of the precolonial period.

Notes

1. Chalchicueyecan is now the city and port of Veracruz, the latter's location having shifted several times during the sixteenth century (Sluyter 1996). In 1519, the Spaniards initially founded, but in name only, La Villa Rica de la Vera Cruz at Chalchicueyecan, the mainland opposite the island of San Juan de Ulúa. They then refounded and built the town fifty-eight kilometers to the north, at present-day Villa Rica. Circa 1525, the Span-

iards dropped Villa Rica from the toponym and moved the port to the left bank of the Antigua River, at present-day La Antigua; launches ferried goods from the deep-water port at San Juan de Ulúa along the coast and across the bar at the river's mouth to Vera Cruz. Beginning with a viceregal order of 1597 and progressing over a transitional period of several years, Vera Cruz shifted back to its first location at Chalchicueyecan, and the toponym eventually contracted to Veracruz, the sixteenth-century site becoming known, first, as La Antigua Vera Cruz and, eventually, as La Antigua.

The five well known *cartas de relación*, or dispatches from Cortés to Charles V, span the years 1519 to 1526. This one, the first, was signed by "La Justicia y Regimiento de La Rica Villa de La Vera Cruz" on 10 July 1519. Cortés wrote or dictated the dispatch, however. The signature of the town council was clearly intended to legitimate breaking with the governor of Cuba, who had sponsored Cortés's mission to the mainland, by establishing an independent governing body.

This and all subsequent Spanish-English translations in this chapter are by the author.

2. The 1580 *relación geográfica*, a standardized geographical report, is in the Joaquin García Icazbalceta Collection of the University of Texas at Austin, herein cited as JGI. We cannot know which league the writer had in mind—the distance a figurative one anyway, no doubt, a type of "within ten miles of here" trope—but readers still require some familiar terms of reference to appreciate such passages. Most sixteenth-century Spaniards would have been familiar with the *legua común*, or common league, equal to 5.6 km. In contrast, the legal definitions of cadastral units employed the *legua legal*, or legal league, equal to 4,180 meters, or 4.2 km (Carrera Stampa 1949; Chardon 1980). Because the land-grants analyzed in chapter 4 employ the legua legal, I have used a conversion factor of 4.2 km throughout in order to be consistent. In the statement of the district governor, therefore, "seven leagues" equals twenty-nine kilometers; assuming the legua común, seven leagues would equal thirty-nine kilometers.

3. These terms have come to have such restrictive meanings, yet ones that vary among literatures, that the complement to material landscape transformation is better communicated by the phrase conceptual landscape transformation, which clearly identifies transformations that relate to what exists in the mind.

4. According to Pratt (1992, 32), the full typology includes six races of *Homo sapiens*: (i) Wild Man; (ii) American; (iii) European; (iv) Asiatic; (v) African; (vi) Monster.

5. In contrast to Harris, other recent research on BC also influenced by postcolonial studies almost entirely ignores material processes (Willems-Braun 1997; Sparke 1998; Clayton 2000). Striking (but unacknowledged) commonalities exist between that BC representationalist school and the school of historical geosophy that J. K. Wright founded more than fifty years ago in order to study changes in knowledge about places (Wright 1947; Lowenthal and Bowden 1976). Bowden (1992), the historical geosopher who has done the most to explicate the emergence of the myth of emptiness for the United States, strongly emphasizes non-native imposition of representation on landscape, doing little to investigate material processes and easily fitting into the ethnohistoricist conceptual structure. The BC representationalists also largely focus on the imposition of representations on landscapes, albeit in some cases with more emphasis on the struggle between natives and Europeans over those representations (Sparke 1998). The BC representationalists certainly are not idealists; in fact, they are rather fond of pronouncements such as "we must always attend to [Nature's] making—rhetorically and materially, and the two al-

ways together" (Willems-Braun 1997, 25). Yet their actions have not matched their homilies, analyses of material processes being limited to, for example, sketchy accounts of courtroom architecture in relation to a native land claim trial (Sparke 1998, 471-72). The BC representationalists nonetheless have much potential to contribute to a comprehensive theory of colonialism and landscape and improve understanding of how, for example, "maps contribute to the construction of spaces that later they seem only to represent" (Sparke 1998, 466). Doing so, however, would require engaging material processes as thoroughly as they have engaged conceptual ones, and it would require forgoing what seems to be an effort to elide prior geographical research in order to construct a theory-free space that can then be filled with a theorization effect (Sluyter 1997a).

2

The Precolonial Landscape

The Aztecs referred to the lands along the Gulf of Mexico as Totonacapan, the land of plenty, and to its people as Totonacs (Kelly and Palerm 1952, 2). Even during years of widespread poor harvests, when droughts or early frosts devastated crops throughout much of central Mexico, the Totonacs had plenty of maize. In 1450, during the reign of Montezuma the elder, an early frost accompanied by snow destroyed the Basin of Mexico's maize crop (Durán 1967, 2:241-44; Alva Ixtlilxóchitl 1985, 2:111). An early frost again the next year and a subsequent series of drought years entirely depleted the Aztec granaries—even the seed stock. Before the rains returned in 1455 and the Great Famine ended, many had died of starvation. Many others had indentured themselves or their children to those with food, four hundred ears of maize for a girl and five hundred for a boy (Torquemada 1969, 1:158). Throughout the Great Famine, Totonacapan continued to be agriculturally productive, and Totonac merchants would arrive in Tenochtitlán, Texcoco, Chalco, and the other cities of the Basin of Mexico with loads of maize and lead away the indentured Aztecs and other Nahuas by "placing collars on their necks, children as well as adults, forming them all into single file" (Durán 1967, 2:243-44).[1]

Such accounts come from native scholars, mostly Nahua and typically through the editorial filter of the Spanish clergy. The earliest two such accounts, edited by the Franciscan Bernardino de Sahagún and the Dominican Diego Durán, date to the second half of the sixteenth century and derive in part from the compilation of native oral and documentary histories (Durán 1967; Sahagún 1950-1982; D'Olwer and Cline 1973, 186-93; Gibson and Glass 1975, 335). Together, Sahagún's *Historia General de las Cosas de Nueva España*, or Florentine Codex, and Durán's *Historia de las Indias de Nueva España y Islas de Tierra Firma* comprise the basic sources for understanding the Aztecs, the other Nahua people of central Mexico, and associated groups such as the Totonacs.

Several less comprehensive works in the same genre provide additional detail, date to the late sixteenth and the seventeenth centuries, and in part derive from the same sources that Sahagún and Durán used (Alvarado Tezozomoc 1944; Velázquez 1945; Torquemada 1969; Alcina Franch 1973, 256-67; Gibson and Glass 1975, 326-38; Alva Ixtlilxóchitl 1985). In general such sources corroborate and support one another.

In addition to narrating how Totonacs took advantage of their plentiful harvests to indenture (some claimed to enslave and even to immolate) Aztecs during the Great Famine, such sources also relate the Totonac origin (Alva Ixtlilxóchitl 1985, 2:111). Apparently, before migrating eastward to settle in the Sierra Madre Oriental and adjacent foothills and coastal plains, the Totonacs too had lived in the Basin of Mexico—during what archaeologists call the Classic period (A.D. 1 to 900), when the metropolis of Teotihuacán dominated much of Mesoamerica.

> Of [the Totonacs] they say that they emerged from the place called Chicomoztoc, or Seven Caves . . . and arrived on the plains beside the lake . . . where now stands Teotihuacán; and they claim that they built those two very high temples and dedicated them to the sun and to the moon. . . . They lived there some time and then . . . left for Atenamitic, which is where the town of Zacatlán now stands, and from there went four leagues further on, down through very rough and high mountains, so that they might better defend themselves against enemies; and there they built their first city, and they expanded throughout all that mountainous country, for many leagues, turning towards the east, and settling in the plains of Zempoala, near the port of Vera Cruz, populating that whole territory with a great many people (Torquemada 1969, 1:278).

Given the timing, "their first city" must have been El Tajín. Its ruins center on a series of plazas and magnificent stone buildings and ball courts in the foothills of the Sierra Madre Oriental less than a hundred kilometers northeast of Zacatlán, and it emerged during the Classic period (García Payón 1971). El Tajín dominated the central Gulf Coast region until roughly A.D. 1200, supplanted by a new urban center a hundred and fifty kilometers to the southeast: Zempoala (García Payón 1949a; Brüggemann 1991). Located on the coastal plain near where Cortés and the conquistadors were to ride their horses up the beach in 1519, Zempoala dominated Totonacapan during the latter half of the Postclassic period (A.D. 900-1521).

Six years after the end of the Great Famine, the army of Montezuma the elder conquered Totonacapan. The Aztecs took sixty-two hundred captives in battles at a pass through the Sierra Madre Oriental near Orizaba and at a ford over the Atoyac River near Cotaxtla (Alvarado Tezozomoc 1944, 114-28; Sahagún 1950-1982, 9:7; Durán 1967, 2:177-83, 198-202, 241-49; Torquemada 1969, 1:160-62). With another battle at the city of Zempoala, the Aztec subjugated Totonacapan, established garrisons, exacted tribute, and sent additional colonists to augment the Nahua population that had become established during the Great Famine (JGI, xxv-8, f. 6; Barlow 1949). When the Basin of Mexico maize crop failed again in 1505 and 1506, during the reign of Montezuma the younger, the Aztecs forced tribute maize from the Totonacs and Nahua colonists of Totonacapan rather than once again indenture themselves (Sluyter 1993; Alva Ixtlilxóchitl 1985, 2:179).

When the conquistadors rode into Zempoala in 1519, they marveled at the architecture, the dense population, and the lush vegetation. Although brief, the comments of Bernal Díaz del Castillo would seem to corroborate that Totonacapan was indeed a land of plenty and Zempoala its chief city.

> [Entering] among the houses, on seeing such a large city, and having seen no other larger, we greatly admired it, and how it was so luxuriant and like a garden, and so populous with men and women, the streets full of those who had come out to see us (Díaz 1986, 76).

Cortés was so impressed that he renamed the city Seville, one of the largest cities of sixteenth-century Europe (Cortés 1988, 32). His biographer, Francisco López de Gómara, described Zempoala as "an orchard, and with such large, tall trees that one can barely see the houses" (Gómara 1987, 97). Overall, the conquistadors give the impression of a large, lush city with tree-lined streets leading through residential suburbs with house gardens into a central plaza flanked by large stone pyramids.

Yet beyond the general sense that late-precolonial Totonacapan was densely settled, urban, and agriculturally productive, more precisely elaborating the relationship between people and landscape remains a challenging task. When reconnoitering near Zempoala, Bernal Díaz del Castillo apparently saw "many books of their paper, folded, like the cloth of Castile" (Díaz 1986, 75). But those Totonac documents disappeared in the following battles and epidemics. The resulting near total desettlement during the sixteenth century precludes oral history. The accounts of the conquistadors themselves clearly provide no more than thin descriptions of a thick landscape. And the region's archaeology has long languished relative to other regions, the environment supposedly determining that nothing of interest had happened around Zempoala (Sanders 1971, 552-54). Recently, however, geographical investigation of the landscape around and between the archaeological sites has begun to elaborate on the relationship between settlement and agriculture (Siemens 1980, 1998; Sluyter and Siemens 1992; Sluyter 1997c). Taken together, the documents, the archaeology, and the geography yield at least a sketch of the late-precolonial interactions between "natives" and landscape, in particular focusing on settlement pattern, population, and agriculture (figure 2.1).

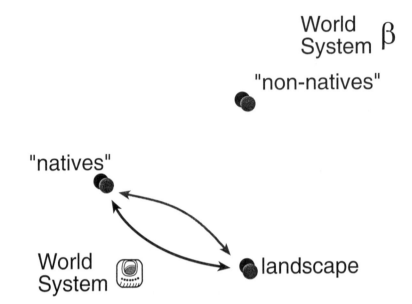

Figure 2.1. Processes and patterns addressed in this chapter are limited to the "natives" element, the landscape element, and their relationships. The quotation marks around "natives" and "non-natives" indicate the relational character of such categories, natives and non-natives not coming into being until their encounter. See figure 1.7 for symbolization.

City, Town, and Village

The slow accumulation of site studies by archaeologists now permits a regional synthesis, at least an interim one, of the late-precolonial settlement pattern and, to some degree, of changes over the prior several thousand years. The archaeology remains limited in scope and utility, with highly generalized, small-scale maps that allow only nominal localization of particular settlements. Other aspects of settlement such as chronology, population, and ethnicity remain even less certain (Tolstoy 1978, 269-72). Nor have all areas received equal attention, with settlement surveys concentrating along major streams (Ruiz Gordillo 1989; Daneels 1990, 1991, 1992; León Pérez 1991). Other than in a few cases, concerted excavations have targeted Zempoala, the main archaeological tourist attraction in the study region. Nonetheless, the broad changes in settlement pattern over what archaeologists call the Preclassic (2500 B.C. to A.D. 1), Classic (A.D. 1 to 900), and Postclassic (A.D. 900 to 1521) periods now seem clear.[2]

During the Preclassic period, the known settlements display a broad scatter across the region (figure 2.2). Settlements occur along the coast, on the coastal plain, and on the piedmont. Ceramic styles suggest ethnic, or at least cultural, affinities to the coeval Olmec of southern Veracruz (García Payón 1971).

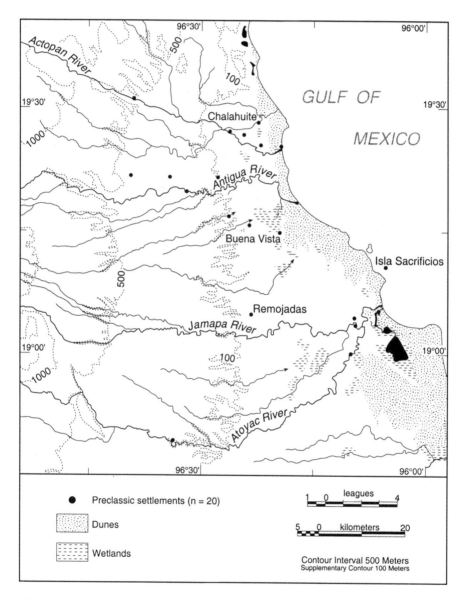

Figure 2.2. Settlement pattern during the Preclassic period (2500 B.C. to A.D. 1). Settlements that fall outside of the study region are not shown.

The overall distribution of settlements during the Classic period remains similar to that of the Preclassic, but with some significant changes in terms of numbers and specific settlements (figure 2.3). Only nine Preclassic settlements continue as Classic settlements at the same time that the total number doubles.

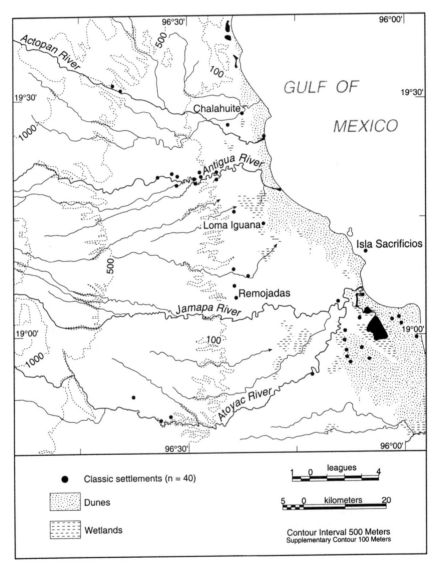

Figure 2.3. Settlement pattern during the Classic period (A.D. 1 to 900). Settlements that fall outside of the study region are not shown.

Whether that change indicates a doubling of population or not, major social changes must have occurred. Although incomplete survey precludes definitive assessment, much of the expansion seems to have focused on the southern dunes. On the basis of the presence of Teotihuacán ceramic styles and the Totonac origin account, the Classic expansion seems to be linked to immigration from the Basin of Mexico.

The number of settlements, and thus perhaps the population, persists into the Postclassic period, albeit again with some significant changes (figure 2.4). Only ten specific settlements persist from Classic to Postclassic. The major shift seems to occur from the southern dunes and central coastal plain to further concentration of settlements along major rivers. Ceramic styles again indicate invasion and immigration by highland peoples (Daneels 1991, 1992).

The only archaeology that directly pertains to the population of any of those settlements derives from Zempoala. Area analysis of land-use classes yields an estimate for Zempoala's core built-up area of eighty-five hundred to twenty-five thousand inhabitants (Brüggemann 1991, 93-95). Uncertainty as to the density of suburban houses dictates the wide range of figures, irresolvable without further excavation.

Several types of documents provide further insight into the population of specific settlements and the entire region, at least for the late precolonial period. Previous studies applying such sources to the Veracruz lowlands draw on a narrow range of primary data, cover only part of the region, or, in several cases, incorporate serious errors of fact and analysis (Kelly and Palerm 1952; Sanders 1953; González Jácome 1988). Yet such studies do, in combination, provide necessary references to and background information on sources (Cook and Simpson 1948; Borah and Cook 1963).

Compilations of Aztec tribute assessments by province comprise the earliest but least useful sources (Cooper Clark 1938; Berdan and Durant-Forest 1980). Cortés seems to have ordered compilation of the Matricula de Tributos in the early 1520s (Barlow 1949, 4). The Codex Mendoza, a copy of the Matricula de Tributos, dates to the 1540s; except for minor differences the two generally agree (Borah and Cook 1963). In both, each tribute province has a separate page with a series of glyphs identifying its principal places and the tribute due by type and amount. But the glyphs do not always correspond to known places, the total provincial assessments do not break down by individual places, and the boundaries between tribute provinces remain vague (Barlow 1949). The Aztecs seem to have divided this part of Totonacapan into at least two tribute provinces: Quauhtochco in the west and Cuetlaxtlan in the east, each of which has its own page. The Quauhtochco page names seven places, and the Cuetlaxtlan page names six. Strangely, given its size, Zempoala does not show up on either the Quauhtochco or the Cuetlaxtlan page, and might have been included in a third tribute province called Zempoalan (Torquemada 1969, 1:197-98). Either one of the pages known to be missing represented Zempoalan, or it was included in Cuetlaxtlan, as mention of "the king of Cuetlaxtlan and Zempoala" suggests

42 Chapter 2

(Alvarado Tezozomoc 1944, 123; Barlow 1949, 4-7). Yet even with a better understanding of the actual areas to which the tributes pertained, methodological obstacles preclude quantification of population. Not only was the tribute in kind, and therefore difficult to relate to a datum value, but the ratio of tribute to

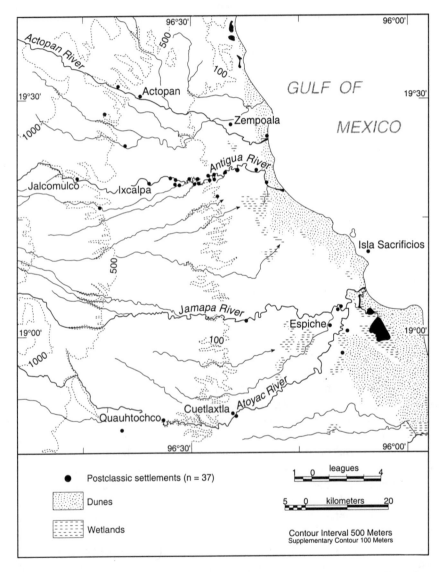

Figure 2.4. Settlement pattern during the Postclassic period (A.D. 900 to 1521). Settlements that fall outside of the study region are not shown.

population varied. The Aztecs levied rebellious or rich provinces higher tributes than complacent or poor provinces. As a consequence, the convoluted attempts to quantify population on the basis of tribute lists remain far from convincing (Borah and Cook 1963; Zambardino 1980). The Matricula de Tributos and Codex Mendoza do, however, rather dramatically confirm the agricultural productivity of the Veracruz lowlands. Beyond food, the inhabitants of Quauhtochco and Cuetlaxtlan paid the Aztecs an annual tribute of 1,600 loads of cotton, 220 loads of cacao, and 7,520 loads of woven cotton mantles, besides various other items such as feathered headdresses and jade necklaces (Barlow 1949, 89-91).

Sixteenth-century accounts by conquistadors and other Spaniards yield the only quantitative population estimates for the late precolonial period. In some cases, such as Hernando Cortés and his biographer Francisco López de Gómara, those accounts probably estimated population rather liberally in order to exaggerate the deeds of conquistadors or the potential for colonization (Cortés 1915, 1988; Gómara 1987; Cook and Borah 1970-1974, 1:7-12). Other accounts, such as the *True History of the Conquest of New Spain* by Bernal Díaz del Castillo, explicitly attempted to refute the supposed exaggerations of prior accounts (Díaz 1986). In still other cases, exaggeration had social rather than personal motives, such as the attempt by Bartolomé de las Casas to paint as black a picture as possible of Spanish behavior and native population decline in order to promote protective legislation (Casas 1951, 1953, 1967). Most likely, the population estimates in such accounts originally derived from native informants or, if not, from fairly loose "guesstimates"—both being notoriously inaccurate (McArthur 1970). Moreover, subsequent accounts that summarized or even simply repeated previous estimates sometimes introduced errors. Even Bernal Díaz and Francisco de Aguilar, conquistadors themselves, wrote well after the Conquest and certainly based their accounts, in part, on earlier ones that themselves sometimes included summaries of reports by others (Aguilar 1938; Díaz 1986; Brooks 1993). Others had not witnessed the Conquest at all, such as Gómara who based his *Conquest of Mexico* on the letters and confidences of Cortés as well as on other accounts (Gómara 1987). Pedro Martir de Angleria, Gonzalo de Fernández de Oviedo y Valdés, Motolinía, Bartolomé de las Casas, Andrés de Pérez de Rivas, and Antonio de Herrera all based their summaries on reports by and interviews of others, such as Cortés, often quoting entire passages verbatim (Pérez de Rivas 1896; Herrera 1944-1947; Casas 1951, 1953, 1967; Oviedo 1959; Martir 1964; Motolinía 1971). Some also had firsthand experience in the Americas; others did not.

Only more than half a century after the Conquest did the Spaniards attempt a more systematic assessment of the precolonial population. The ranking crown official of each district answered a series of questions that resulted in a geographical report, a *relación geográfica*. Question five asked whether a district had "many or few natives, and if it has had more or less in other times, and the causes thereof" (Cline 1972, 183-94; Acuña 1985, 19). The district governors of Vera Cruz and Xalapa, the next district inland, responded in 1580 with regional geographies accompanied by maps (JGI, xxv-8; Acuña 1985, 343-74). Both seem to have relied on native informants to some degree, with the governor of Vera Cruz claiming to have requested native assistance in producing a map, and the map included in the Xalapa report clearly displaying native stylistic elements (JGI, xxv-8, f. 20; Harley 1992). Such oral history complements the reports of the conquistadors, although the district governors no doubt were familiar with those as well and might, in part, have been drawing on them.

None of the documents yield more than surrogate population figures, such as numbers of houses at Zempoala, and require assumptions about family size before conversion to total population. In general, the accounts use the terms *casas*, *vecinos*, and *indios*—literally houses, citizens, and Indians. Because veci-nos and indios quite clearly refer to male heads of households, the three terms roughly equate to numbers of households. Since the equivocal nature of the data suggests simplicity rather than complex statistical manipulations, in what fol-lows, total population equals the number of casas, vecinos, or indios multiplied by 4.5, the assumed average family size, plus twenty percent for non-family household members such as slaves or servants (Borah and Cook 1963, 67-72, 81-82).

The population estimates tied to specific places seem most precise, albeit still with a generous margin of error—perhaps as much as fifty percent more or less (figure 2.5). Bernal Díaz did not put a number to the population of the city he described as being "so populous with men and women" (Díaz 1986, 76). But others did, and Zempoala clearly was the metropolis of the region. Las Casas, predictably, gave the high estimate of twenty to thirty thousand vecinos, a me-dian of twenty-five thousand (Casas 1951, 251; 1967, 261). Arias Hernández, a priest who had served at Vera Cruz and dictated a description to a scribe in Spain in 1571, also mentions thirty thousand indios, but he probably derived that figure from reading Las Casas (Paso y Troncoso 1905, 5:201). Torquemada, even more obviously following Las Casas, virtually quoting verbatim, inaccu-rately modifies the range to twenty-five to thirty thousand vecinos (Torquemada 1969, 251). Martir recorded the lowest estimate, fifteen thousand, a figure of unknown origin but presumably based on an interview with one of the conquis-tadors (Martir 1964, 1:427). Aguilar, who rode into Zempoala beside Cortés and Díaz, estimated twenty thousand—significantly the only figure known to have been provided by one of the eyewitnesses (Aguilar 1938, 39). The 1580 geo-graphical report supplies a similar "middle-of-the-road" estimate: twenty thou-sand vecinos (JGI, xxv-8, ff. 5v-6). Aguilar's status as an eyewitness and the median position of 20,000, midway between the low of Martir (15,000) and the high of Las Casas (25,000), suggests veracity; application of the conversion for-mula yields a total population of 108,000.

Other large places did not receive the attention of Zempoala, but a scatter-ing of estimates provides some notion of the populations of principal towns. The Aztec governor came to greet Cortés from Cuetlaxtla, renamed Cotaxtla during the colonial period, a garrison that guarded a major route to the highlands and a town that according to Martir had five hundred casas (JGI, xxv-8, ff. 5v-6; Barlow 1949, 91-92; Martir 1964, 1:421-22). Applying the conversion formula, the derived population of 2,700 seems reasonable, even low given Martir's con-

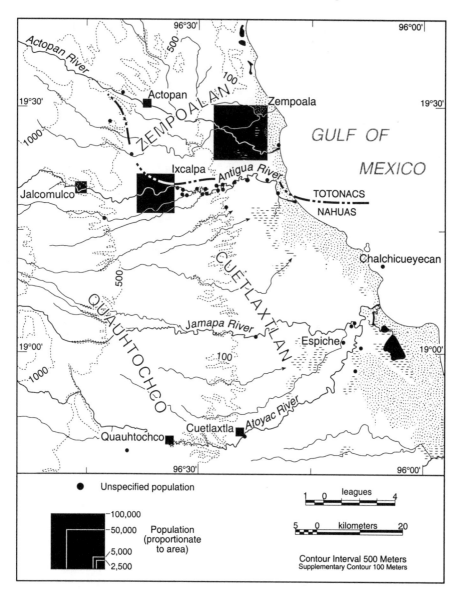

Figure 2.5. Settlement pattern and population of the Veracruz lowlands during the late precolonial period. Settlements above the 500-meter contour, south of the drainage of the Atoyac River, and north of the drainage of the Actopan River fall outside of the study region and are not shown.

servative estimate for Zempoala. No estimates exist for the other known Aztec garrisons, Actopan and Quauhtochco (colonial Huatusco), but presumably they must have at least equaled Cuetlaxtla (JGI, xxv-8, ff. 5v-6; Barlow 1949, 89-91). According to the two 1580 geographical reports, Jalcomulco "had more than a thousand indios" and Ixcalpa, later known as Rinconada, more than ten thousand indios, yielding population estimates for Jalcomulco of 5,400 and for Ixcalpa of 54,000 (JGI, xxv-8, ff. 5v-6; Acuña 1985, 120-21).

Estimates for the broader region and unspecified settlements seem less precise but nonetheless useful. A full century after the Conquest, the comment by the historian of the Jesuits in New Spain that the region around the port of Veracruz previously had places "so populous and large, that some came to sixty thousand vecinos" can only be hyperbole given the earlier, much lower estimates even for the metropolis of Zempoala, and even by Las Casas himself (Pérez de Rivas 1896, 2:195; also Alegre 1841-1842, 1:150). Nonetheless, the archaeological map of Postclassic settlement, no matter how incomplete and tentative, and the Aztec tribute lists do make clear that the region contained many more settlements, and of a range of sizes, than those with surviving population estimates.

Although the province of Quauhtochco remains largely mysterious, Aguilar claimed that Cuetlaxtlan had forty thousand casas—a population of some 216,000, or nearly a quarter of a million people (Aguilar 1938, 38). The Aztec garrisons of Quauhtochco and Cuetlaxtla were possibly the largest towns south of the Antigua River. Depopulation and time have obscured the locations of many of the others, but the toponyms persist in the archives: Alcocahua, Espiche, Jamapa, Mictanguautla (JGI-xxv-8; AGN-T, vol. 32, exp. 4; vol. 2672, exp. 8; vol. 2678, exp. 12; vol. 2782, exp. 16; vol. 2680, exp. 20; vol. 2764, exp. 17; vol. 2764, exp. 18). Some of those names might attach to the four or five Nahua towns of "no more than two hundred houses" each that the Spaniards came across along the lower Jamapa River, a total population of some five thousand people (Gómara 1987, 91). In further corroboration of a provincial population estimate of nearly a quarter million, Gómara claimed that the Aztec governor came with four thousand men to parley with the Spaniards on the beach at Chalchicueyecan, then ordered two thousand men and women to camp nearby (Gómara 1987, 83-86).

Whether or not Zempoalan formed a separate province in the north or not, by 1519 the Totonacs dominated north of the Antigua River, Nahuatl speakers south of the river and inland (Díaz 1986, 75, 102; Gómara 1987, 89; Cortés 1988, 34). How long that ethnic geography had been established and what preceded it remains unknown, awaiting much archaeology, but it presumably dated at least to the Aztec conquest of Totonacapan in the mid 1400s. Other aspects of the settlement pattern are equally murky. Cortés estimated that "all the province of Zempoala and all the mountains neighboring [Villa Rica], would amount to fifty thousand soldiers and fifty towns and forts" (Cortés 1988, 32); Oviedo parroted Cortés (Oviedo 1959, 4:11); Gómara inflated the number of soldiers to a hundred thousand (Gómara 1987, 106); and Herrera and Torquemada converted the soldiers into a hundred and twenty thousand vecinos (Herrera 1944-1947, 3:374; Torquemada 1969, libro iv, cap. lxxix). Díaz more modestly proposed that in all of Totonacapan, "all that land of the Totonac language," existed thirty settlements (Díaz 1986, 78). Thus a comparison of the only two eyewitness accounts, on which all the others are based, and the map of Postclassic settlement does little more than confirm many towns and the tentative state of the region's archaeology.

The archaeological estimate of Zempoala's population provides the only alternative type of evidence against which to judge the veracity of the documents (Brüggemann 1991, 93-95). That estimate of 8,500 to 25,000 inhabitants pertains to the core built-up area of the city, roughly a square some two-and-a-half kilometers on a side focused on a series of plazas and pyramids. Thus the population densities implied by that estimate, from 1,360 to 4,000 per square kilometer, are lower by far than the roughly 15,000 per square kilometer estimate for the coeval Aztec capital of Tenochtitlán, for which better data exist (Sanders 1992, 149). On the other hand, the documentary-based estimate of 108,000 yields a density of 17,280 per square kilometer for the same core area, more similar to the Tenochtitlán estimate. Whether Aguilar's "twenty thousand casas" pertains to a larger area than the archaeological estimate and therefore reflects a lower density is unknowable without a more concerted excavation effort. In any case, such comparisons make the Zempoala estimate of about a hundred thousand seem quite reasonable.

Accurately estimating the late-precolonial population of the study region as a whole remains impossible—but necessary and doable. The only true cities, Zempoala and Ixcalpa had populations, respectively, of about 100,000 and 50,000. Several large towns spanned the region from north to south and east to west, all of them seemingly aligned along the major river valleys that connected the lowlands to the highlands. Jalcomulco had a population of some 5,000 and Cuetlaxtla, an Aztec garrison, of about half that. The other known Aztec garrisons, Actopan and Quauhtochco, likely had similar populations of 2,500 each. The largest known settlements, then, had an approximate combined population of some 162,500. Given the dispersed character of much Mesoamerican settlement, however, the settlement hierarchy likely did not stop at the rank of towns. To assume a whole constellation of villages of about a thousand people each, such as the Spaniards came across along the lower Jamapa River, seems reasonable. To further assume an additional rank of hamlets of a hundred inhabitants or so each, such as the "fishing huts" that Cortés noted near the mouth of the Antigua River, also seems reasonable (Gómara 1987, 95-96). In sum, considering the estimate of the population of the province of Cuetlaxtlan alone, some 216,000 derived from Aguilar's claim of forty thousand houses, and considering that the Spaniards did not penetrate or report on the province of Quauhtochco, a population estimate for all three provinces combined of half a million seems entirely reasonable.

Canal Irrigation, Hill Lands, and Wetlands

That clear evidence of dense population certainly did not dissuade the archaeological community from marginalizing the Totonacapan lowlands. By western
terms of reference, the subhumid climate *must* have precluded intensive agriculture. The long dry season *must* have limited urbanization and "social evolution."
Zempoala, undeniably an urban center by the accounts of the conquistadors, was
late in developing, derivative of highland centers, and *must* have relied on canal
irrigation for its food and tribute production.

Canal Irrigation

Despite that enthusiasm for canal irrigation—and little else—the actual evidence
for it remains scant. The most obvious source has been the statement by Gómara
that Zempoala was "completely covered in gardens and freshness, and with fine
irrigated gardens" (Gómara 1987, 97). Despite Lesley Byrd Simpson's mistrans-
lation of "huertas de regadío" as "well-watered orchards" instead of "irrigated
gardens" and the possibility of hand irrigation, the statement clearly implies
canal irrigation (Palerm 1955, 34; 1961, 260; Gómara 1964, 70). Gómara, of
course, had never been to Zempoala and must have relied on an informant,
probably Cortés. The only applicable written statement by him, however, refers
to "water wells and cisterns" inside the principal houses, not to irrigation, and
forces the conclusion that Gómara drew either on his own imagination or on a
personal communication from Cortés (Cortés 1988, 21). Torquemada does no
more than combine Gómara and Díaz when writing his account around 1600,
adding nothing of real substance: "in each house there was a garden, with its
standing water, altogether appearing a delightful paradise" (Torquemada 1969,
libro iv, cap. xix). Canal irrigation would certainly help to explain how Zempoala could appear "so luxuriant and like a garden" when the Spaniards arrived in
April, towards the end the dry season, but so would early rains that particular
year.
    Archaeology, despite considerable obsession with canal irrigation, has done
nothing to demonstrate it, with all the physical evidence to date confirming a
domestic water system in the central precinct rather than agricultural irrigation.
Following Strebel's rediscovery of the location of Zempoala, the Paso y Troncoso project of the 1890s first located hydraulic features at Zempoala: a series of
"desagües del muro," or wall drains, spaced at regular intervals around the low
walls enclosing the main precinct (Strebel 1883; Paso y Troncoso 1892-1893,
2:8-9, 298-99; Galindo y Villa 1912, figs. 19, 23). Half a century later, another
archaeologist uncovered "a network of small underground aqueducts which, by
gravity, circulated crystalline water and distributed it to the entire ancient city"
(García Payón 1949a, 453-54; 1971, 538). "Crystalline water" aside, García
Payón did not describe the sizes and locations of these subterranean ducts other

than as being under the central precinct, but he did assert "that by means of gradual inclines these aqueducts emptied into house- or enclosure-cisterns and from them, through another passageway, to other cisterns, until they finally discharged into an irrigation canal" (García Payón 1971, 537-38). He also relocated Paso y Troncoso's wall drains and interpreted them as having carried "running water from the [Actopan River], each section of the merloned wall having had drain holes underneath its base where required" (García Payón 1949a, 455).

García Payón's interpretation of his and the Paso y Troncoso excavations remains hopelessly unclear, with water supply and drainage functions seemingly confounded. On the one hand, the use of waste water drained from a residential area to irrigate crops did occur elsewhere in Mesoamerica (Doolittle 1990, 138-39). On the other hand, Zempoala's main precinct seems to have had ceremonial and, perhaps, defensive functions. Not many people would have lived within the merloned perimeter wall, and the waste water discharge involved and, consequently, the area of crops irrigated, if any, would have been small. The small size and regular spacing of the wall drains suggest that they drained the plazas during summer rain storms, hurricanes, and floods (García Payón 1971, fig. 32b). Even if the wall drains did discharge into some sort of ditches, they would not have been irrigation canals. Irrigation, after all, would have pertained to the long dry season, not to the summer wet-season.

The Paso y Troncoso project also produced a map of the central precinct and environs that indicates a canal irrigation system used by farmers who had settled the area in the mid-nineteenth century (Paso y Troncoso 1892-1893, 2:291-92; Galindo y Villa 1912, fig. 12). That system drew water from a side channel of the Actopan River to irrigate about a hundred hectares in total and certainly demonstrates the potential for canal irrigation at Zempoala. But suggestions that the postcolonial canals represent "remnants of one of the irrigation systems" used by the Zempoalans is pure fantasy (Wilkerson 1983, 58, 81, fig. 17). Comparison of the 1891 map with maps and air photos from 1973 demonstrates that the Actopan River has undergone substantial channel changes over the past century (SRH 1973a, 1973b, 1973c). A 1942 flood even destroyed the nineteenth-century main irrigation canal, or *zanja madre* (García Payón 1950, 90; 1971, 513). Even greater channel changes must have occurred since 1519. The nineteenth-century settlers would have had to engineer and construct their own canals within the context of a hydrology substantially altered since the conquistadors rode into Zempoala.

In summary, the archaeology at most amounts to having uncovered a system of storm-water drains and the water supply for the principal houses of the city that Cortés reported. No evidence exists for an elaborate canal irrigation system, in which "each house had a garden with flowing water, and everything appeared like an earthly paradise," as asserted by so many archaeologists for so many years (Paso y Troncoso 1892-1893, 2:297; Fewkes 1907, 236; Krikeberg 1933, 41-44; García Payón 1949a, 1971; Melgarejo Vivanco 1949, 1976, 1980; Sanders 1953, 67; 1971, 547; Palerm 1955, 33; 1961, 259; Palerm and Wolf

1957, 16; Wolf 1959, 13; Sanders and Price 1968, 160; Adams 1977, 287; Wilkerson 1983). García Payón even went so far as to speculate that the origin of the canal irrigation system, for which barely an iota of evidence exists even for the Postclassic period, dates to the Classic (García Payón 1966, 18). In the most imaginative variant of all, an ephemeral brush, wood, and stone dam on the Actopan River fed water into the canal irrigation system during the dry season (Melgarejo Vivanco 1949, 188; 1980, 24). During the wet season, floods would have destroyed the dam and inundated the downstream fields. As the floodwaters receded, the canals would have aided drainage and permitted earlier planting. In the subsequent dry season, the rebuilt dam would again divert water into the canal system. Furthermore, the system had an enormous extent—apparently.

> [When] the Spaniards arrived at Zempoala, they marveled at an irrigation system which not only watered its plots but distributed water to the patios of the houses; it was a system comprising the lower basin of the [Actopan River], beginning at Descabezadero and even higher, at Almolonga [, some forty kilometers upstream from Zempoala] (Melgarejo Vivanco 1976, 35).

In reality, the existing evidence demonstrates that the Totonac elite enjoyed indoor plumbing. The potential for a canal irrigation system certainly existed, as demonstrated by the small nineteenth-century system and the much more extensive one that now irrigates several thousand hectares of sugar cane. But recent attempts to use false-color infrared, aerial photography to confirm even one precolonial canal have failed to detect so much as a trace (unpublished data). Further ground reconnaissance and excavation have also failed to corroborate a century of assertion (Doolittle 1990, 114; Cortés Hernández 1991; unpublished data).

Five other places have equally as good or better evidence as Zempoala for precolonial canal irrigation (figure 2.6). In 1580, the district governor for Jalapa reported that Atezca, also spelled Atesca, "through irrigation harvests lots of maize twice per year and has cacao fields" (Acuña 1985, 367). Irrigation would in fact have been essential for cacao cultivation in the subhumid climate (Palerm 1961, 262-63). Besides Atezca, cacao orchards occurred near Espiche, Cuetlaxtla, and Quauhtochco during the early sixteenth century and at Chicuasen during the 1730s (AGN-T, vol. 511, exp. 12, f. 18v; AGN-Hospital de Jesús, leg. 400, exp. 12; BAGN 1936, 215; 1940, 206, 209). Given the explicit reference linking cacao cultivation and irrigation at Atezca, the water requirements of cacao, and the confirmation of precolonial cacao production in these subhumid lowlands by the Matricula de Tributos and Codex Mendoza, irrigation almost certainly occurred at some of those places and others during late precolonial times. Whether large canal irrigation systems were involved remains entirely unclear, however.

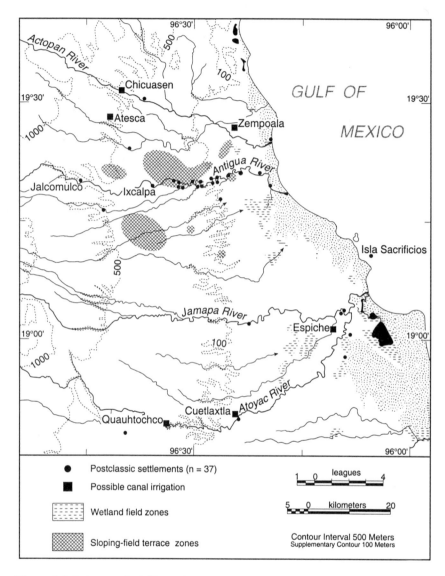

Figure 2.6. Late precolonial intensive agriculture.

Terracing

But if canal irrigation has proven a relatively fruitless obsession, at least so far, geographical analysis of the piedmont to the southwest of Zempoala has revealed complexes of relict sloping-field terraces scattered throughout some thousand square-kilometers of hill lands (Siemens 1985, 143). From the air these vestiges appear as light lines against the dark soil of recently plowed fields. Indiscernible when approached on the ground, the lines comprise no more than a scatter of stones smaller than twenty centimeters in diameter and exhibit no appreciable relief (Sluyter and Siemens 1992). Superficially at least, they resemble the so-called stone lines of the Petén savanna (Rice and Rice 1979).

Ground survey and photogrammetry facilitated the mapping of nine field complexes and an assessment of their morphology (Sluyter and Siemens 1992). Most characteristically, the linear concentrations of stones vary from three to five meters in width and form rectilinear networks that trend parallel to slope contours (figure 2.7). The intervals between the centers of the lines vary from five to twenty-five meters on slopes ranging from four degrees to three-quarters of a degree but with no clear relationship between interval and slope. The lengths of the lines range from fifteen to five hundred meters. Relatively contiguous networks of lines occupy areas from three to fifty hectares. Moreover, at La Gloria a suite of such fragments consistently orient to between thirteen and fifteen degrees east of north, suggesting the unity of the fragments (Sluyter and Siemens 1992, fig. 4). The builders seem to have ignored microvariations in slope direction in order to conform to an overall orientational scheme. Presumably, other complexes underlie the intervening spaces but were covered in crops and secondary vegetation during mapping. If so, the entire La Gloria complex would cover a minimum of one hundred and fifty hectares, and the similar complex near Tamarindo with an orientation of about ten degrees west of north would cover a minimum of three hundred hectares (Sluyter and Siemens 1992, fig. 2).

The characteristic contouring on gentle slopes suggests the *metepantli* terraces of the Mesa Central as an analog to gain insights into the function of the relict lowland features. Metepantli farmers construct parallel flights of low banks, or *bordos*, that trend parallel to the contours of gentle slopes (West 1970; Patrick 1977, 1985; Denevan 1980, 626). The metepantli certainly dates from as early as the Classic period, quite possibly earlier. Farmers still employ the technique throughout the Mesa Central but not in the Veracruz lowlands (Patrick 1977, 214-19). Near Apan, Hidalgo, metepantli fields vary from fifteen to a hundred and fifty meters long and from twelve to thirty meters wide on slopes of three to six degrees to less than three meters wide on slopes of fifteen degrees but with no general relationship between interval and slope (West 1970, 367; Patrick 1977, 50). In Tlaxcala, the bordos are nominally one meter thick and forty centimeters high (Wilken 1987, 106-7). While the bordos slow runoff and accumulate soil in the intervening fields, they never attain the near horizontal surfaces of bench terraces. The resulting deeper soils and increased infiltration do, however, provide for greater soil moisture storage throughout the year. The bordos themselves drain better than the fields and support various xerophytes, principally *maguey*.[3]

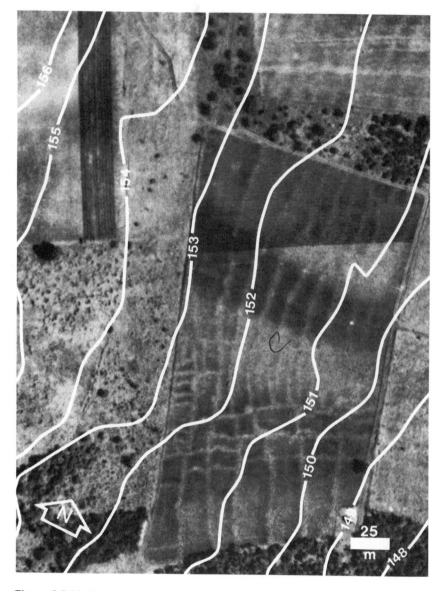

Figure 2.7. Vertical aerial photograph of relict sloping-field terrace complex with overlay of contour lines. Photograph by Secretaría de Recursos Hidráulicos (SRH 1973c).

Metepantli and the lowland vestiges, then, seem strikingly similar. Field widths, lengths, and slopes correspond. The cultural contexts and the climates have much in common, although the highlands are subject to frosts during the dry season. That farmers incorporate many of the stones they clear from their fields into their bordos, simultaneously strengthening them and utilizing them as a dump, further suggests that the lines of stones in the lowlands might be relict metepantli (Sluyter and Siemens 1992, fig. 6). Upon abandonment, breaches might develop in a bordo. Then soil creep, rainsplash erosion, and slope wash would carry soil particles downslope while leaving behind a linear concentration of stones. Subsequent plowing would attenuate the resulting parallel stone strips into a pattern similar to the vestiges, broader than a bordo and with no appreciable relief.

Nonetheless, the putative Veracruz bordos might never have been as substantial as those typical of present-day, highland metepantli. A closer analog might be the low stone alignments which farmers in Guerrero and Sonora employ to distribute runoff evenly over field surfaces to increase infiltration and slow soil erosion (Doolittle 1984, 129, fig. 3).

In light of those two analogs, the relict features might most basically represent field-stone clearance dumps but also sloping-field terrace bordos. The cost-benefit equation of stone clearance is complex. On the one hand, stones can form a beneficial mulch which increases infiltration, decreases evaporation, and mitigates rainsplash erosion (Lightfoot 1993). On the other hand, stones can hinder tillage and plant growth, breaking and deflecting tools and competing with plants for space. Farmers therefore tend to clear the larger stones and leave the smaller ones, the exact balance varying with technological, cultural, and environmental context. Stones also have an intrinsic value as building material, and linear dumps can demarcate field boundaries and form terrace walls. The metepantli analog and the gently sloping vertisols, a type of soil which does not erode easily, suggest that the vestiges were sloping-field terraces rather than bench terraces, the latter typically employed to mitigate soil erosion on steep or highly erodable slopes and to facilitate canal irrigation (Wilken 1987, 104-24). As with the metepantli, increases in infiltration and soil moisture storage probably were the major motivations for the Veracruz sloping-field terraces (Patrick 1977, 114-21).

That those vestiges pertain to the precolonial period seems clear from the accounts of three Germans sojourning in the region during the nineteenth century. Hugo Fink, Brantz Mayer, and Carl Sartorius all observed relict terracing, similar to but apparently more intact than the present lines of stones.

> The whole country is interlaced with parallel lines of stones, which were intended, during the heavy showers of the rainy season, to keep the earth from washing away. The number of these lines of stones shows clearly that even the poorest land, which in our days nobody would cultivate, was put under requisition (Fink 1871, 373).

It is true, that traces of old cultivation are yet to be found, and also the remains of a former dense population. The sides of the hills, in many places, as in Chile and Peru, are cut into terraces (Mayer 1847, 11).

When the tall grass is burnt down, we can see that the whole country was formed into terraces with the assistance of masonry, everywhere provision had been made against the ravages of the tropical rains; they were carried out on every slope, descending even to the steepest spots, where they are often only a few feet in width. In the flat valleys are countless remains of dams and reservoirs, mostly of large stones and clay, many of solid masonry, naturally all rent by the floods at the lowest part, and filled with earth. On the dry flat ridges the remains of large cities are found, forming for miles regular roads. . . . All is now concealed by trees or tall grass; for many miles scarcely a hut is built, where formerly every foot of land was as diligently cultivated as the banks of the Nile or the Euphrates in Solomon's time. We know not whether a plague of hunger, or warlike tribes from the North, or some great convulsion of nature destroyed the numerous population, indeed we have not the slightest clue, which could enable us to decide to what people these relics of great industrial activity belong (Sartorius 1961, 10).

Since by the nineteenth century, the origin of the vestiges was already uncertain, and since livestock rather than agriculture dominated during the intervening three centuries of the colonial period, the features must be precolonial. Sartorius, Mayer, and Fink clearly collaborated with one another and jointly deduced as much. Further refining that chronology and understanding how the sloping-field terraces relate to the changing settlement pattern will require excavations beyond the four test pits completed so far, none of which yielded pottery sherds that might indicate chronology.

Documentary data and crop ecology indicate the possibilities of cotton, maize, and agave cultivation for the sloping-field terraces.[4] The Aztec tribute lists indicate that Totonacapan was a major cotton producer (Barlow 1949, 89-92). Although not now evident, cotton cultivation continued at least into the sixteenth-century (AGN-Hospital de Jesús, leg. 400, exp. 12). Cotton's precipitation requirements and crop cycle accord well with the subhumid climate. Bolls would have developed during the wet season, then ripened and yielded their fiber during the dry season. Moreover, the vertisols that dominate much of the terrace area are well suited to cotton cultivation. Some sources suggest that the cotton of the tribute lists might refer to "tree cotton," one sixteenth-century source describing how Zempoalans wove cloth from the fibers of the ceiba tree (Paso y Troncoso 1905, 5:195, 200).[5] But ceibas would hardly be likely to produce enough to meet the annual tribute of 1,600 loads of raw fiber and 7,520 loads of woven mantles.

Unlike cotton, which cannot grow in the highlands due to frosts, maize can and did; and it therefore does not appear in the Aztec tribute lists for Quauhtochco and Cuetlaxtlan. Maize's bulk, weight, and near ubiquity in Mesoamerica did not encourage long-distance transport from Totonacapan to the Basin of Mexico except during the periodic famines (Sluyter 1993). Given an average precipitation of some eight hundred millimeters during the hundred and thirty days from mid May to late September, a rain-fed maize crop is certainly possible despite the subhumid climate of the lowland environs of Zempoala. However, the coincidence of the canícula, the August dry period, with the maturation of the tassels and silks makes pollination problematic. Depending on the timing and severity of the canícula, yields might be low or the entire crop lost (Claassen and Shaw 1970). Sloping-field terracing reduces the risk of growing rain-fed maize by enhancing soil moisture storage to weather severe canículas.

Although not much in evidence at present, a sixteenth-century source reports agave cultivation in the Veracruz lowlands (Paso y Troncoso 1905, 5:194, 200). Drawing on the metepantli analog, the stony bordos would have been the best microenvironment for this economically important xerophyte (Patrick 1977, table 3.7, 130-31). Suggestively, Sartorius noted that "agaves start up from heaps of stones" throughout the piedmont (Sartorius 1961, 9).

Those three crops would have complemented one another in the context of sloping-field terracing. Past practice among the Teenek of northern Veracruz and others included intercropping and rotating cotton with maize to reduce losses to pests and increase yields (Sartorius 1961, 175; Alcorn 1984, 390; Fisher 1989). In the deepened, more humid soils of the sloping fields, then, farmers might have intercropped maize and cotton. They would have harvested the maize at the end of the wet season, thus exposing the cotton to additional sun to aid boll ripening during the dry season. Cotton, as a perennial shrub, would have mitigated topsoil loss during the winter northers. Along the stony, more rapidly draining, and therefore less humid bordos, agave would have formed a living windbreak, reducing maize lodging, cotton lint loss, and evapotranspiration (Davis and Norman 1988).

None of the test pits yielded diagnostic botanical remains to confirm the cultivation of any of those three possible crops (unpublished data). Phytoliths do occur but cotton and agave do not produce identifiable phytoliths (Pearsall 1989). Maize phytoliths, which might be distinguishable from those of other grasses, did not occur either (Piperno 1988; Doolittle and Frederick 1991). Pollen preservation is very poor, with low concentrations and severe degradation. Ironically, the same clearance and deep plowing of the last several decades that has exposed the vestiges to view from the air has disrupted them and threatens their preservation for further study.

Wetland Fields

That archaeologists have equally failed to recognize precolonial agricultural use of wetlands is entirely consistent with the effects of the pristine myth. If westerners have had a long-standing obsession with canal irrigation, they have had an equally long-standing aversion towards wetlands. Yet geographical analysis, including air and ground survey as well as excavation, has revealed several thousand hectares of relict field complexes scattered throughout the wetlands of the coastal plain (Siemens 1980, 1998; Siemens et al. 1988). As elsewhere in the Americas, those labyrinthine complexes of relict planting platforms and intervening canals appear as patterning of microtopography and vegetation in wetlands (Denevan 1970; Denevan and Turner 1974; Sluyter 1994).

The general methods of construction and functions of such intensive wetland agriculture seem clear enough, the details much less so. The major extant occurrence, the highly productive chinampas of the Basin of Mexico, provides the best analog to model function and construction (Sluyter 1994). Farmers constructed fields by both ditching into and mounding above ground surfaces that intersected the water table for at least part of the year. The most general functions involved regulation of soil moisture in the rooting zone and maintenance of nutrient and heat sumps in the intervening canals to serve as a source of fertilizing muck and to mitigate frost damage, the latter clearly not applicable to tropical lowlands. In some cases, farmers may have lowered a perennially high water table or raised the planting surface above the water surface, as in the case of the chinampas. There, permanent dams controlled water levels and salinities in the interconnected lakes of the Basin of Mexico, the surfaces of the large rectilinear planting platforms never becoming submerged (Palerm 1973). In other cases, planting platforms seem to have been entirely submerged during the wet season, with farmers managing drainage to allow cropping as early in the dry season as possible yet retain enough water for splash and subirrigation later in the dry season.

The small, typically curvilinear fields of lowland Veracruz occur in seasonal backswamps rather than in perennial lakes and seem to have functioned in the latter manner (figure 2.8). The labyrinthine canal system, possibly interrupted by ephemeral dams, allowed a delicate balance between drainage during the early dry season and irrigation during the late dry season (Siemens 1983b, 1998). Moreover, as the annual floodwaters receded, they left behind a soil that was weeded and renewed in nutrients from an increment of fresh mud. The benefits—cropping during the dry season, increased productivity, and reduced risk—would have been worth the labor cost of construction and maintenance.

The general chronology of the fields also seems clear enough, albeit with much room for refinement. Most basically the fields date to the precolonial period (Siemens 1980). More specifically, the dominant orientation of the field complexes indicates origins during the Classic period (Siemens 1983b). The orientation of fifteen degrees east of north mimics the orientation of the main avenue and pyramids at Teotihuacán, the highland center that dominated much of Mesoamerica during the Classic period and that seems to have imposed that azimuth on landscape orientations in other parts of the highlands and, seemingly, the lowlands (Tichy 1976). The fields' general orientation cannot, of

Figure 2.8. The relict planting platforms and canals of a complex of intensive wetland agricultural fields. Photograph by the author, May 1989.

course, reveal whether Teotihuacán exercised direct control over field construction, the Totonacs brought a cosmological imperative with them on their migration, or the connection was more culturally diffuse.

Excavations confirm cultivation during the Classic period (Siemens et al. 1988). At two distinct field complexes in backswamps of the San Juan River, maize phytoliths occur about a meter beneath the surface of planting platforms in association with sherds of Classic pottery styles. A pollen record of maize cultivation from a core at nearby Laguna Catarina confirms that relative, ceramic chronology with absolute, radiocarbon dates (Sluyter 1997c). Maize cultivation in the general area began during the Preclassic period, when a saline coastal lagoon fringed by mangrove forest occupied the basin that the San Juan River now drains. Upward trends in the proportion of phosphorous and clay in the core reflect increasing population and the sort of slash-and-burn forest clearance associated with shifting cultivation (Eidt 1977; Deevey et al. 1979; Binford 1983). A layer of charcoal indicates that around 450 B.C., by when the basin had become isolated from the Gulf of Mexico and occupied by freshwater backswamps along the San Juan River, people began to clear trees from wetlands and convert them into agricultural fields. Just as for the phytolith record, maize cultivation in the wetlands does not seem to persist into the late precolonial period. Around A.D. 500, a pulse of carbon, phosphorous, and freshly eroded sand indicate, at least tentatively, that protracted intensification of land use eventually resulted in slope destabilization in the piedmont. During the subsequent, 500-year hiatus in maize pollen, downward trends in the proportion of phosphorous and carbon indicate a decrease in population and a restabilization of slopes. Maize pollen resumes after A.D. 1100, but sporadically and perhaps, given the lack of Postclassic pottery sherds and phytoliths from the wetland field complexes themselves, it derives from fields on the hill lands bordering the wetlands. Maize cultivation using intensive wetland agriculture, then, clearly had begun by the Classic period but, at least on the basis of the limited research so far, might not have persisted into the Postclassic.

Because the numerous precolonial settlements in and around the San Juan wetlands have lacked archaeological attention, further refining that chronology and understanding the relationship between changing settlement pattern and agriculture awaits much additional research. Only the archaeological sites of Buena Vista and Loma Iguana have yielded relevant data, and then quite little and without the use of radiocarbon dating. People living at Buena Vista beginning in the Preclassic, on what then was the shore of an estuarine lagoon fringed by mangrove forest, fished and gathered mollusks as well as employing agriculture (Casimir 1990). During the Classic period, after freshwater wetlands had formed, Buena Vista was abandoned and people moved to Loma Iguana, near one of the test pits that yielded maize phytoliths and Classic pottery sherds. By the Postclassic, people had moved away from Loma Iguana.

Landscape

In terms of the intensive agriculture necessary to sustain the population and tribute production of Totonacapan, sloping-field terraces and wetland fields seem much more likely than canal irrigation. The chronologies of both terracing and wetland fields remain far from certain, but at least firm evidence exists for both—as opposed to the supposed canal irrigation. Just what Sartorius meant by "countless remains of dams and reservoirs, mostly of large stones and clay, many of solid masonry" in the "flat valleys" remains obscure (Sartorius 1961, 10). So does his seeming reference to stone walled bench terraces: "formed into terraces with the assistance of masonry, . . . carried out on every slope, descending even to the steepest spots, where they are often only a few feet in width (Sartorius 1961, 10). As yet, apparently, we know approximately nothing about the region's late-precolonial intensive agriculture compared to what continued research might yield.

Moreover, little evidence exists for other precolonial land uses, both agricultural and others, and little potential even for uncovering such evidence. Flood recessional and shifting, rain-fed cultivation of maize do not require the same investment of labor in field infrastructure as intensive agriculture and do not result in persistent landscape modifications such as canals and bordos. Both might well have occurred, however. Only a little archaeological evidence demonstrates precolonial fishing and mollusk collection, but Cortés noted some "fishing huts" not far from the mouth of the Antigua River and turtles, fish, and shellfish all seem to have been used (Gómara 1987, 95-96; Alvarado Tezozomoc 1944, 122; Navarrete Hernández 1988; Casimir 1990). The conquistadors also commented on native hunting, with deer and turkey seemingly plentiful in 1519 (Díaz 1986, 75; Gómara 1987, 96; Cortés 1988, 20-21). The sixteenth-century geographical reports provide further insight into possible precolonial resource uses. The surviving natives fished the major streams; had available a wide range of game, including waterfowl, turkey, rabbit, and deer; and gathered fruits and medicinals (Paso y Troncoso 1905, 5:193, 195-99; JGI, xxv-8, ff. 10v-13v). They might also have mined the guano of the islands just off Chalchicueyecan for use as fertilizer (JGI, xxv-8, f. 16v).

Taking a landscape perspective, the heterogeneity of contrasting environmental patches in close juxtaposition would have given people access to diverse floral, faunal, and mineral resources: lagoons, lakes, ponds, marshes, salt pans, woodlands and meadows in basins; dunes, interdunes, and beaches along shorelines; reefs and open water in the Gulf of Mexico; channels, floodplains, levees, and gallery forests along streams; and woodlands and savannas on the piedmont. Moreover, the annual rhythm of the rains would have added a temporal heterogeneity. Vegetation and soil moisture, for example, would have spatially varied from wetland margins to centers and temporally from dry season to wet season. As in the Amazon Basin, annual flooding of gallery forest would have provided habitat for and access to fish and crustaceans, and the wetlands would have yielded a seasonal round of floral and faunal resources (Wilken 1970; Nietschmann 1972; Goulding 1980).

Even more speculatively, given the lack of a chronology for the sloping-field terraces, the various agroecosystems might have had spatial and temporal ecological relationships. For example, sloping-field terraces on the piedmont overlook a complex of wetland fields in a backswamp of Arroyo Naranjillo, only a couple of kilometers from the putative canal irrigation system at Zempoala. On the one hand, the vestiges might represent different periods of agricultural intensification. On the other hand, the wetland fields might have provided dry-season crops to complement the wet-season crops of the piedmont fields. Also, a recent agricultural practice suggests the possibility of a more complex ecological interrelationship. Some farmers who cultivate the margins of the Naranjillo wetland employ seed-beds in the wetland to germinate their piedmont, wet-season maize crops (Siemens 1990b). This strategy advances the crop's growth far enough by transplanting time in May to ameliorate the worst effects of the canícula. The addition of canal irrigation would only have made highly productive harvests throughout the year even more possible, enormously reducing the risk of famine.

1519/Ce Acatl

That archaeologists so badly miscategorized this tropical lowland is, of course, a particular case of a broader phenomenon associated with European colonization: namely, the pristine myth. Their implicit assumptions reflect the colonizer's model of the world, the global categorization of colonized regions as backwards, that has paralleled and naturalized the material redistribution of global resources, labor, and capital. The fascination with the possibility of irrigation canals at Zempoala is especially symptomatic of such miscategorization. A preoccupation with the significance of irrigation in the emergence of urban societies typically parallels the assumption that tropical lowlands are somehow marginal (Steward 1955; Sanders and Price 1968; Wittfogel 1972). Above all, then, that archaeologists miscategorized this tropical lowland reflects the western assumption that changes in productivity must have progressed from the tropical idyll of the precolonial period, through the extensive ranching of the colonial period, to the intensive commodity agriculture of the present.

On the contrary, when Cortés arrived in 1519—the year Ce Acatl, or One Reed, in the Nahua calendar—he and the other conquistadors encountered a landscape that was densely rather than sparsely settled. Zempoala stood out as a metropolis of a hundred thousand, at the top of the settlement hierarchy of a region with a population of perhaps half a million people. Little wonder that Cortés dubbed it Seville and Bernal Díaz marveled at its luxuriance and streets full of women and men. The subhumid lowland climate clearly did not preclude intensive agriculture, whatever the details of function and chronology for the various agroecosystems that will emerge as research goes on. Those systems, the settlement pattern, its ethnic differentiation, and tribute exaction by the Aztec were the culmination of millennia of precolonial processes.

The coming of the Spaniards and the establishment of the colonial triangle dramatically transformed the late-precolonial landscape. At present the regional population is about three-quarters of a million, less than double the late-precolonial population.[6] More than half of those people live in and immediately around the industrial port of Veracruz, built where the conquistadors unloaded their horses on the then-empty beach of Chalchicueyecan. Drive inland from that port, one of Mexico's largest, and you encounter cattle ranches and irrigated sugar cane fields and mango orchards, exotic biota domesticated in Asia and brought to the Americas by Europeans.

Notes

1. This and all subsequent Spanish-English translations in this chapter are by the author.

2. The maps of precolonial settlement synthesize the following sources: Esteva 1843; Heller 1853; Sartorius 1869; Fink 1871; Bancroft 1875; Strebel 1883; Paso y Tron-

coso 1892-1893, 2:317; Nuttal 1910; Galindo y Villa 1912; García Payón 1947, 1949a, 1949b, 1950, 1966, 1971; Medellín Zenil and Torres Guzmán 1951; Medellín Zenil 1952, 1953, 1955, 1960; Ekholm 1953; Medellín Zenil and Peterson 1954; Molina Feal 1985; Ruiz Gordillo 1985, 1989, 1992; Brüggemann 1989, 1991; Casimir 1990, 1991; Daneels 1990, 1991, 1992; León Pérez 1991; Stark and Arnold 1997.

3. *Maguey* (*Agave* spp.), agave or century plant in English.

4. Cotton (*Gossypium* spp.); maize (*Zea mays*); agave (*Agave* spp.).

5. Ceiba (*Ceiba pentandra*), silk-cotton tree or kapok tree in English.

6. The figure of 776,066 people is the sum of populations for the following seventeen *municipios*, as estimated by the XI Censo General de Población y Vivienda of 1990: Actopan (40,541), Adelberto Tejeda (5,195), Apazapan (3,651), Boca del Río (144,549), Carrillo Puerto (12,035), Cotaxtla (16,624), Cuitlahuac (21,897), Jamapa (9,177), La Antigua (21,555), Manlio Fabio Altamirano (19,345), Medellín (29,298), Paso de Ovejas (28,646), Paso del Macho (23,104), Puente Nacional (17,741), Soledad de Doblado (26,612), Ursulo Galván (27,489), and Veracruz (328,607). The populations of the municipios of Veracruz and Boca del Río define the population living in and immediately around the port of Veracruz: 473,156 people.

3

Colonization

The enormous material/conceptual transformation involved in the colonization of these lowlands and of New Spain began with a prospectus that quickly became reality. Cortés, in his 1519 dispatch, wrote of country "very apt and agreeable for traveling through and for pasturing all kinds of livestock" (Cortés 1988, 20).[1] And by 1580, when the district governor claimed "150,000 head of livestock," that vision clearly had materialized (JGI, ms. xxv-8, f. 5). Cortés, however, had not envisioned the other major material transformation: the devastation of the native population that paralleled the increase in livestock, as reported by the same governor.

> According to the tradition of the oldest residents of this land, at the time that the Spaniards came, there were many places and large Indian populations within six leagues [twenty-five kilometers] all around this city [of Vera Cruz]. These have become so diminished that many have become completely depopulated, leaving no trace except the memory of a name; and others now have so few residents and people that, compared to what was, the extreme to which they have been reduced is sad to see. . . . In this notable way the natives of this district have declined since the Spaniards mastered the land; and each day the towns continue to disappear, two or three places joining together into one in order better to preserve themselves, in such a way as one cannot expect anything but that those remaining will come to total ruin and destruction (JGI, ms. xxv-8, ff. 5v-6v).

The governor conveys the overall impression of vast herds and flocks grazing lush pastures amid deserted cities and villages, recalling Oliver Goldsmith's epitaph for another landscape: "The country blooms, a garden and a grave."

The orthodox explanation of the causal relationship between that increase in livestock and decrease in natives, not just for Veracruz but for New Spain more generally, presumes that the rise in livestock population was the dependent variable. In other words, as the native population declined due to a series of disease epidemics, agricultural fields could become pastures and livestock population could increase—and did so.

> Only as lands became unoccupied through depopulation did Spaniards become interested in acquiring them. . . . The denuded landscape of much of modern Spanish America is thus related to Indian abandonment of land and the replacement of a human population with grazing animals (Gibson 1966, 152).

> We do not contend that open-range grazing was without negative consequences for Indian livelihood, settlement continuity, or demography. But government policy in the matter was benign and basically effective, and damages were contained. . . . Indian demographic decline was overwhelmingly due to epidemic disease . . . , and it was that decline which made possible the expansion of Spanish livestock and agricultural activity, not vice versa (Butzer and Butzer 1995, 169).

Those scholars clearly cannot deny that some livestock negatively impacted some native communities because the documents demonstrate that conflicts between natives and ranchers abounded in Tlaxcala, Oaxaca, the Basin of Mexico and other highland regions (Gibson 1964, 278-82; Gibson 1967, 80-84; Taylor 1972, 119; Super 1988, 55). Those disputes concerned both land tenure and damages to crops and infrastructure, the latter mainly due to large rather than small stock. Cattle entered native fields of maize, vegetables, and fruit just before harvest and devoured or spoiled all while trampling and destroying fences, canals, and terrace walls; entire towns were demolished and abandoned (Gibson 1967, 152-53).

Yet such scholars do argue that the Crown generally succeeded in limiting such destruction through legislation. A 1567 decree, for example, stipulated that native settlements were to encompass a minimum area of one square league (*Recopilación* 1987, libro 6, titulo 3, ley 20). Subsequent legislation mandated that no cattle ranch should locate within one and a half leagues of any native settlement and no sheep ranch within half a league (McBride 1923, 123-24).

Such highly generalized conclusions, however, caricature colonialism in an effort to claim a single "root cause" for native depopulation and livestock expansion that applies to all of New Spain for all of the sixteenth century. Colonization, in that view, becomes an unavoidable tragedy caused by pathogens. Such overly simplified analysis obviates understanding complex interactions among natives, non-natives, and landscape. Clearly, for almost any large region of the Americas, in comparison to depopulation attributable to disease epidemics, any other cause simply pales. But just as clearly, such trite generalities do little to explain the colonization process. In terms of the colonial triangle, the conceptual structure of such non-explanations conforms to figure 1.5, with the implicit assumptions that the result of the colonization process is immanent to characteristics of the non-natives, that native agency is relatively inconsequential, and that environment is determinative for natives but not for non-natives. Interminably rehearsing the humanitarian efforts of some viceroys, the ministrations of some clergy, or the legislation intended to protect natives does not serve any explanatory role in such a framework. The only intention can be to demonstrate "good intentions" in order to claim an "enlightened colonialism" which minimized the "price of progress" as much as humanly possible. In other words, the effectiveness or ineffectiveness of good deeds or legislation intended to protect natives from livestock becomes irrelevant to explaining the expansion of livestock ranches when the conclusion is that native population "decline was overwhelmingly due to epidemic disease" anyway, and that pathogens thus made possible the expansion of livestock ranches (Butzer and Butzer 1995, 169). In that view, native depopulation was simply, if unfortunately, part of a necessary and natural teleological progression, with westernization as the telos.

In contrast, analysis focused on interactions among natives, non-natives, and landscape can begin to explain colonization as a dynamic, reciprocal, spatial process. For example, Sauer observes that on Hispaniola the arrogation of native labor for placer mining, agriculture, and domestic service so disrupted native ecologies that malnutrition resulted (Sauer 1966, 203-5). In order to concentrate and control labor, the Spaniards resettled natives at the gold placers and prohibited hunting and fishing trips. That settlement nucleation, entailing virtual incarceration and forced labor, necessitated a focus on manioc cultivation. Cassava, the bread made from manioc flour, thus became nearly the sole food of the natives. By abstracting that single element out of a complex subsistence ecology, the Spaniards enforced a diet with so little protein and fat that malnutrition became endemic. The Taino's "excellent but delicate ecologic balance broke down, quickly and inadvertently," and native population declined precipitously (Sauer 1966, 203). At the same time, the Spaniards retained a monopoly on raising livestock, prohibited natives from integrating that new source of protein and fat into their subsistence ecology. Then, just as Crown officials had started to understand the process of native decline and promote the integration of livestock into native agriculture, the smallpox epidemic of 1518 virtually extirpated the last of the Tainos. The relationship between native population, livestock, and epidemic disease thus becomes understandable as a complex, dynamic spatial process rather than as natural, unavoidable, and categorically predetermined.

Beyond such direct impacts on native subsistence and population due to non-native arrogation of native labor and land, environmental changes had indirect impacts. For the Valle de Mezquital in the central highlands of New Spain, for example, Melville argues that the sixteenth-century expansion of sheep ranches preceded and precipitated the native population decline (Melville 1994, 6-15). An exponential increase in the sheep population resulted in extreme overgrazing, a decrease in vegetation cover, more frequent and greater floods, dramatic soil erosion, and reduced spring flow. That environmental degradation negatively impacted native food production and thus caused population decline. Recognition of such complex interactions among non-natives, natives, and landscape reemphasizes the importance of considering the landscape patterning of such environmental variables as soil, for example, as both resulting from transformative processes and constituting a parameter for further transformations.

The sixteenth-century environmental impacts of the introduction of livestock into New Spain nonetheless remain far from clear. Some scholars have claimed that a metaphorical plague of sheep and cows early, persistently, and pervasively degraded environments (Simpson 1952; Crosby 1972; Melville 1994). Others have claimed the opposite, that the livestock introduction coincided with environmental recovery (Butzer and Butzer 1993). In that view, by the coming of the Spaniards, high native population densities were already testing environmental thresholds, with agriculture periodically disrupting vegetation and causing the erosion of soil from hillside fields. As native population declined due to disease epidemics, vegetation invaded abandoned fields and restabilized slopes. Only then did the flocks and herds expand; and through use of conservationist management practices, such as transhumance, overgrazing rarely occurred. Livestock, in the latter view, remain innocent of any immediate, widespread degradational effect beyond influencing vegetation composition—that is, the particular plant species involved as opposed to the vegetation type, be it woodland or grassland. The much later environmental depredations of the nineteenth and twentieth centuries have resulted from increasing integration into the global economy rather than from the sixteenth-century diffusion of Iberian pastoralism (Butzer and Butzer 1995).

Despite that prominence of livestock in the colonization process, whether related to scholarly debates over environmental impact or native depopulation, ranching's sixteenth-century beginnings have remained as obscure for New Spain as a whole as for Veracruz itself—little wonder since, as will become apparent, they are the same beginnings. While not discounting the horses and sheep noted in the 1580 report, the livestock that came to dominate the Veracruz lowlands were cattle. By the end of the first century of colonization, the Gulf Coast had become the quintessential cattle range of New Spain (Chevalier 1952, 1963; Simpson 1952; Doolittle 1987, figs. 3-5). Establishing the initial spatial characteristics of the lowland ranching ecology that became so dominant deserves considerable effort because the land-use patterns initially established constituted a parameter for subsequent colonization processes. This chapter therefore treats the introduction of cattle and a particular ranching ecology into the Veracruz lowlands, the earliest interactions between natives and ranchers, and changes in landscape patterns (figure 3.1). Subsequent chapters focus on later interactions among natives, non-natives, and landscape.

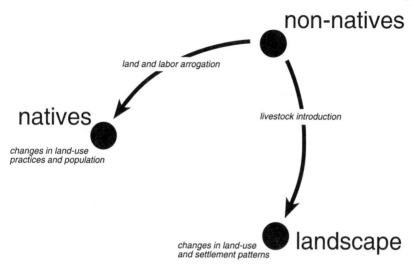

Figure 3.1. Processes and patterns addressed in this chapter.

The First Cattle

While the first cattle have left no more than a few archival tracks, enough exist to trail the first herd of New Spain through the marshes and hills of the Gulf Coast lowlands. An anonymous testimonial of 22 October 1554, preserved in Seville's Archivo General de Indias, posthumously recounts the deeds of a conquistador and yields a solitary, brief reference to the first cattle to reach New Spain.

> After the pacification of Mexico City and the other provinces of this New Spain, the said Gregorio de Villalobos, with the intention of remaining in it permanently, at the time that he came from the islands of Santo Domingo brought a number of yearlings, so that there might be cattle, he being the first to bring them to New Spain (Hackett 1923, 1:40).[2]

Accepting that anonymous assertion for the moment, a certain Gregorio de Villalobos apparently introduced the first cattle. And he landed his yearlings after August 1521, since in that month the Spaniards took the Aztec capital of Tenochtitlán, later rebuilding it as the colonial capital and renaming it Mexico City. But no matter how closely scrutinized, the sentence reveals nothing about precisely when this Villalobos introduced the yearlings, where he introduced them, how many he introduced, or how he propagated them.

Other such biographical fragments about Villalobos neither directly confirm nor directly contradict his claim to introducing the first cattle. Unlike some of the conquistadors, he has left a meager record of his life. He wrote no chronicles; he conducted no voluminous correspondence. The few biographical deeds and dates mainly derive from posthumous *probanzas de servicios y méritos*, similar to the so many other "proofs of meritorious service" that lauded the past deeds of conquistadors in order to secure lasting privilege for their scions. Consequently, while the assertion that Villalobos introduced some cattle early in the history of the colony is a long recognized clue to the beginnings of cattle ranching in New Spain (Brand 1961), it is equally a long uninvestigated clue.

While yielding no further references to cattle per se, the archival vestiges of Villalobos's life do assemble into a brief biography (Icaza 1923, 1:223; Hackett 1923, 1:40-41). He hailed from the Andalusian town of Almonte, on the northern margin of the Marismas, a large area of wetlands along the lower reaches of the Guadalquivir River (figure 3.2). His parents had come from Jerez de la Frontera, just south of the Marismas. The shipping lists of Seville record his passage to the Antilles in 1516, only twenty-two years old (Boyd-Bowman 1964, 59). In Cuba two years later, he must have heard of Grijalva's 1518 encounter with Montezuma's emissaries at Chalchicueyecan, now the site of the port of Veracruz. In early 1521, two years after Cortés had left Cuba to follow up on Grijalva's report and six months before the fall of Tenochtitlán, Villalobos sailed for Mexico to ride with the conquistadors (Boyd-Bowman 1968, 150). He arrived at Villa Rica de la Vera Cruz aboard a ship of reinforcements, probably the same one that brought Julián Alderete, the Royal Treasurer who was to ensure that Charles V would get his share of any booty (Díaz del Castillo 1986, 310). Rather than proceeding inland to take part in the battle for Tenochtitlán, though, Villalobos remained as part of the garrison at Villa Rica. Kept there by the direct orders of Cortés, Villalobos became one of Villa Rica's vecinos, or citizens, and he served as alderman and mayor. By 1526, he was serving as "majordomo" to Cortés at Medellín, a Spanish settlement along the lower Jamapa River founded around 1524 (Díaz del Castillo 1986, 505; Cortés 1988, 199). As his primary reward for helping to conquer Mexico, like so many other conquistadors, he received a grant of native labor and tribute, an *encomienda*. The natives so commended to Villalobos lived in Ixhuatlán, midway between Puebla de los Angeles and Medellín (Scholes and Adams 1955, 33). Eventually, the year being uncertain, he relocated from the lowlands to the highlands, moving to Puebla. There, as he had done in Villa Rica, he became a vecino and served as a *regidor* and as *alcalde* (Dorantes de Carranza 1987, 173). In 1542, he received a grant to establish a farm near Puebla and another for a garden plot (AGN-M, vol. 1, ff. 68-68v). The occasion for that move to a more urbane locale might well have been marriage to Beatriz García de la Fuente. They married sometime after 1527, that being the year her first husband died, and raised a daughter and two sons. Villalobos had died by 1547, the encomienda of Ixhuatlán going to one of the sons. As late as 1560, that successor was receiving 110 pesos per year

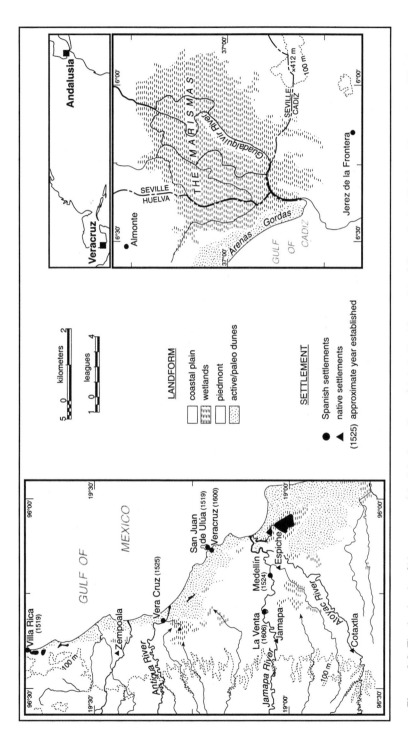

Figure 3.2. The lowlands of Veracruz and Andalusia as they pertain to the biography of Gregorio de Villalobos. The scales of the two maps are identical. The legal league of 4.2 kilometers is used. Medellín had a different location during the 1520s than at present.[3]

from the natives of Ixhuatlán, but by 1565 he had also died and the encomienda escheated (Paso y Troncoso 1939-1940, 9:18; Himmerich y Valencia 1991, 261).

That spare biography certainly does not directly help to fix the date that Villalobos imported the cattle with any greater precision than does the phrase "after the pacification of Mexico City." In fact, too literal an interpretation of such disparate biographical fragments only confuses the issue. Villalobos could not literally, after all, have come from Cuba half a year before the fall of Tenochtitlán, imported the cattle at some time after the fall of Tenochtitlán, and have brought some caves "at the time that he came from the islands of Santo Domingo." Clearly the last statement must be figurative, the context implying that Villalobos either made more than one voyage between the Antilles, then known as "the islands of Santo Domingo," and New Spain or that he had someone ship him the yearlings once he had become established. Such archival fragments clearly lack precision and consistency. Lacunae certainly abound. And exaggerations probably do as well; after all, the conquistadors' descendants wrote such posthumous biographies in order to profit by their forbears' services to the Crown, the motive for inflation thus being ample.

Yet while not directly addressing the issue of cattle introduction, by sketching Villalobos's background and peregrinations the biography does provide context and thus facilitates some reasonable inferences. Quite significantly, and somewhat uncharacteristically for a conquistador, Villalobos seems to have lived in the Veracruz lowlands continuously from his arrival in the spring of 1521 until at least 1526, possibly even somewhat longer. Beginning that lowland residence at Villa Rica in the north, Villalobos later moved south to Medellín. Although Cortés himself had scouted out Medellín's site around 1524, intending for that settlement on the Jamapa River to become the principal port of New Spain, Spaniards had largely abandoned it by 1527 (Oviedo 1959, 4:188-89, 244; Cortés 1988, 199). Its former residents moved to a refounded Villa Rica de la Vera Cruz: established about 1525 on the left bank of the Antigua River (García Icazbalceta 1858-1866, 1:495; Oviedo 1959, 4:244). That refounded Vera Cruz remained the sole Atlantic port of New Spain for the rest of the sixteenth century, with launches ferrying goods from the deep-water anchorage at San Juan de Ulúa along the coast and up the Antigua River (Sluyter 1996, 174-75). Together with other residents of Medellín, then, Villalobos might have moved to Vera Cruz by 1527, relocating to the highlands only later. Or, given Medellín's abandonment, he might have seized on the opportunity to leave the lowlands altogether and move directly to Puebla in 1527 or soon thereafter. In either case, he would by that date have had not only a long familiarity with these lowlands but a broad one: half a decade split between Villa Rica in the north and the lower drainage of the Jamapa River in the south. Villalobos seems primarily to have lived in the lowlands that long in order to serve his employer, Cortés. Yet that residence might well have yielded the knowledge, motive, and opportunity to import some yearlings and found a cattle ranch, or estancia, to propagate them.

Further context helps to hone such inference, particularly as to when and where Villalobos might have imported those cattle. In 1523, the ranchers of Hispaniola and Cuba began to prohibit livestock exports to the mainland (Cortés 1988, 204). As a measure of the Antillean ranchers' determination to stymie potential competition by the new colony, a death penalty enforced that embargo. As a measure of its success, the cattle population of New Spain remained almost nil until after a royal decree of 1526 ended the embargo. Consequently, the residents of Mexico City, despite constituting a major concentration of meat eaters, did not establish even a small beef market until 1526 (Matesanz 1965). And only in 1526 did Cortés report that he had begun raising cattle in the Toluca Valley, near Mexico City (Cortés 1963, 471-72). By the seventeenth century, however, the cattle population of New Spain had boomed and two dominant cattle districts had emerged: the environs of the port of Veracruz and the lowlands along the Pánuco River, some four hundred kilometers to the northwest of Veracruz. The progenitors of the vast Pánuco herds certainly did not arrive until after the embargo had ended. Spaniards had conquered and settled the Pánuco region in 1523, just as the embargo was beginning, and did not import cattle until after 1526 (Doolittle 1987). In the Veracruz lowlands, however, Villalobos apparently beat the embargo. He probably did not bring the yearlings on his initial voyage to join the conquistadors, six months before the fall of Tenochtitlán, when he still lacked firsthand knowledge of potential pastures and, more pointedly, would have had looting rather than ranching in mind. Yet he must have shipped the yearlings before the embargo began sometime in 1523, either making another trip himself or sending for them. He therefore must have landed the cattle in late 1521, in 1522, or possibly as late as 1523. Given his residence in Villa Rica until at least 1524 or so, he would have landed the yearlings there and pastured them nearby. Accepting for the moment the veracity of those inferences, his initiative combined with the success of the embargo would have made the Villalobos yearlings not only the first cattle to reach New Spain but quite likely the only ones to arrive during the first half decade of the colony.

If the year and place that Villalobos introduced those cattle remain somewhat inferential and imprecise at this point, estimating the number of head and how quickly they might have multiplied enters the realm of blatant speculation. Nonetheless, only setting some informed limits to the size of the herd and its rate of increase can gauge its significance to the establishment of cattle ranching in New Spain. As already inferred from his biography, Villalobos must have initially pastured the yearlings near Villa Rica, increased the size and maturity of the herd, and then moved it south after Cortés founded Medellín about 1524. Since the anonymous writer of the 1554 testimonial uses the term *becerras* rather than *terneras*, and does not indicate a milk cow aboard ship, the cattle must have been weaned, yearlings, and therefore quite capable of breeding on arrival. Moreover, the use of *becerras* rather than *becerros* implies a preponderance of heifers over bulls. All in all, such a herd would have been appropriate to ship on one of the small vessels available and to seed a ranch with: still relatively small individuals so that more could fit in the hold; already mature enough that they would have been weaned, not need a milk cow aboard, and be ready to breed on arrival; and mainly female, since one or two bulls could service all of the heifers. According to all accounts, such livestock had a remarkable fecundity in the Antilles and New Spain (Simpson 1952; Sauer 1966; Watts 1987). While herds of cattle likely did not double every fifteen months, as some contemporaries claimed, birth rates did so far outstrip death rates that annual growth rates must have approached ten percent (Chevalier 1952, 115). For Pánuco, a fairly analogous context to the Veracruz lowlands, Doolittle has argued for a doubling time of between eight and nine years (Doolittle 1987, 6-7). Using that same rate of increase for the Villalobos cattle and assuming an initial herd of ten yearlings in 1521 yields fourteen head by 1525 and twenty by 1529. Assuming an initial herd of twenty yields twenty-eight head by 1525 and thirty-nine by 1529.

The herd that Villalobos led southward from Villa Rica to Medellín, then, would have been small. Even by the end of the Antillean embargo in 1526, the Villalobos herd could have contained no more than a couple of dozen animals, and they therefore cannot have been the direct progenitors of the subsequently vast herds of New Spain. With the end of the Antillean embargo, further cattle imports to Pánuco and elsewhere populated New Spain with cattle. Even so, the cattle population of New Spain grew but slowly. By 1531, five years after the end of the embargo and the establishment of a beef market in Mexico City, an ordinance still prohibited the slaughter of cattle (Chevalier 1952, 103). Presumably the market's beef came from animals that died of natural causes. Only with another half decade of increasing herds did the price of beef begin to fall, costing in 1538 a quarter what it had in 1532 (Chevalier 1952, 103, 114-15).

The First Cattle Ranch

The Villalobos herd nonetheless remains notable for an impact out of all proportion to its reproductive impact, its cold trail well worth tracking from the rather tenuous clues of published biographical fragments into the depths of the archives. Accepting the inferences regarding approximately when and where Villalobos introduced and raised his cattle, as based on the posthumous assertion regarding that introduction and on the biographical and more general contextual information, requires also accepting that he introduced ranching. More pertinently, he would have established a particular way of raising cattle—a particular ranching ecology. Its characteristics, namely its elements and their spatial patterning, would thus have influenced the subsequent expansion of cattle herding and associated landscape transformations. Establishing those characteristics, as well as testing the inferences about when and where Villalobos grazed his herd, most basically requires locating his estancia—New Spain's prototypic cattle ranch.

Locating any of the estancias of sixteenth-century New Spain generally requires finding the relevant *real merced,* the royal grant awarded to cattle and sheep ranchers. Spaniards also established estancias through arrogation of native or Crown lands, so-called squatting, and through purchase or lease from natives or other land holders such as the Marquesado del Valle (Chevalier 1952, 134-35). But grants of Crown land—itself, of course, native land usurped through conquest—dominated the establishment of titles for estancias (Prem 1992). The volumes in the Mercedes section of the Archivo General de la Nación in Mexico City contain the bulk of such *mercedes,* the official copies of the originals retained by the grantees (Simpson 1952; Prem 1988; Sluyter 1997b). The Kraus collection of the Library of Congress in Washington and the Ayer collection of the Newberry Library in Chicago each contain an additional volume of mercedes (LOC-Kraus, ms. 140; NLC-Ayer, ms. 1121). Those two errant volumes and AGN-Mercedes primarily contain grants for livestock estancias and for farms but also for building lots and other land uses. Besides actual mercedes, the volumes contain *mandamientos acordados,* the viceregal writs ordering inspections in response to requests for grants, and other documents related to land tenure and use. The grants for livestock estancias specify the date of the award, the awardee, the location, the number of land units, and whether the land units were for *ganado mayor* or *ganado menor,* for large livestock or small livestock. Large stock included cattle, horses, and mules; small stock included sheep, goats, and pigs.

Unfortunately, the viceregal scribes did not begin recording grants for estancias until the early 1540s, well after Gregorio de Villalobos had moved to Puebla and just before he died; therefore, the mercedes volumes contain no grant for an estancia in his name. The earliest livestock enterprises did not even involve a formal title to the land—simply a permit, if anything at all—to run stock in a general locale (Chevalier 1952, 108-13). Municipal councils in some regions issued such grazing licenses during the 1520s and 1530s, and when Antonio de Mendoza became the first viceroy of New Spain in 1535, he soon standardized and took central control of everything from currency to land grants (Chevalier 1952, 120). With a 1536 ordinance, for example, he stipulated minimum distances between *asientos,* or *sitios de estancias* (Galván 1851, 121). Even by that time, however, the only property rights were attached to the animals themselves and to the actual sitio de estancia, the centrally located cattle or sheep station where ranchers gathered animals in corrals for branding, sheering, or culling. The space between those sitios remained Crown land that all could graze in common. But despite seemingly making such grants as early as 1536, only in the early 1540s did Mendoza instruct his scribes to begin recording grants in the central register that eventually became the eighty-six volumes of AGN-Mercedes. That half-decade lag between the viceroy taking control of the granting process and systematic recording of grants seems logical: meeting the

demand for estancias would not have become significant and require systemati-
zation until several years after the Antillean embargo had ended and livestock
numbers had substantially increased. In fact, the number of grants for cattle estancias went from less than twenty per year during the early 1540s to a peak of
nearly eighty per year during the early 1580s. Granting declined thereafter and
virtually ceased during the period of *composición*, or Crown vetting and confirmation of individual mercedes, during the 1630s and 1640s (McBride 1923, 56-
57; Chevalier 1952, 16, 264-65; Prem 1988, 124-31).

One of those grants in AGN-Mercedes, despite considerably postdating
Gregorio de Villalobos, does contain a clue to the location of his estancia. A
grant of 1583 for a cattle estancia along the Jamapa River refers to previous occupance by a Gabriel de Villalobos.

> We, the Royal President and Justices [of the Governing High Court], in the
> name of his Majesty, hereby grant Juan de la Párraga one cattle estancia in the
> district of the city of Vera Cruz, between the estancia of Gonzalo de Alegría
> and [that of] Francisco de Cocas, that was wont to be that of Gabriel de
> Villalobos, on the other side of the Jamapa River, such as was inspected by
> Diego Rodríguez, lieutenant to the district governor of the city and port of Vera
> Cruz, by the command and commission of the most excellent Viceroy, the
> Count of Coruña [Lorenzo Suárez de Mendoza] (AGN-M, vol. 13, f. 20).

The reference to Gabriel rather than Gregorio de Villalobos might signify
nothing more than a scribe's error; but, more likely, Gabriel was one of
Gregorio's sons. The sources remain vague regarding the children of Gregorio
de Villalobos and García de la Fuente, but a document of 1591 names a Baltasar
de Padilla and a Luisa de Villalobos as son and daughter (O'Gorman 1941, 214).
Baltasar must have been the eldest son since he inherited the encomienda of
Ixhuatlán as well as taking his paternal grandfather's name, Gregorio de
Villalobos having been the son of Diego de Padilla and Teresa de Villalobos
(Icaza 1923, 1:223). No document so clearly refers to a younger son, the one to
take over the family estancia, but a Gabriel de Villalobos was a vecino of Puebla
in 1555 and thus almost certainly was Baltasar's brother (AGN-M, 4:107). The
connection between Gregorio and Gabriel thus remains somewhat conjectural
but seems sound given the paucity of families named Villalobos in New Spain
during the early sixteenth century (Icaza 1923; O'Gorman 1941; Boyd-Bowman
1964, 1968; Himmerich y Valencia 1991). In fact, only one other male
Villalobos is associated with the Veracruz lowlands, namely Pedro de
Villalobos, but he was involved in gold mining and returned to Spain a rich man
without having married (Millares Carlo and Mantecón 1945, 1:28-29, 333;
Boyd-Bowman 1964, 162; Himmerich y Valencia 1991, 187). During the mid-
1530s, a Francisca Mejía de Villalobos held the encomienda of Tenampa, Tla-
cotepec, and Tlatela, about fifty kilometers inland from Vera Cruz (Himmerich
y Valencia 1991, 189). She had married Diego Marmolejo, the first *en-*

comendero, in the mid-1520s and inherited the encomienda when he died around 1533 (Gerhard 1993, 363, 366). She remarried to Juan de Miranda and the encomienda escheated on Miranda's death in 1564 (González de Cossío 1952, 276-77). Francisca Mejía de Villalobos does not seem to have been closely related to Gregorio de Villalobos, and she bore no children by either Marmolejo or Miranda, so Gabriel de Villalobos could not have been her son. Both Baltasar and Gabriel, unlike their sister, Luisa, seem to have died without heirs (O'Gorman 1941, 214).

Locating the 1583 grant to Juan de la Párraga, "between the estancia of Gonzalo de Alegría and [that of] Francisco de Cocas," thus serves to locate the preexisting estancia founded by Gregorio de Villalobos. Unfortunately, the mercedes volumes do not record any grant along the Jamapa River in the name of Francisco de Cocas, probably because he purchased his estancia from the original grantee. Nor do the mercedes volumes record any grant along the Jamapa River in the name of Gonzalo de Alegría. Only the writ that ordered the inspection of the estancia that Alegría requested seems to survive. And even that mandamiento acordado, as if the clues nest within a maze of folios, survives only as a copy within yet another document: an inspection report prompted by Juan Rodríguez de Villegas's 1575 request for an estancia along the Jamapa River (AGN-T, vol. 2764, exp. 18, ff. 225-60). Due to the opposition of a neighboring rancher, Pedro Núñez de Móntalban, the viceroy apparently never granted Villegas his request. But Gonzalo de Alegría did receive his estancia, as a series of documents makes clear. First, on 10 March 1573, the *alcalde mayor*, or district governor, responded to the mandamiento acordado by recommending that the viceroy make the grant (AGN-T, vol. 2764, exp. 18, ff. 258-58v). Second, a map accompanying the Villegas inspection report confirms the existence by 1575 of the Alegría estancia (figure 3.3). Third, a map from another inspection report refers to an "estancia de Pedro de Alegría" in the lower Jamapa drainage around 1573, the reason for the different first name being obscure but probably signifying nothing more than a scribe's error (figure 3.4). Fourth, the 1583 Párraga merced itself confirms the award to Alegría (AGN-M, vol. 13, f. 20). Moreover, the 1575 Villegas map not only confirms the award but locates the Alegría estancia and, by association, the neighboring Párraga estancia "that was wont to be that of Gabriel de Villalobos." It was somewhere south of the Jamapa River—"on the other side of the Jamapa River," as the lieutenant to the governor of Vera Cruz put it. But it was also north of the Atoyac River, named "El Río Grande de Medellín" on the 1575 map. In general terms, then, the Villalobos estancia was between the Jamapa and Atoyac rivers, somewhat upstream from their confluence.

A 1606 grant to Francisco Párraga for a license to open an inn confirms and more closely specifies the location of the Párraga estancia and, thereby, the Villalobos estancia.

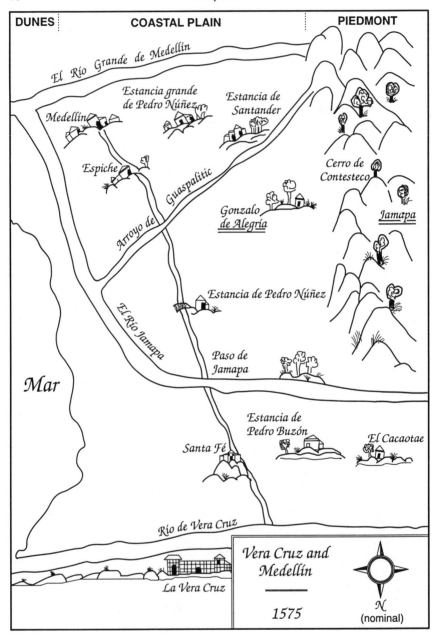

DUNES | **COASTAL PLAIN** | **PIEDMONT**

El Río Grande de Medellín

Estancia grande
de Pedro Núñez

Estancia de
Santander

Medellín

Espiche

Cerro de
Contesteco

Jamapa

Arroyo de Guaspalitic

Gonzalo
de Alegría

Estancia de Pedro Núñez

El Río Jamapa

Paso de
Jamapa

Mar

Estancia de
Pedro Buzón

El Cacaotae

Santa Fé

Río de Vera Cruz

*Vera Cruz and
Medellín*

1575

N
(nominal)

La Vera Cruz

Figure 3.3. A sketch of the 1575 map related to Juan Rodríguez de Villegas's request for an estancia along the Jamapa River. Note landform zonation across top: dunes, coastal plain, piedmont. The original is in AGN-Tierras (vol. 2764, exp. 18, f. 260).

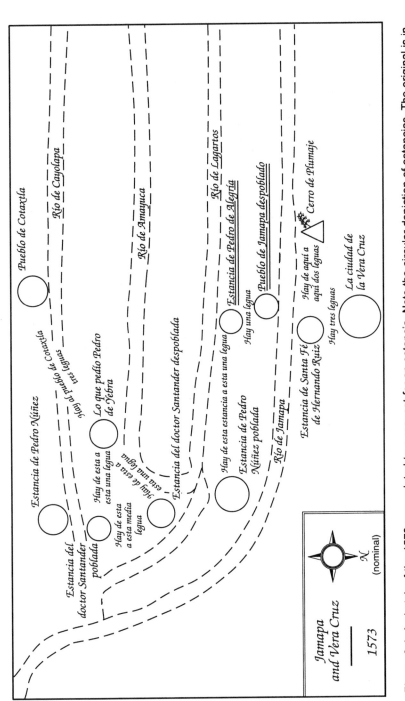

Figure 3.4. A sketch of the 1573 map related to a request for an estancia. Note the circular depiction of estancias. The original is in AGN-Tierras (vol. 2672, exp. 8, f. 21).

Because Licenciado Francisco Párraga vecino of the new city of Veracruz . . . has his stocked cattle estancias in the district of the old city of Vera Cruz near the river called Jamapa along the royal highway that goes from the said new city to Mexico [City, and because] many persons of those who cart goods and travel on the said highway during the rainy season are not able to cross and continue there due to the river rising [, and because] in order to prevent that damage . . . he endeavored to build and found an inn and a boat or canoes for people to cross and proceed . . . , that well within the limits and bounds of the said estancias, next to the river that they call Jamapa, he can found, build, and establish an inn (AGN-M, vol. 25, f. 143).

Presumably Francisco Párraga was a son of Juan de la Párraga. By 1606, the Párragas had more than one estancia, seemingly contiguous. And in the midst of them, on the banks of the Jamapa River, Francisco Párraga founded a ferry service and inn, or *venta*, and called it the Venta de Jamapa. The route of the highway subsequently changed, however, and the establishment of a second Venta de Jamapa at the ford on the new highway has muddied the location of Párraga's inn. Fortunately, several eighteenth-century maps help to sort out that toponymic confusion—a naming, renaming, and moving of places that characterizes these lowlands (AGN-Ríos y Acequias, vol. 2, fc. 286-87; AGN-Fomento Caminos, vol. 1, fc. 91; AGN-Indiferente de Guerra, vol. 452A, f. last). During the eighteenth century, people distinguished the two inns as the Venta Nueva de Jamapa versus the Venta Vieja—the New Inn versus the Old Inn. The Venta Nueva was at the present-day town of Jamapa. The Venta Vieja was eight kilometers upstream; that location, now the small village of La Venta, retains the toponym if not the seventeenth-century inn. The Jamapa marked along the right margin of the 1575 map refers to a native settlement of that name, further upstream than either of the ventas (AGN-M, vol. 13, ff. 81v-82; AGN-T, vol. 2764, exp. 17, fc. 223; exp. 18, ff. 238, 245, 257v; Paso y Troncoso 1939-1940, 14:82). That the cartographer did not indicate houses at Jamapa signifies abandonment, a condition stipulated more explicitly by the adjective "despoblado" on the 1573 map. Native Jamapa had, as the district governor of Vera Cruz put it a few years later, "become completely depopulated, leaving no trace except the memory of a name" (JGI, ms. xxv-8, f. 5v).

During the first decade of the colonial period, then, Gregorio de Villalobos grazed cattle along the Jamapa River near Medellín after having moved his herd south from Villa Rica. Despite lacking formal title, a son named Gabriel de Villalobos might have taken over operation of the estancia upon Gregorio's death, sometime before 1547. By 1555, however, Gabriel was a *vecino* of Puebla and received a grant for a sheep estancia near that city (AGN-M, vol. 4, 107). During the early 1560s, Viceroy Luis de Velasco began the formal granting of estancias in the lower Jamapa drainage. As that ranching frontier boomed, the Villalobos estancia lay abandoned but still remembered, somewhere in the environs of the place that was to become the Párraga estancia in 1583, the Venta de Jamapa in 1606, the Venta Vieja during the nineteenth century, and then the village of La Venta. There the hilly fringe of the piedmont abuts the coastal plain, a site well suited to the spatial characteristics of the ranching ecology of Villalobos's boyhood home—the Marismas of Andalusia.

The First Cattle Ranching Ecology

To Gregorio de Villalobos, the country along the lower reaches of the Jamapa River must have seemed strangely parallel to the place where he had grown up. As he drove his small herd southward from Villa Rica, where the mountains virtually plunge into the Gulf of Mexico, he traveled a narrow coastal plain crossed by the streams that drain the escarpment of the Sierra Madre Oriental to the west. Upon reaching the Jamapa drainage, however, the coastal plain suddenly widens considerably, not as wide as the Andalusian coastal plain but nonetheless a broad expanse of floodplains inscribed by meandering streams and punctuated by wetlands. Moreover, like the Arenas Gordas of the Andalusian coast, dunes cut off that coastal plain from the sea. Like the Sierra Morena north of Almonte, mountains rise inland. And like the Marismas themselves, the wetlands of Veracruz flood annually. Surely the seasons are reversed, with the rains coming in a tropical summer rather than a Mediterranean winter, but the terrain and the rhythm of the floods would have inspired a *paisano* of Almonte. Perhaps just as inspiring would have been the thrill of being first; although the Marismas dwarf the Veracruz wetlands, in the 1520s the former already swarmed with cattle while the latter had never been grazed.

As the land grant documents make clear, Villalobos headquartered his estancia near where the Jamapa River emerges from the hilly fringe of the piedmont and breaks onto the coastal plain, that strategic straddling of the wet and the dry thus suggesting an adaptation of the ranching ecology of the Marismas (figure 3.5). From that location, ten kilometers upstream from Medellín, the piedmont slopes up toward the Sierra Madre Oriental. For the traveler, the only respite from the piedmont's dry savanna and patches of deciduous woodland and shrubland comes when the road dips into the comparatively verdant *barrancas*, or ravines, of the streams that drain the escarpment and have dissected the Tertiary conglomerates into a ragged apron abutting the coastal plain. Those streams, before cutting through the cordon of sand dunes along the coast, meander across the coastal plain and form a belt of backswamps that harbor wet savanna studded with palm trees and evergreen woodlands. The coast itself is a jumble of longitudinal dunes, some cresting at over a hundred meters and trending north-south for several kilometers, interspersed with the stagnant ponds that during the nineteenth century harbored the mosquito vectors of yellow fever (Arreola 1982).

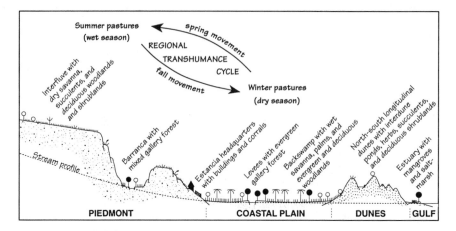

Figure 3.5. A sketch of a generalized transect across the lowlands illustrates the regional-scale transhumance of the ranching ecology. Compare the landform zonation across the bottom with figure 3.2 and figure 3.3.

The ranchers of the sixteenth-century Marismas also straddled the wet and the dry (Doolittle 1987). Their cattle made an annual circuit between hill land and wetland in a system of regional-scale transhumance, or *travesío*. As the floodwaters of the Guadalquivir River receded each spring, herders branded their calves and drove the stock into the Marismas to graze the lush new growth. Largely untended during the long dry season, uncastrated and isolated among a labyrinth of sloughs, the animals became semiferal. Solanos blowing out of Africa parched the oak-pine savannas of the surrounding hills, and the ranchers set them ablaze in late summer (Fernández Alés et al. 1995, 366). As the rains returned each October, herders rounded up the semiferal stock and drove them upslope before the Guadalquivir flooded, the wildness of the cattle dictating the use of horses and pikes, or *garrochas*. Before being turned into the fresh regrowth of the hill pastures, ranchers collected their cattle in corrals scattered around the margins of the Marismas in order to cull the herds for marketable animals (Jordan 1993, 23-26). The same corrals served for calf branding in the spring. Something like that ranching ecology had been in place since at least Roman times, when Strabo commented on the hazards of pasturing cattle in the Marismas: when they flood "the cattle . . . have at times actually been engulfed; at other times they have merely been cut off, and in their struggle to get back to the land lacked the strength to do so, and perished" (Strabo 1923, 2:28-29; Butzer 1988).

Sartorius, the nineteenth-century German inhabitant of Veracruz, provides a provocative description of the spatial relations between the dry savanna of the piedmont and the wet savanna of the coastal plain, giving a sense of how Villalobos would have adapted the ranching ecology of the Marismas (Sartorius

1961, 4-10, 182-85). During the summer wet season, the cattle could graze up on the piedmont. But with "the cessation of the rains, the prairies fade, the soil dries up, the trees lose their foliage, the herds seek the forests and chasms, and in the cloudless skies, the sun scorches up the unsheltered plains" (Sartorius 1961, 9). As the winter dry season progressed and the floodwaters receded from the backswamps, ranchers would drive their cattle downslope to graze the wet savanna (figure 3.6). The vaqueros would wait until the piedmont pastures had become tinder dry and set them alight, "partly to destroy the clouds of torment-ing ticks and tarantulas, partly to call forth a new crop from beneath the ashes" (Sartorius 1961, 9). Around June, as the flooding streams once again inundated the backswamps and threatened to strand the semiferal cattle on quickly forming islands, mounted vaqueros rounded up their herds and drove them upslope (fig-ure 3.7). Unlike the Marismas, where saline waters provided the cattle with salt, the vaqueros of Veracruz could use salt as a lure but nonetheless employed horses in the roundups. Like the Marismas, corrals of wooden poles or stones located near ecological transition points on the annual transhumant circuit served for culling and branding, the cattle passing the corrals twice yearly (fig-ure 3.8).

At least some elements of that nineteenth-century ranching ecology also pertained to the sixteenth century, most notably the regular burning of pastures and the wildness of the cattle. In 1571, the former priest of Vera Cruz noted that ranchers used fire to open and maintain pasture and that the burning tended to

Figure 3.6. Cows graze on the coastal plain during the dry season, standing water in foreground, higher and drier terrain behind. Photograph by the author, January 1992.

Figure 3.7. An engraving of a sketch by Johann Moritz Rugendas illustrates a nineteenth-century roundup on the coastal plain, standing water in the foreground, higher and drier terrain behind (from Sartorius 1961: plate opposite page 4).

Figure 3.8. The buildings and corral of a cattle estancia toward the end of the dry season. Most of the few cows present in that season are sheltering from the midday sun in the shade of sheds or trees. Photograph by the author, April 1994.

occur during the dry season: "plains, all made into pastures," "wont to be burned around Christmas time" (Paso y Troncoso 1905, 5:194-95). Radiocarbon-dated remains of charred vegetation exhumed from the sediments of the wetlands confirm such extensive and persistent colonial burning (Siemens et al. 1988; Sluyter 1997c). The priest, Arias Hernández, also portrays the majority of the cattle as semiferal: "many cows and many wild ones, and many bulls and very fierce" (Paso y Troncoso 1905, 5:199). As in the Marismas and in nineteenth-century Veracruz, the sixteenth-century cattle also went largely untended. Hernández also remarks that the main profit was in veal, "the meat that's worthwhile, that is the best eating of all" (Paso y Troncoso 1905, 5:199). The excess bulls—uncastrated, uncontrollable, and unnecessary to veal production—were hunted with the *desjarretadera*, the Andalusian garrocha but modified with a crescent blade (Paso y Troncoso 1905, 5:199; Jordan 1993, 25-26, 77). Riding behind a fleeing bull, the hunter used the desjarretadera to sever a hamstring and drop the animal in its tracks. The cattle hunters, not necessarily the legitimate owners, took only the hides and tallow, leaving the carcasses to their dogs and the buzzards.

The form of the estancia, as its legal definition emerged during the first century of colonization, also implies that some of the characteristics of the sixteenth-century ranching ecology paralleled that of the Marismas. Beginning with Viceroy Mendoza in 1536 and continuing through reaffirmations and elaborations by Gastón de Peralta in 1567 and Martín Enríquez de Almansa in 1574 and 1580, those ordinances stipulate a north-south oriented square a league on a side for large stock and two-thirds of league on a side for small stock (Galván 1851, 121-41, 165-67; Hackett 1923, 1:174-89; Carrera Stampa 1949, 19-21; Simpson 1952, 17; Prem 1988, 295-96). They also stipulate that the ranch headquarters—with its *casas y corrales*, its buildings and corrals—be at the center of the estancia. Excerpts from the ordinances of 1567 and 1580 illustrate (figure 3.9).

An estancia for large stock . . . has 5,000 *varas* [1 league] from east to west, and another 5,000 from north to south, and 2,500 varas [1/2 league] from the center to each of its four sides . . . , squared with four equal corners (Hackett 1923, 1:178-82).

An estancia for large stock has 3000 *pasos de marca* [1 league] from the structures and house of such estancia to the structures and house of the next, and 2,000 of the said pasos [2/3 league] for estancias for small stock . . . , each one of the said estancias being understood as having to include within it 1,500 pasos [1/2 league] from the houses and structures to all its parts for those for large stock, and 1,000 [1/3 league] for those for small stock (Galván 1851, 166-67).

Curiously, that legally defined square conceptualization seems to have suffered competition from a lay circular conceptualization. The notion of a circular form probably derived from Andalusian and Antillean antecedents and from the

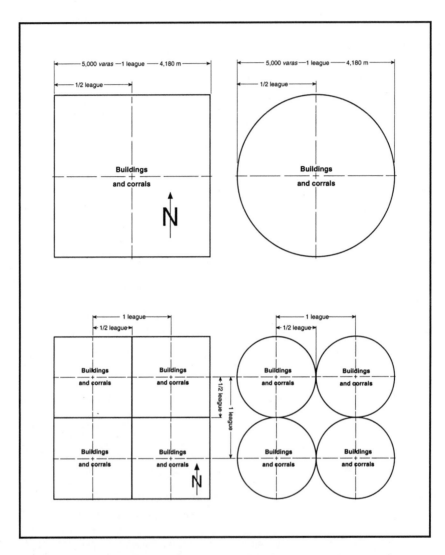

Figure 3.9. The legal definition of the sitio de estancia para ganado mayor, the estancia for large stock such as cattle and horses, was a north-south oriented square a league on a side (top left). That form was specified in ordinances by various viceroys: Antonio de Mendoza, in 1536; Gastón de Peralta, in 1567; and Martín Enríquez de Almansa, in 1574 and 1580. The circular form (top right) was a lay misinterpretation of the stipulation that all parts of the estancia must be within half a league of the buildings and corrals at its center, clearly impossible with the square form. The bottom half of the figure shows how such estancia forms would adjoin.

stipulation that each cattle estancia have half a league "from the houses and structures to all its parts," the corners of a square league clearly being further than half a league from its center (Galván 1851, 166-67). Despite clearly contradicting the legal definition, at least one high official sanctioned the circular form as late as the 1590s (AGN-T, vol. 3460, exp. 2, ff. 10-14v; also AGN-T, vol. 3185, exp. 2, ff. 62-63v). And maps specifically relevant to the Veracruz lowlands variously employ circular or square representations of estancias (figure 3.4, figure 3.10). Given the circular and square alternatives, then, and especially given that the rudimentary surveying techniques of the sixteenth century could not precisely transfer conceptual estancias to the ground in any case, the stipulations of the ordinances must have remained ideals.

The central location of the headquarters remains a consistent feature of both the square and the circular conceptualizations of the estancia, and that location would have been consistent with the spatial fluxes of regional-scale transhumance. Ideally, as ranchers moved cattle between hill land and wetland, they would pass the centrally located corrals. As stock moved upslope with the onset of the rains in the spring, the corrals served for culling. As stock moved downslope with the deepening of the dry season in the fall, the same corrals served for branding. That spatial pattern also pertained to the Marismas, albeit with a reversal of the seasons. In Veracruz, the great annual branding, or *herradero*, that punctuated the downslope portion of the annual cycle took place in fall rather than spring (Sartorius 1961, 183-84).

Most significantly of all, the Andalusian origins of the ranchers who followed Villalobos entailed transfer and adaptation of an entire suite of characteristics pertaining to the ranching ecology of the Marismas, as echoed for nineteenth-century Veracruz in Sartorius's detailed description and more than hinted at by the sixteenth-century evidence. An orthodox literature long emphasized Spain's semiarid plateau as the model for New Spain's ranching ecology (Bishko 1952; Brand 1961; Rouse 1977). But the image of Estremadurans on horseback herding cattle across semiarid grasslands has come to seem as much myth as icon. That sheep predominated on the plateau contradicts the claim that a fully developed cattle ranching ecology involving mounted herders diffused southward with the Reconquista and, ultimately, through Seville and across the Atlantic to New Spain (Doolittle 1987; Butzer 1988; Jordan 1993). In contrast, cattle did predominate in Andalusia, and the Marismas with their semiferal cattle and mounted herders thus seem to provide a more realistic model for New Spain's cattle ranching ecology. The Andalusian provenance of many of the original conquistadors, the some four hundred who sailed with Cortés, further supports that inference. Nearly a third of them, just like Villalobos, hailed from the Andalusian provinces bordering the Marismas—Seville, Huelva, Cádiz— and knew its transhumant pulse (Boyd-Bowman 1964, XLI). Both Almonte and Jerez de la Frontera, respectively the hometowns of Gregorio de Villalobos and

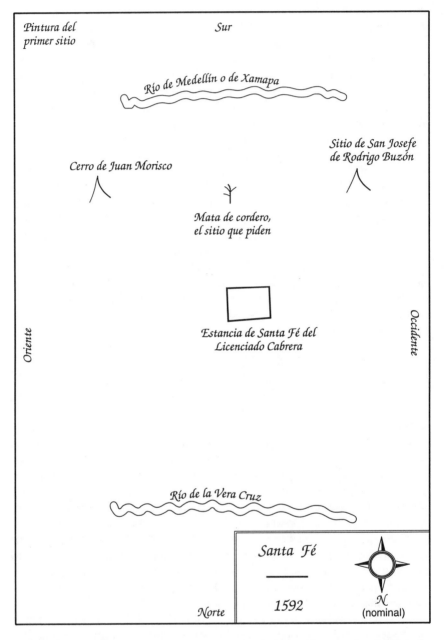

Figure 3.10. A sketch of the 1592 map related to a request for an estancia. Note the square depiction of the estancia; compare with the circular depiction of estancias in figure 3.4. The original is in AGN-Tierras (vol. 2764, exp. 15, fc. 188).

his parents, were significant centers in a long-standing cattle economy (Jordan 1993, 29, 33). Such Andalusians continued to dominate emigration to the Indies throughout the sixteenth century (Boyd-Bowman 1976).

Having witnessed the fecundity of the cattle Columbus had introduced into Hispaniola in 1493, Andalusians diffused the Marismas ranching ecology to New Spain together with elements of Antillean origin such as the *desjarreta-dera*. During the 1520s, Villalobos established that model in the environs of the port of Veracruz. During the 1530s, other Andalusians established that model in the Pánuco district, also a seasonally inundated coastal plain (Doolittle 1987). During the 1550s, escalating a process begun by Viceroy Mendoza because of damages to native agriculture, Viceroy Velasco virtually eliminated cattle ranches from the more densely settled parts of the highlands—around Mexico City, Puebla, and Oaxaca (Chevalier 1952, 133-35). Then, with the mining boom and a consequent surge in immigration from Spain, the colonial economy soared in the second half of the sixteenth century. As demand increased for meat, tallow, and hides in parallel with Velasco's attempts to banish cattle from the highlands, the Gulf Coast emerged as prime cattle country. By the seventeenth century, Veracruz and Pánuco had emerged as the two dominant cattle districts of New Spain. From Pánuco, the practice of herding cattle from horseback, fairly unique among ranching ecologies on a worldwide basis, diffused northward into Texas (Doolittle 1987; Jordan 1993).

Early Interactions Between Ranchers and Natives

Early interactions between natives and ranchers could have involved labor, land, or both. Until the 1550s, encomenderos like Villalobos controlled much of the labor in New Spain. By the time of the spread of estancias along the Gulf Coast during the 1560s, New Spain had changed considerably. A series of epidemics had devastated the native population. The Crown had undercut the power of the conquistadors, especially their control of native labor through the encomienda system. And viceroys Mendoza and Velasco had centralized the control of land use through the award of mercedes. Understanding of the interactions among natives, non-natives, and landscape after midcentury can therefore lean on analysis of the mercedes record, as explicated in the next two chapters. Much less can ever be clear about the preceding, anarchic period—when ranchers grazed cattle on land without any sort of formal title, before the landscape had become so horribly depopulated, and while encomenderos still grasped tight to their awards of native labor and tribute.

Encomienda served as the "master institution" of New Spain until the 1550s (Himmerich y Valencia 1991, 15-17): it encompassed the primary flux of capital and labor; it articulated the power of the state; and it interfaced between natives and non-natives. Encomienda loosely simulated the political, economic, and settlement patterns that the Spaniards had usurped from the Aztecs (Gibson 1964, 194-97; Lockhart 1992, 428-35). Rooted in the feudalism of medieval Spain and sharpened during the colonization of the Canaries and the Antilles, encomienda at once placated the greed of the conquistadors and accumulated capital for the Crown (Simpson 1950, 6-13; Sauer 1966, 10-11, 199-204). Although not a grant of land, encomienda connoted spatial as well as temporal dimensions. As reward for taking part in the conquest of New Spain, the encomendero received license to exploit the natives settled in a particular place for a specific period (Simpson 1950, 56-64; Gibson 1966, 49-67). In return, the Crown expected the encomenderos to subjugate the natives through physical force and psychological indoctrination. The natives were to be industrious Christians, serving God and state under the lash of the encomendero. The encomendero forwarded a percentage of the tribute to the Crown, including the church tithe of ten percent, the *diezmo*, as a surcharge on all tribute except services (Borah 1941, 387-99). All natives were either in an encomienda and administered by an encomendero, or they were in the Crown's *real corona* and administered by a *corregidor* at the local level and by a district governor, or alcalde mayor, at the district level (Gerhard 1993, 9).

Two persistent trends brought the encomienda system to a nominal close around midcentury and to virtual extinction by 1600. First, as native population declined in a series of devastating epidemics, tribute revenue also declined. Second, as the Spanish state consolidated power, the focus of capital accumulation shifted from tribute to silver mining. Regular troops replaced conquistadors and native labor became required for mining and infrastructure construction. Encomenderos thus became a liability and an object of state suppression (Simpson 1952, 84-145; Gibson 1966, 103-7). A series of laws with often lagging enforcement suppressed encomendero power and inheritance (Gibson 1968, 7, 109-12, 123). Beginning with the New Laws of 1542, encomenderos were increasingly limited in the exploitation of their encomiendas (Zavala 1935; Simpson 1950; Miranda 1965). The New Laws required residence in the same province as the encomienda to encourage encomenderos to fulfill their obligation to control and indoctrinate the natives. But at the same time, encomenderos were not supposed to live among those natives, nor even to spend more than a single night in their villages, nor to build houses or storage buildings there—all to limit demands for labor. Most germane to the issue of interactions between natives and ranchers, the New Laws forbad encomenderos to graze livestock on the lands of their natives (*Recopilación* 1987, book 6, title 9, laws 10-14, 17-20). As enforcement of the New Laws improved through the 1540s and 1550s, encomenderos were able to monopolize less and less native labor. With the reform of 1557, the Crown commuted tribute from goods and services to a standardized head tax of one *peso de oro común* plus half a *fanega* of maize per year (Cook and Simpson 1948, 11; Sanders 1992, 89-91). Control of native labor became the prerogative of the Crown, institutionalized as the *repartimiento* system in which individual entrepreneurs applied to the viceroy for an allotment of workers for a specific purpose and period (Gibson 1966, 143-45). As encomiendas escheated for lack of legitimate heirs, having "run out of lives," state officials replaced the encomenderos. Those corregidores and alcalde mayores directly funneled the native head tax into Crown coffers (Gibson 1966, 147-48; Gerhard 1993, 9-10). By 1600, only a few encomiendas survived (Himmerich y Valencia 1991, 15-17). The Marquesado del Valle, the Cortés family estate, proved an exception that would endure the full span of the colonial period (García Martínez 1969). After a series of struggles with other conquistador factions and the Crown, Cortés became the Marqués del Valle in 1529, his estate retaining only a fraction of the encomiendas he originally had awarded himself but in perpetuity (Simpson 1950, 64-66, 164-67; García Martínez 1969).

Only those circumstances and propinquity suggest that Villalobos might have grazed cattle on encomienda lands. He probably did not do so on land belonging to his own encomienda of Ixhuatlán, which perched at an elevation of twelve hundred meters on the escarpment of the Sierra Madre Oriental, about seventy kilometers inland from the Villalobos estancia. Despite preceding the New Laws that would have prohibited grazing on Ixhuatlán lands, that distance and difference in elevation probably precluded doing so. But Cortés held the encomienda of Mictanguautla and Espiche near Medellín until it escheated in 1532 (AGN-T, vol. 2782, exp. 16, f. 3v; Paso y Troncoso 1939-1940, 13:38; Gerhard 1993, 360). As Cortés's agent in Medellín, Villalobos would have managed that encomienda at the same time he herded cattle nearby (figure 3.11). The 1525 attempt by the Medellín town council to secure title to the lands of the community of Espiche might have been an attempt to generate revenue from such a situation by renting pasture to Villalobos. In 1525, Gonzalo de Salazar and Pedro Almidez Cherino, who had assumed power in New Spain while Cortés went on an expedition to Honduras, petitioned the Crown to grant lands to various town councils, including that of Medellín (Paso y Troncoso 1939-1940, 1:83-84). The intention seems to have been to provide municipalities with public lands, or *propios*, that they could then rent out in order to generate funds for public works. Those potential propios, however, belonged to neighboring native communities and whether the Crown actually granted the request in any given case remains unclear. In Spain, propios were part of a more general class of community commons, or ejidos (Butzer 1988, 44). Much of any ejido provided communal pasture for draft animals and woodlot for fuel. In order to generate funds for public works, however, a town council could rent out some of the ejido to vecinos, such rented lands being termed propios. Villalobos, as the sole rancher among the vecinos of Medellín, would have been the only potential renter for its propios. How Villalobos related to the other nearby Cortés encomienda, Cotaxtla, remains even less clear. Cotaxtla escheated around 1525, but it became part of the Marquesado del Valle in 1529 (García Martínez 1969, 137-40, 157-60).

The use of encomienda labor—either from Ixhuatlán, from Mictanguautla and Espiche, or even from Cotaxtla—seems less likely than grazing on encomienda lands. The only available tribute assessments date so late as to be nearly meaningless in addressing this issue, but none of them include service. By the 1560s, Ixhuatlán's tribute had been commuted to 110 pesos per year (Paso y Troncoso 1939-1940, 9:18). Espiche paid a tribute of 300 pesos worth of clothing and cacao plus the diezmo during the late 1550s (BAGN 1940, 209). And Cotaxtla paid tribute in textiles and maize during the 1540s and 1550s, commuted to 24 pesos and twelve fanegas of maize in 1569 (Paso y Troncoso

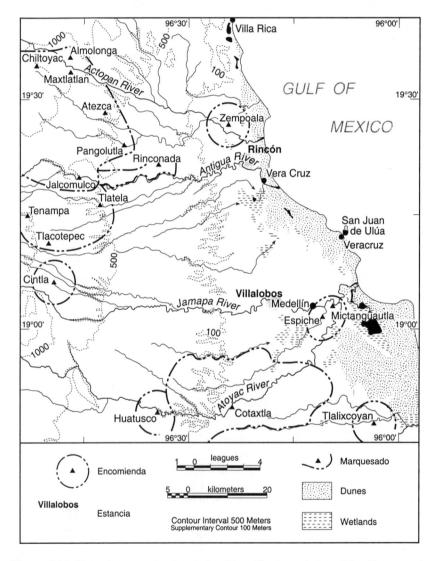

Figure 3.11. Estancia-encomienda relationships. The boundaries of the Marquesado del Valle follow Gerhard (1993, 340–42).

1939-1940, 11:32-33; González de Cossío 1952, 581-82). More significantly, the labor requirements of the ranching ecology were so low that beyond the initial construction of a rudimentary house and corrals, the use of native labor seems unnecessary. In sixteenth-century Andalusia, the law stipulated only four vaqueros for every five hundred head (Jordan 1993, 34). The ratio of herders to cattle might have been even lower in nineteenth-century Veracruz, Sartorius claiming only one vaquero for every five hundred to eight hundred head (Sartorius 1961, 182). Moreover, in both the Marismas and New Spain during the sixteenth century, African slaves made up the bulk of the vaqueros (Jordan 1993, 34; Melville 1994, 30). Arias Hernández confirms that situation for late sixteenth-century Veracruz, reporting that the large Hernán Ruiz de Córdova estancia near Vera Cruz had a workforce of two hundred Africans (Paso y Troncoso 1905, 5:195).

One other encomendero besides Villalobos seems to have operated an early estancia in the lowlands, with less than thirty-five kilometers separating her native communities from her ranch. María del Rincón, upon the death of her first husband, Alvaro Maldonado, briefly became the *encomendera* of Tlalixcoyan, south of Medellín, but lost it to Governor Estrada around 1528 (Himmerich y Valencia 1991, 187-88). She had soon remarried to the encomendero of Jalcomulco, Pangolutla, and Atezca, about forty-five kilometers west of Vera Cruz. When that second husband, Pedro de Maldonado, possibly the brother of her first husband, died around 1544, Rincón inherited the encomienda and married Gonzalo Rodríguez de Villafuerte, the holder of an encomienda in far southern Veracruz (Simpson 1950, 160-61). When Rodríguez died around 1575, all of the family encomiendas escheated (Cook and Simpson 1948; Scholes and Adams 1955, 37; Gerhard 1993, 360-62, 373-75). Besides the string of encomiendas, Rincón also ran an early estancia. A document of 1563 refers to a place near Vera Cruz that "was wont to be the cow estancia of doña María del Rincón" (AGN-M, vol. 6, f. 218v). A 1553 report more precisely locates that "Hato de Doña María," *hato* signifying cattle herd, as being about a league northwest of Vera Cruz (Paso y Troncoso 1939-1940, 7:37-38). During the 1530s through the 1550s, then, María del Rincón controlled the natives of Jalcomulco, Pangolutla, and Atezca. She lived in nearby Vera Cruz at least part of the year, and she ran cattle on an estancia located between the encomienda and Vera Cruz (González de Cossío 1952, 277); yet, while less than thirty-five kilometers separated the Rincón estancia and encomienda, she does not seem to have used native labor to herd cattle. At least the encomienda assessment of 1544, instead of ranch labor, specifies a tribute of maize, turkeys, eggs, and servants in Vera Cruz (González de Cossío 1952, 277-79). By the late 1550s, such tribute in kind had been commuted to cash (Paso y Troncoso 1939-1940, 9:22). While she might have directed some of the servants, or *indios de servicio*, to work her herd, again, the particular ranching ecology Villalobos introduced had low labor requirements. Given the propinquity, however, Rincón might well have grazed cattle on encomienda land.

By the 1540s, the Villalobos and Rincón estancias were not the only cattle ranches in the lowlands. In 1542, Viceroy Mendoza ordered that six or seven unspecified vecinos of Vera Cruz who were grazing cattle in its environs establish estancias a minimum of three leagues from town (AGN-M, vol. 1, ff. 31, 36v). One of those ranchers must have been María del Rincón, but the others were not necessarily encomenderos. While none of those early ranchers necessarily used native labor, or even had access to it, they all must have used native land. If the viceroy had to establish a protective buffer around Vera Cruz, there were presumably enough semiferal cattle by the 1540s to cause damage to native agriculture as they made the annual transit from coastal plain to hill land and back again.

For the initial period of ranching, then, preceding the centralized granting of land, interactions between natives and ranchers remain as unclear for Veracruz as for New Spain more generally. Based on scant data, the early ranchers probably did not use native labor to herd cattle, but they inescapably arrogated native lands, although not necessarily the lands of their own encomienda communities. By the period of the mercedes volumes, numerous conflicts over land between natives and cattle ranchers certainly began to be documented, and while suggestive of undocumented disputes during the 1920s and 1930s in terms of types of conflict, the number of conflicts must have been escalating as the cattle population of New Spain dramatically increased. As further developed in the following chapters, those later disputes include both complaints by native communities against ranchers and vice versa. In 1542, for example, the community of Quiotepec in Oaxaca sued Pedro de Santiago because his cattle continuously destroyed the natives' crops (AGN-M, vol. 1, f. 11; Simpson 1952, 4). In 1551, Alonso de Villaseca sued the natives of Toluca for fencing their maize fields to prevent his cattle from grazing the harvest stubble—a common practice in Spain (AGN-M, vol. 3, f. 328). Given the difficulty and cost of bringing such disputes before the court, many more than the documented cases must have occurred (Chevalier 1952, 115-16). That Viceroy Velasco virtually eliminated cattle ranches from the more densely settled parts of the highlands during the 1550s emphasizes just how desperate the situation had become by midcentury (Chevalier 1952, 133-35).

Spatial analysis of the land-grant record, as detailed in the next two chapters, provides a much fuller understanding of the interactions among natives, non-natives, and landscape for the second half of the sixteenth century. With the highlands becoming so unfriendly for cattle ranchers after midcentury, a land rush engulfed the lowlands. The mercedes record that resulted from the new imperative to secure land title, documents that process. With the exception of the exceptional Marquesado del Valle, most of the encomiendas in the study region had escheated by 1544, all by 1600 (García Martínez 1969, 137-40, 157-60; Himmerich y Valencia 1991, 145-48). And native communities had continued to lose population, so that by 1580 the alcalde mayor of Vera Cruz saw little hope to expect anything but "that those remaining will come to total ruin and destruction" (JGI, ms. xxv-8, f. 6v).

Notes

1. This and all subsequent Spanish-English translations in this chapter are by the author.

2. The original, in part, reads "contidad de bezerras para que oviese ganado" (Hackett 1923, 1:40). Hackett translates that phrase as "a number of calves, so that there might be cattle." In contrast, I translate "bezerras" as "yearlings" because the Spanish word for calf is *ternero*; *becerro* clearly signifies yearling. The distinction is significant. Calves would have required a milk cow aboard, and cattle cannot breed until almost a year of age. Yearling heifers and bulls are already weaned and can breed. Moreover, the use of *becerras* rather than *becerros* implies a preponderance of heifers over bulls.

The following sketch provides some general context for readers not familiar with cattle terminology and life cycle, as pertinent to the above point as well as to subsequent analysis. See the classic *Beef Cattle* (Neumann and Snapp 1969) for more detailed information. Calving occurs in either spring or fall, depending on fodder availability and other variables. Single calves are typical, twins relatively rare. The male is called a bull calf (ternero), the female a heifer calf (*ternera*). Veal (ternera) typically comes from calves between one and three months of age but technically can come from any unweaned calf. Weaning takes place between six and ten months of age. Between one and two years of age, females are called yearling heifers (becerras); males are called yearling bulls (becerros) or, if castrated, yearling steers or bullocks (*bueyes jovenes*). Between two and three years of age, the adjectival phrase two-year-old is used: two-year-old bull (*novillo*), two-year-old steer or bullock (novillo or buey joven), and two-year-old heifer (*novilla*). Beef typically comes from yearling and two-year-old steers; but it can also come from yearling and two-year-old heifers, termed slaughter stock. Yearling and two-year-old heifers retained to replenish the herd are termed replacement stock (*hembras de vientre*). Some, but many fewer, yearling and two-year-old bulls are also retained. Once cattle reach maturity at about three years of age, heifers begin to be called cows (*vacas*), steers begin to be called oxen (*bueyes*), and two-year-old bulls begin to be called bulls (*toros*). Significantly for beef operations, once cattle reach maturity they no longer put on much weight but they do keep right on eating; therefore, only those intended for breeding stock (many cows plus a few bulls) or traction stock (oxen) survive their third birthday. Nonetheless, by one year of age cattle have reached puberty, and yearling heifers and bulls can already breed. Typically, however, a heifer is first bred at between fifteen and eighteen months of age, thus having its first calf at between two and three years of age, the gestation period being approximately nine months. Similarly, while yearling bulls can breed, mature bulls can service much larger herds. In uncontrolled breeding systems, each bull typically serves twenty-five cows in open country, as few as a dozen in mountainous terrain.

3. The location of Medellín shifted several times during the sixteenth century. The Spaniards first founded Medellín in 1521 at about 1,600 meters elevation on the escarpment of the Sierra Madre Oriental, possibly at present-day Tataltetelco (Paso y Troncoso 1892-1893, 2:331; Aguilar 1938, 94; Gómara 1964, 300; Cortés 1988, 165, 199). Circa

1524, Cortés moved Medellín to the lower Jamapa River (Oviedo 1959, 4:188-89). This second location was somewhere near Espiche (Paso y Troncoso 1905, 5:194; Paso y Troncoso 1939-1940, 1:84). Gómara, following Cortés, identifies the site as two leagues from San Juan de Ulúa (Gómara 1964, 326). Cortés also provides a detailed, firsthand description of the location: "the said place is by a river, which I took a canoe down to see if boats would be able to pass up to the town and if it flows out to the sea, and it flows into a river that does flow out to the sea, and the mouth of that river has more than a fathom of water; by clearing the river of the many tree trunks in it, the boats will be able to go up to unload among the very buildings of the town" (Cortés 1988, 199). A grant inspection report of 1592 more closely specifies the location of the second Medellín— known as Old Medellín, or Medellín Viejo, by that time—on the left bank of the Jamapa River about five kilometers west of present-day Medellín (AGN-T, vol. 2764, exp. 15, f. 189v). In about 1525, the Spaniards began abandoning Medellín for the newly founded Vera Cruz on the Antigua River (see chapter 1, note 1). By 1527, Medellín seems to have survived only as a native settlement (JGI, xxv-8, ff. 2v-3; Paso y Troncoso 1905, 5:191; Cuevas 1914, 3; Paso y Troncoso 1939-1940, 15:83; Oviedo 1959, 4:244; Cervantes de Salazar 1985, 811). By the early 1570s if not soon after 1527, Medellín had moved to its current location on the right bank of the Jamapa River, one kilometer upstream from its junction with the Atoyac River (AGN-T, vol. 32, exp. 4, ff. 87, 97; vol. 2764, exp. 15, fc. 193; figure 3.3). In moving to that third location, Medellín seems to have subsumed the native settlement of Mictanguautla that had occupied that site (AGN-T, vol. 2680, exp. 20, f. 253).

4

From Archive to Map to Landscape

In the 1540s, as ranchers increasingly sought title to their estancias and as Viceroy Mendoza instituted a centralized grant register, data began to accumulate that now permit analysis of some of the sixteenth-century interactions among natives, livestock ranching, and the Veracruz landscape. Carl Sauer, the renowned Berkeley geographer, had as early as the 1940s noted that wealth of archival data—not just any kind of data, but spatial data.

> Factual data, precisely localized, of enumerations of persons and goods, of land titles, assessments, production, lie neglected in various archives to await exploitation. There is an embarrassment of such riches in the old Spanish records for New Spain (Sauer 1941, 13).

As V. S. Naipaul exults in another context, perhaps a little too ambitiously, while "the documents last we can hunt up the story of every strip of occupied land. I can give you that historical bird's eye view" (Naipaul 1995, 11).

On both sides of the controversy over the effects of the livestock invasion on natives and landscape, the most convincing interpretations derive from quantitative analysis of just such systematic data, not from narratives strung together out of the anecdotal opinions of sixteenth-century observers. The voluminous records of the colonial administration invite such quantitative analysis: most immediately through calculation of changes in livestock density in space and time for comparison with archival and field evidence of changes in environment and native population. The primary database consists of the grants for estancias collected in the eighty-six volumes of AGN-Mercedes plus the two errant volumes in the Library of Congress and the Newberry Library (Prem 1988; Sluyter 1997b). As noted during the hunt for the Villalobos estancia, those grants specify the date of award, the awardee, the location, the number of land units, and whether the land units were for large stock or small stock—for, respectively, ganado mayor or ganado menor. Ganado mayor grants imply cattle, unless specified as being for horses or mules, and ganado menor grants imply sheep, unless specified as being for goats or pigs. Beginning in 1536, a series of vicere-gal ordinances also make clear that estancias for ganado mayor had a legal area, despite not strictly being a grant for a tract of land, of 1,747 hectares and, begin-ning in the early 1560s, a minimum stocking rate of five hundred head. Estan-cias for ganado menor had a legal area of 776 hectares and a minimum stocking rate of two thousand head.

As Sauer had noted, such data represent a scholarly trove—at that time, a neglected "embarrassment" of riches. Yet he surely had little cause for embar-rassment, certainly not for the riches but neither for their scholarly neglect. True, the Mexican archives do contain a wealth of data pertinent to a spatial perspec-tive on long-term ecological change. True, no one with a sensibility for land-scape and ecology had by 1941 systematically engaged those data. Yet those were years of exploration and discovery, for the gleaning of the pithy fragments that would frame the great research problems of succeeding generations. Lesley Byrd Simpson, the prodigious Berkeley "historian," within a decade had in fact taken up his colleague's challenge by systematically analyzing the grants pre-served in AGN-Mercedes.[1] The resulting monograph, published in the *Ibero-Americana* series, provided the first quantitative overview of the spatial distribu-tion of livestock during the early colonial period, a fine complement to Cheva-lier's contemporaneous socioeconomic history (Simpson 1952; Chevalier 1952,

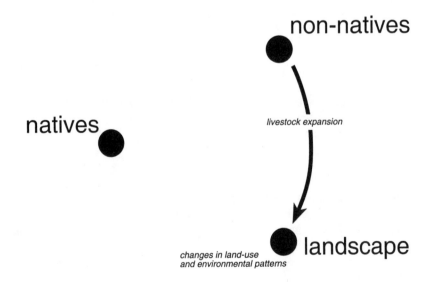

Figure 4.1. Processes and patterns addressed in this chapter.

1963). Those two seminal works have provided the impetus for a series of subsequent studies that contribute more particular, regional understandings of the livestock invasion and its relation to changes in native population and environment (Licate 1981; Piñón Flores 1984; Prem 1988; Widmer 1990; Butzer and Butzer 1993; Melville 1994).

This chapter uses that same spatial database of land grants in order to address how the earliest interactions between non-natives and landscape continued to change as livestock ranching expanded over the remainder of the first century of colonization (figure 4.1). Chapter 4 also begins to address how that livestock expansion impacted environment. Chapter 5 will address how the earliest interactions between non-natives and natives, as covered in chapter 3, continued to change and integrate analysis of the three sides of the colonial triangle while considering both material and conceptual processes.

Methodological Difficulties

On beginning analysis of the mercedes, an awareness settles in that the relatively substantial literature based on that database has not, despite by now spanning half a century, resolved three fundamental methodological issues. First, the extant mercedes in AGN-Mercedes, the Library of Congress, and the Newberry Library might represent only a fraction of all the grants that the scribes originally recorded in the viceregal register. Second, the de facto areas of the grants might not have been the de jure 1,747 hectares for ganado mayor and 776 hectares for ganado menor. Third, the de facto stocking rates might not have been the de jure, minimum rates of five hundred head for ganado mayor and two thousand head for ganado menor.

Without resolution, all three issues compromise any analysis. Simpson confronted but did not resolve them in 1952. Neither has the long series of subsequent studies resulted in any resolution of method nor, consequently, of the controversy over the environmental effects of the livestock invasion or its relation to native depopulation. As a recent and prominent example of that controversy, Melville posits that a "plague of sheep" descended on the sixteenth-century Valle de Mezquital and wreaked environmental havoc (Melville 1994). In contrast—even while relying on the same database of land grants as Melville—the Butzers claim much lower livestock densities and a lack of environmental degradation until much later in the colonial period (Butzer and Butzer 1993).

The completeness of the extant record remains the most trenchant issue. AGN-Mercedes (vols. 1-35, 84), LOC-Kraus (ms. 140), and NLC-Ayer (ms. 1121) span roughly the first century of Spanish colonization and comprise some ten thousand copies of grants, the originals having been retained by the grantees (Simpson 1952). The viceregal scribes only began to keep that register in 1542, however, two decades after Villalobos first introduced cattle, at least a decade after town councils began to issue grazing licenses, and several years after Vice-roy Mendoza began to grant estancias. Furthermore, seven lacunae totaling twelve years occur between 1542 and the virtual end of granting during the period of composición, or Crown vetting and confirmation of individual mercedes, during the 1630s and 1640s: 1544-1546, 1557, 1562, 1569-1571, 1578, 1580, and 1610-1611 (Prem 1988, 130). Moreover, due to the simultaneous use of several register volumes and due to possible loss of some but not all of those parallel volumes for any given period, even years with some extant grants might not necessarily indicate complete, or even good, preservation. Indeed, the occasional copies of mercedes that do not appear in AGN-Mercedes but do appear elsewhere, such as the tenure litigations in AGN-Tierras, indicate the incompleteness of the AGN-Mercedes register. In addition, Cortés and his heirs leased out land within the Marquesado del Valle (García Martínez 1969). Those leases, or *censos*, provided ranchers with title to land in exchange for an annual rent paid in perpetuity, but while therefore effectively land grants, those censos do not appear in AGN-Mercedes (Chevalier 1952, 173-74). Estancias as a whole, of course, represent only capitalist enterprises; individuals kept small numbers of pigs, goats, sheep, donkeys, horses, mules, and cattle on other lands, and the mercedes cannot directly address those livestock (Gibson 1964, 345).

The issue of the areal extent of the land units remains equally unresolved. Despite a few references in the archival documents to circular estancias, viceregal ordinances of 1536, 1567, 1574, and 1580 clearly specify north-south oriented squares (AGN-T, vol. 3460, exp. 2, ff. 10-14v; vol. 3185, exp. 2, ff. 62-63v; Galván 1851, 123-41, 166-67; Hackett 1923, 1:178-82; West 1949, 120). Technically, the spaces between the centrally located cattle or sheep stations remained open range, but the estancia for large stock came to have a de jure definition of one legal league on a side, encompassing an area of 1,747 hectares (figure 3.9). And the estancia for small stock was two-thirds of a league on a side, or 776 hectares. Simpson nonetheless, citing the stipulation that estancias for large stock be one league apart and those for small stock be two-thirds of a league apart, infers that "each estancia was surrounded by a belt of open land at least double the size of the piece granted" (Simpson 1952, 21). That stipulation, however, seems to have referred to the distance between the headquarters idealized as being at the centers of estancias, rather than to a distance between boundaries, and thus makes no provision for some sort of presumed buffer zone between estancias.

> An estancia for large stock has 3000 pasos de marca [1 league] from the structures and house of such estancia to the structures and house of the next, and 2,000 of the said pasos [2/3 league] for estancias for small stock (Galván 1851, 166-67).[2]

Even so, because of the rudimentary surveying techniques of the sixteenth century, the reality on the ground could have only approximated the stipulations of the ordinances. How close the de facto approached the de jure therefore has remained an open question.

The issue of stocking rates relates particularly closely to the controversy over environmental degradation or its lack because assumptions about stocking rates effect calculations of livestock density, a measure of grazing pressure on pasture. As mercedes never prescribed upper stocking limits, the stocking rates of five hundred head of cattle and two thousand head of sheep specified beginning in the 1560s, clearly refer to the minima necessary to secure and retain tenure—to, in the dialect of another frontier, "prove up":

> that within one year [by 1576] the said estancia be stocked with two thousand head of the said small stock and . . . at no time may be abandoned nor with fewer number of stock on pain of this grant becoming null and void (AGN-M, vol. 10, f. 61);

> that within one year [by 1577] the said ranch has been stocked with the said large stock, which will be at least five hundred head (AGN-M, vol. 10, f. 182);

> that within the next year [by 1618] each one of the said ranches has been stocked with two thousand head of the said small livestock (AGN-M, vol. 33, f. 113).

Yet some interpretations characterize those figures as *the* legal stocking rates, as if they were the maximum "prescribed stocking rates" rather than the *minima* required to retain tenure (Butzer and Butzer 1993, 93; Butzer and Butzer 1995, 156). Determinations of regional livestock densities based on that assumption have relied on multiplying the number of estancias by the legally stipulated, minimum stocking rates and dividing by the area of the entire region (Simpson 1952; Butzer and Butzer 1993, 1995). Using the entire area of a region in such exercises recognizes that until composición, the range remained open and livestock could graze far beyond their home estancias—at least in theory. While that method is entrenched in the literature, multiple examples illustrate how de facto stocking rates often exceeded the de jure minima, sometimes by an order of magnitude (Morrisey 1957, 24-29). Even more troublesome in the context of analyses of livestock density in relation to environmental change, high densities do not necessarily equate with overstocking, which implies exceeding the sustainable grazing density and destroying the range. Different environments and herding ecologies in fact entail a wide range of sustainable stocking rates, so-called carrying capacities. Since the Spaniards had considerable experience in the use of transhumance to manage livestock densities in time and space, any analysis of livestock densities should accommodate cultural as well as environmental variables.

Methodological Solutions

Two deductive methodological solutions have emerged to address the issue of completeness versus incompleteness of the archival record. Both methods assume that AGN-Mercedes preserves only a fraction of the original grants. Both attempt to deduce the original number of grants from the number of extant grants.

Simpson, assuming that years with zero-to-few grants in AGN-Mercedes represent "lost volumes," interpolates between "years of fullest coverage" (Simpson 1952). He then employs the interpolated data to derive correction factors for each class of grant for all of New Spain between 1536 and 1620: extant grants plus 40.5% for "Spanish cattle grants," plus 25% for "Spanish sheep grants," and plus 26.3% for "Indian sheep grants." Given Simpson's frustratingly brief explanation of method, replication on the basis of his highly aggregated data remains elusive. He further proposes correction factors to account for additional under-representation in AGN-Mercedes: plus 6.86% for sheep estancias in Tlaxcala; and plus 5.45% for leases within the autonomous Marquesado del Valle. The vague correspondence between Simpson's data and conclusions, even between his in-text calculations and tabular summaries, hardly encourages confidence—especially to two decimal places. Nonetheless, Simpson estimates that for all of New Spain only seventy-five percent of the mercedes for livestock and agricultural lands granted between 1536 and 1620 are preserved in AGN-Mercedes. And, as a final correction factor, he derives the areal extent of livestock estancias in 1620 by multiplying the number of grants in each class by the de jure area for that class, summing the products, and multiplying by three—a final "correction" based on his assumption that "each estancia was surrounded by a belt of open land at least double the size of the piece granted" (Simpson 1952, 21).

Prem proposes an alternative deductive solution (Prem 1988, 1992). He reasons that since the viceregal scribes recorded mandamientos acordados and mercedes in the same volumes, the probability of preservation should be the same for those writs of inspection that actually resulted in grants as for the grants themselves. Therefore, the extant documents of AGN-Mercedes "can be treated as a binomial distribution" (Prem 1988, 131). In other words, the number of extant writs with corresponding extant grants divided by the number of extant grants should equal the number of extant grants divided by the unknown, original number of grants. For the eastern Basin of Puebla, that quotient is 0.6, and the deduced, original number of grants is 256 (Prem 1992, 449). On that basis, Prem concludes that for the period 1587-1620 only sixty percent of the original grants for livestock and agricultural land are extant in AGN-Mercedes.

Both of those deductive methods have serious limitations. Efforts to reconstruct the record by interpolating between years with seemingly fullest coverage ignore the possibility of real fluctuations in granting due to changes in political and economic variables, including complete cessation of granting in some years. Assuming that the proportion of extant writs that actually resulted in grants equals the proportion of extant grants seems a dubious stretch of logic: certainly arguable and possible, but hardly demonstrable or plausible. Assuming a vast web of undocumented buffer zones between the estancias seems even less plausible.

Intensive study of regions within New Spain has produced two inductive methodological solutions that avoid the limitations inherent in the deductive methods. First, research in regional archives recovers copies of mercedes not preserved in AGN-Mercedes. Second, cross-referencing regional databases allows inferring estancias that lack extant mercedes themselves but receive mention as neighboring estancias in extant mercedes.

Several researchers working at a regional scale have searched out copies of mercedes in addition to those preserved in AGN-Mercedes (Prem 1984, 1988, 1992; Licate 1981; Melville 1983, 1990, 1994; Piñón Flores 1984; Widmer 1990). Copies of mercedes appear in regional archives and in other sections of the AGN—such as in regional notarial archives, where records of property transfers provide details of the original land grants; and in AGN-Tierras, where litigants in tenure disputes entered copies of their original mercedes into evidence. Some of those copies preserve mercedes not extant in AGN-Mercedes. Unlike studies at the scale of New Spain, which have typically relied on microfilm copies of AGN-Mercedes, regional studies permit searching, networking, and cross-checking several archives. Even in the AGN, much relevant documentation remains "in its still unexplored parts, and they are very large" (Martínez 1992, 132). For example, a thousand AGN-Tierras volumes remain entirely uncataloged (Melville 1983, 82). Only research in the archives themselves, as opposed to reliance on the incomplete microfilm copies held by various institutions north of the Rio Grande, will uncover documents and insights that extend rather than mimic Simpson's and Chevalier's seminal research.

Intensive regional studies also permit cross-referencing the estancias that themselves lack extant mercedes but are referred to as neighboring estancias in extant mercedes. For the Valle de Mezquital, Melville infers fully fifty-six percent of her claimed total of 776 sheep estancias on the basis of such mention as neighboring estancias (Melville 1983, 80). The proportion of grants the Butzers infer to "compensate for the lost titles" in the Bajío remains unclear (Butzer and Butzer 1993, 93; Butzer and Butzer 1995, 153). Regardless, the assumption that an estancia belonging to Fulano de Tal mentioned as a neighboring estancia in an extant merced represents a "lost" grant simply because no grant in the name of Fulano de Tal is extant seems fraught with hazards. Most essentially, many grants changed owners soon after award, legally or illegally, and mentions of such estancias as neighboring estancias in subsequent mercedes would name the current owner rather than the original grantee. The names of estancias themselves—often quite generic, such as El Hato Grande or El Rincón—also changed and provide but tentative identifications of specific tracts. Melville thus might have inferred many more grants than ever existed and grossly overesti-mated the number of estancias in the Valle de Mezquital, counting the same tract several times over because the owner changed several times—but not necessar-ily. She does try to minimize the hazards of duplication by comparing landscape referents and by applying a downward adjustment for one period to "take into account the possibility of confusion with earlier holdings"; but the often am-biguous character of the referents seriously compromises rigor (Melville 1994, 125-27). Although rooted in the data and thus essentially inductive, inferring neighboring estancias necessitates careful consideration of assumptions and spa-tial analysis.

Only a cartographic methodological solution can ensure rigor in inferring mercedes from neighboring estancias, as well as directly addressing the issues of de facto areal extent and stocking rate. Mapping grants as area symbols prevents assigning the same location to more than one inferred estancia and, at the same time, directly relates the number of grants, their areal extent, and the number of head of livestock to the area of pasture in a given region. Area-symbol maps represent the phenomenon being mapped with a symbol that covers, at the map scale, the same area as the phenomenon. For, example, a square symbol one league on a side at the map scale would represent a single cattle estancia, a square two-thirds of a league on a side, a single sheep estancia. In contrast, point symbols use an icon to represent phenomena. For example, open symbols might represent cattle estancias and filled symbols sheep estancias, a circle one unit and a triangle ten units. Clearly phenomena as small as individual estancias can only be mapped as area symbols at an appropriately large map scale.

While Simpson produced a series of maps for his seminal monograph, their small scale cannot delineate individual estancias (Simpson 1952, 28-87). More-over, the maps simply assign quantities for each class of grant to each of twenty-nine regions, ranging in area from 5,250 to 48,000 square kilometers. Doolittle usefully converts Simpson's numbers to a series of choropleth maps (Doolittle 1987). Developed at the scale of New Spain in order to address a quite different research problem, however, such highly generalized maps cannot address the methodological issue of inferring mercedes at the regional scale.

Curiously, those regional-scale studies that have used cartographic methods have tended to employ point-symbol rather than area-symbol mapping. Licate, for example, maps 68 out of 178 estancias for the eastern Mesa Central as indi-vidual point symbols but does not differentiate between cattle and sheep estan-cias (Licate 1981, 114-17). Prem similarly maps estancias as point symbols for the western Basin of Puebla (Prem 1988, 235-84). And the Butzers map some 744 estancias for the Bajío, aggregating five per point symbol (Butzer and Butzer 1993). They have produced other such aggregated point-symbol maps for the Mesa Central and the Gulf Coast (Butzer and Butzer 1995).

In a seminal departure from that tendency, Prem maps estancias as area symbols for two thousand square kilometers of the western Basin of Puebla by combining archival work at the AGN and regional archives with field work and air photo interpretation (Prem 1984, 1988). Those maps indicate that by 1619, grants for farmland fully occupied much of the bottomlands and grants for estancias much of the Popocatépetl and Iztaccíhuatl piedmont (Prem 1988, 137-45, 156-74). Few spatial gaps existed by 1619 except around Atlixco, suggesting recovery of the vast majority of grants. Prem thus demonstrates the feasibility and utility of an area-symbol analysis. Nonetheless, over ninety-one percent of the some 1,250 grants are for farmland rather than livestock, demonstrating little about the de facto areal extent of estancias.

Those same regional studies suggest an inductive methodological solution to the issue of stocking rates. Scouring documents related to wills, court cases, and censuses, Melville notes scattered references to livestock numbers, extrapolates those numbers to the entire Valle de Mezquital, and calculates livestock densities for ten subregions (Melville 1994, 49-51, 78-84). She calculates livestock densities for each subregion by abstracting scattered references to livestock numbers grazing particular areas or estancias throughout that region, multiplying by the total number of estancias for each subregion for each decade, and dividing by the area of each subregion to allow for grazing on commonage beyond the estancias themselves. The highest calculated density is 7.85 sheep per hectare for the Tula subregion during the 1570s. The highest calculated density for the Valle de Mezquital as a whole is 4.36 sheep per hectare during the 1580s. That regional density far exceeds the 2.6 head per hectare derived deductively by dividing the minimum 2,000 sheep by 776 hectares, that difference being the basis for the debate with the Butzers. The inductive method entails its own assumptions, of course, possibly overestimating livestock densities by relying on the nonsystematic data of law suits. For example, most of Melville's livestock numbers derive from complaints of crop damage lodged against ranchers by native communities, suggesting possible exaggeration of livestock numbers to support those charges.

From Archive to Map

As suggested by Prem's research on farms in the Puebla Basin, only regional-scale, area-symbol mapping can address the compounded methodological issues associated with the mercedes database. Area-symbol mapping of the land grants for the Veracruz lowlands advances resolution of all three methodological issues and thereby allows a rigorous analysis of some of the interactions among natives, non-natives, and landscape.

Several partial listings of mercedes facilitated archival recovery of documentation for 233 livestock estancias for the Veracruz lowlands (Sluyter 1997b).[3] Of those, 204 have extant copies of the titles in AGN-Mercedes. Twenty-five only have extant mercedes or other documentation demonstrating grants in repositories other than AGN-Mercedes, namely in AGN-Tierras and in the Protocolo volumes of the Archivo Notarial de Xalapa (ANX-Protocolo). And four estancias are inferred from mention as neighboring estancias in mercedes or associated documents. The two errant volumes of mercedes in the Library of Congress and the Newberry Library did not reward folio-by-folio inspection with any grants for pertinent estancias. Of the 233 estancias, 118 were for large stock and 115 for small stock.

In essence, because locational information varies from grant to grant, localizing those 233 estancias with acceptable precision to permit area-symbol mapping requires spatially reconciling the overall granting pattern. At one extreme, generic details, lack of extant toponym and landscape referents, and lack of associated maps lowers individual precision to plus/minus ten kilometers. For example, the 1588 grant to Pedro García del Valle includes no references to any but the most general location.

> Don Alvaro Manrique de Zúñiga, in the name of his Majesty, hereby grants one sitio de estancia for small stock to Pedro García del Valle in the limits of the village of Guatusco, in an open savanna by a small stone pyramid, on top of which are two trees, one small and one large; and next to the said pyramid are three or four small hills, all of stone; and towards the east is a thicket of bamboo and other trees (AGN-M, vol. 14, ff. 161v-62v).

The naming of Guatusco provides the only certain locational referent. In another example of the dynamic toponyms that characterize these lowlands, Guatusco became the current village of Santiago Huatusco in the eighteenth century (AGN-Fomento Caminos, vol. 1, fc. 91; AGN-Indiferente de Guerra, vol. 452A, f. last; Ajofrín 1958-1959, 2:31). During the sixteenth and early seventeenth centuries, the now much larger and better known town of Huatusco, which perches on the escarpment of the Sierra Madre Oriental above and to the west of Santiago Huatusco, had a succession of toponyms dominated by variations on San Antonio—not Huatusco (Mota y Escobar 1939-1940, 209-10, 289; Gerhard 1993, 84). Neither the scattering of stone-faced mounds nor the vegetation descriptions, no matter how evocative in other ways, do more than confirm a location for the estancia somewhere on the savanna plains in the environs of Santiago Huatusco.

At the other extreme, the detailed locational information of some mercedes and associated inspection reports—including landmarks, distances, extant toponyms, and associated maps—facilitate an individual precision of plus/minus two kilometers. Thus the mercedes to the Párraga family, associated inspection reports, and maps made possible the localization of the Villalobos estancia (AGN-M, vol. 13, f. 20; vol. 25, f. 143; AGN-T, vol. 2764, exp. 18, ff. 225-60). As another example of high precision localization, the 1592 merced to Nicolás de Salazar for two estancias includes locational referents that survive to the present (AGN-M, vol. 19, ff. 81-81v). In addition, the inspection report survives, including two maps drawn by the lieutenant to the district governor of Vera

Cruz (AGN-T, vol. 2764, exp. 15, ff. 181-95v). That report and its maps clarify such issues as that particular inspector's use of "River of Medellín" as an alternative name for the Jamapa River (figure 3.10, figure 4.2, figure 4.3).

> Don Luis de Velasco [the younger], in the name of his Majesty and without injury to Him or any third party, hereby grants two sitios de estancia for large stock to Nicolás de Salazar in the limits of the jurisdiction of the city of Vera Cruz, between its river and that of Jamapa. The one [estancia] is named Mata de Cordero, which towards the north is four leagues from the said city and one from Estancia Santa Fé; and towards the south, little more than one league separate it from the said Jamapa River; and towards the west is the ranch named San Josefe; and towards where the sun rises is Juan Morrisco Hill. And the other ranch is in Laguna Moreno, which towards the north is six leagues from the said city and more or less one league from Estancia Moreno; and towards the said river, it would be a league to the village of Medellín, in which southeasterly direction is a great thicket; and little less than half a league separates it from the said river of Medellín, between the said Laguna Moreno and about where the old village of Medellín was wont to be (AGN-M, vol. 19, f. 81).

> Being hard by a *laguna* called Moreno, which has a large thicket, it would be a league towards the southeast to the village of Medellín and another league to the cattle ranch called Moreno, said Estancia Moreno being towards the north [illegible] of the said laguna; and the said laguna would be separated from the Jamapa River, also known as the River of Medellín, by a league and a half; and from the palm they call palm of Guinea it would be a little more or less than half a league, standing in the said place that is two harquebus shots from where the old village of Medellín was wont to be (AGN-T, vol. 2764, exp. 15, f. 189v).

Even those two brief excerpts and the two maps demonstrate that the first Salazar estancia was at a place then called Mata de Cordero, about a league north of the Jamapa River and four leagues south of the Antigua River. The present-day village of Mata Corderos confirms that location, as does a hill named Cerro del Maize that seems formerly to have been Juan Morrisco Hill. The claim of a single league between Mata de Cordero and Estancia Santa Fé, also relatively well localized, thus seems to be an underestimate by the inspector. The location of San Josefe, a popular estancia name in the region, offers no sure guide to the western limit of the Salazar estancia, but by the 1570s a Pedro Buzón had purchased or otherwise acquired several estancias in the district, including the one immediately to the west (AGN-M, vol. 12, ff. 87-87v; AGN-T, vol. 2764, exp. 17, fc. 223). Some twenty years later, the Rodrigo Buzón referred to on the Salazar map must have been Pedro Buzón's son, the name of the present-day village of El Buzón confirming the family's presence. The second Salazar estancia was between the Jamapa River and a seasonal wetland called Laguna Moreno,

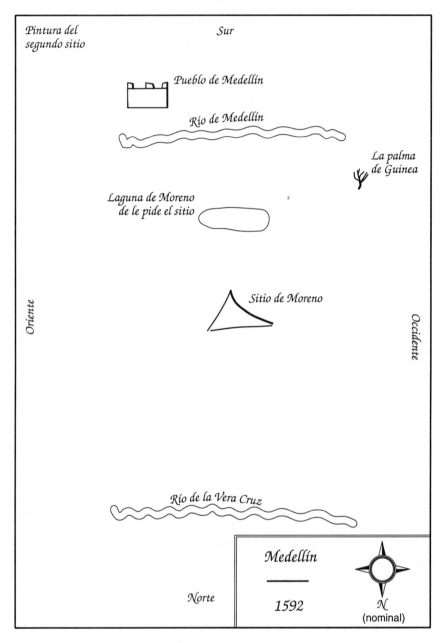

Figure 4.2. A sketch of a map related to a 1592 request for an estancia. The original is in AGN-Tierras (vol. 2764, exp. 15, fc. 193).

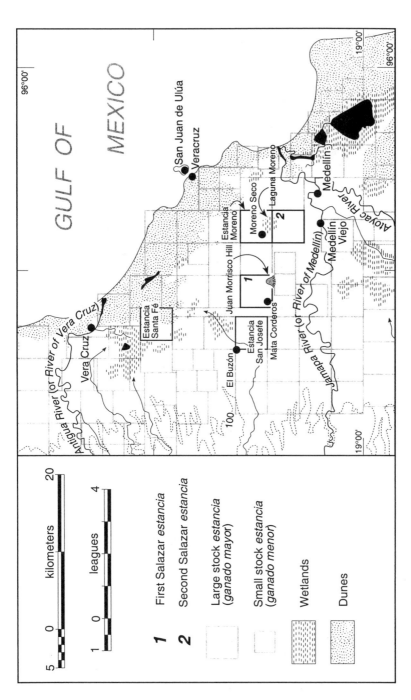

Figure 4.3. Localization of the two estancias granted to Nicolás de Salazar in 1592 (AGN-M, vol. 19, ff. 81-81v). Compare figures 3.10 and 4.2.

about six leagues south of the Antigua River, a league northwest of Medellín, and just north of Medellín Viejo, the old town site that had been abandoned in the 1520s (chapter 3, note 3). The present-day village of Moreno Seco marks the location of the Estancia Moreno, just north of Laguna Moreno.

Overall, the higher precision localizations establish a series of subregional grids of area symbols that, collectively, more closely define the location of lower precision mercedes (figure 4.4). Grants such as the ones to Párraga and Salazar define such grids. Grants such as the one to García del Valle fit into those grids. The García del Valle sheep ranch, for example, finds a place in the grid of area symbols on the open savanna plains just west of Huatusco. The result is a fair cartographic representation of the land grants—not, by any methodological stretch, a cadastral map. In fact, while land disputes among neighboring ranchers indicate that they quickly began to think of the boundaries implied by the stipulated minimum distances between headquarters as delimiting private property, until composición in the seventeenth century, they did not (AGN-T, vol. 32, exp. 4; vol. 2764, exp. 18). The spaces between the ranch headquarters legally remained an open range where different herds mixed, distinguished only by their brands (Chevalier 1952, 16, 264-65). Thus the map's locational grid cannot be cadastral. And even if it were, pacing off distances on horseback and gauging direction by the sun could not have precisely mapped the boundaries.

From Map to Landscape

When mapped by decade, the space-time patterning of the land granting process emerges out of archival obscurity (figure 4.5). The synoptic area-symbol maps demonstrate that the lacunae in the mercedes register represent the actual rhythm of the granting process, a function of changing politics and economy rather than an artifact of missing documents (figure 4.6).

The 1540s and 1550s represent a transitional period between the few precocious estancias of the 1520s and 1530s, as detailed in the preceding chapter, and the land rush of the 1560s. The 1540s and 1550s cattle estancias cluster in the environs of Vera Cruz except for one grant on the southern margin of the study region near Huatusco. The grants near Vera Cruz probably reflect Viceroy Mendoza's 1542 order that several of its vecinos who were grazing cattle nearby, one of them surely being María del Rincón, establish estancias a minimum of three leagues from town (AGN-M, vol. 1, ff. 31, 36v). They thus reflect absorption of local grazing arrangements into Viceroy Mendoza's centralization of control over land use during the 1540s. The northern coastal plain, open savanna on vertisolic plains interrupted by streams, made for prime cattle range. Just as importantly, the royal highway from Vera Cruz through Rinconada and on to Xalapa and Mexico City provided access to developing urban markets. With the

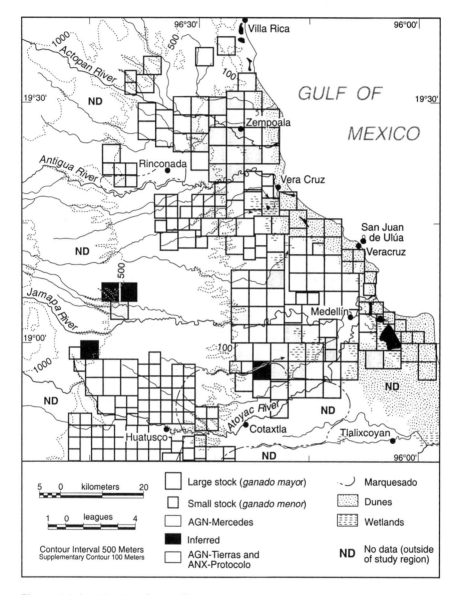

Figure 4.4. Localization of grants for cattle and sheep estancias, 1540s-1620s.

end of the Antillean embargo, continued but modest immigration from Spain, and consolidation of the colonial economy, the livestock industry diversified but remained relatively small. The two earliest lacunae in the mercedes record, 1544-1546 and 1557, reflect changes in viceregal policy in response to cattle damages to native crops in the densely settled districts of the highlands. Viceroy Mendoza spent 1544-1546 converting cattle estancias to sheep in Puebla and Oaxaca rather than granting new ones (Butzer and Butzer 1995, 167). And Viceroy Velasco halted granting during 1557 as part of a broader policy to shift cattle ranching away from the most densely settled zones of the Central Highlands (Chevalier 1952, 124-25).

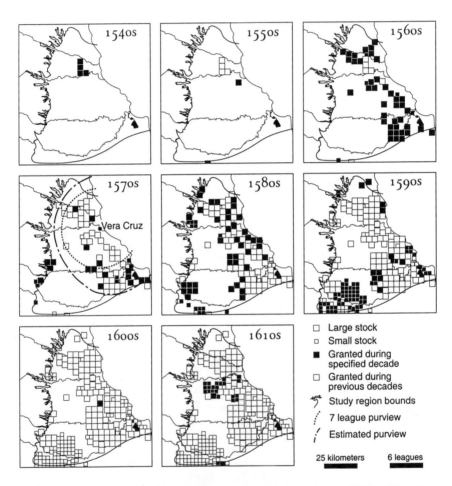

Figure 4.5. Grants for cattle and sheep estancias by decade, 1540s-1610s. The 1570s panel includes the purview of the district governor for Vera Cruz who, in his 1580 report, estimated 150,000 head of large stock at the close of that decade. The seven league purview is the district governor's own claim. The slightly larger purview derives from analysis of the offices of the grant inspectors.

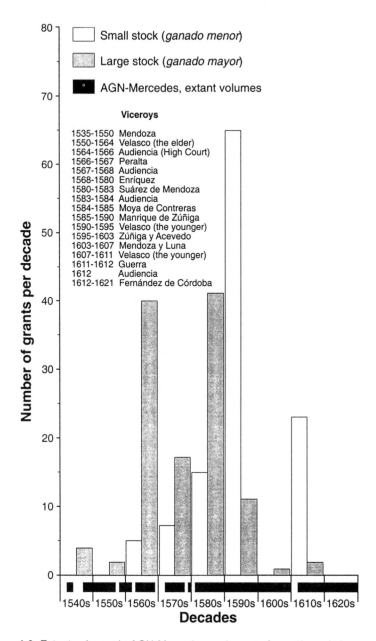

Figure 4.6. Extant volumes in AGN-Mercedes and grants for cattle and sheep estancias, 1540s-1620s. The viceroy list derives from Gerhard (1993, 405).

The flood of granting during the 1560s came in response to new silver strikes, the development of an efficient refining technology, and the beginning of the mining boom. In parallel with increased immigration from Spain, the urbanized, meat-eating populations of Mexico City and Puebla grew exponentially, and the mines themselves demanded tallow for candles and hides for ore and water containers. The colonial economy and demand for cattle products soared. With cattle having been banished from the highlands, even if only temporarily, the Gulf Coast emerged as prime cattle country and a land rush stretched the length of the narrow coastal plain. The increased competition for pasture prompted ranchers to seek legal title after years of de facto occupation, and informal estancias dating to earlier decades continued to absorb into the formal granting process. For example, the 1563 grant of a cattle *estancia* to Gonzalo Ruiz de Córdova notes that "it appears to have already been populated with the said livestock for many years" (AGN-M, vol. 7, f. 136). Cattle must have streamed down the passes through the Sierra Madre Oriental to populate those estancias. Even assuming that Villalobos and Rincón had a hundred head of cattle between them by 1530, natural increase would only have amounted to about a thousand head by the late 1550s (Doolittle 1987, table 1). To achieve the stipulated minimum stocking rate of five hundred head per estancia, the forty-six ganado mayor estancias of 1569 would have required a total of twenty-three thousand head. The five sheep estancias probably supplied the local and naval mutton markets, two of them being near the deep-water port of San Juan de Ulúa. The sand dunes of the coast rather than the wetlands of the coastal plain made the better sheep range, wet pastures encouraging sheep parasites and infectious diseases such as foot rot.

A relative hiatus during the 1570s reflects a change in viceroy and policy in response to suits by native communities throughout New Spain against livestock damages to their agricultural fields (Chevalier 1952, 115). The consequent caution of Viceroy Enríquez resulted in periodic halts to granting, explaining the lacunae of 1569-71 and 1578 (Butzer and Butzer 1995, 167). Much of the granting that did occur filled in the interstices between existing estancias in the prime zones of the coastal plain. But some granting for both ganado mayor and ganado menor began in the environs of Huatusco as well. That activity might reflect early speculation regarding the possibility of a new southern *camino real*, or royal highway, from Veracruz to Puebla through Orizaba (Rees 1975; Driever 1991). Estancias along the new route would have ready access to the domestic market for meat, wool, hides, and tallow and to the export market for leather. The military campaigns of Philip II generated a vast demand for leather, and 74,352 cow hides shipped through Veracruz in 1587 alone (Chevalier 1952, 134-35).

After a change of viceroy in 1580, granting once again boomed. As the native population throughout New Spain approached its nadir after the epidemics of the 1570s, reduced food supplies, inflation, and high food prices stimulated a flood of grants in the lowlands (Chevalier 1952, 131). Grants for cattle estancias continued to fill in gaps on the coastal plain and push up the piedmont and into the dunes. Cattle and sheep estancias proliferated along the camino real running from Vera Cruz through Rinconada and on to Mexico City as well as near Huatusco, where speculation continued over a possible southern camino real. The learned and respected Doctor Palacio, who in his role as confidant to Viceroy Manrique de Zúñiga promoted the southern route for a new highway, had also, hardly coincidentally, acquired some estancias northwest of Huatusco during the 1580s (AGN-M, vol. 13, f. 29v; vol. 15, ff. 86-87; vol. 21, ff. 6v-7; AGN-T, vol. 2702, exp. 13-14; Driever 1991).[4] The vertisolic savanna plains northwest of Huatusco comprised the prime range, co-opted for cattle estancias.

The 1590s land rush for sheep estancias reflected the continuing growth of the colony's textile industry and the need for lowland pastures as the flocks of the Central Highlands pressed the limits of their home pastures, perhaps in the context of a series of drought years (Chevalier 1952, 135-36; Salvucci 1987, 135-36; Metcalfe 1987; Melville 1990). A few cattle grants filled most of the remaining interstices on the coastal plain and lower piedmont, but most of the sheep grants focused on the upper piedmont near Huatusco. They generally occupied rougher terrain than the plains that cattle ranchers had co-opted during the 1580s. Sheep grants also filled the dunes near the relocated port of Veracruz, officially transferred from the Antigua River to the mainland opposite San Juan de Ulúa in 1597 (Paso y Troncoso 1939-1940, 13:1-3). Many of the ganado menor grants probably represent *agostadero* for sheep from the Central Highlands. The term *agostadero*, or dry-season pasture, is named for the summer dry season of Spain and derives from *agosto*, or August. In the context of New Spain, however, agostadero refers to winter dry-season pastures. If by 1580 the district governor of Vera Cruz had already remarked on "the innumerable sheep that descend from the highlands to over-winter," by the 1590s even more than innumerable flocks must have streamed across the Sierra Madre Oriental every year (JGI, ms. xxv-8, f. 5).

Most of the good cattle pasture had been occupied by the 1600s, but filling in continued through the 1600s and 1610s, with interstices too small for ganado mayor estancias granted as ganado menor. During the 1610s, a lagging rush for sheep grants spread up the central piedmont, relatively near the northern camino real and with good access to the Central Highlands but not as ideally situated as the Huatusco zone. The cessation of granting during the 1620s reflected the decline in silver production, modest population growth, and economic stagnation relative to the previous century of growth (Gibson 1966, 103-5). And the landscape was full. By 1619, some 2,954 square kilometers of estancias occupied more than fifty percent of the lowlands and nearly all of the prime range.

Regarding the issue of completeness of the mercedes record, then, the rhythm of the granting process evident in the extant documents is real, a function of changing politics and economy rather than an artifact of supposedly lost volumes. As policy changed, granting engulfed a series of frontiers, preceded by a scatter of pioneers and succeeded by filling in. Only the autonomous enclaves of the Marquesado del Valle, around Cotaxtla and Rinconada, and the central piedmont remain as significant blanks on the map by 1619. The former blank reflects occupation by censos rather than mercedes. The grants that do intrude on the enclaves largely date to the period 1567 through 1593, when the Crown had sequestered the Marquesado (García Martínez 1969, 137-40, 157-60). The latter blank relates to the inaccessibility of the central piedmont, the difficulty of north-south movement in a zone dissected by deep ravines and the distance from the royal highways to the north and south. Of the total of 233 estancias mapped, only four represent inference from mention as neighboring estancias and only twenty-five exclusively derive from repositories other than AGN-Mercedes. Given the space-time pattern evident in the area-symbol maps, the spatial distribution of grants in 1619 confirms that all of the precocious estancias of the 1520s through 1550s eventually absorbed into the formal granting process and that no significant spatial lacunae match the temporal lacunae in AGN-Mercedes. The patterning also suggests that Spanish space accumulation largely proceeded through viceregal granting rather than through other processes, such as purchase from natives or permanent "squatting."

Thus, at least for the Veracruz lowlands, "correcting" for "lost" mercedes is unjustified and results in spurious analyses. Few if any estancias additional to those documented seem warranted or, indeed, even possible. Adding forty percent to cattle estancias and twenty-five percent to sheep estancias for New Spain as a whole thus comes to seem an egregious distortion of reality (Simpson 1952). Similarly, accounting for putative squatters or lost grants by inference from neighboring estancias, more than doubling the documented estancias, comes to seem flagrant folly (Melville 1983). Melville infers 455 out of 862 estancias for a region of 10,029 square kilometers versus the 4 out of 233 for the Veracruz lowlands, a region of 5,250 square kilometers. The large proportion of inferred estancias for the Valle de Mezquital compared to Veracruz suggests the need for mapping the Valle de Mezquital grants in order to preclude counting the same location several times simply because ownership changed. While arguably the distinct environmental and cultural contexts of other regions, particularly in predominantly sheep rather than cattle districts, might have resulted in different processes of space accumulation than those of the lowlands, only further research can demonstrate those differences. Most essentially, that research must employ cartographic methods or fail the most basic standards of rigor.

Regarding the areal extent of the land units, the de jure areas of 1,747 hectares for ganado mayor and 776 hectares for ganado menor represent a close approximation of reality. The blanks among the densest groups of estancias on the coastal plain or around Huatusco might represent a few missing mercedes but more likely represent the difference between the conceptual and the operational, the neighboring estancias and a scattering of *caballerías*, the forty-three hectare farm tracts, co-opting the interstices. The Spanish and surviving native communities might also have retained minimal buffer zones, accounting for other interstices. Regardless, in no case could any estancia have been "surrounded by a belt of open land at least double the size of the piece granted" and thus justify multiplying the de jure areal extent by three (Simpson 1952, 21). To varying degrees in space and time, the central piedmont might well have served as common range during the wet season, the cattle retreating to their home estancias on the coastal plain during the dry season. But that seasonal round between piedmont and coastal plain in no way equates with Simpson's hypothesized buffer zone around each estancia.

The issue of stocking rates remains the most thorny of the three methodological problems. Employing the standard deductive method, multiplying the number of estancias by the de jure minimum stocking rates, the 118 cattle and 115 sheep estancias granted by 1619 amount to 59,000 head of cattle and 230,000 head of sheep. Assuming grazing on granted lands only, the cattle would have occupied 206,146 hectares at a density of 0.29 head per hectare, and the sheep 89,240 hectares at a density of 2.6 head per hectare. Assuming grazing throughout the entire 525,000 hectare region, densities would have been nearly half that, 0.16 head per hectare for cattle and 1.5 head per hectare for sheep, each species assumed to graze non-granted lands in proportion to granted lands: 366,391 hectares for cattle and 158,609 hectares for sheep.

Melville's inductive method cannot be applied in the lowlands because, in comparison to the Central Highlands, apparently more rapid and extreme native depopulation seems to have resulted in a lack of records of community complaints against ranchers. Instead, a single observation made by the district governor of Vera Cruz in 1580 provides a gross estimate of the livestock population: some 150,000 cows and mares (undoubtedly brood mares to provide mules for the port traffic) grazed within little more than twenty-nine kilometers of Veracruz and "innumerable sheep" descended to agostadero pastures every winter (JGI, ms. xxv-8, f. 5). Since no precise jurisdictional boundaries existed and since this particular governor displayed a tendency to progressively shorten leagues with increasing distance from his desk, as evident from locational references to several settlements, the exact area of his purview remains uncertain. An analysis of the offices of grant inspectors provides a rough delineation, however, and reveals that the Vera Cruz jurisdiction included the entire study region exclusive of the southwest quadrant, those grants mainly being inspected out of Huatusco. Since the viceroy did not grant any estancias in 1580, the report must relate to the situation in the late 1570s. By then the purview of the governor included fifty-seven cattle and eight sheep estancias. On the basis of the minimum stocking rates, those grants represented 28,500 cattle and horses together with 16,000 sheep. Even allowing for additional head grazing on leases in the two enclaves of the Marquesado, even allowing for a few unrecovered or nonextant mercedes, even allowing for some exaggeration on the part of the governor— 28,500 remains a far cry from 150,000, and 16,000 is hardly "innumerable."

Together the deductive and inductive methods establish a range of probable estimates. For large stock alone, the inductive method raises the possibility of stocking rates more than five times the legal minimum. Ignoring, at least for the moment, the possibility of grazing beyond granted estancias, the range of densities for cattle would have been between 0.29 head per hectare and 1.43 head per hectare, respectively the legal minimum and five times that minimum. Similarly for sheep, although much more tentatively given the vague "innumerable" of the geographical report, grazing density would have ranged between 2.6 and 12.9 head per hectare. Assuming grazing throughout the ungranted central piedmont and other spatial lacunae, the lower end of the range would fall to, as previously calculated, 0.16 head per hectare for cattle and 1.5 head per hectare for sheep. The upper end of the range would fall to 0.8 head per hectare for cattle and 7.5 head per hectare for sheep.

Given the paucity of data, such a range of gross estimates remains the most credible reconstruction of probable livestock densities; but determining which end of such a range might be the most probable, and thus evaluating the environmental consequences, requires comparison with an analogous context with better data. In an early effort at such comparison, Simpson contrasted the de jure minimum density of 0.29 head of cattle per hectare against twentieth-century range management practices in the United States and concluded that it "seems altogether improbable that any grazing land could support" such densities "for any length of time" (Simpson 1952, 21). Such a specious comparison between tropical and temperate environments was perhaps the best possible at the time. A better environmental analog would be tropical and subtropical Africa, with cattle densities there ranging between 0.6 and 2.4 head per hectare (Rattray 1987, 113-22; Holmes 1987, 91-100; White 1987, 227-38; Edwards and Tainton 1990, 99-128; Gatenby 1991, 12). Yet even that comparison biologizes pastoralism (Turner 1993, 402-21). Even a comparison with the current livestock density of the Veracruz region itself, 0.5 to 2.0 head per hectare, would ignore many changes in environment, technology, culture, and other variables since the colonial period (INEGI 1984).

The first Mexican livestock census provides the most appropriate analog for comparison: relatively accurate, high resolution data for the environs of Veracruz during a time—the early twentieth century—when ranching was quite similar to the colonial period. At the time of that 1902 census, during the last decade of the Porfiriato, the region's livestock economy prospered, focusing on beef production for urban markets (*Estadística Ganadera* 1903; Skerritt Gardner 1989, 29-33). Sheep production had declined with liberalization of international trade and competition from imported textiles (Salvucci 1987, 135-67; Chávez Orozco and Florescano 1965, 194). Otherwise the ranching ecology remained similar to that of the colonial period, the major adjustments being improvement of transportation infrastructure, the nineteenth-century introduction of more productive and palatable African grasses, principally Guinea and Pará grass, and the beginnings of the replacement of *criollo* stock with specialized breeds (*La Ganadería* 1965, 13; Parsons 1970, 141-53). Rural population was beginning to rise from its colonial nadir but remained relatively low until after the impending revolution and subsequent agrarian reform (*Estadísticas Históricas* 1990, 21,

48-51). The livestock densities of 1902 should therefore represent the apogee of the colonial-type pastoral ecology and provide a reasonable analog to evaluate the range of estimates of colonial livestock densities and their potential for environmental degradation.

The 1902 census provides counts for cattle, horses, mules, sheep, goats, donkeys, and pigs by municipio, the municipalities of Mexico roughly equating to U.S. counties (*Estadística Ganadera* 1903). Aggregation at the municipal level therefore dictates the smallest unit of analysis. The analysis categorizes cattle, horses, and mules as large livestock, sheep and goats as small livestock, and disregards donkeys and pigs as domestic livestock. The analysis also subsumes immature livestock—calves, lambs, colts, and kids—under the mother-juvenile pair since both the stipulations of the mercedes and the 1902 census concern the livestock capital rather than the annual product.

Comparing those data with the estimates for the colonial period requires normalization to standard livestock units (SLU) and further mapping. The conversion of all livestock to SLU considers feed intake and cultural context to normalize head of small livestock to head of large livestock, thus factoring out the changing proportions of sheep and cattle over space and time as well as any possible bias arising from grants for cattle estancias actually supporting sheep and vice versa. The feed intake of livestock varies widely. Even within taxa such variables as feed type, breed, weight, maturity, environment, gender, gestation, and lactation all affect feeding (NRC 1987). As a gross generalization, however, a standard ewe unit of fifty kilograms would consume some 1.69 kilograms of dry matter per day, and a standard cow unit of 350 kilograms would consume some 7.28 kilograms per day, the relationship between ungulate weight and forage consumption being nonlinear (NRC 1987, 75; Chesworth 1992, 138). Those live weights approximate those of the small criollo cattle and Merino and criollo sheep of sixteenth-century New Spain (Chevalier 1952, 133; Wilson and Burns 1973, 677-89; Gatenby 1991, 37, 41; Jordan 1993, 67; Rouse 1977, 253-54). The consumption ratio of large to small livestock, 1 to 4.3, suggests a similar stocking ratio and a factor for normalizing number of sheep to number of cattle. In contrast, the mercedes specify a minimum of 0.29 head per hectare for cattle and 2.6 for sheep, a ratio of 1 to 9—roughly twice the ratio derived through consumption analysis. Seemingly, then, the stipulated minimum stocking rates took the transhumance of Spanish pastoralism into account. As opposed to relatively parochial cattle, the peripatetic sheep grazed a given estancia for only half a year, moving between summer and winter estancias, and thus could maintain approximately twice the stocking rate that the consumption analysis suggests. That assumption does not ignore the evidence for regional-scale cattle transhumance but recognizes that such travesío occurred at the scale of the municipality—in other words, within the boundaries of the statistical unit of analysis. Given that transhumance, the ratio of sheep to cattle densities that the mercedes themselves specify yields the most appropriate normalization factor: 1.0 large stock to 1.0 SLU, and 9.0 small stock to 1.0 SLU. That normalization factor has the credibility of deriving inductively from the primary data themselves, the mercedes, and of being deducible from biological and cultural processes: ungulate consumption and Spanish transhumance. Employing SLU thus not only factors out the changing proportions of sheep, cattle, and other livestock over space and time, but factors out the confounding effect of transhumance, a central trait of Spanish pastoralism.

In comparison to the 5,250 square kilometer study region, the included municipalities have a combined area of 4,814 square kilometers (*Los Municipios* 1988). Several of the municipalities extend beyond the study region, but minimally; several others only slightly impinge on its margins and thus do not warrant inclusion (figure 4.7).[5] Because the entire area of each municipality does not comprise pasture but data aggregation dictates the municipality as the smallest unit of analysis, the calculations must assume grazing throughout the entire area rather than on the granted estancias alone. The statistics therefore inescapably underestimate the livestock densities for pasture lands. That bias affects mountainous municipalities such as Actopan more than such floodplain municipalities as Jamapa, but the primary goal remains an evaluation of the range of densities for 1619 through comparison with the analogous pastroecosystem of 1902—not an explanation of differences among municipalities except as that issue relates to the primary goal.

Figure 4.8 summarizes the 1902 and 1619 minimum livestock densities in SLU per hectare. Much higher livestock densities generally obtained in 1619 than in 1902. The minimum regional estimate for 1619, as defined by the de jure minimum stocking rates, is more than twice the 1902 regional density: 0.16 SLU per hectare compared to 0.071 SLU per hectare. The maximum regional estimate for 1619, as defined by five times the de jure minimum stocking rates on the basis of the estimate of the district governor, is more than eleven times the 1902 regional density: 0.79 SLU per hectare compared to 0.071. Only the municipality of Adalberto Tejeda had a higher density in 1902 than its maximum 1619 estimate: 0.085 SLU per hectare compared to 0.013. Only Boca del Río has a 1902 density enough higher than its minimum 1619 estimate to graduate to the next higher density class from the 1619 to the 1902 map. Five of the other municipalities have the same density class on both maps. Eight drop one density class from the 1619 to the 1902 map. And Carrillo Puerto drops two density classes.

That comparison suggests that even the minimum estimate for 1619 is high relative to the 1902 livestock density and, by analogy, relative to the 1902 "carrying capacity" and thus to the 1619 "carrying capacity." The maximum estimate for 1619 implies environmental disaster. Direct evidence of environmental degradation should therefore be preserved in the sediments of the lakes and lagoons of the coastal plain. Overgrazing should have resulted in devegetation, soil compaction, increased runoff, and gullying. Yet analysis of the sediments of Laguna Catarina reveals no such soil erosion during the colonial period. The sediments record no more than a sharp rise in the influx of carbon and phosphorous (Sluyter 1997c). Albeit that sediment core represents only a single point, it occurs near the center of a basin into which flow streams draining the entire central zone of the study region. Laguna Catarina would not have recorded any erosion in the sheep zone around Huatusco or the cattle zones in the lower drainages of the Jamapa, Atoyac, and Actopan rivers. Nonetheless, its sediments

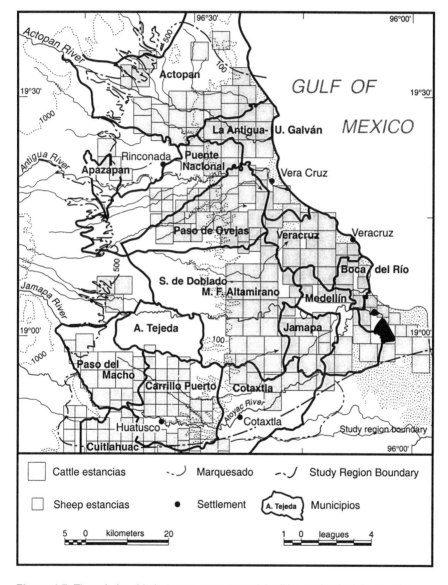

Figure 4.7. The relationship between current municipalities and colonial estancias.

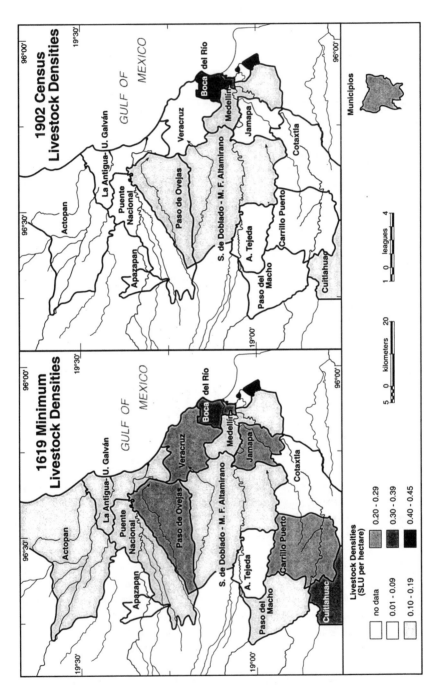

Figure 4.8. Livestock densities in Standard Livestock Units per hectare for 1619 and 1902.

would have recorded erosion in the central zone, from the coastal plain that had been granted for cattle in the 1560s to the central piedmont grants for sheep of the 1610s. Yet Laguna Catarina records no evidence of major disruptions in the vegetation cover, changes in the runoff regime of the streams, or failures of slopes. Burning of pasture and tons of ruminant faeces resulted in dramatic influxes of carbon and phosphorous and no doubt were, in conjunction with introduced plants, altering the region's vegetation composition, but vegetation cover seems to have remained intact.

Conversely, the relative differences in livestock densities between 1619 and 1902 might be misleading, thus explaining away the incongruous correlation between environmental stability and apparently extreme livestock densities during the sixteenth and early seventeenth centuries. The much lower regional SLU population of 1902 might have grazed on a proportionately smaller area of pasture than available in 1619. Postulating more comparable 1619 and 1902 livestock densities, however, would demand assuming a vast reduction in pasture area, the 34,204 SLU of 1902 grazing on only forty-five percent of the pasture lands of 1619. That seems unlikely given that in 1902 the livestock economy was booming while the pastoral ecology remained similar to that of the colonial period except for additional transport infrastructure and the introduction of African grasses. If anything, the area of pasture lands should have been higher in 1902. Supporting that logic, Adalberto Tejeda counters the general pattern of lower densities in 1902 than in 1619 only because during the sixteenth and seventeenth centuries the central piedmont remained isolated from the main transport axes and that municipality remained virtually ungranted. Boca del Río also gained livestock but presents a different sort of special case, the high 1902 density probably due to break-of-bulk feedlot operations near the port of Veracruz.

Even so, some might argue that the lower 1902 densities reflect a decline in livestock population because of degradation of pasture quality due to overgrazing during the intervening centuries. Livestock populations throughout New Spain do in fact seem to have declined somewhat in the seventeenth century, at least according to the scattered accounts of contemporaries, although none from the Veracruz lowlands. Chevalier attributes that decline to either deterioration of range productivity or "degeneration of the species" due to a "lack of new blood" (Chevalier 1952, 130). A more likely cause, though, seems to have been that the silver boom of the sixteenth century so inflated the price of hides, tallow, beef, and veal that ranchers began to slaughter not only their excess males, but their female animals—the replacement stock itself. As rates of herd growth slowed and demand continued, prices increased even more and so did the slaughter of hembras de vientre. With a bust to the mining boom ever imminent, ranchers would have had great incentive to increase cull rates while high prices lasted. A similarly high demand for mutton impacted the sheep population. As a consequence, the viceroy issued several edicts throughout the early 1590s that prohibited the slaughter of cows and ewes in an attempt to increase herd size and secure the meat supply (Chevalier 1952, 131-32). Whatever the cause of the gen-

eral decline in the herds of New Spain, though, the cattle population seems to
have restabilized during the seventeenth century. In those districts where mixed
farming haciendas emerged, livestock populations probably never recovered to
the levels of the late sixteenth century. But in those districts such as the Veracruz lowlands where cattle ranching continued to predominate and did not
have to compete with crops for land, high cattle populations persisted.

In fact, the vast Veracruz herds persisted throughout the colonial period and
into the postcolonial period until the agrarian revolution of the 1910s. In 1580,
of course, the district governor of Vera Cruz had reported some 150,000 cows
and mares and "innumerable sheep" for a somewhat smaller district than the
entire region (JGI, ms. xxv-8, f. 5). The results of the comparison to the 1902
census suggest some exaggeration on the part of the governor, however, favor-
ing the lower end of the range of SLU estimates for 1619 for the entire region—
closer to 76,222 SLU than to 381,110. And livestock densities were as high or
higher through the eighteenth century, as noted in the "Relación de Corral" for a
somewhat larger region.

> From Veracruz and other places along the coast, roads go to Mexico [City]
> through Orizaba, Jalapa, and Ixhuatlán de los Reyes. . . . In the haciendas and
> ranches of that aforesaid region during the years 1765 and 1766 there were
> more than 200,000 head of cattle, more than half of them feral (Siemens and
> Brinckmann 1976, 311).

And with some fluctuations that situation persisted through the nineteenth century (Chávez Orozco and Florescano 1965, 54, 194; Del Angel P. 1994). At
midcentury, Sartorius reported that "thousands of cows pasture" and that neither
"towns nor villages are found in these extensive districts, but merely here and
there the solitary farms of the cattle-proprietors, or of the herdsmen" (Sartorius
1961, 9-10). A traveler also observed the persistent preponderance of cattle, at
least on the basis of the herds of a single rancher, albeit the most infamous one:

> much of this land is of good quality, and would produce cotton and sugar most
> profitably. Very little of it is in cultivation, with the trifling exception of the
> chili and corn patches. General Santa Anna owns immense herds of cattle,
> some forty or fifty thousand head, which graze upon it (Thompson 1846, 12-
> 13).

Equally, sixteenth-century intensification of the livestock ecology to alleviate grazing pressure through fodder cultivation is an improbable explanation for
the conjunction of environmental stability and seemingly extreme livestock densities. The mercedes record does not substantiate the possibility of such intensification. By 1619, the viceroys had granted only ninety-two caballerías of farmland in the region. The annual harvest from those farms might have approached
some 1,849,000 kilograms of maize. Thus even if dedicated to maize fodder
production, as a liberal estimate those farms could have fed only some 2,233

SLU. That estimate ignores the additional fodder available through grazing crop stubble, but 2,233 SLU represents only three percent of the minimum estimate of the 1619 SLU population, less than the population of five estancias for ganado mayor stocked at the minimum rate.[6]

The cartographic method thus allows evaluation of the range of probable densities—from low values based on the minimum stocking rates stipulated in the mercedes to high values based on the observation of the district governor—with the closest environmental and cultural analog for which relatively precise data are available. On the basis of comparison with the 1902 census, even if the de facto 1619 density did not exceed the de jure minimum, the first century of colonization ended with livestock occupying most of the best pasture lands in extremely high densities. In comparison, the high estimate thus comes to seem entirely improbable. Other such estimates based on fragmentary data, such as the observation of the district governor, thus also raise suspicion—for example, the estimates for the Valle de Mezquital that Melville bases on a few lawsuits. Perhaps a more detailed, municipality-by-municipality study of the Veracruz lowlands will eventually reveal a more complex process in which sheep-dominated zones suffered degradation of the range, as suggested by the great drop in livestock densities between 1619 and 1902 for the two municipalities that were the near exclusive domain of sheep in 1619: Cuitlahuac and Carrillo Puerto. Even so, those two municipalities represent less than eight percent of the study region's area.

Melville's proposal, to extrapolate the "ungulate irruptions model" from the Valle de Mezquital to all of New Spain, thus seems inappropriate:

> as predicted by the model of ungulate irruptions, wherever grazing animals were introduced in New Spain their population history mirrored the experience for the Valle de Mezquital; that is, they increased exponentially, peaked, crashed, and finally stabilized (Melville 1994, 162-63);

> contemporaries correlated the decline in the animal populations with environmental deterioration and overexploitation (Melville 1994, 47-55).

Whether the Valle de Mezquital represents a special case, whether Melville's model applies even there, or whether the Veracruz lowlands represent a special case—all remain open empirical questions. But the Veracruz lowlands clearly did not undergo the sequence of environmental degradation predicted by the ungulate irruptions model. The livestock population did increase rapidly during the sixteenth century, but it did not overshoot the range "carrying capacity," did not devastate the environment, and did not suffer a population crash. Instead, the high densities of the sixteenth century persisted through the colonial period.

Landscape: Pastoral Ecology and Environment

Beyond evaluation of estimates of livestock density, spatial analysis of the archival database begins to address land as landscape and thus to manifest Naipaul's "historical bird's eye view" and address the colonial triangle. The insight and rigor possible through analyzing both temporal and spatial patterning of cultural ecological elements contrasts markedly with simplistic deductions based on the monodimensional "ungulate irruptions model." Even biological ecologists, the long-time promoters of such models, have come to recognize their ahistorical and aspatial character as serious epistemological flaws. Perspectives such as landscape ecology and historical ecology have thus begun to become established among biological ecologists, built on foundations that geographers such as Carl Sauer and Carl Troll laid decades ago (Sauer 1969; Troll 1971; Forman and Gordon 1986; Pickett and Cadenasso 1995; Russell 1997).

From a landscape perspective, the correlation between environmental stability and apparently extreme livestock densities begins to become understandable. The Spaniards might have been able to maintain high livestock densities because their pastoral ecologies exploited seasonally available pasture through transhumance at a range of scales. Long-distance transhumance moved sheep between the Mesa Central and the Veracruz lowlands. Regional-scale transhumance moved cattle between the dry savanna of the piedmont and the wet savanna of the coastal plain. Both types of transhumance were based on Iberian antecedents (Butzer 1988). Both would have mitigated grazing pressure by reducing livestock density during the season in which pastures were most sensitive to degradation.

The land grant record demonstrates the proliferation of inter-regional sheep transhumance. A few of the sheep estancias, those congregated in the dunes near Veracruz, probably supplied the local and naval mutton markets. But the majority, located on the upper piedmont, would have served as agostadero for highland flocks. By the 1590s' land rush for sheep estancias, cattle estancias already had preempted most of the coastal plain. The piedmont made better sheep pasture anyway, the wetter conditions of the coastal plain being conducive to sheep parasites. The piedmont around Huatusco also had good access to the pass through the Sierra Madre Oriental that the camino real would eventually use. The district governor of Vera Cruz certainly noted the annual descent of the sheep to the lowlands, and certain toponyms such as Paso de Ovejas suggest sheep transhumance, but the land grant documents themselves add spatial substance and detail that confirms the practice. Maps from grant inspection reports show two major drove trails for sheep near Huatusco, one running generally east-west and the other northeast-southwest (figure 4.9, figure 4.10). The mercedes themselves specify the connections between lowland agostadero and highland districts. In 1595, Francisco López, a vecino of Puebla who had run a sheep

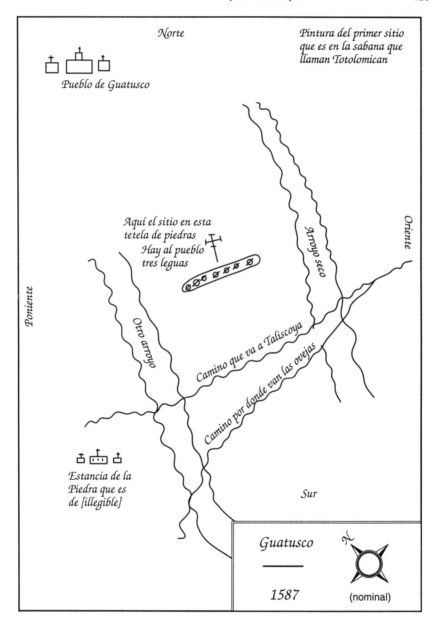

Figure 4.9. A sketch of a map related to a 1587 request for an estancia near Huatusco, rendered as "Guatusco" in the sixteenth century. Note the "camino por donde van las ovejas," or sheep drove trail. The original is in AGN-Tierras (vol. 2702, exp. 12, f. 7v).

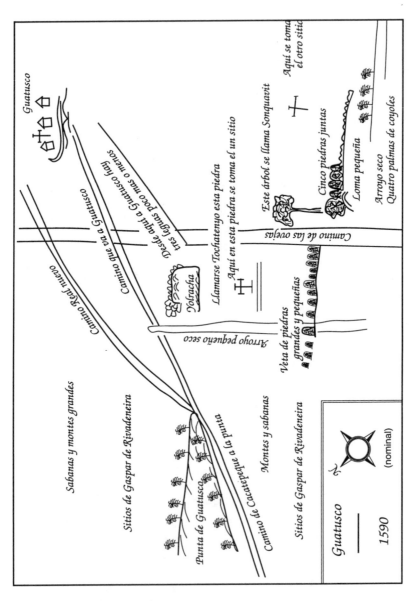

Figure 4.10. A sketch of a map related to a 1590 request for an estancia near Huatusco, rendered as "Guatusco" in the sixteenth century. Note the "camino de las ovejas," or sheep drove trail. The original is in AGN-Tierras (vol. 3331, exp. 1, f. 9).

ranch there since 1589, received grants for two sheep ranches near Huatusco (AGN-M, vol. 20, ff. 144-45; Prem 1988, 271). At least five more holders of ganado menor grants in the lowlands can be confirmed as vecinos of the highland districts that together formed the center of gravity for the flocks of New Spain: Puebla, Tecamachalco, and the Llanos de Ozumba (AGN-M, vol. 10, ff. 45v-46, 61-61v, 68v-69; vol. 20, ff. 21v-22, 144-45; vol. 21, ff. 7v-8). Those summer pastures were more than a hundred kilometers to the west and fifteen hundred meters in elevation above the Huatusco district. During the seventeenth century, the great sheep drives to agostadero in Nuevo León would begin to eclipse the Veracruz pole of the system in terms of both distance and size (Butzer and Butzer 1995, 182).

The mercedes also demonstrate the sixteenth-century proliferation of the cattle ranching ecology that Villalobos diffused and adapted from the Marismas of Andalusia. Forty-one out of the 118 cattle estancias in the region, or thirty-five percent, straddled the transition zone between piedmont and coastal plain (figure 4.11). Just as for Villalobos, that strategic location would have provided access to pasture during both the wet and the dry seasons. More tellingly, in some cases the spatial relations among multiple grants to individuals or families reveal the success of the Andalusian model of regional-scale transhumance. The analysis probably reveals only some of the spatial connections among suites of estancias that encompassed hill land and wetland. Many more such distributed estancias might be obscured by unclear family relationships because of common last names such as García, the use of surrogates to acquire land grants, and subsequent land purchases. Thus only some of the grouped estancias in figure 4.11 reveal systems that transect coastal plain and piedmont; in some cases, one or more estancias might be missing from a system. The Núñez de Montalván brothers, Juan and Pedro, became the first land barons in the south of the region by acquiring a string of at least six estancias between 1564 and 1567 (AGN-M, vol. 7, ff. 272-73; vol. 8, f. 189; vol. 9, f. 107; vol. 9, ff. 115-16; AGN-T, vol. 32, exp. 4, f. 102). They stretched from the wetlands up onto the lower fringes of the piedmont. Spanning nearly the entire region, the Ruiz de Córdova family ran cattle on at least sixteen tracts (AGN-M, vol. 7, ff. 136-36v, 272v; vol. 8, ff. 30-30v; vol. 9, ff. 33v-34; vol. 12, f. 119; vol. 13, ff. 40-40v; vol. 17, ff. 116v-17; vol. 18, ff. 240v-41v; vol. 19, ff. 81-81v; ANX-Protocolo, vol. 1600-1608, ff. 414-15v). Some of the estancia systems indicate that as the lower piedmont zone was taken up, the cordon of dunes became alternative wet-season pasture. Although vast seasonal movements of cattle imply the existence of drove trails similar to those of the Marismas, only a few suggestive toponyms remain, as indicated on figure 4.11: Paso Vaquero and Paso del Toro.

During the first half of the seventeenth century, a very few families came to control the vast herds that seasonally ranged across piedmont, coastal plain, and dune lands. With the decline in silver production, modest immigration, and nadir in native population, families that had accumulated capital through their control of encomienda and repartimiento labor, either through tribute or in such enter-

prises as sugar mills and silver mines, turned to real estate. The wealthiest families acquired enormous haciendas and entailed them (Wobeser 1989, 63-64).[7]
The monastic orders, as well, came to control vast tracts.

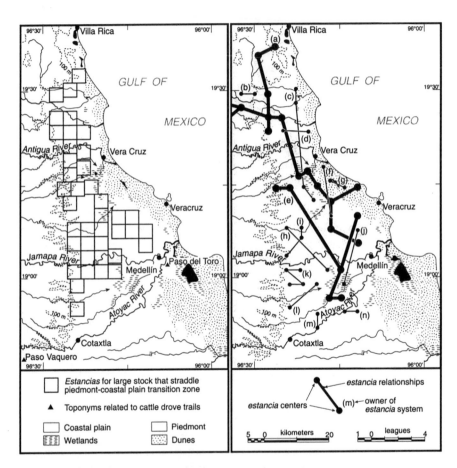

Figure 4.11. Proliferation of the Marismas ranching ecology. The left panel shows
estancias for large stock that straddled the piedmont-coastal plain transition zone.
The right panel shows groups of estancias for large stock belonging to the same individual or family: (a) Ruiz de Córdova; (b) Sayas; (c) Castañeda y León; (d) Luna; (e)
Núñez de Montalván; (f) Avendaño; (g) Bautista de Torres; (h) Alegría; (i) Losada; (j)
Salvatierra; (k) Villanueva; (l) Herrera; (m) Méndez; (n) Pedraza. Contrasting line
thickness and dot size distinguishes networks; it does not signify different characteristics. Three more estancias belonging to the Ruiz de Córdova family occur upslope of
the western edge of the map.

The origins of the haciendas, however, lay in the awards of mercedes. That a few individuals might acquire vast holdings ran counter to the official rationale for awarding mercedes: to reward those who had rendered services to the Crown and to promote the development of the colony (Prem 1988, 120). Formulaic clauses within each merced reiterated royal decrees that attempted to promote that intent (*Recopilación* 1987, book 4, title 12, laws 3, 10-11). Those clauses required productive use of the land to retain tenure, prohibited speculation, and specifically excluded churches or monastic orders from owning estancias, the last clearly intended to limit the power of the major potential challenger to Crown authority.

> [Viceroy] Don Diego Fernández de Córdoba etc., in the name of His Majesty and without injury to His or any third party's rights, do hereby grant Luis Ochoa four estancias for small stock in the district of the old city of Vera Cruz . . ., with the obligation and condition that inside of the following year each one of the tracts be stocked with 2,000 head of the said small livestock, and inside of four years they cannot be sold, traded, or given to anyone on pain of this grant being declared null and void. And by the same token, neither he nor subsequent owners, can ever leave any of the estancias unstocked nor with less than 500 head of the said large stock [sic] for more than four years running on pain of this grant being declared null and void. The said four estancias belonging to the said Luis Ochoa and his descendants . . . , once the said time has passed can be disposed of to whomever, except not to any church, monastery, nor ecclesiastic (AGN-M, vol. 33, ff. 114-15v).

The transposition of "500 head of large stock" for "2000 head of small stock" attests to both the seriousness and the futility of such prohibitions. The scribe, numbed by writing out the same formulaic clauses merced after merced momentarily forgot that the grant was for sheep estancias. Yet no one seemed to notice. Similarly, although the Crown's intent seems to have been to award no more than a few estancias to any one person, some individuals acquired dozens (Chevalier 1952, 176-81). For Hispaniola, Charles V had ordered that "no person can have more than three asientos," or sitios de estancia, but for New Spain the maximum number of grants that any one individual might hold never received such formal stipulation. Consequently, circumvention of the official desire, far from a determined one in any case, appears to have been common (González de Cossio 1957, 306-7; Prem 1988, 120-24). In fact, some grantees served as premeditated surrogates for the eventual title holders.

As the most successful of the early land grabbers in the Veracruz lowlands, the Ruiz de Córdova family exemplifies the process. Gonzalo Ruiz de Córdova was a merchant in New Spain by 1535 and a vecino of Vera Cruz and Mexico City (Boyd-Bowman 1968, 2:118). By 1556 he had, as the English merchant Tomson reported, become "a very rich man of the saide Towne of Vera cruz" (Hakluyt 1904, 9:346). From 1547 to 1593, between father Gonzalo and sons Hernando and Gaspar, the Ruiz de Córdovas personally received mercedes for twelve cattle estancias and one sheep estancia (AGN-M, vol. 7, ff. 136-36v, 272v; vol. 8, ff. 30-30v; vol. 9, ff. 33v-34; vol. 12, f. 119; vol. 17, ff. 116v-17; vol. 18, ff. 240v-41v; vol. 19, ff. 81-81v; ANX-Protocolo, vol. 1600-1608, ff. 414-15v). They also bought further estancias, Gonzalo receiving a dispensation in 1558 to purchase an estancia from Ana de Vergara, who had inherited it when her son died (ANX-Protocolo, vol. 1600-1608, f. 415v; Bermúdez Gorrochotegui 1987, 77). The dispensation seems to have been necessary because the Vergaras had not yet owned the estancia for the stipulated four years. In addition, the Ruiz de Córdovas employed surrogate grant applicants. In 1592, Nicolás de Salazar blatantly acted as a dummy for son Hernando in the acquisition of two cattle estancias (AGN-T, vol. 2764, exp. 15, f. 182v). And after receiving a cattle estancia in 1583, a former encomendero named Baltasar de Obregón sold son Gaspar the title for seventy pesos (AGN-M, vol. 13, ff. 40-40v; Chevalier 1952, 179-80). Seemingly Gaspar, who went by Gaspar Ruiz de Cabrera, had premeditated the entire deal.

> I [Baltasar de Obregón] do so because Licenciado Gaspar Ruiz de Cabrera has shown me the site of the estancia and because I have requested said grant in his name and for his sake. I have pledged my word to cede and transfer it to him if successful. Moreover, the aforementioned has paid the fees for the grant and the petition, as well as expenses. For my trouble and the steps I have had to take in the said affair, he has paid me seventy gold pesos, with which sum I declare myself to be paid to my satisfaction (AGN-Vínculos, vol. 269; Chevalier 1952, 180).

With a single hide fetching almost a peso and a half wholesale in Mexico City in 1575 and more than five pesos in Spain by 1585, seventy pesos was nothing, recoverable with the sale of a few dozen hides (Chevalier 1952, 134-35). Already by 1571, Arias Hernández had attributed twenty estancias and two hundred African slaves to the Ruiz de Córdova family (Paso y Troncoso 1905, 5:195). Sometime after the death of father Gonzalo in 1581 or earlier, son Gaspar entailed the family holdings as the Mayorazgo de Santa Fé: thirty-three estancias, thirteen caballerías, and various other holdings (AGN-Vínculos, vol. 269; Chevalier 1952, 180; Fernández de Recas 1965, 399-400).

The other large private land owner to emerge was the Higuera family. Like Gonzalo Ruiz de Córdova, Francisco de la Higuera lacked an encomienda. He accumulated capital with the family sugar enterprises in the environs of Xalapa through the labor of African slaves and repartimientos of native labor (Frank 1979, 23; Bermúdez Gorrochotegui 1987, 24-31, 51-52). Santísima Trinidad, at a thousand meters elevation on the escarpment of the Sierra Madre, was one of the largest sugar mills of the early colonial period. In 1588, Francisco acquired six estancias, five for sheep and one for cattle, west of Rinconada. Entailment as the Mayorazgo de la Higuera occurred in 1606 (AGN-Vínculos, vol. 56; Fernández de Recas 1965, 379-80). The holdings included a few estancias in the lowlands but also sugar mills, or *ingenios*, near Xalapa and many more holdings even further upslope, such as 20,000 head of sheep grazing the Llanos de Ozumba (ANX-Protocolo, vol. 1600-1608, ff. 383v-87). In 1607, don Francisco's son, Andrés Pérez de la Higuera, purchased twenty-one cattle estancias, two farm tracts, and one inn from the Ruiz de Córdova family, possibly contravening the entail of the Mayorazgo de Santa Fé. With that purchase the Mayorazgo de la Higuera became one of the major land owners in the lowlands (Bermúdez Gorrochotegui 1987, 75-77).

In 1634, the Ruiz de Córdova and Higuera families intermarried. By that time the Mayorazgo de la Higuera had purchased three more cattle estancias near Vera Cruz, and the Mayorazgo de Santa Fé included thirty cattle estancias, four going in dowry to the Higuera family (AGN-T, vol. 589, exp. 1; Bermúdez Gorrochotegui 1987, 35-44, 86). Through mercedes, surrogates, purchases, and intermarriage, the two entailed estates comprised a vast swath of land stretching the length of the coastal plain and extending up the piedmont toward Xalapa.

Despite prohibitions on sales, trades, or gifts of estancias "to any church, monastery, or ecclesiastic," the monastic orders also acquired vast haciendas through purchases by surrogates, donations, and mortgages (McBride 1923, 59-69; Chevalier 1952, 301-9). The Jesuit hacienda of Acazónica, fifty kilometers due east of Veracruz, probably functioned as agostadero for the Jesuit flocks of Puebla, numbering 40,000 sheep by 1603 (Fonseca and Urrutia 1852, 5:231; Chevalier 1952, 315; Wobeser 1989, 100). The Crown had expelled the Jesuits from New Spain by 1767, but in the 1790s a subsequent owner of Hacienda Acazónica came into conflict with the Mayorazgo de Santa Fé over prime pasture lands near Vera Cruz (AGN-T, vol. 3058, exp. 3). The court documentation indicates the extent of Acazónica's holdings: a large slice of the central piedmont between the Jamapa and Antigua rivers.

The composición process, peaking during the 1630s and 1640s, only further aided those with capital to subsume small-holders, including natives (McBride 1923, 56-58; Prem 1988, 124-25). In contrast to the early grazing licenses, which conceived pasture as usufruct, the mercedes had at least implied an award of inheritable private property. While the league of land that theoretically separated the centers of estancias for large stock legally remained Crown property, the viceregal ordinances that stipulated a square that was a league on a side and oriented to the cardinal directions certainly implied boundaries around those estancias. Yet without Crown ratification of such colonial practices, the mercedes remained but dubious land titles (Chevalier 1952, 106-21, 263-64). Composición, after a century of colonization, effected that ratification. During composición, Crown officials confirmed land grants, resolved boundary disputes, and issued legal land titles. Those with cash to pay the surveying fee and settlement tax—or, just as likely, to bribe the inspector—not only consolidated and legitimized their own already enormous tracts but were able to absorb smaller neighbors.

Space accumulation thus proceeded through three stages during the first century of colonization (González de Cossio 1957). First, encomenderos controlled native labor within spatially ill-defined locales. Second, those entrepreneurs who accumulated capital in trade, in silver mines, or in sugar and textile mills on the basis of native or African slave labor, began to control land use on estancias, relatively well-defined spaces but legally remaining Crown land. Some of that capital, through donation and other means, also accumulated estancias for the Church. Third, the most successful families consolidated and entailed their estancias, acquired legal title to them through composición, and thus became the owners of haciendas, immense private properties. The families of encomenderos who had run livestock during the sixteenth century, such as María del Rincón and Gregorio de Villalobos, did not become the owners of haciendas, or *hacendados*, of the seventeenth century. In the lowlands, the early and nearly absolute decline of the native population seems to have prevented encomenderos from accumulating sufficient capital to control much private property, an extreme case of the more general pattern in New Spain (Chevalier 1952, 188-93; Lockhart 1969). During the seventeenth century, the hacienda became New Spain's new master institution, replacing the estancia that itself had replaced the encomienda and acting as the interface and encompassing the primary flux of capital and labor between the Spanish town and the native countryside (Lockhart 1969).

New Spain had gone from a franchise colony in which the feudal institution of encomienda dominated to a settler colony in which private property became institutionalized. In eliminating nearly all of the encomiendas, the Crown had begun to achieve quite effective control over space; then, in need of cash to support its military campaigns, it relinquished control to those with the capital to pay the composición fees. Space came under the control of a minority of individuals; the haciendas came into being; and, at an already low ebb in the colonial economy, the Crown arrogated an enormous amount of capital. Two centuries later, out of the ferment of the battles that ended Europe's sovereign power in Mexico, Generalissimo Santa Anna emerged to dominate the Veracruz lowlands as thoroughly as he did Mexican politics (Siemens 1990a). That his tens of thousands of cattle continued to follow the same seasonal round between wetland and hill land as had those of the sixteenth century explains a good deal about the lack of environmental degradation attributable to the livestock invasion in these lowlands. The buildings of El Lencero—the upper pole of his hacienda, between Xalapa and Cerro Gordo—are now a museum. The buildings of Manga de Clavo, the lower pole near the port of Veracruz, no longer exist. But if you drive inland from the old fortress at San Juan de Ulúa in April, crest the dune field, and look westward you will appreciate their former setting. The piedmont still stretches upward toward the glacial cap of Mount Orizaba, and the grass and low thickets sprawl parched and leafless and brown under the cloudless sky of the dry season. The buildings and corrals of Manga de Clavo occupied the fringe of the verdant belt of wetlands that divides the piedmont and the dune cordon, their uniqueness and ecological significance still as clear as it must have been to Gregorio de Villalobos, the hacendados such as Santa Anna who followed him, and the natives who preceded all of them. The next chapter addresses what happened to those natives, the interactions of natives and non-natives, and integrates all three sides of the colonial triangle in terms of both material and conceptual processes.

Notes

1. Although Lesley Byrd Simpson, Sherburne F. Cook, and Woodrow Borah have made many seminal contributions and can justly be characterized as the Berkeley School of Mexican Colonial History, only Borah actually held an appointment as historian, Cook being a physiologist and Simpson being a scholar of literature.

2. This and all subsequent Spanish-English translations in this chapter are by the author.

3. Table 4.1 includes all known estancias granted for the Veracruz lowlands. The recent availability of a searchable CD-ROM index for AGN-Mercedes (*Argena II*, published in 1995) now makes recovery of pertinent grants infinitely easier than perusing the various partial indexes—ranging from card files, to handwritten manuscripts, to published lists (Sluyter 1997b). *Argena II* includes ninety-eight sections of the AGN. The original CD-ROM index (*Argena*, published in 1993) included only twenty-two sections and did not include AGN-Mercedes. In November 1999, the AGN began to implement an on-line version of the *Argena II* CD-ROM (www.agn.gob.mx). Also in 1999, several volumes that had long been under restoration or in the microfilming department of the AGN again became accessible, accounting for the minor difference between previous publications (Sluyter 1997b, 1998) and this one; the current version is the definitive one.

Table 4.1. Known mercedes for estancias.

Date (d/m/y)	Grantee	Ganado mayor (no.)	Ganado menor (no.)	Documentation
10/5/1541	Francisco de Avila	1		ANX-Protocolo, vol. 1600-1608, f. 414
27/8/1541	Diego de Ojeda	1		ANX-Protocolo, vol. 1600-1608, f. 413v
27/9/1547	Gerónimo Ruiz de Córdova	2		ANX-Protocolo, vol. 1600-1608, f. 414
7/7/1550	Bernardo de Castillo	1		AGN-M, vol. 3, ff. 115-15v
1554-1558	Hernando de Vergara	1		ANX-Protocolo, vol. 1600-1608, f. 415v
16/4/1563	Diego de Acevedo	1		AGN-M, vol. 6, ff. 193-93v
20/4/1563	Alonso Nortes de Sosa	1		AGN-M, vol. 6, ff. 199-99v

Table 4.1, continued.

Date (d/m/y)	Grantee	Ganado mayor (no.)	Ganado menor (no.)	Documentation
28/4/1563	Simon de Herrera	1		AGN-M, vol. 6, ff. 213v-14
12/5/1563	Juan García Calleza		1	AGN-M, vol. 6, ff. 227-27v
22/5/1563	Julián de Olmedo	1		AGN-M, vol. 6, f. 249
8/10/1563	Gonzalo Ruiz de Córdova	1		AGN-M, vol. 7, f. 136
8/10/1563	Gonzalo Ruiz de Córdova	1		AGN-M, vol. 7, ff. 136-36v; ANX-Protocolo, vol. 1600-1608, f. 415v
9/10/1563	Gonzalo Ruiz de Córdova	1		AGN-M, vol. 7, f. 136v
17/11/1563	Luis de Monzón	1		ANX-Protocolo, vol. 1600-1608, f. 414
20/11/1563	Gonzalo de Molino	1		AGN-M, vol. 7, f. 211v
8/1/1564	Hernán Ruiz		1	AGN-M, vol. 7, f. 272v
8/1/1564	Juan Núñez	1		AGN-M, vol. 7, ff. 272v-73
18/2/1564	Francisco Martínez	1		AGN-M, vol. 7, ff. 345-45v; ANX-Protocolo, vol. 1600-1608, ff. 414v-15
30/1/1565	Unknown	1		ANX-Protocolo, vol. 1600-1608, ff. 414v-15
4/6/1565	Gonzalo Ruiz de Córdova (a regranting of 2 estancias previously held by Juan de Madrigas and Gerónimo Hernández)	2		AGN-M, vol. 8, ff. 30-30v
14/11/1565	Pedro Núñez de Montalván	1		AGN-M, vol. 8, f. 189
14/11/1565	Francisco López	1		AGN-M, vol. 8, ff. 190-90v
8/5/1566	Juan Núñez de Montalván	1		AGN-T, vol. 32, exp. 4, f. 102
25/1/1567	Luis Belmonte	1		AGN-M, vol. 9, f. 5
25/1/1567	Agustín de Abrego	1		AGN-M, vol. 9, ff. 5-5v
18/3/1567	Antonio de Sotomayor		1	AGN-M, vol. 9, ff. 29-29v

Table 4.1, continued.

Date (d/m/y)	Grantee	Ganado mayor (no.)	Ganado menor (no.)	Documentation
20/3/1567	Hernando de Ribadeneira		1	AGN-M, vol. 9, ff. 30v-31
22/3/1567	Pedro Gutiérrez de Alcocer	1		AGN-M, vol. 9, ff. 33-33v; ANX-Protocolo, vol. 1600-1608, f. 415
22/3/1567	Hernán Ruiz	1		AGN-M, vol. 9, ff. 33v-34; ANX- Protocolo, vol. 1600-1608, f. 414v
12/4/1567	Jerónimo de Benavides	1		AGN-M, vol. 9, ff. 50v-51; ANX-Protocolo, vol. 1600-1608, f. 415
18/4/1567	Alonso Franques	1	1	AGN-M, vol. 9, ff. 60v-61
28/4/1567	Diego de Ludueña	1		AGN-M, vol. 9, f. 65v
28/4/1567	Cristóbal Ortiz	1		AGN-M, vol. 9, ff. 67-67v
3/6/1567	Antonio de Pedraza	2		AGN-M, vol. 9, f. 91v
3/6/1567	Rodrigo Hernández	1		AGN-M, vol. 9, ff. 91v-92
3/7/1567	Tomás Pérez	1		AGN-M, vol. 9, ff. 106v-7
3/7/1567	Pedro Núñez de Montalván	1		AGN-M, vol. 9, ff. 107-7v
3/7/1567	Nicolás de Igarca	1		AGN-M, vol. 9, ff. 107v-8
3/7/1567	Diego de May-orga	1		AGN-M, vol. 9, ff. 108v-9
5/7/1567	Hernando Sal-vatierra	1		AGN-M, vol. 9, ff. 114v-15
7/7/1567	Juan Núñez	1		AGN-M, vol. 9, ff. 115-15v
7/7/1567	Pedro Núñez de Montalván	1		AGN-M, vol. 9, ff. 115v-16
12/7/1567	Alonso de Cas-tilla	1		AGN-M, vol. 9, ff. 106-6v
22/9/1567	Francisco de Bustamante	1		AGN-M, vol. 9, ff. 163v-65
7/11/1567	Gonzalo Ruiz de Córdova	1		ANX-Protocolo, vol. 1600-1608, ff. 414-14v
27/1/1568	Hernando Sal-vatierra	1		AGN-M, vol. 9, ff. 275v-76
28/2/1568	Pedro Palomino	1		ANX-Protocolo, vol. 1600-1608, f. 414v
3-4/1573	Gonzalo de Ale-gría	1		AGN-T, vol. 2764, exp. 18, ff. 225-60

Table 4.1, continued.

Date (d/m/y)	Grantee	Ganado mayor (no.)	Ganado menor (no.)	Documentation
6/1573	Bernaldo de Losada	1		AGN-T, vol. 2764, exp. 17, ff. 212-24v
7/7/1573	Pedro de Yebra	1		AGN-T, vol. 2672, 1a pte., exp. 8, f. 230
9/7/1574	Isabel de Vergara		1	AGN-T, vol. 32, exp. 4, ff. 11v-12v
7/1574	Juan de Ocón		1	AGN-T, vol. 32, exp. 4, ff. no pagination
10/9/1574	Juan Martínez Plasencia		1	AGN-M, vol. 10, ff. 45v-46
by 1575	Juan Rodríguez (inferred: neighbor to a 17/6/1575 grant to Melchor de Avila)	1		AGN-M, vol. 10, ff. 65v-66
12/4/1575	Juan Sarmiento		1	AGN-M, vol. 10, ff. 61-61v
12/4/1575	Alonso de Segura	1		AGN-M, vol. 10, ff. 61v-62
17/6/1575	Melchor de Avila		1	AGN-M, vol. 10, ff. 65v-66
16/7/1575	Juan de Madina		1	AGN-M, vol. 10, ff. 68v-69
by 1576	Isabel de Eozar (inferred: neighbor to a 1576 grant to Isabel de Silva)	2		AGN-T, vol. 2777, exp. 3, ff. 1-9v
circa 1576	Isabel de Silva	1		AGN-T, vol. 2777, exp. 3, ff. 1-9v
5/4/1576	Pedro Rodríguez de Moral	1		AGN-T, vol. 2769, exp. 14, ff. 225-33; ANX-Protocolo, vol. 1600-1608, f. 414v
30/10/1576	Juan Ruiz Pastrana	1		AGN-M, vol. 10, ff. 182-82v
7/11/1576	Juana Delgado	1		AGN-M, vol. 10, ff. 184v-85
11/12/1576	Bernardino Santacruz	1		AGN-M, vol. 10, ff. 191-91v
12/1/1577	Juan Sarmiento		1	AGN-M, vol. 10, f. 203v
22/5/1577	Toribio Calderón	1		AGN-M, vol. 10, ff. 244-44v
29/5/1577	Jerónimo González de Alorbolla	1		AGN-M, vol. 10, ff. 244v-45
1/6/1577	Antonio Galeote	1		AGN-M, vol. 10, ff. 245-46v

Table 4.1, continued.

Date (d/m/y)	Grantee	Ganado mayor (no.)	Ganado menor (no.)	Documentation
circa 1579	Francisco de León Coronado	1		AGN-T, vol. 2678, exp. 12, ff. 1-13v
14/1/1579	Diego Daza	1		ANX-Protocolo, vol. 1600-1608, f. 415
13/4/1581	Alonso Pérez de Arteaga	1		AGN-M, vol. 11, ff. 19-19v
10/7/1581	Alonso Villanueva		1	AGN-M, vol. 11, ff. 39-40
12/7/1581	Leonor de Cayas	1		AGN-M, vol. 11, ff. 42v-43
6/10/1581	Juan Sarmiento	1		AGN-M, vol. 11, f. 66
18/7/1583	Sebastián Díaz	1		AGN-M, vol. 11, ff. 275v-76v
26/7/1583	Francisco Hernández	1		AGN-M, vol. 11, ff. 280v-81
29/7/1583	Francisco Or-duña	1		AGN-M, vol. 11, ff. 281v-82
17/10/1583	Pedro de Castañeda y León	2		AGN-M, vol. 12, ff. 5-5v; ANX-Protocolo, vol. 1600-1608, ff. 415-15v
17/10/1583	Rodrigo de Luna	2		AGN-M, vol. 12, ff. 5v-6; ANX-Protocolo, vol. 1600-1608, ff. 415v-16
14/11/1583	Juan de Párraga	1		AGN-M, vol. 13, ff. 20-20v
20/11/1583	Juan Bautista de Torres	2		AGN-M, vol. 12, ff. 20v-21
26/11/1583	Francisco Ramírez	2		AGN-M, vol. 13, f. 29v
17/12/1583	Baltasar de Obregón	1		AGN-M, vol. 13, ff. 40-40v
by 1584	Hernán Jerónimo (inferred: neighbor to a 16/5/1584 grant to Leonor de Herrera)	1		AGN-M, vol. 13, ff. 81v-82
16/1/1584	Pedro Camúz	1		AGN-M, vol. 12, ff. 45v-46
20/4/1584	Gonzalo de Ale-gría	1		AGN-M, vol. 13, ff. 73v-74
16/5/1584	Leonor de Herrera	2		AGN-M, vol. 13, ff. 81v-82
26/5/1584	Bernardo de Losada	2		AGN-M, vol. 12, ff. 87-87v

Table 4.1, continued.

Date (d/m/y)	Grantee	Ganado mayor (no.)	Ganado menor (no.)	Documentation
3/8/1584	Marcos de Sayas	2		AGN-M, vol. 12, ff. 96-96v
14/9/1584	Juan Méndez de Sotomayor	2		AGN-M, vol. 13, ff. 113-13v
22/1/1585	Pedro de Castañeda y León	2		AGN-M, vol. 12, ff. 118-18v
4/2/1585	Diego de Avendaño y Mendoza	2		AGN-M, vol. 13, ff. 132v-33
8/10/1587	Hernando Ruiz de Córdova	1		ANX-Protocolo, vol. 1600-1608, f. 415v
by 1588	Francisco Hernández de la Higuera (purchases and donations of 5 estancias originally held by Rodrigo Hernández, Juan de la Peña, Juan de Zúñiga Azcaray, and Antonio González)	1	4	ANX-Protocolo, vol. 1578-1594, ff. 405v-6; ANX-Protocolo, vol. 1600-1608, f. 389v
24/2/1588	María de Naveda Villavicencio		3	AGN-M, vol. 14, ff. 80v-81v
30/4/1588	Juan Bernal	1		AGN-M, vol. 14, ff. 96v-97v
19/8/1588	Agustín Meléndez		1	AGN-M, vol. 14, ff. 125-26
11/11/1588	Pedro García del Valle		1	AGN-M, vol. 14, ff. 161v-62v
31/7/1589	Antonio Corte		3	AGN-M, vol. 15, ff. 25v-26v
18/8/1589	Juan López Mellado		2	AGN-M, vol. 14, ff. 359v-60v
14/9/1589	Francisco de León Coronado	2		AGN-M, vol. 15, ff. 43v-45
29/11/1589	Melchor García	5		AGN-M, vol. 15, ff. 86-87
16/4/1590	Diego de Yebra	2		AGN-M, vol. 15, ff. 169-69v
29/5/1590	Francisco Orduña		2	AGN-M, vol. 16, f. 27v

Table 4.1, continued.

Date (d/m/y)	Grantee	Ganado mayor (no.)	Ganado menor (no.)	Documentation
29/5/1590	Martín de Pedrosa, for the natives of Santiago Huatusco		2	AGN-M, vol. 15, ff. 182v-83v; AGN-T, vol. 3331, exp. 1, ff. 1-9
19/6/1590	Lucas Hernández		2	AGN-M, vol. 15, ff. 191-92
4/7/1591	Gaspar de Ribadeneira		4	AGN-M, vol. 17, ff. 25v-26v; AGN-T, vol. 2702, exp. 12, ff. 386-97v
7/7/1592	Gaspar Covarrubias		1	AGN-M, vol. 19, f. 25
9/7/1592	Antonia de Herrera		2	AGN-M, vol. 19, ff. 28-28v
10/7/1592	Gaspar de Covarrubias		1	AGN-M, vol. 19, f. 30
10/7/1592	Andrés Rodríguez		1	AGN-M, vol. 19, ff. 30v-31
27/8/1592	Alonso Villanueva	4		AGN-M, vol. 19, ff. 48-49
14/11/1592	Nicolás de Salazar	2		AGN-M, vol. 19, ff. 81-81v
6/7/1593	Juan de Burgos		2	AGN-M, vol. 19, ff. 130-31
15/7/1593	Isabel de Almodovar		1	AGN-M, vol. 19, ff. 133v-34v
30/5/1593	Hernán Ruiz de Córdova	2		AGN-M, vol. 18, ff. 240v-41v
15/12/1593	Alonso Pardo		2	AGN-M, vol. 18, ff. 373v-74; AGN-T, vol. 2702, exp. 13, ff. 398-406v
26/4/1594	Sebastián de Luna		4	AGN-M, vol. 21, ff. 6v-7
26/4/1594	Cristóbal Romero		2	AGN-M, vol. 21, ff. 7v-8
10/7/1594	Diego de Cubire		1	AGN-M, vol. 19, ff. 243-43v
7/12/1594	Miguel de Acurcia		2	AGN-M, vol. 21, ff. 47-48
7/12/1594	Alonso Pérez Carreno		2	AGN-M, vol. 21, ff. 48-48v
22/12/1594	Nicolás Rodríguez		2	AGN-M, vol. 21, ff. 55-55v
30/12/1594	Juan Sánchez Bermejo		2	AGN-M, vol. 20, ff. 20-20v
30/12/1594	Juan Muñoz		2	AGN-M, vol. 20, ff. 21v-22

Table 4.1, continued.

Date (d/m/y)	Grantee	Ganado mayor (no.)	Ganado menor (no.)	Documentation
30/12/1594	Bartolomé Vallejo		2	AGN-M, vol. 20, ff. 22-23v
16/2/1595	Juan Martínez		2	AGN-M, vol. 20, ff. 36-36v
7/8/1595	Juan Martínez		2	AGN-M, vol. 20, ff. 112v-13
7/8/1595	Juan de Estrada		2	AGN-M, vol. 20, ff. 113-13v
7/8/1595	Juan Gómez		2	AGN-M, vol. 20, ff. 114-14v
7/8/1595	Juan de Estrada		2	AGN-M, vol. 20, ff. 117-18
7/8/1595	Agustín de Balsa		2	AGN-M, vol. 20, ff. 118-18v
7/8/1595	Juan Gómez		1	AGN-M, vol. 20, ff. 119-19v
7/8/1595	Juan Gómez		2	AGN-M, vol. 20, ff. 119v-20v
31/8/1595	Pedro Hernández de Asperilla	1		AGN-M, vol. 21, ff. 103v-4
18/9/1595	Luis de Heraso		2	AGN-M, vol. 20, ff. 141-42
16/9/1595	Luis de Heraso		1	AGN-M, vol. 21, ff. 110v-11
23/9/1595	Francisco López		2	AGN-M, vol. 20, ff. 144-45
16/10/1595	Juan Sánchez Bermejo		2	AGN-M, vol. 20, ff. 182-82v
21/10/1595	Juan Sánchez Bermejo		2	AGN-M, vol. 20, ff. 198v-99
23/10/1595	Juan Muñoz		2	AGN-M, vol. 20, ff. 198-98v
29/5/1606	Alonso del Moral	1		AGN-M, vol. 25, ff. 64-64v
11/10/1614	Domingo Xavier	1	2	AGN-M, vol. 29, ff. 128v-29
16/10/1614	Domingo Xavier	1	1	AGN-M, vol. 29, ff. 139-39v
3/9/1616	Juan de Castro		4	AGN-M, vol. 31, ff. 192-92v
7/7/1617	Francisco Hernández		4	AGN-M, vol. 33, ff. 112v-14
7/7/1617	Luis Ochoa		4	AGN-M, vol. 33, ff. 114-15v
7/7/1617	Luis Ochoa		4	AGN-M, vol. 33, ff. 115v-16v
7/7/1617	Francisco Hernández		4	AGN-M, vol. 33, ff. 116v-18v

4. Diego García de Palacio, *Diálogos militares, de la formación, è información de personas, instrumentos, y cosas nescessarias para el buen uso de la guerra*, Mexico City, 1583. Diego García de Palacio, *Instrucción naútica para navegar*, Mexico City, 1587 (Chevalier 1952, 164).

5. Table 4.2 summarizes the minimum and maximum 1619 and the 1902 livestock density estimates in SLU per hectare. In 1902, the included municipalities enumerated 30,481 cattle, 3,090 horses, 596 mules, 138 sheep, and 189 goats, as well as 1,405 donkeys and 1,217 pigs. Some of the municipalities have changed names or boundaries since

Table 4.2. Municipio livestock densities.

Municipio	Area hectares	1619 Minimum SLU	SLU/ha	1619 Maximum SLU	SLU/ha	1902 Count SLU	SLU/ha
Actopan	82,254	10,167	0.12	50,835	0.62	1,701	0.021
A. Tejeda	17,438	222	0.013	1,110	0.064	1,496	0.085
Apazapan	6,580	222	0.034	1,110	0.17	148	0.023
Boca del Río	4,277	1,389	0.33	6,945	1.6	1,930	0.45
Carrillo Puerto	24,676	6,889	0.28	34,445	1.4	1,127	0.046
Cotaxtla	65,968	4,667	0.071	23,335	0.35	903	0.014
Cuitlahuac	12,996	3,833	0.30	19,165	1.5	1,405	0.11
Jamapa	16,368	3,944	0.24	19,720	1.2	1,086	0.066
La Antigua-U. Galván	25,663	4,722	0.18	23,610	0.92	1,634	0.064
Medellín	37,014	4,222	0.11	21,110	0.57	4,271	0.12
Paso de Ovejas	38,895	8,667	0.22	43,335	1.1	6,685	0.17
Paso del Macho	32,326	6,000	0.19	30,000	0.93	1,727	0.053
Puente Nacional	33,313	4,639	0.14	23,195	0.70	1,688	0.051
S. de Doblado-M.F. Altamirano	59,551	10,750	0.18	53,750	0.90	7,615	0.13
Veracruz	24,100	5,889	0.24	29,445	1.2	788	0.033
Totals	481,419	76,222	0.16	381,110	0.79	34,204	0.071

1902, necessitating aggregation to conform with current boundaries: Soledad de Doblado-Manlio Fabio Altamirano and La Antigua-Ursulo Galván, the last not listed in the 1902 census even under its previous name of San Carlos and presumably included in the count for La Antigua. In any case, municipal boundaries are nominal, no precise map yet being available (Cambrezy and Lascuráin 1992, 155-56). The included grants comprise some eighty-nine percent of the 233 grants in the study region. In terms of counting protocol, an estancia falling more than half within a municipality counts as one; an estancia falling half within a municipality counts as half; and an estancia falling more than half outside of a municipality counts as zero. Estancias for large stock equal 500 SLU. Estancias for small stock equal 222.222 SLU (2000 ÷ 9). The minimum 1619 livestock density equals the area of a municipality divided into the total SLU for that municipality. The maximum 1619 livestock density equals the area of a municipality divided into five times the total SLU for that municipality. See chapter 5 for densities in the 1990s, averaging 0.486 SLU per hectare for these same municipalities.

6. The 1580 report claims a return of 100 to 150 fanegas of maize from each fanega planted (JGI, xxv-8, f. 11v). The fanega denotes both quantity of grain and area of cultivation: one *fanega de maíz* equals 46 kilograms or 55.5 liters of maize; one *fanega de sembradura de maíz* equals one-twelfth of a caballería, the forty-three acre farming tracts, or 3.58 hectares (Carrera Stampa 1949, 20; Barnes et al. 1981, 73; Prem 1988, 295). Therefore, one hectare would have required 12.8 kilograms of seed maize and returned 1,285 to 1,927 kilograms. Considering that livestock grazing the maize stubble after har-

vest probably manured the fields each year, such a yield seems possible. Placing that range in context, the mean annual maize yield for all reporting Mexican agroecosystems has risen from some 575 kilograms per hectare in the 1890s to some 1,800 kilograms per hectare in the 1980s, and shifting cultivators in the Laja Valley in lowland Guerrero seed at fifteen to twenty kilograms per hectare and obtain yields from 500 to 1,800 kilograms per hectare, depending on the ratio of cultivation to fallow (*Estadísticas Históricas* 1990, 1:407-8; Lambert 1992, 163). Considering that at least some of the forty-three caballerías would have been fallow in some years, an estimated yield of 1,500 kilograms per hectare seems liberal. Ninety-two caballerías of forty-three hectares each could thus have produced 5,934,000 kilograms of maize per year. As a gross generalization, livestock have a daily dry matter intake equivalent of some 90 g/kg $^{0.75}$ of live weight/day (NRC 1987, 75; Chesworth 1992, 138). Thus the SLU of 350 kilograms would consume some 7.28 kilograms per day, or 2,657 kilograms of maize per year. And the total production of the ninety-two farm tracts, even if dedicated to fodder production, would have fed a liberal estimate of 2,233 SLU, exclusive of the minimal additional feed intake available through grazing in fallow fields.

7. I use hacienda to denote a large, entailed property without implying any of that constellation of socioeconomic and political characteristics that came to be associated with "the" hacienda—debt peonage and the *tienda de raya*, or company store, for example. The history of the hacienda, typically couched in such terms as its genetic relationship to encomienda and economic cycles of the world system, remains far from clear (Lockhart 1969; Mörner 1973; Frank 1979; Van Young 1983; Florescano 1987). But if hacienda historiography has produced no definitive answers, hacienda geography barely exists, despite Magnus Mörner's call for an interdisciplinary, cartographic approach a quarter century ago and despite its importance to understanding development and environmental issues throughout Latin America.

> To understand the role and development of the haciendas, it seems even more important to place them, or the entire agrarian structure in a certain district, in an ecological context and to determine the cartographical dimensions through time. . . . It would seem that interdisciplinary teamwork between historians and geographers, rural sociologists or other social scientists would often be the rational solution (Mörner 1973, 215-16).

5

Material/Conceptual Colonization

To return to the opening of the first chapter, Cortés writing in 1519, the district governor in 1580, and Sartorius about 1850 together seem to sketch out the transformation of the Veracruz lowlands through several centuries of colonization. Apparently impressed by the openness of the country, Cortés conceived a prospectus for the pastoral landscape that within the first century of colonization was to become the material reality. Yet by the beginning of the postcolonial period, thickets of thorny shrubs and low trees grew over most of the region. Once through the cordon of dunes and the belt of wetlands with its evergreen woodlands, travelers confronted the long climb through what Sartorius categorized as the "dreary wilderness" of the savanna country (figure 5.1). While, as addressed in the next chapter, the irrigation and drainage projects of the twentieth century have obliterated much of the landscape Sartorius once rode through, especially on the coastal plain, his savanna with low thorny mimosas still dominates the piedmont.

More precisely delineating that landscape transformation and the processes involved, even in material terms alone, quickly leads into figurative as well as literal thickets. Combining the certainty of high livestock densities by the end of the first century of colonization, as demonstrated in the previous chapter, with the long-standing thesis that "hoofed locusts" generally degrade vegetation certainly suggests that overgrazing by cattle and sheep destroyed the range and, eventually, created a "wilderness" (Muir 1894, frontispiece; Simpson 1952; Crosby 1972; Melville 1994). As the previous chapter demonstrates, however, impacts on slope stability and hydrology, such as Melville believes were so general, were actually minimal. Overgrazing and trampling over any substantial area would have resulted in fragmentation of vegetation cover, compaction of soils, sheet erosion, and gullying. No evidence of such impacts is preserved, neither as scars on the landscape nor as sediments in Laguna Catarina. That lack

143

Figure 5.1. The view westward across the savanna country of the piedmont toward the Sierra Madre Oriental, characterized by grasslands with thickets of shrubs and low trees except where cut by deep ravines, or barrancas. A few cows and cacti appear in the foreground. Original representation sketched around 1833 by Johann Moritz Rugendas; engraving originally published in 1859 (Sartorius 1961: plate opposite p. 40).

of evidence for substantial soil erosion suggests that because the ranching ecology Villalobos had implanted was well adapted to the seasonal availability of pasture, vegetation cover persisted despite the rapid increase in the livestock population during the second half of the sixteenth century. Yet while the livestock might not have destroyed the vegetation cover, overgrazing could well have changed the vegetation type by promoting the invasion of thickets of thorny and woody plants into grasslands.

As one end-member in a range of possibilities, then, Sartorius's thorny thickets might be the result of several centuries of overgrazing of the open grassland that Cortés implies: "beautiful bottomlands and river banks . . . very apt and agreeable for traveling through and for pasturing all kinds of livestock" (Cortés 1988, 20).[1] A 1529 description corroborates and elaborates on Cortés by claiming a vast extent for such grasslands: "there are ten or twenty leagues of plain as flat as a floorboard, and in some places forty to eighty leagues, with grass as high as your knee or higher" (Lockhart and Otte 1976, 196). Moreover, only a decade after the land rush of the 1560s, Arias Hernández emphasized the need to burn pastures every second Christmas to keep them palatable and thus hints that range quality quickly began to deteriorate as grazing pressure increased (Paso y Troncoso 1905, 5:201). And within another several decades, Bishop Mota y Escobar despaired at how the fields of Zempoala had been "converted into cattle estancias . . . , all laid waste and ruined by a lot of thorny woods and *sacas* [coarse grasses or cacti] due to the livestock" (Mota y Escobar 1939-1940, 218).

As the opposite end-member in the range of possibilities, the seemingly degraded grasslands or savannas that Sartorius noted for the piedmont in the nineteenth century might already have existed when the Spaniards arrived—the result of native land use, of climate, or of both. Cortés, in an effort to gain Crown support for his colonization project, might well have exaggerated the potential for a pastoral economy by extrapolating from the verdant, open environs of major riverine settlements such as Zempoala. After all, his effusive description is as locationally ambiguous as it is tantalizingly brief, and it rests on a minimum of experience with the native vegetation and a maximum of boosterism. Besides, Cortés hailed from Estremadura and thus took one of the dustiest corners of Spain as his environmental benchmark. The writer of the 1529 description might also have exaggerated, the eighty leagues of "plain as flat as a floorboard" that he cites being an entirely improbable stretch of such country given the region's topography.

Just as tellingly, as elaborated in the second chapter, a dense agricultural population had occupied these lowlands for millennia before the Spaniards even arrived. Between the several cities and many villages, the region's population seems to have totaled some half a million. Those people not only fed themselves but produced a surplus in excess of subsistence, mainly cotton tribute for the Aztecs. Relict earthen mounds, stone pyramids, agricultural terraces, and ditches still litter the landscape and attest to the density of that agricultural occupance, at least for those who search for such faint spoor of ancient labor. Although the chronologies of many such vestiges remain uncertain, the sediments of Laguna Catarina preserve a pollen record of maize agriculture several millennia long. Precolonial agriculturalists, long and densely settled on the land, would have had ample opportunity to modify the vegetation.

Moreover, the savanna and its thorny thickets of shrubs and trees that Sartorius describes might derive, at least in part, from the subhumid climate itself. The prolonged winter dry season alone could account for such a patchwork of low deciduous forest and, where vertisols inhibit tree growth, savannas (Gómez-Pompa 1973; Lauer 1978). How climate might have changed in these lowlands over the last five hundred years remains unknown (Brown 1985). Nonetheless, some data indicate that the cold period known as the Little Ice Age in midlatitudes might have expressed itself as a drier-than-present period in Mexico (Florescano 1980; Metcalfe 1987). Most of the evidence for such climate change comes from the Central Highlands and indicates drying beginning in the second half of the sixteenth century and not abating until about 1850 (Ouweneel 1996). Such data at least raise the possibility that lowland ranching might have been expanding just as climate was becoming drier.

Between those relatively simplistic end-members lie complex possibilities about which we know approximately nothing—even focusing on material transformation, let alone beginning to integrate conceptual processes and material-conceptual feedbacks. Nonetheless, Sauer's inference that many tropical savannas might be cultural rather than climatic or edaphic, at least in part a product of precolonial land use, suggests that the Veracruz landscape is not the result of any single factor per se, be it climate, precolonial agriculture, or colonial grazing (Sauer 1950, 1958, 1966). Hypothetically, then, Cortés's 1519 dispatch and the 1529 description of "ten or twenty leagues of plain . . . with grass as high as your knee" might refer to a cultural savanna, the product of several millennia of native forest clearance, burning, agriculture, and game management. With native depopulation and old-field succession to shrubs and trees in the first few decades of colonization, the vegetation the livestock invaded when ranching boomed in the second half of the sixteenth century might already have been similar to the seemingly degraded vegetation that Sartorius described in the nineteenth century. Such consideration of the complex interrelationships among the roles of climate and land uses spanning the precolonial through postcolonial periods has more generally begun to counter the prevailing thesis that ranching in New Spain invariably entailed overgrazing and environmental degradation (Sluyter 1998).

Just as compellingly but even more intractably, Cortés, the district governor, and Sartorius seem to sketch out a conceptual transformation of these lowlands. Cortés's "beautiful bottomlands" and Sartorius's "dreary wilderness" bracket the process of recategorization that came to characterize precolonial landscapes as sparsely populated and little used, as "wilderness" in the "classic European sense of uninhabited land" (Bowden 1992, 6). In that pristine myth, natives became conceptualized as denizens of Edenic, primordial landscapes, as lacking the rationality to effectively use, modify, and humanize their lands. And, as the binary complement to that conceptual transformation of the Americas, Europe became categorized as the source of rationality and enlightened innovation diffusing into the vacuum of its colonies. The colonial reconfiguration of the global distribution of resources, labor, and capital thus became naturalized and justified through a parallel redistribution of oppositional categories: cultivated versus wilderness, civilized versus savage, enlightened versus despotic, social versus natural, progressive versus traditional, developed versus developing, core versus periphery, innovative versus imitative, and other synonyms for, essentially, advanced versus retarded (Said 1979; Wolf 1982). To Europeans, after all, the category "New World" came to mean a region both new*ly* brought within the European purview as well as a new*er* version of Europe, one with immature cultures and resources that through improvement eventually would become just like Europe. Colonization was the process through which the savagery of the New World would catch up to the civilization of the Old, through which the irrational, natural, and static would develop into the rational, social, and dynamic (O'Gorman 1958, 1961; Todorov 1984; Hulme 1992). Because such colonial categorizations were integral to the process of escalating material redistributions rather than derivative ideological props, they infused and became axiomatic to every expression of the western world view, from science to literature (Said 1993; Lowe 1991; Hulme 1992; Latour 1993).

Again, Sauer's insight into the relationship between native depopulation and forest invasion of cultural savannas in the tropics most directly suggests a possible feedback loop connecting material and conceptual landscape transformations in Veracruz. In the Caribbean, material/conceptual landscape transformation during the colonial period seems to have created a naturalized landscape of reforested native fields that "appears primeval" (Sauer 1966, 68). Cronon's suggestion that colonial old-field succession in New England validated early postcolonial categories such as "forest primeval" extends that hypothesis to temperate latitudes (Cronon 1983).

As a test of that hypothesis, this chapter examines material processes such as disease introduction, native desettlement and non-native resettlement, non-native arrogation of native labor and land, and expansion of livestock ranching (figure 5.2). In parallel, it examines conceptual processes such as the recategorization of landscape from productive to wilderness. It therefore elaborates on and extends forward in time the analysis of the early interactions between non-natives and natives covered in the third chapter at the same time as integrating all three sides of the colonial triangle in terms of material processes, conceptual processes, and material-conceptual feedbacks.

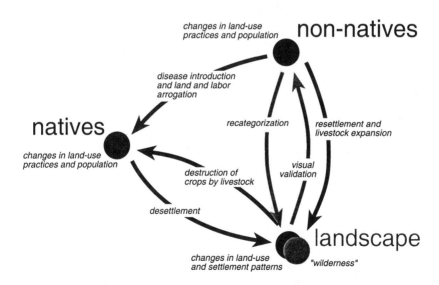

Figure 5.2. Processes and patterns addressed in this chapter.

Chapter 5
The Demography of Colonization

Andrés Pérez de Rivas, the historian of the Jesuits in New Spain, remarked on the greatest single material transformation that had taken place by the end of the first century of colonization. He claimed that by the 1620s not a single native was to be seen within sixteen leagues of Vera Cruz (Pérez de Rivas 1896, 2:195). Native population—from numbering in the hundreds of thousands living in cities and their constellations of smaller towns and villages—had reached a shocking nadir. Just as the regional governor had predicted in 1580, even the few native communities that had survived until then would within a few more decades "come to total ruin and destruction" (JGI, ms. xxv-8, f. 6v). By 1620, the non-native population, largely Spaniards and Africans, had increased but had not even begun to approach the native population of a century before. Nor had the colonizers replicated the native settlement pattern, concentrating instead at the port of Veracruz. To the colonizers, most of the lowlands simply constituted a ranching hinterland bisected by a short segment of the transportation link that stretched from Spain across the Atlantic to Veracruz and on to the viceregal capital of Mexico City.

Accurately describing and understanding that demographic transformation and reconfiguration in settlement pattern is part of the broader, and controversial, investigation of the native depopulation of the Americas (Roberts 1989; Denevan 1992b; Brooks 1993; Henige 1998). Median estimates for the population of New Spain at the end of the precolonial period converge on some twenty million, with collapse to one million by around 1620, the nominal population nadir (Denevan 1992b, 3; Whitmore 1992; Gerhard 1993, 24). But given the equivocal character of the data, the range of estimates remains broad, a general consensus forming on little more than the need for many more regional studies drawing on a wide range of sources and methods (Denevan 1992b, 289).

Since the Mexican general census began in only 1895, the demographic data for the first century of colonization necessarily derive from diverse proto-statistical sources, albeit somewhat different from those used to reconstruct pre-colonial population in the second chapter. While the existing literature does not directly bear on understanding changes in the population and settlement pattern of the Veracruz lowlands, it does provide necessary background information on the documentary database. The few studies that have focused on the region tend to rely on secondary sources, to ignore spatial patterns, to draw on a narrow range of primary data, to cover only part of the region or, in several cases, to incorporate serious errors of fact and analysis (Kelly and Palerm 1952, 7-14, 249-63; Sanders 1953; González Jácome 1988). More usefully, the seminal reconstructions by the Berkeley "historians" of the sixteenth-century population decline for all of New Spain provide references to sources organized by settlement (Cook and Simpson 1948; Borah and Cook 1960, 1963; Cook and Borah 1960, 1970-1974). The resulting database of published tribute assessments and ecclesiastical reports, in combination with other documents such as travel journals and with archival documents, forms the basis for the following reconstruction.[2]

Of all such protostatistical sources, the series of tribute assessments that civil and ecclesiastical officials compiled beginning with the consolidation of Crown power in the 1530s provides the most systematic data on population change. The earliest such assessment that pertains to the Veracruz lowlands is the Libro de las Tasaciones, or Book of Appraisals, that Viceroy Mendoza began during the 1530s and subsequent viceroys periodically revised until 1570 (González de Cossio 1952; Cook and Borah 1960, 7-8). The viceregal scribes also incorporated summaries of assessments from an earlier but not extant volume. A whole series of such compilations of tribute assessments up until the early 1570s contributes data to the population reconstruction, sometimes only an oblique and qualitative reference, sometimes quantitative time series (García Pimentel 1904; Paso y Troncoso 1905, vol. 1 passim; 5:202-72; Paso y Troncoso 1939-1940, 9:2-43; 11:5-60; 14:70-101; BAGN 1936, 185-226; BAGN 1940, 195-243; Cook and Simpson 1948; Cook and Borah 1960). After a gap of nearly three decades, a 1597 petition to extend encomienda inheritance summarizes counts from preceding years in order to make a case for declining encomienda populations and thus for declining encomendero revenue and resulting hardship (Paso y Troncoso 1939-1940, 13:3-48; Cook and Simpson 1948, 8-9; Cook and Borah 1960, 10).

While indisputably a rich database, such tribute assessments do not translate into a reconstruction of population change without first addressing several methodological issues. Most basically, such sources yield no more than surrogate population figures. As the following examples illustrate, assessments record the tribute appraised in kind or in cash, or they record numbers of tributaries rather than people, the various classes of tributaries never being more than a subset of the total population.

> Zempoala, near Vera Cruz, is appraised at twelve pesos cash (BAGN 1940, 204).

> Rinconada, also known as Iscalpa, . . . to pay in tribute to the Marqués del Valle, . . . the following things: Firstly, they have to pay him sixty pesos de oro común in *tostones* every eighty days; they have to pay him a thousand salted fish every year (González de Cossio 1952, 580).

> Actopan . . . has 110 *indios tributarios*. . . . They speak the Totonac language (Paso y Troncoso 1939-1940, 14:81).

The basic accuracy of such data, the meaning of the different classes of tributaries such as *casados* (married males) and tributarios (male tributaries), their relation to the amount of tribute assessed, and the conversion of figures relating to such tributary classes or amounts of tribute into total population all require careful consideration.

Lacking any independent benchmark, the absolute accuracy of the tribute assessments remains unknowable, with some thus free to argue for systematic inflation of head counts and others for deflation. Cook and Simpson argue that in order to conceal assets and gain sympathy for their lobby, encomenderos used their local influence to minimize the number of tributaries the inspectors recorded, presumably by conspiring to hide some natives during head counts or by bribing inspectors to falsify records. In support of that argument, Cook and Simpson demonstrate that Cortés deflated counts of tributaries in the Marquesado del Valle to approximately fifty percent of the actual figure (Cook and Simpson 1948, 5-6). In contrast, Sanders argues that Cortés constituted a special case because as the most powerful of the encomenderos he would have wanted to reassure the Crown that he did not control as many natives as he actually did (Cook and Borah 1970-1974; Sanders 1992, 92-93). Unlike Cortés, argues Sanders, most encomenderos would actually have attempted to inflate head counts in order to gain higher appraisals and increase tribute revenues. The *Breve y Sumaria Relación* by Alonso de Zorita, an ecclesiastical judge of the midsixteenth century, supports Sanders's position by enumerating the ways in which encomenderos inflated the head counts to gain higher tribute assessments (Zorita 1963, 220-27). Sanders's argument seems the more logical one because the natives rather than the encomenderos were the tribute payers. With the populations of encomiendas declining so markedly throughout the sixteenth century, encomenderos would have had little reason to exaggerate that decline, even in the 1597 petition to extend encomienda inheritance on the grounds that encomienda populations, and therefore revenues, were low. As native population approached its nadir early in the seventeenth century, encomienda revenues must in fact have been extremely low (Paso y Troncoso 1939-1940, 13:3-48; Cook and Simpson 1948, 8-9; Cook and Borah 1960, 10). Church officials such as Zorita, on the other hand, might well have deflated head counts in order to protect their charges from onerous tribute assessments, as would have the natives themselves. On the whole, then, while various special interest groups had reasons to either inflate or deflate counts, the struggles between those groups probably kept the counts fairly honest.

The methodological contributions of Cook, Simpson, Borah, Sanders, and others facilitates interpreting the categories of tributaries named in the assessments, the amounts of tribute each paid, and the changes in such categories over the sixteenth century (Cook and Simpson 1948, 11-12; Cook and Borah 1960, 16, 37; Cook and Borah 1970-1974, 1:125-29). Immediately following the conquest, the ratio of tribute to tributaries was spatially variable. Generally, however, married men were termed tributarios and paid at a full rate. Widows, widowers, and unmarried adults who held land paid at a lower rate. And nobles, their "serfs," and their slaves were exempt, as they had been under native rule (Borah and Cook 1960, 65; Cook and Borah 1960, 16, 37, 65). The tribute reform of 1557 seems to have echoed that poorly specified, early system except that nobles lost their exempt status, effectively destroying the native social hierarchy (Borah and Cook 1960, 65). In addition, the Crown standardized the rate of tribute at one peso de oro común plus half a fanega of maize per year per tributario—or, in a few cases, at half a peso de oro común and one fanega of maize (Cook and Simpson 1948, 11; Sanders 1992, 89-91). That alternate rate suggests the equivalence of one peso de oro común and one fanega of maize, setting the standard rate at 1 1/2 pesos per tributary per year, the rate therefore used throughout the following analysis. Widows, widowers, and unmarried adults who held land paid half that tributario rate (Cook and Simpson 1948, 11; Cook and Borah 1960, 16, 37; Sanders 1992, 89-91). Cook and Borah assume the standard rate was in effect by the mid-1560s (Cook and Borah 1970-1974, 1:19). Sanders proposes a longer lag between proclamation and enforcement, with the standard rate not effective until 1576. The crown also collected the standard church tithe of ten percent as a surcharge on all tribute except services and turned the proceeds over to the church (Borah 1941, 387-89, 397-99). That tenth, or diezmo, applied to tribute collected by encomenderos, by Crown officials such as corregidores and district governors, and by majordomos in the Marquesado del Valle.

To convert such known, albeit always imprecisely known, relationships between the amount of tribute and the number of natives in a particular tributary class to total population requires determination of general conversion factors and algorithms. Sometimes the approach to determining a suitable conversion factor has been inductive, comparing tribute appraisals and total population counts from places with both sorts of data (Borah and Cook 1960; Butzer 1991). Sometimes the approach has been deductive, based on presumed rates of depopulation (Cook and Simpson 1948; Borah and Cook 1963). In general, conversion protocols incorporate a ratio of levied tributary population to total tributary population and a percentage for non-tributary population (Cook and Simpson 1948, 12-13; Cook and Borah 1960, 38, 68-74, 88-102; Borah and Cook 1963, 67-72, 81-82). The resulting algorithms take the following form: number of levied heads of tributary families multiplied by a conversion ratio equals the total tributary population; then that total tributary population plus the percentage of the total population exempt from tribute, or the non-tributary population, equals the total population. The conversion factors employed in reconstructing population change for the Veracruz lowlands are similar in form to those used to reconstruct the late precolonial population and follow those established in the literature on the colonial demography of New Spain but respect the equivocal character of the data with a cautious minimum of arithmetic manipulation (Cook and Borah 1970-1974, 1:238-40; Cook and Borah 1970-1974, 2:196-98; Zambardino 1980; Butzer 1991, 207).

The reform of 1557 marks a significant change in the algorithm. From the earliest tribute assessments of the 1530s until the reform, the conversion assumes a ratio of 1 to 3.3 to convert from figures for tributarios to total tributary population. In addition, the non-tributary population of native nobles, their workers, and their households adds a further fifty percent (total population 1530-1557 = [number of tributarios x 3.3] + 50%). After the reform—itself a result of the dramatic decline in native population, of course—all natives became part of the tributary population at the same time as family size decreased. The conversion therefore assumes a ratio of 1 to 2.8 to convert from figures for tributarios to total tributary population (total population 1558-1619 = number of tributarios x 2.8). For those cases in which the number of tributaries was not recorded, only the amount of tribute levied in cash, the standard conversion of 1 1/2 pesos per tributary is used to arrive at a figure for tributarios before application of the appropriate algorithm.[3] Tribute recorded in kind requires an additional prior conversion, from various goods into cash.[4] All results have an estimated error margin of plus/minus fifty percent.

A diverse body of reports, travel journals, and other documents from throughout the early colonial period supplements the tribute assessments, providing cross-checks as well as data pertinent to non-native population change. Beginning in the 1560s, as part of the increasing professionalization and bureaucratization of geographical knowledge, the Crown further consolidated surveillance and control through systematic, spatially referenced compilations of land use, resources, population, and many other variables. Juan López de Velasco based the prototype of those geographies, his *Geografía y Descripción Universal de las Indias*, written between 1571 and 1574, on reports collected over the previous quarter-century, heavily relying on responses by local officials to a 1569 questionnaire (Cook and Borah 1970-1974, 1:31; Velasco 1971; Cline 1972, 189; Warren 1973, 48-49; Butzer 1992, 553-57). Three somewhat later geographies also pertain to the Veracruz lowlands: Antonio de Herrera's *Historia General*, written between 1596 and 1615; Antonio Vázquez de Espinosa's *Compendio y Descripción*, written between 1622 and 1630; and Juan Díez de la Calle's *Memorial y Noticias*, published in 1646 (Díez de la Calle 1932; Herrera 1944-1947; Vázquez de Espinosa 1948; Ballesteros Gaibrois 1973, 240-50; Warren 1973, 53-55; Butzer 1992, 554). Such geographies can only be as reliable as the reports and censuses used to compile them, of course; the same cautions therefore apply as to the tribute assessments. Moreover, some of the geographies compile counts made over several decades and do not always assign specific years to individual entries. To treat such sources consistently, their terminal dates—1574 for López de Velasco's *Geografía*, for example—provide the year for pertinent counts unless other sources allow more precise inference.

A more systematic project to gather comparable data from across New Spain required a geographical report, or *relación geográfica*, from the ranking crown official of each district. Dating to 1580, three of those reports and associated maps pertain to the Veracruz lowlands, the district governors of Vera Cruz, Xalapa, and Tlacotalpan responding to the detailed questionnaire of 1577 sent out by López de Velasco (JGI, xxv-8; Paso y Troncoso 1905, vol. 5 passim; Ramírez Cabañas 1943; Pasquel 1958; Cline 1972, 183-94; Acuña 1985, 279-

374). All three reports seem to have relied on native informants to some degree. While many of the same cautions apply as to the tribute assessments, the relaciones geográficas do provide a regional overview for about 1580 by local writers whose duties, including collecting tribute and inspecting requests for mercedes, gave them firsthand experience with surviving native communities and with the landscape beyond the Spanish settlements and royal highways.

Other diverse sources provide even more fragmentary but still valuable information. In terms of travel journals, three English merchants passed through Vera Cruz, as did nearly every visitor to New Spain: Robert Tomson in 1556, John Chilton in 1568, and Henry Hawks around 1570 (Hakluyt 1904, 9:338-58, 360-97; Warren 1973, 59-60). Several ecclesiastics kept diaries during their tours of inspection in the lowlands (Pérez de Rivas 1896; Gage 1928; Mota y Escobar 1939-1940, 1987; Burrus 1973, 162-63; Ciudad Real 1976). The population data contained in such documents are sporadic and not strictly commensurable with the other sources. Rather, the journals and diaries serve to corroborate and fill gaps in the geographies and censuses.

The geographies, relaciones geográficas, and diverse diaries and travel journals also yield data on non-native population changes that require development of conversion factors similar to those for the native demographic analysis. Such sources tend to report non-native population in terms of vecinos, or citizens, typically the adult males of a town. In early New Spain, the Spaniards were almost all adult males and the ratio of vecinos to total non-native population was 1 to 1 (Boyd-Bowman 1976, 582). As Spanish women immigrated, as African slaves were imported, and as miscegenation increased through the sixteenth century, the ratio of total non-native population to vecinos also increased. Given the uncertainty of such trends and progressive ambiguity of the category non-native, two conversion factors paired with a large margin of error seem sufficient. As based on the relevant literature, they reflect the different household sizes in small settlements versus urban centers of more than 750 vecinos: for towns, total non-native population = vecinos x 4.0; for urban centers, total non-native population = vecinos x 4.5 (Butzer 1991, 207). With an estimated error margin of plus/minus fifty percent, the resulting population reconstructions have much greater value for discerning relative changes and trends than for determining absolute values.

Native Desettlement

Even allowing for the largely relative value of such population reconstructions, the tragedy that the regional governor lamented in 1580 is certain: depopulation exceed ninety percent throughout these lowlands, from Zempoala to Jalcomulco and from Cotaxtla to Iscalpa (table 5.1). The large Totonac and Nahua communities of 1519 all but disappeared within the first sixty years of colonization. But beyond quantification of that demographic apocalypse, reconstructions of depopulation trends for individual settlements facilitate more sophisticated understanding. Excursions from trend lines reveal spurious data points. Fluctuations in trends and differences among trends reveal processes related to the sequence of epidemics, to the institutions of encomienda, repartimiento, and *congregación*, and to the expansion of livestock ranching.

Eight data points, the first deriving from the reconstruction of late precolonial population in chapter 2, plot the depopulation trajectory of Iscalpa, renamed Rinconada by the Spaniards (figure 5.3). The striking dip in population during the 1550s reveals a spurious data point. It relies on Robert Tomson's claim of five or six houses, totaling some twenty-five to thirty people. But the sharp downward excursion from the otherwise smooth trend sounds an alert: Tomson must have been referring to the houses around the Venta de Rinconada, the inn on the royal highway he took from Vera Cruz to Xalapa. He never even saw the larger native community of Rinconada because of its location a few kilometers off the main road. The rest of the data points derive from tribute assessments, are therefore commensurable, and form a smooth trend. Tomson's anomalous figure must be ignored.

The population of Rinconada seems to have declined in direct response to the series of epidemics. The first and greatest scourge, smallpox, arrived at Zempoala in 1520 (Motolinía 1971, 10-11, 294; Florescano and Malvido 1982; Crosby 1986, 199-207; Brooks 1993). An African quickly became the scapegoat carrier, an unverifiable detail in an epidemic that between 1520 and 1521 spread throughout the lowlands and highlands killing hundreds of thousands of people (Gómara 1964, 204-5; Díaz 1986, 244). At Rinconada, only twenty kilometers from Zempoala, smallpox had destroyed most of the population by the early 1530s. A series of such epidemics climaxed in the Great Cocolixtle of the late 1570s, a return of the typhus epidemic of the 1540s or possibly the measles epidemic of the 1530s (Ocaranza 1982; Gerhard 1993, 22-24; Prem 1991). Each epidemic in the series occurred among an ever smaller population with ever greater immunity. Each epidemic in the series thus probably resulted in somewhat smaller relative declines and, certainly, much smaller absolute declines. But the decline was nonetheless inexorable. By 1580 fewer than 200 people remained at Rinconada, by 1600 fewer than 150. Even if the latter count, drawn

Table 5.1. Native population decline in four major settlements.

Settlement	1519 Population	1580 Population	Absolute Decline	Relative Decline
Cotaxtla	2,700	53	2,647	98.0%
Jalcomulco	5,400	280	5,120	94.8%
Iscalpa/Rinconada	54,000	165	53,835	99.7%
Zempoala	121,500	99	121,401	99.9%
Totals	183,600	597	183,003	99.8%

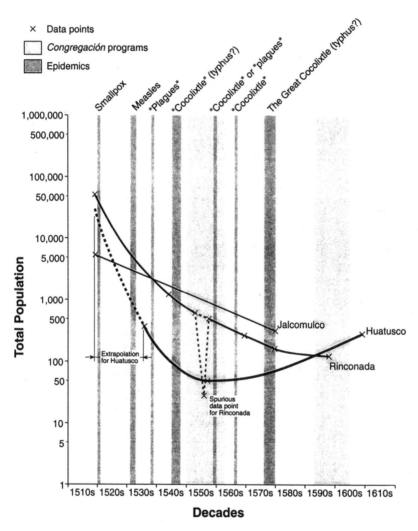

Figure 5.3. Epidemics, congregación programs, and population trends for three major native settlements: Rinconada, Jalcomulco, and Huatusco.

from the 1597 petition to extend encomienda inheritance, deflates the number of inhabitants, by 1580 they already numbered less than one percent of the population on the eve of the initial smallpox epidemic.

Only two data points pertain to Jalcomulco, but the overall trend appears similar to Rinconada. The series of epidemics resulted in dramatic depopulation. More removed than Rinconada from the main road between Veracruz and Xalapa, Jalcomulco seems to have fared slightly better. Nonetheless, even relative isolation did not protect Jalcomulco from over ninety percent population decline during the first sixty years of the colonial period.

Rinconada and Jalcomulco thus reflect the overall trend of native depopulation and its primary cause in the Veracruz lowlands as well as in New Spain and the Americas more generally. Natives lacked antibodies to exotic epidemic pathogens. Many therefore died of introduced diseases. Just as significantly, they did not have children; and within decades entire communities had disappeared. While deaths through massacre, forced transport and labor, famine, battle, torture, and suicide all contributed to the native toll, epidemic diseases by far wrought the greatest loss (Cook and Lovell 1991; Denevan 1992b, 4-7). The people of these lowlands had suffered precolonial epidemics, generically known as *cocolixtle* in Nahuatl—meaning plague, epidemic, or pestilence (Herrera 1944-1947, 3:374). But, as elsewhere throughout the Americas, the diseases brought by non-native hosts caused the apocalypse associated with initial colonization. The long separation of the Old and New World pathogenic realms ensured a lack of antibodies and the exceptional virulence of such diseases as smallpox, typhus, and even measles (Crosby 1986, 196-216).

Although lacking a good 1519 population estimate, extrapolation of the depopulation trend indicates that disease introductions had a similarly grim consequence for Huatusco's natives. In fact, extrapolation suggests at least an order of magnitude higher 1519 population than inferred in chapter 2. Moreover, the nadir seems to have arrived earlier than at Rinconada. The upward trend after 1560 probably relates to the institutionalized settlement consolidation program, known as congregación, implemented partially because of such extreme depopulation (Gibson 1966, 153-54). Like encomienda, the Spaniards' experiences on the Antilles had already sharpened the institution of congregación by the time of New Spain's colonization (Simpson 1950, 6-13). The state, ecclesiastics, encomenderos, and aspiring land owners all united in the effort to nucleate the declining native population through forced resettlement (Gerhard 1977). Through control of space, congregación facilitated indoctrination, surveillance, and labor exploitation at the same time as opening land to granting for livestock estancias (*Recopilación* 1987, libro 6, titulo 3, ley 10). Two concerted congregación programs occurred during the sixteenth century: 1550-1563 and 1593-1605 (Pezzat 1980; *Recopilación* 1987, libro 6, titulo 3, leyes 1-29). During both resettlement programs, scattered communities seem to have been moved to Huatusco from the surrounding district (AGN-M, vol. 7, ff. 236v-37; AGN-Indios, vol. 6, 2a pt., f. 236). The effect of the Great Cocolixtle that intervened between the two congregación programs remains unclear for Huatusco, the lack of data points dictating a smooth curve and precluding further interpretation.

The overall downward trends for Zempoala and Cotaxtla also reflect the sequence of epidemics, but the greater number of data points reveal striking fluctuations that allow a clearer understanding of the congregación process (figure 5.4). Zempoala lost ninety-nine percent of its population during the first decade

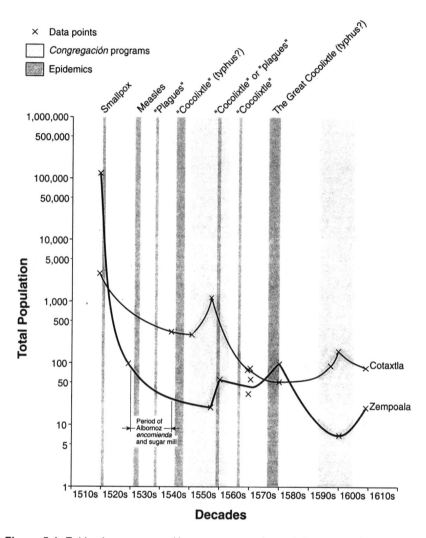

Figure 5.4. Epidemics, congregación programs, and population trends for two major native settlements: Zempoala and Cotaxtla.

of colonization, mostly to the smallpox epidemic of 1520. Between 1529 and 1600, its population fell a further ninety-three percent, but on a base of only ninety-nine inhabitants. Nonetheless, a period of population recovery began in the late 1550s. The initially steep upward trend followed by a decade of relative stability seems to relate to the first congregación program, the relocation to Zempoala of natives from surrounding communities (AGN-M, vol. 4, ff. 65v-

66). During the 1570s, natural increase seems to have doubled population to around a hundred. Then, apparently due to the Great Cocolixtle, population plummeted. By the turn of the century so few families remained that the second congregación program supposedly resettled them near Xalapa (Torquemada 1975-1983, 2:82-83). Given that Mota y Escobar reported some twenty natives at Zempoala a decade later, however, they probably never left at all or had returned in the interim (Mota y Escobar 1939-1940, 218, 220). Changes in population at Cotaxtla display many of the same characteristics as at Zempoala. The initial series of epidemics devastated population. The first congregación program somewhat rebuilt population by relocating natives from surrounding communities. Further epidemics again reduced population. And the second congregación program again rebuilt population. Congregación clearly did not increase the total population of these lowlands; it merely concentrated the surviving population in fewer and fewer settlements. In some cases such settlement consolidation seems to have been voluntary. For example, epidemics had so reduced the population of Alcocahua by 1578 that the survivors moved to Mictanguautla and Espiche (AGN-T, vol. 2678, exp. 12, ff. 5-7). All such population nucleation, of course, voluntary or involuntary, only increased the virulence of smallpox and typhus epidemics (Prem 1991, 47).

Besides disease, arrogation of native labor might have contributed to depopulation. As concluded in the third chapter, that possibility seems unlikely in relation to, specifically, the use of encomienda labor on early ranches. But general demands for cash, food, or direct labor by encomenderos or the Crown might well have negatively impacted native subsistence and therefore health and population. The encomiendas focused on the zones of densest precolonial settlement: a northern cluster encompassing Zempoala, Rinconada, Santa María Tlatela, Atezca, Jalcomulco, and Pangolutla; and a southern axis along the Atoyac River from Espiche and Mictanguautla to Cotaxtla and Huatusco (figure 3.11). As native population and tribute revenues declined in parallel throughout New Spain, the institutional relationship between the colonizers and native labor changed. By midcentury, encomenderos began to lose control of native labor and the colonial economy, with most of the encomiendas having escheated by 1600 and many long before then (Himmerich y Valencia 1991, 15-17). In the Veracruz lowlands, only Cotaxtla and Rinconada, as perpetual components of the Marquesado del Valle, remained beyond Crown control. But Huatusco escheated in 1535, Zempoala in 1544, Santa María Tlatela in 1564, Jalcomulco and Pangolutla in 1575, and Mictanguautla and Espiche around 1600 (Himmerich y Valencia 1991). The Crown, of course, continued to demand tribute from natives that came directly under its control and also began to allocate their labor through the repartimiento, a system in which individual entrepreneurs could apply to the viceroy for an allotment of workers for a specific purpose and period (Gibson 1966, 143-45).

Direct evidence for the negative impact of encomienda or repartimiento labor demands on native population pertains only to Zempoala. After losing most of its population to smallpox in 1520, subsequent epidemics no doubt played a role in further decline, but so did encomienda. Rodrigo de Albornoz, the third encomendero, founded a sugar mill at Zempoala around 1530 and exploited native labor in the operation of that ingenio (AGN-M, vol. 2, ff. 173v-74; Díaz 1986, 531). By 1544, Albornoz had abandoned the sugar mill and the encomienda had escheated. When he then requested a license for a new mill and a large tract of land to grow sugar cane near Xalapa, the local natives objected by citing the Zempoalans' fate, which they particularly ascribed to African slaves: Zempoala had been, in the words of the natives, "completely destroyed and depopulated" (AGN-M, vol. 2, ff. 250v-53, 259; Paso y Troncoso 1939-1940, 4:76-78). In the words of Bernal Díaz, "with a license from His Majesty, Rodrigo de Albornoz built a sugar mill at Zempoala, the said town being destroyed in a few years" (Díaz 1986, 531). Once freed from encomienda, however, population stabilized and then somewhat rebounded with the first congregación program. During the 1560s some Spaniards living at Zempoala reportedly exploited the natives: "the said Spaniards live among the natives in the town of Zempoala, which is one league from Vera Cruz, and have them build houses, from which follow many damages to the detriment of the natives" (AGN-M, vol. 6, ff. 218v-19). Whether that use of native labor was through the repartimiento system, and therefore legal, or not remains unknown. Regardless, at a minimum, native population remained stagnant, and it might even have somewhat declined. Then, over the following decade, population doubled to around a hundred before plummeting during or after the Great Cocolixtle. Repartimientos of native labor continued despite such low populations. For example, the Crown ordered four Jalcomulco natives to work at the Higuera family's Santísima Trinidad sugar mill in 1599 (Zavala and Castelo 1939-n.d., 4:302-4).

Non-Native Resettlement

Meanwhile non-natives had resettled these lowlands (figure 5.5). Yet the newcomers had not replaced the native population in number, nor had they replicated the precolonial settlement pattern. After hesitant beginnings at Villa Rica and Medellín, the Spaniards made Vera Cruz the Atlantic port of New Spain for much of the sixteenth century. Although the main non-native settlement in the lowlands, the population of Vera Cruz peaked at only about eighteen hundred inhabitants. As Vera Cruz lost population after 1570, its deepwater port gained. The viceregal order of 1597 that officially made the mainland shore opposite the island of San Juan de Ulúa into "the new city and port of Veracruz" simply recognized the reality of that ongoing settlement re-focusing. The flood of mercedes during the 1590s and 1600s for house lots, or *solares*, at Veracruz reflects that relocation process (AGN-M, vols. 18-26 passim). By 1609, Mota y Escobar reported the old port of Vera Cruz as being "deserted, the houses ruined, less than eight Spaniards remaining, most of the people being free Negroes" (Mota y

Escobar 1939-1940, 217). A century later, Gemelli Careri found no more than the "small fishing village" that remains today (Gemelli Careri 1745, 522).

Even Vera Cruz's peak population estimate of eighteen hundred provides a misleadingly high impression of the degree of non-native resettlement because many of those people were seasonal inhabitants. They remained at Vera Cruz only during the winter, when the annual fleet unloaded and reloaded between the end of August and the beginning of April (Hakluyt 1904, 9:361). Various

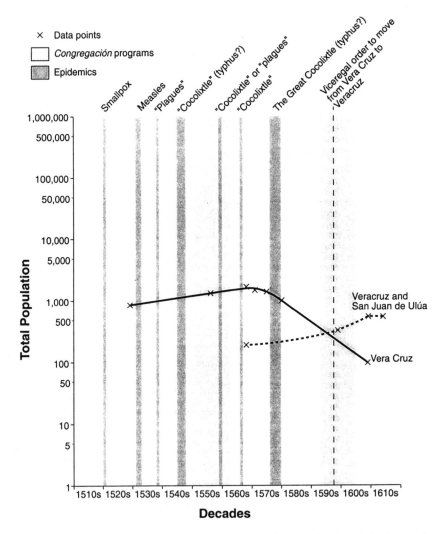

Figure 5.5. Epidemics, congregación programs, and population trends for two major non-native settlements: Vera Cruz and Veracruz/San Juan de Ulúa.

contemporaries who remained year-round bemoaned the summer health rigors, especially the humidity and "putrid infirmities" supposedly emanating from the wetlands (JGI, xxv-8, f. 3). The coming of the summer rains did in fact stimulate the mosquito vectors that spread another introduced disease, malaria (Crosby 1986, 140-42). The Spaniards—as implied by their word for malaria, *paludismo*—related that disease to the wetlands where mosquitoes bred and, even more perceptively, to "the miserable plague of mosquitoes" itself (JGI, xxv-8, f. 6v; Paso y Troncoso 1905, 5:199). Much of the permanent non-native population of the lowlands was African, such as the 150 slaves laboring at the fort of San Juan de Ulúa when John Chilton passed through in 1569 (Hakluyt 1904, 9:361). The natives must also have been as susceptible to malaria as the Spaniards, but the Africans were relatively more immune (Friedlander 1969). Yellow fever, also transmitted via a mosquito vector, was the disease that eventually gave Veracruz its macabre reputation but probably did not arrive until the seventeenth century at the earliest (Arreola 1982, 5-7; Alegre 1841-1842, 3:109; Kiple and Higgins 1992, 239).

Beyond the pale of the settlement nucleations themselves, vaguer extrapolation must suffice. As the sixteenth century passed, more and more estancias occupied the environs of the port of Vera Cruz, and the native settlement pattern faded to a shadow on the landscape. Even by 1580, livestock had replaced people throughout much of these lowlands (figure 5.6). Spaniards and their African slaves only occupied the central coast and a string of ventas connecting the coastal enclave to Mexico City, controlling the study region as a ranching hinterland and transportation corridor. Beyond the ranchers themselves, invariably Spaniards and few in number, Africans seem to have comprised the bulk of the labor force on the ranches just as in the port. By 1571, the Ruiz de Córdova family alone owned twenty estancias and two hundred African slaves (Paso y Troncoso 1905, 5:195). A string of inns did mark the transportation route between the deep water port of San Juan de Ulúa and the viceregal capital of Mexico City but were no more than way stations of a few buildings each in the hinterland between the coast and Xalapa (Hakluyt 1904, 9:355). An unknowable but probably minimal population of natives and Africans lived in refuges beyond the reach of colonial surveillance. Those escaped slaves and their descendants, or *cimarrones*, despite viceregal efforts at elimination, raided Spanish estancias and native settlements (AGN-Reales Cédulas Duplicados, vol. 5, exp. 803, ff. 197v-98v; Pérez de Rivas 1896, 1:282-93; Davidson 1966, 246-50; Aguirre Beltrán 1972; Carroll 1991). Never assessed for tribute, such outlaw communities by definition remain beyond the law, beyond the protostatistical sources, and therefore largely unknowable in terms of population.

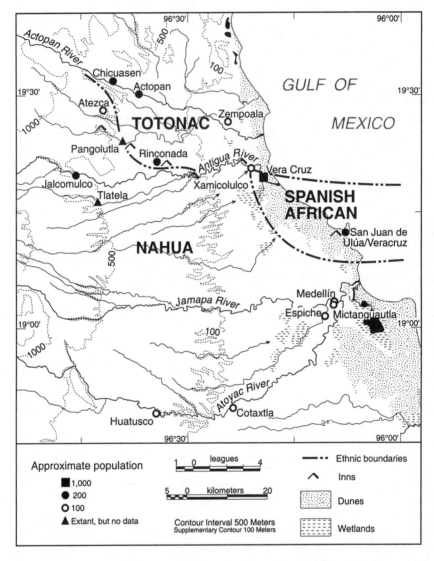

Figure 5.6. Settlement pattern of the Veracruz lowlands about 1580. Settlements that fall outside of the study region are not shown.

Late Interactions Between Ranchers and Natives

By the end of the first century of colonization, livestock ranches had thoroughly replaced native settlements. Hundreds of thousands of people were gone. Tens of thousands of head of cattle and, seasonally, hundreds of thousands of head of sheep grazed among deserted cites and villages. No more than a few thousand non-natives had resettled the region. Yet the processes that had so radically transformed land-use and settlement patterning have remained unclear—not just for these lowlands but for New Spain as a whole.

Going no further than the orthodox explanation, the overall pattern of native depopulation and livestock expansion seems to support the simplistic conclusion that ranchers expanded their herds only after disease epidemics caused native depopulation. Gregorio de Villalobos, of course, had introduced livestock in the 1520s, when native population was still high. And, while early ranchers such as Villalobos and María del Rincón probably did not use native labor to herd cattle, they inescapably occupied native lands. Until at least the 1550s, however, as demonstrated in chapter 3, the ranchers and livestock in the lowlands remained so few that conflicts with natives over land must have been just as few. By the time that Viceroy Velasco banished cattle from the Central Highlands due to increasing conflicts with natives there, by the time that lowland cattle ranching boomed, by the time that a land rush engulfed the Veracruz coastal plain, by the 1560s—the region's native population had already declined by at least three-quarters. Ranchers expanded into a largely depopulated landscape. Just as critically, as enforcement of the New Laws improved through the 1550s, the remaining encomenderos were increasingly prevented from grazing livestock on the lands of their encomienda communities, a pervasive source of conflict in the highlands during the first half of the century (*Recopilación* 1987, book 6, title 9, laws 10-14, 17-20; Chevalier 1952, 155-56).

That complicit perspective caricatures the colonization process as nothing more than an unforeseeable and unavoidable tragedy caused by pathogens that supposedly were the so-called root cause of, in sequence, native depopulation and livestock expansion. Such trite generalities do little to explain the complex suite of processes that constitute colonization. Such trite generalities simplistically and aspatially correlate two categories—namely pathogen-bearing-Spaniards and disease-susceptible-natives—in order to explain away colonization as a predetermined, natural process.

Rather than such overly simplistic "explanations," understanding colonialism demands analysis of the complex interactions among natives, non-natives, and landscape. When analyzed at the scale of decades and the immediate environs of individual settlements, the relationship between the livestock invasion and native depopulation does in fact begin to appear much more reciprocal, dynamic, and complex. Unlike the Valle de Mezquital, livestock do not seem to have degraded the environment of the Veracruz lowlands and thereby negatively impacted native ecology, food supply, and population. Yet livestock also had more direct negative impacts on native communities, as the documentation of conflicts between natives and ranchers well demonstrates for districts in the Central and Southern Highlands (Gibson 1964, 278-82; Gibson 1967, 80-84; Taylor 1972, 119; Super 1988, 55). Large stock in particular entered native fields and destroyed crops and infrastructure (Gibson 1967, 152-53). For communities attempting to recover after an epidemic such impacts could have been critical. Only analysis at the scale of individual settlements, however, can address such processes as cows destroying the maize crop that a native community had been relying on.

At Huatusco, a trickle of estancias during the 1580s led to a flood of grants during the 1590s, and that expansion of sheep ranches seems to be related to changes in native settlement pattern and, perhaps, population (figure 5.7). The mode in granting, as measured by grants for estancias that impinge on a square of four leagues on a side centered on Huatusco, correlates with the increase in its population after midcentury. The low temporal resolution of the population data, only three data points, prohibits discerning decadal-scale associations. As explored in chapter 4, the land rush around Huatusco relates to much broader processes: a change of viceroy, continuing growth of the textile industry, speculation over a possible southern camino real, and perhaps climatic drying that reduced pasture availability in the Central Highlands. The increase in Huatusco's population also relates to a broader process, namely the second congregación program (AGN-Indios, vol. 6, 2a pt., f. 236). That conjunction suggests that even as late as the 1590s, sheep ranchers were not invading a landscape that had been completely depopulated decades before. Small villages were still disappearing, their populations congregated at Huatusco. The processes involved and the effect of the expansion of sheep ranching on the aggregate, district population remain unclear, however. On the one hand, forced settlement nucleation might have preceded land granting, the sheep occupying spatial gaps left in the wake of the congregación program. The mercedes and associated inspection reports certainly suggest occupation of an already depopulated landscape, as developed in the next section. In that case, the sheep would have had no direct effect on the district population. On the other hand, native communities might have attempted to resist the sheep invasion. In that case, the sheep might have negatively impacted the district population before the surviving natives, faced with de facto loss of their lands, gave in to the pressure to congregate at Huatusco. By virtue of its location at the bottom of the canyon of the Atoyac River, Huatusco offered protection from livestock. But which of those two alternative processes pertained remains an open question, unresolvable because of the low temporal resolution of the population data for Huatusco. The opposite data issue pertains to Cotaxtla, where higher resolution population data would allow decadal-scale correlation with land grants, or censuses, if the latter did not remain so elusive for the Marquesado del Valle.

Zempoala, in contrast, has both population and land-use data of sufficient temporal resolution to provide firmer evidence of more complex and dynamic interactions between native population change and ranching (figure 5.8). The first mode in granting, during the 1560s, definitely follows the rise in Zempoala's population associated with the congregation of natives from surrounding

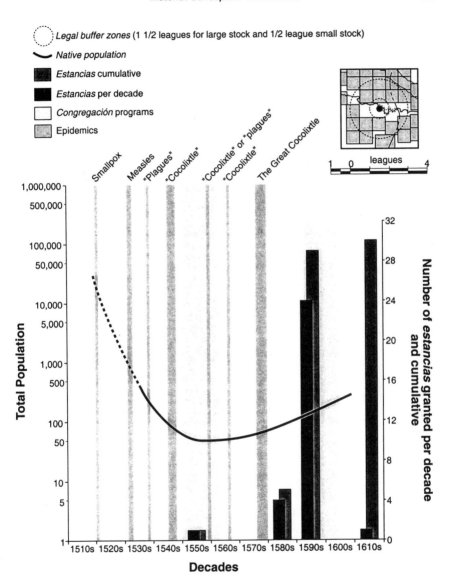

Figure 5.7. Epidemics, congregación programs, granting for livestock estancias, and population trends for Huatusco. Compare figure 4.4 for the estancia grid around Huatusco. Available temporal precision limits graphing the estancias to the nearest decade because stocking could have preceded or lagged the actual merced by several years. Available spatial precision limits locating the estancias as to either being more than half within the four-by-four-league square or not because even mercedes with detailed locational information have an individual precision of no better than plus/minus two kilometers.

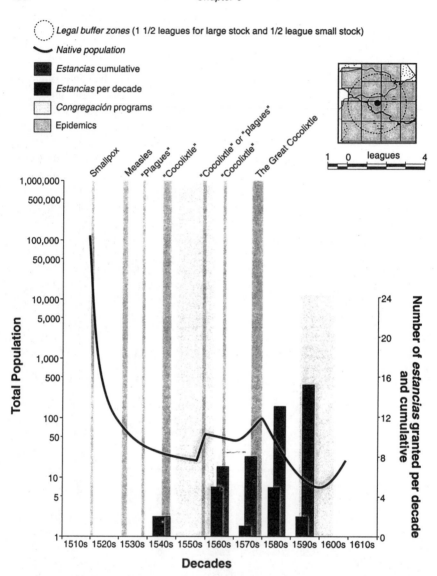

Figure 5.8. Epidemics, congregación programs, granting for livestock estancias, and population trends for Zempoala. Compare figure 4.4 for the estancia grid around Zempoala. Available temporal precision limits graphing the estancias to the nearest decade because stocking could have preceded or lagged the actual merced by several years. Available spatial precision limits locating the estancias as to either being more than half within the four-by-four-league square or not because even mercedes with detailed locational information have an individual precision of no better than plus/minus two kilometers.

villages during the prior decade (AGN-M, vol. 4, ff. 65v-66). With land abandonment, the ranchers moved in. Native depopulation thus seems to precede ranching, although some of the grants—in contrast to Huatusco, almost exclusively for large stock—might have formalized estancias actually occupied in the 1550s. The possible decline in Zempoala's population during the 1560s might be related to a cocolixtle epidemic, although no documents specifically link Zempoala to cocolixtle at that time. The decline might also be related to labor arrogation by cattle ranchers; one document does specifically link damages to the natives with their being forced to build "houses," likely by ranchers intent on establishing the requisite infrastructure of buildings and corrals on their estancias (AGN-M, vol. 6, ff. 218v-19). A lull in land grating and in epidemics during the early 1570s coincides with a doubling of population. That increase clearly signals recovery of the district population, not simply relocation to Zempoala, since the surrounding villages had already been congregated during the 1550s. Then, during the 1580s, population crashed and a renewal of granting seems to completely occlude Zempoala. Again, livestock invasion seems to follow native depopulation due to an epidemic, this time the Great Cocolixtle. With no data points between 1580 and 1600, uncertainty persists as to whether disease destroyed Zempoala before ranchers completely took over its lands, whether estancias so hemmed in the natives that crop damage destroyed their subsistence base, or whether the two processes acted in concert. In any case, the second congregación program supposedly relocated the few survivors to the Xalapa district in the 1590s, although perhaps not permanently (Mota y Escobar 1939-1940, 218, 220).

> [Zempoala] does not have . . . anybody left because since then it became so diminished that there were no more than three or four *personas*. And in the congregación of towns that the count of Monterey made [between 1593 and 1605], those few vecinos went to a town in the curacy and parish of Xalapa. . . . All of [Zempoala's] plains and fields are now full of the cattle of estancias belonging to men who requested them as grants or who bought them since (Torquemada 1975-1983, 2:82-83).

Unlike Huatusco in its canyon, Zempoala's location on the open coastal plain simply offered no protection from livestock.

The documents record one unambiguous, graphic, direct conflict between natives and ranchers that illustrates a process at which the Zempoala and Huatusco data only hint (figure 5.9). In 1574, the viceroy granted Juan de Ocón and Isabel de Vergara two sheep estancias on the coastal plain near Espiche, harbingers of the land rush for lowland sheep pasture (AGN-T, vol. 32, exp. 4). The Núñez de Montalván brothers protested, claiming that the sheep estancias conflicted with their own, preexisting cattle ranches. For good measure, one Montalván brother charged that Ocón had actually conspired to coerce native

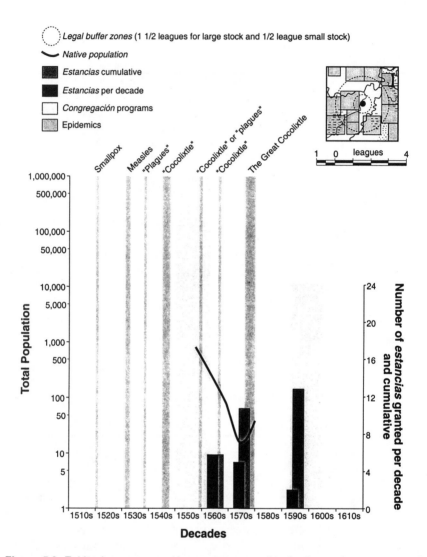

Figure 5.9. Epidemics, congregación programs, granting for livestock estancias, and population trends for Espiche. Compare figure 4.4 for the estancia grid around Espiche, near Medellín. Available temporal precision limits graphing the estancias to the nearest decade because stocking could have preceded or lagged the actual merced by several years. Available spatial precision limits locating the estancias as to either being more than half within the four-by-four-league square or not because even mercedes with detailed locational information have an individual precision of no better than plus/minus two kilometers.

acquiescence to the grants: "Juan de Ocón bribed the natives and made them drunk so that . . . they would not protest" (AGN-T, vol. 32, exp. 4, without pagination). Equally pithy, during the ensuing investigation the natives of Espiche testified that cattle had long posed a threat to their crops and livelihood: "there are some cattle estancias three or four leagues from this town that do great damage eating the crops and destroying the fruit trees" (AGN-T, vol. 32, exp. 4, without pagination). While the viceroy nonetheless allowed the two sheep estancias, further granting around Espiche ceased. Two further grants went in during the 1590s but across the Jamapa River from Espiche, and a spatial interstice of several square leagues persisted around Espiche and Mictanguautla/Medellín. Those communities must have survived the Great Cocolixtle because Martín de Mafra became the encomendero of Espiche and Mictanguautla from the 1580s until the encomienda escheated around 1600 (AGN-T, vol. 2782, exp. 16, f. 3v; Paso y Troncoso 1939-1940, 13:38). Mercedes in Mafra's name occur from Pánuco to Acapulco to Xalapa, where he held another encomienda, but unless he purchased an estancia in the Veracruz lowlands, he did not have one near Espiche or Mictanguautla (AGN-M, vol. 11, f. 66v; vol. 13, f. 164; vol. 17, f. 95; vol. 19, f. 157v). The paucity of data limits analysis of changes in Espiche's population, but it seems to have reached nadir around the mid-1570s and then increased when the surviving natives of nearby Alcocahua moved to Mictanguautla and Espiche during the Great Cocolixtle (JGI, xxv-8, ff. 5v-6; AGN-T, vol. 2678, exp. 12, ff. 5-7). Exposed to the depredations of roaming cattle on the open coastal plain, just like the Zempoalans, the testimony of the Espiche natives offers a graphic illustration of the resulting crop damages. Surrounded by a buffer of ungranted land, like Huatusco in its canyon, Espiche nonetheless survived the sixteenth century.

Because the timing of native depopulation and livestock expansion differed between the highlands and the lowlands, the latter did not experience the same degree of direct conflict between natives and ranchers that characterized highland livestock districts. The expansion of cattle ranching hit the highlands in the 1540s, lagging the end of the Antillean embargo by little more than a decade and coming into conflict with the still dense native population. That timing produced a rich record of litigation between natives and ranchers in Tlaxcala, Oaxaca, and other highland regions (Zorita 1963, 268-70; Gibson 1967, 80-84; Taylor 1972, 119). Those disputes concerned both land tenure and crop damages, the latter mainly related to large stock. In Tlaxcala, for example, cattle entered fields of mature maize, vegetables, and fruit before harvest, devouring and trampling what was intended to be the natives' food supply through the coming year and damaging infrastructure such as fences, canals, and terraces (Gibson 1967, 152-53). As livestock destroyed crops, natives became impoverished and sold land to ranchers in order to earn cash. More cattle resulted in more damages and more sales in a vicious positive feedback process. Entire towns were destroyed and abandoned. Natives could sue, as the community of Quiotepec did in 1542 after Pedro de Santiago's cattle repeatedly destroyed crops (AGN-M, vol. 1, f. 11;

Simpson 1952, 4). But litigation was both slow and expensive, and Spaniards could also sue, as Alonso de Villaseca did in 1551 when the natives of Toluca fenced his cattle out of their maize fields to prevent grazing of harvest stubble (AGN-M, vol. 3, f. 328). That Viceroy Velasco attempted to eliminate cattle ranches from much of the highlands during the 1550s emphasizes just how poorly the courts served natives and how desperate the situation had become by midcentury (Chevalier 1952, 133-35).

In contrast, livestock ranching began expanding through the lowlands only in the 1560s, after Velasco virtually banished cattle from the highlands exactly because of their depredations. By then, epidemics had so reduced the native population and the first congregación program somewhat nucleated the survivors that direct conflict between ranchers and natives rarely if ever reached litigation (Gibson 1967, 82-83, 152-53). Only a few faint echoes of conflicts—crop damages at Espiche, forced labor at Zempoala—therefore entered the documentary record. Yet those clues suggest that while the overall upward trend in livestock population followed the devastating decline in native population, the livestock expansion hindered the recovery of surviving communities. As in the highlands, cattle would have been much more destructive of native crops than sheep. Seasonal movement between coastal plain and piedmont, semiferal stock, and uncastrated bulls all figured in the ranching ecology that Villalobos had implanted. And all of those characteristics would have been disastrous to any native field or orchard in the path of a roaming herd (Zorita 1963, 270). In addition, at least some Spaniards employed bribery and deceit to accumulate space at the expense of surviving native communities.

Legislation protected native communities, at least in theory, from such fraud and crop damages. Velasco's expulsion of cattle from highland districts, albeit no more than a temporary exile in some cases, well demonstrates the Crown's determination to protect native communities and, far from incidentally, revenue from the head tax. But just as tellingly as such dramatic campaigns, the Crown institutionalized protection within the land-granting process itself. From the beginning of centralized granting in the 1540s, the mercedes themselves stipulated that no estancia should damage the interests of the Crown or any third party, including native communities. The formulaic clauses follow a series of decrees codified in the *Recopilación de Leyes de los Reynos de las Indias* of 1618 (AGN-M, passim; *Recopilación* 1987, libro 4, titulo 12, ley 9, ley 12; libro 6, titulo 3, ley 20; Chevalier 1952, 122). Moreover, the merced itself was but the final document in a process that began with a request to the viceroy for a writ to order an inspection of a specific tract for a specific purpose. Inspection by a Crown official would then determine the suitability of the tract for that purpose. In several cases that pertain to the Veracruz lowlands, the resulting paper trail survives in its entirety. On 19 January 1617, for example, Viceroy Fernández de Córdoba issued a writ, or mandamiento acordado, ordering the corregidor of Vera Cruz to inspect four tracts requested by Luis Ochoa as sheep estancias (AGN-T, vol. 2784, pt. 1, exp. 3). The writ specified that the corregidor immediately post it on the door of the Vera Cruz church, within a month inspect the tracts accompanied by local land owners and the representatives of nearby native communities, take depositions regarding conflicts of interest, and allow any third parties four months from the date of posting to file objections to granting the estancias. On 8 February, the lieutenant of the corregidor in fact did post a copy of the writ on the church door. On 13 February, the lieutenant, his scribe, and several third parties inspected the tracts and visited the surrounding native settlements and estancias. The scribe recorded the depositions of a series of Spanish and native witnesses and draughted a map of the tracts. On 30 June, after waiting the stipulated four months, the lieutenant wrote a report that recommended granting the estancias. And on 7 July, the viceroy did grant all four tracts to Luis Ochoa (AGN-M, vol. 33, ff. 114-15v).

In addition, several decrees stipulated buffers between estancias and native communities. In 1556, Viceroy Velasco granted some communities a buffer radius of one league (Chevalier 1952, 125). In 1567, Viceroy Peralta decreed that native settlements were to encompass a minimum area of one square league, including both town and surrounding fields (McBride 1923, 123-24). Other legislation stipulated that no cattle estancia should locate within one and a half leagues of any native settlement and no sheep estancia within half a league (*Recopilación* 1987, libro 6, titulo 3, ley 20). Huatusco seems to have maintained such a buffer, perhaps largely due to its location at the bottom of a canyon. In contrast, exposed on the open coastal plain, ranches completely occluded Zempoala. Yet Espiche and Mictanguautla, despite a similar site, did maintain a nominal buffer. The case of Espiche, however, raises the issue of the effectiveness of such buffers. The natives complained about "some cattle estancias three or four leagues" distant, well outside any legislated buffer. Nor did legal buffers offer effective protection from semiferal stock that ranged far from their home estancias.

Most tellingly, despite the Great Cocolixtle of the late 1570s marking the last in a series of devastating epidemics, despite the grant inspections, despite the restrictive clauses of the mercedes, despite the protective legislation—Pérez de Rivas could by 1620 claim that not a single native was to be seen within sixteen leagues of Vera Cruz (Pérez de Rivas 1896, 2:195). Nearly half of the grants for cattle estancias and most of those for sheep estancias came after the Great Cocolixtle. Confronted with that explosion of livestock ranching, the native population that had survived into the 1580s declined to virtually zero, and a desettled landscape grazed by immense herds persisted for the next several centuries. By the early postcolonial period the back country of Veracruz constituted a "wilderness," Sartorius's categorization based in part on the low population density but also on the vegetation. Understanding how colonization created that landscape, in spite of legislation clearly intended to halt and even reverse desettlement, therefore requires understanding not only desettlement but vegetation change.

Old Field Succession

Beyond reconstructing the spatial and temporal dimensions of the livestock invasion, the land-grant documents permit a systematic analysis of the complex process of vegetation change that lies somewhere between presuming that the thorny thickets of Sartorius's "wilderness" must have preceded colonization, the result of climate or native land use, and presuming that several centuries of overgrazing or climate change must have degraded once open grasslands. Many of the Crown officials who inspected tracts requested as estancias wrote reports that included descriptions of settlement, terrain, and vegetation. Some also drew maps with graphic and textual landscape representations. While only some of the inspection reports survive, most of the actual grants are extant and include vegetation descriptions the viceregal scribes copied from the reports. Those data cannot compare to the much later, more systematic land-surveys of the United States, so amenable to statistical analysis. But mapping the vegetation references in the land grants does yield a perspective on the vegetation of a particular place at the time of livestock invasion. The coverage of the grants clearly must be biased in favor of areas supporting at least some grasslands, that resource being what prospective ranchers were after. Yet, despite that caveat, the grants do cover more than half of the region and, equally as critical, by definition cover the lands that would have been most affected by the livestock invasion. As another caveat, informal grazing might have impacted the vegetation of a particular locale before a rancher obtained a grant to it. Yet the vegetation descriptions are contemporaneous with the major influx of livestock in any particular district and thus indicate the condition of the vegetation as each successive wave of the invasion engulfed a new ranching frontier.

The grants and attendant vegetation descriptions initially focused on the coastal plain, then shifted into the dunes and onto the piedmont (figure 5.10).[5] From hesitant beginnings in the north during the 1540s and 1550s, granting spread southward between the dunes and the piedmont during the 1560s. The vegetation references associated with the coastal plain, though brief, refer to savannas, *matas*, *montes*, and *matas de monte*—grasslands with scattered solitary trees and patches of open woodland or shrubland. The Hispanic term monte designates fragmented, open woodland or shrubland; and mata de monte, often abbreviated as mata, indicates a patch of such woodland in a savanna (Santamaría 1959; Corominas 1973; Rzedowski 1983). And, as one inspector put it in 1574, there was "nothing except montes and savanna" (AGN-T, vol. 32, exp. 4). The subsequent expansion into the dunes reveals a similarly open vegetation of grasses, other herbaceous vegetation, and woody thickets. On the piedmont, the inspectors encountered stands of evergreen oaks at higher elevations but also the familiar savannas with matas de monte and mimosas, typically acacias. Throughout the region, as at present, evergreen trees fringed rivers and seasonal

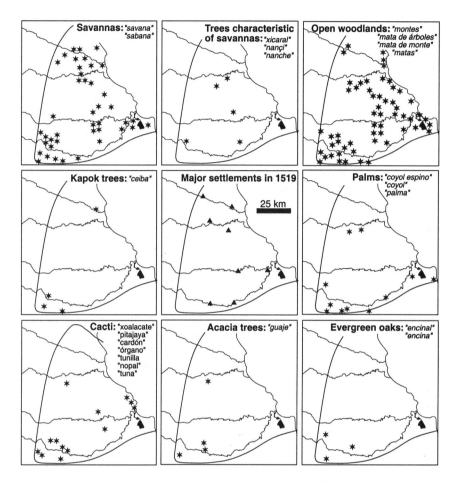

Figure 5.10. Vegetation references from land grant documents. See figure 2.5 regarding the major settlements of the late precolonial period. The line encloses the Veracruz lowland study region.

wetlands. Mangroves bordered the brackish lagoons among the dunes to the south of San Juan de Ulúa. And deciduous trees and shrubs dominated the woody vegetation elsewhere.

At the regional scale, then, the land-grant documents echo Sartorius's nineteenth-century description as well as climatic and edaphic patterning, and therefore the sixteenth-century livestock invasion must have occupied the deciduous woodlands and thickets rather than creating them through degrading open savanna. The sand substrate of the dunes, despite receipt of over 1,000 millimeters of precipitation, precludes even low deciduous forest except on the finer substrates of interdunal basins; shrubs and herbs therefore dominate much of the dune cordon. Similarly, the vertisols of the upper piedmont, despite receipt of over 1,200 millimeters of precipitation, due to waterlogging during the wet season and deep cracking during the dry season, support a patchwork of savanna and low deciduous woodland, expectably grading into shrubland on the drier, lower piedmont. Only the wetlands of the coastal plain can harbor extensive hydrophytic and evergreen communities. On the northern coastal plain, vertisols and the rainshadow suggest savanna with sparse tree growth as the precursor to the present-day irrigated cane fields, although with gallery forests bordering streams and wetlands. To the south, increasing precipitation and phaeozems also suggest savanna but with the possibility of extensive low deciduous woodland and shrubland as well as taller evergreens bordering streams and wetlands.

Scrutinizing more specific vegetation references—literally at the species level—the grants also reveal that precolonial land use had affected the vegetation that the Spaniards encountered. As native population rapidly declined in the first two decades of colonization, from some half a million to less than one hundred thousand after the initial smallpox and measles epidemics, vegetation invaded former agricultural fields and communities. The grants record the palm trees that marked those fields (figure 5.11). More specifically, the coyol palm noted in the documents characteristically invades disturbed vegetation, especially when periodically burned (Pennington and Sarukhan 1968).[6] Because the coyol bears edible fruit, the natives even encouraged its growth, the 1580 geographical report classifying it as a "cultivated tree of this land" (JGI, xxv-8, f. 11). In several cases, the grants clearly associate coyol palms with savannas near former native settlements (AGN-T, vol. 3331, exp. 1, ff. 1-9; AGN-M, vol. 33, ff. 112v-14, 115v-16v). One grant even notes "a savanna where there is a round mata that in the middle of it has a large clearing with two palms" (AGN-M, vol. 14, ff. 80v-81v)—a striking, but at the time seemingly unappreciated, description of thickets invading former agricultural fields.

If the coyol palm marked moribund agricultural fields, the ceiba marked the former settlements themselves (figure 5.12).[7] Natives protected the ceiba, the kapok or silk-cotton tree, its enormous canopy providing shade, its seed pods fiber, and its bark medicine (Santamaría 1959; Mason and Mason 1987; Niembro Rocas 1986). Sacred among the Maya as the World Tree, towering ceibas still grace the plazas of towns throughout the lowlands. The grants note ceibas near Zempoala and Huatusco as well as more generally associated with the stone and earthen mounds, the so-called *cúes*, that marked former settlements (AGN-M, vol. 9, ff. 33-33v; vol. 10, ff. 45v-46; vol. 14, ff. 161v-62v; vol. 15, ff. 25v-26v, 86-87; vol. 17, ff. 25v-26v). Significantly, lone ceibas rose above thickets of low trees and shrubs: "in a savanna where there is a large mata, and in the middle of it a large ceiba rising above the trees of the said mata"; "a round mata and in it a very large ceiba" (AGN-M, vol. 15, f. 26; vol. 17, ff. 25v-26). The

Figure 5.11. Coyol palms in recently burned pasture just after the beginning of the rainy season and the greening of the piedmont vegetation. Photograph by the author, June 1999.

Figure 5.12. A ceiba tree, majestic even during the dry season when its leaves have fallen, marks a precolonial mound amid irrigated fields of sugar cane on the otherwise level coastal plain. Photograph by the author, January 1992.

ceibas—and, more significantly, the matas de monte in which ceibas occurred—marked the overgrown settlements of the former native population, signposts to a moribund cultural landscape.

The land-grant documents yield a more systematic analysis of landscape transformation than such particularistic observations as Mota y Escobar's, who despaired at how thorny woodlands had wasted the once verdant fields of Zempoala, can ever provide. The analysis reveals that the livestock invaded a largely moribund cultural savanna, as opposed to a purely climatic or edaphic savanna. By the second half of the sixteenth century, these lowlands had become a matrix of savanna with patches of former settlement and agriculture undergoing old-field succession. Regardless of whether climatic drying associated with the Little Ice Age might have been modulating that succession, where the landscape had been most thoroughly disturbed, in agricultural fields and settlements, the thickets had invaded before the livestock. Livestock might well have influenced the floristic composition of the invading vegetation but seemingly not the structure—that is, the particular species involved but not the vegetation type. Exotic weeds certainly followed the livestock and displaced native species. For example, European clover became so widespread in New Spain by 1555 that the Nahua coined a new term: *Castillan ocoxichitli*, after the Castilian invaders and a native weed of similar appearance (Crosby 1986, 152).

But the struggle between grasslands and thickets would not have hinged so much on the particular flora involved as on the balance between disturbance by livestock versus disturbance by fire in a context of, possibly, a drier climate than at present (Harris 1966; Cházaro Basáñez 1977; Anderson 1982). Heavy grazing would have promoted the thickets. Grazing reduces the supply of fine fuels necessary to frequent, low intensity fires that suppress the seedlings of woody plants. At the same time, browsing by cattle of the leguminous pods of mimosas disperses their seeds in fertilizing cow flops and thus further promotes thicket invasion. In contrast, repeated, active burning of pastures by ranchers would have consumed the woody species and favored the grasses. Despite viceregal prohibitions, such burning seems to have been regular practice during the sixteenth century, with Arias Hernández reporting that the pastures were "wont to be burned around Christmas time" (Paso y Troncoso 1905, 5:194-95). Sedimentary charcoal from Laguna Catarina confirms the annual burning if not its seasonal timing (Sluyter 1997c). Such December burns, relatively early in the dry season, would have resulted in the localized, low intensity fires that fragment landscape and promote a mosaic of grassland and woodland patches. The practice Sartorius implies predominated during the nineteenth century—burning late in the dry season, when woody vegetation and grass are driest—would have resulted in the much more extensive, intense fires that favor more homogenous grasslands. Drier wet seasons during the Little Ice Age would only have further favored the herbaceous over the woody.

As the relatively minor role of cacti in the region's vegetation reveals, whatever the complex balance between grazing and burning in particular places and times, the livestock and cultural practices of the ranchers at most modulated the old-field succession toward "dreary wilderness, overgrown with low thorny mimosas." Cacti, sharply armed against even the most determined cow, provide the most certain diagnostic of overgrazing and vegetation degradation. As livestock assault the palatable plants, cacti displace them. Yet the grants reveal cacti as a relatively minor element of the landscape the livestock were invading, even as cacti remain generally unobtrusive at present, probably more related to the long dry season than to land-use history (Gómez-Pompa 1973).

Millennia of native land use, then, had not degraded the lowland vegetation by the time the Spaniards arrived. Rather, native peoples had created a cultural savanna, one that because of its openness impressed Cortés with its grazing potential. But the subsequent livestock invasion did not have a major degradational impact on the vegetation either. Rather, livestock seem to have refilled a long vacated ecological niche. Before human occupance of the Veracruz lowlands, the vegetation had co-evolved with Pleistocene herbivores. Until the Holocene, such herbivores as glyptodonts and horses propagated many of the thorny deciduous trees—such as the acacias and xícaros noted in some of the grants—eating the pods and fruits, dispersing the seeds through digestive tracts, and fertilizing the seedlings with feces (Janzen and Martin 1982).[8] With the exception of deer, most of those herbivores became extinct, and the palatable fruits containing indigestible seeds became an ecological anachronism. Evolved to propagate through extinct dispersal agents and increasingly assaulted by agricultural clearance and burning, the populations of xícaros and similar species must have become minor elements in the emerging cultural savanna. Only culturally valued trees, such as the coyol and ceiba, would have thrived. To some degree, then, native depopulation and livestock invasion reinstated the Pleistocene ecology and re-expanded the thorny thickets.

From "Wastelands" to Estancias

The Spaniards not only diffused epidemic diseases that depopulated and materially transformed settlement and vegetation patterns; they not only diffused livestock that contributed to the emergence of a sparsely populated "dreary wilderness, overgrown with low thorny mimosas" (Sartorius 1961, 9); they also implanted conceptual models, categories, and other habits of thought that were just as integral to the landscape transformation as the smallpox and the cattle. In doing so, they largely ignored or remained oblivious to precolonial concepts and categories. Where natives had seen agricultural lands, as clearly demonstrated by the remains of wetland fields and terraces, Spaniards saw pasture lands and populated them with livestock. Cortés initially did so in rhetoric, and others later did so in fact. As two erstwhile critics of modern culture and agriculture have observed, Europeans colonized the Americas with visions to the exclusion of sight, with visions of former places but without the sight to appreciate the environments and cultures they were colonizing (Berry 1977; Jackson 1994). That imposition of erroneous categories, that failure to understand and value native land use on its own terms, ultimately proved more fatal to the recovery of native populations and ecologies than the exercise of sovereign power. Charles V and his successors, after all, were the embodiments of that sovereign power, and they persistently strove to protect native peoples.

After an initial period of intellectual ferment, the Spanish Crown and Christian Church reconciled the existence of Native Americans with prior ontological assumptions and implemented laws that recognized native rights to freedom and property. To Christians, the Americas did not easily fit into the model of the *Orbis Terrarum*, the Island of the Earth that constituted the world inhabited by human beings, themselves defined as the progeny of Adam and Eve (O'Gorman 1958, 1961). Europe, Asia, and Africa made up that world, each of those contiguous continents having been populated by one of Noah's three sons when the biblical flood receded. No ontological enigma arose as long as Columbus could maintain the fiction that he had reached Asia. But when Amerigo Vespucci coasted far southward along the Patagonian shore without finding an entrance to the Indian Ocean, he concluded that Christians had encountered a *Mundus Novus*, a New World. In 1507, however, the *Cosmographiae Introductio* reconciled the several ontological speculations about that New World by conceiving the Americas not as a world distinct from the Orbis Terrarum, not as an actual Mundus Novus, but as a fourth part of the Orbis Terrarum that had newly come into the European purview. Yet considerable ontological ambiguity persisted. The Americas might have become comparable in cosmographic status to Europe, Asia, and Africa as individual entities. But, simultaneously, the Americas quite obviously remained distinct from those three contiguous parts of the reconceptualized Orbis Terrarum.

That ambiguity in the adjusted Christian ontology equally pertained to the status of the people of the Americas. Native Americans clearly appeared to be cast in God's own image and therefore must be human beings. Yet at the same time they lived in a world that seemed, fourth part of the Orbis Terrarum or not, to be entirely surrounded by water rather than being contiguous with the three continents populated by Shem, Ham, and Japheth. Historians have typically, if facilely, personified the resolution of that ontological conundrum as a marathon debate between Ginés de Sepúlveda and Bartolomé de Las Casas at Valladolid in 1550 (O'Gorman 1961; Todorov 1987). Sepúlveda, following Aristotelian categories, argued that the natives were immutably inferior, the natural slaves of Christians. Las Casas argued for natives as fully rational and spiritual beings, therefore capable of becoming Christians and subject to the same obligations and protections of divine and natural law as Christians. In both intellectual and legal terms, however, that confrontation was but a late echo of a broader process of resolution that emerged over the first half of the sixteenth century. Already by 1537, a papal bull commanded that "the aforesaid Indians and all other nations which come to the knowledge of Christians in the future must not be deprived of their freedom and ownership of their property" (Todorov 1987, 162). That position well fit the Spanish Crown's desire to reduce the power of the encomenderos and promote the stabilization and recovery of the native population that would have to provide the tribute and labor to develop New Spain. Just five years after the papal bull, the Crown had codified the revised ontological model in the New Laws, legislating the protection of specific aspects of native freedom and property. Half a century later, Acosta's *Historia Natural y Moral de las Indias* was to systematize understanding of the Americas as the fourth part of a single world and of Native Americans as human beings, different than Europeans to be sure but nonetheless progeny of Adam and Eve (Acosta 1590; Butzer 1992). Native Americans, argued Acosta, in the earliest version of the Bering Land Bridge theory, must have migrated to the New World from Asia via a land connection in far northern latitudes.

But reconciling the existence of Native Americans with the prior ontological model, conceiving of them as human beings, and recognizing their rights to freedom and property entailed an enormous cost. Ontologically, for Native Americans to be human demanded that the New World could not be an alien world, another world, a world that Europeans must therefore strive to understand on its own terms. The New World could only be a new*ly* encountered part of the same old world and, moreover, a new*er* part of that world, in the sense of being less mature than the three older parts (O'Gorman 1961). As the binary complement of that New World, then, the three contiguous continents became categorized as the Old World. In gaining the status of human beings and accompanying rights under natural and divine law, Native Americans lost their own identities. They became categorized as immature human beings, as potential Europeans, as puerile students aspiring first and foremost to become Christians and to become, most basically of all, westerners.

That process afforded little significance to native terms of reference and even less to reconciling the existence of Europeans with native ontological models (Todorov 1987). Any attempts to understand natives from their own perspectives were attempts to eliminate those perspectives. Diego Durán thus intended his treatise on native beliefs to provide a guide to recognizing and replacing their vestiges with Christian beliefs (Durán 1967). Bernardino de Sahagún had the same purpose (Sahagún 1950-1982). Franciscans who so assiduously learned Nahuatl did so to westernize natives rather than to Nahuatlize westerners. Conversion, not going native, remained the goal. Ironically, in attempting to learn about natives in order to obliterate native knowledge, Durán and Sahagún preserved at least a few faint sketches of native ontological models (León-Portilla 1959). Perhaps exactly for that reason, neither Durán's *Historia de las Indias* nor Sahagún's *Historia General* were published until the nineteenth century.

In an aspect of that process more directly related to the transformation of the lowland landscape, Spaniards deployed a particular conceptualization of the relationship between land use and land tenure in combination with a failure to understand, recognize, or even consider native categories of land use. That fatal combination of a particular "vision" with a failure to "see" constituted lands beyond the immediate environs of surviving native communities as unused grasslands and shrublands that could most rationally be used for grazing. The grant inspectors characteristically described such prospective estancia lands as *yermas* and, most often, as *baldíos* or *tierras baldías* (AGN-M, vol. 8, ff. 190-90v; vol. 9, f. 91v; AGN-T, vol. 2702, exp. 12, ff. 386-97v; vol. 2702, exp. 13, ff. 398-406v; vol. 2764, exp. 15, ff. 181-95v; vol. 2777, exp. 3, ff. 1-9v; vol. 3331, exp. 1, ff. 1-9). The term baldío equates to wasteland, to the *wasta est* that described idle lands in the eleventh-century Domesday Book of England (Darby 1973). Both baldío and waste designate lands once productive but made idle by plague or war. In eleventh-century England, the Norman conquest had laid waste such lands. In eleventh-century Iberia, the Reconquista turned Muslim lands into baldíos that the Crown then granted to Christian settlers. All lands not actively used became Crown lands, or *realengos*, and were open to public grazing until granted to an individual for a specific purpose such as farming (Chevalier 1952, 105-6). That category echoed Roman law, in which *res nullis* designated lands either abandoned or never cultivated and thus available. The privilege to graze lands not actively used extended even to crop stubble after the harvest, an arrangement in which transhumant flocks gained access to valuable fodder and left behind an equally valuable deposit of manure.

The term baldío thus did not necessarily categorize lands as pristine, as lacking any prior productive use. On the contrary, baldío connoted that a calamity had laid waste the land. The grant inspectors certainly recognized moribund settlements by the many *cúes* that dotted the landscape and knew that a dense native population had once occupied the lowlands. Yet the associated agricultural fields, undergoing old-field succession, went unremarked. The Spaniards seem to have been unaware that natives had once excavated a labyrinth of ditches to manage the hydrology of the wetlands of the coastal plain. Only one grant inspector recorded those earthworks: "a small lake which appears in the rainy season . . . and marshes ditched straight southward" (AGN-M, vol. 15, ff. 191v). Not a single inspector noted the even more extensive agricultural terraces of the lower piedmont.

In contrast, lands that natives clearly and actively used did not merit categorization as baldíos, but conflict arose when Spaniards insisted on access to crop stubble, a seasonal application of the privilege to graze lands not actively used. Elsewhere in New Spain, ranchers went so far as to sue natives for fencing their maize fields to exclude cattle (AGN-M, vol. 3, f. 328). Some of that conflict arose from a failure to appreciate essential differences between Spanish and native agroecologies. Wheat scythed at harvest leaves only the butts of stalks in the fields. Livestock can graze that stubble without damaging the crop while leaving behind manure essential to the next crop. Maize undergoes a much more protracted harvest, however. At the end of the growing season, the stalks sometimes are doubled over without removing the ears (Alcorn 1984, 361). The inverted husks shield the ears while drying. Even fields of yellowed, doubled over stalks, which a Spaniard might have equated with the stubble of a harvested wheat field, could retain a substantial number of drying ears. While ranchers won their suits and access to maize fields, the conflict so threatened native crops that Viceroy Velasco began to restrict the legal grazing period to January and February (Chevalier 1952, 119, 125).

The case of Espiche illustrates another process, however—one that pertained to landscape patches such as fallow fields and diverse resource gathering zones that fit more ambiguously into the Spanish conceptualization of the relationship between land use and land tenure. The grant inspector had claimed that the natives themselves categorized the land under inspection as baldíos and so labeled them on the accompanying map (AGN-T, vol. 32, exp. 4, without pagination; figure 5.13). But the ensuing investigation revealed that cattle were destroying native crops and orchards. Rather than baldíos, some of the lands being granted around Espiche in reality were native agricultural fields and orchards or groves of fruit trees. Ocón had used alcohol to coerce the natives into categorizing the lands as baldíos. They might have been fallow at the time and thus overgrown and categorized as matas de monte but they remained part of the native subsistence system nonetheless. Fallow fields and communal resource gathering zones also existed in Spain, of course, but when confronted with unfamiliar agroecologies and an exuberant tropical vegetation, the category baldíos became exceptionally plastic. Such manipulation of the category wasteland and its application to fallow lands pertained more widely to Spanish space accumulation throughout New Spain (Chevalier 1952, 279; Rojas Rabiela 1988, 64-65).

Thus, in accumulating space, at least some Spaniards circumvented the legislation intended to protect native land tenure and thereby helped to make such legislation superfluous, on the books but with few native communities left to protect by the end of the first century of colonization. The most vulnerable lands were probably the most critical—not those far from surviving villages and not those in their immediate environs, but those fallow fields and managed groves of trees in an intermediate orbit. The plasticity of the category baldío could incorporate such landscape patches, neither abandoned due to depopulation nor actively cultivated just at the time when a grant inspector came along. Significantly, in circumventing explicit laws, individuals were able to draw on the implicit, taken-for-granted environmental and spatial categories that formed the conceptual parameters for colonial space accumulation. Lands beyond the immediate confines of native communities, even if still utilized by those communities, equaled wastelands. Space itself equaled a map, the maps of the land grants at once recording space accumulation and land use as well as manifesting the conceptual parameters for the articulation of power through space in order to exert power over space: "cartography is part of the process by which territory becomes" (Harley 1992, 532). The maps therefore did more than delineate the

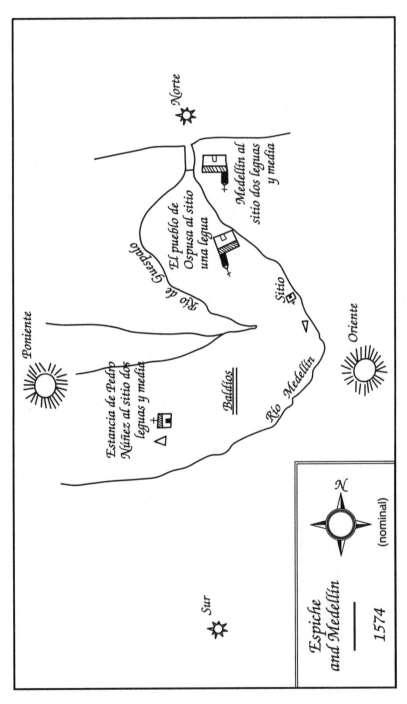

Figure 5.13. Transcription of a map from 1574 relating to a dispute over two sheep estancias near Espiche, here rendered "Ospusa" (AGN-T, vol. 23, exp. 4).

grid of Spanish space accumulation and record landscape patterns; like the categorical baldíos in the texts of the land grants, cartographic representation was part of the transformative process resulting in those patterns.

Native cultures clearly had their own cartographic traditions and terms that equated to baldío, but their modes of representation differed so radically from Spanish mapping that they did not constitute a basis for immediate resistance. Native cartographies were rooted in the genesis of place, combining genealogical with spatial representations (Harley 1992). In that tradition, too, maps inescapably manifested power as knowledge that constituted conceptual parameters for the articulation of power through space in order to control space. But the native tradition had more in common with Medieval cartography than the land-grant maps, the latter akin to other maps of the Renaissance and part of the emerging Cartesian representation of absolute, georeferenced space. Natives eventually learned how to employ Spanish landscape representations in order to resist the appropriation of territory by the ranchers—but too little and too late, just before the period of granting came to a close at the end of the colony's first century. Only by 1590, in fact, did the natives of Huatusco finally request two sheep estancias (AGN-T, vol. 3331, exp. 1). In doing so, they employed the Spanish conceptualization of the landscape, both in categorizing the requested lands as baldíos and in representing space as a map (figure 4.10). Even so, although the map seems to include native representational elements, a district Crown official actually drafted it.

Further upslope, around Huatusco de Chicuellar (the Huatusco at 1,300 meters elevation known as San Antonio during the sixteenth century), that process of effective resistance began by the 1560s and continued through the turn of the century. The native communities of the escarpment had better weathered the epidemics than those of the piedmont and coastal plain—for as yet unknown reasons—and received many grants for sheep estancias (AGN-M, vol. 7, ff. 217v, 219v-20; vol. 8, ff. 194-94v; vol. 11, f. 302; vol. 14, ff. 359v-60v; AGN-T, vol. 2687, exp. 28-29; vol. 2688, exp. 6; vol. 2702, exp. 15; vol. 2723, exp. 10; vol. 2735, pt. 2, exp. 3; vol. 2742, exp. 14; vol. 2773, exp. 11; vol. 2776, exp. 5; vol. 2782, exp. 11; vol. 2809, exp. 6.). Nonetheless, Huatusco de Chicuellar lost all but a small townsite, or fundo legal, as a result of fraud by ranchers during composición (Chevalier 1952, 358). The Valley of Oaxaca, where natives successfully retained control over many of their lands, owned sheep and cattle estancias, and even entailed estates, might represent the extreme of native resistance to Spanish space accumulation—but, again, only through adopting non-native terms of reference (Taylor 1972, 33-48). In other highland regions, such as the Valley of Mexico, Spaniards quickly and thoroughly usurped native lands (Gibson 1964, 274-79).

Material-Conceptual Feedback

Ultimately, the issue is not simply that taken-for-granted environmental and spatial categories allowed a few Spaniards to exploit the plasticity of land-use categorization, circumvent legislation intended to protect native communities, and thereby accumulate space. It is not simply that natives took decades to learn the effective use of those land-use categories to resist non-native space accumulation. And it is not simply that non-natives never learned native land-use categories, never saw the native landscape to which they applied their non-native conceptual models. Ultimately, the issue is that western categories became the taken-for-granted, be-all and end-all measures of productive land use. Understanding how, through a material-conceptual feedback process, they became and so doggedly remain dominant in global development/conservation discourse remains central to learning about alternatives and how to appreciate them.

To summarize the material and conceptual landscape transformations while rejoining them into a single material/conceptual process, systematic analysis of the land-grant documents demonstrates that the livestock invasion did not directly degrade the precolonial vegetation into the "dreary wilderness" that Sartorius reported in the nineteenth century. Nor had the interaction of precolonial land use, climate, and soils already produced such a landscape by 1519. Instead, precolonial land use had created a matrix of cultural savanna with patches of settlement and agriculture. That material landscape patterning together with landscape concepts diffused from Spain through the Antilles constituted the parameters for Cortés's vision of a pastoral landscape. Depopulation due to epidemics of introduced diseases created a moribund landscape, thickets invading former fields, cultural savannas, and settlements before the livestock. As the ranchers accumulated space and increasingly occupied the landscape with their herds and flocks after midcentury, they preempted the recovery of the surviving native population. By the turn of the century, livestock had almost entirely replaced people, thickets and pastures had replaced agriculture, and Cortés's colonial prospectus had become reality. Epidemiological and old-field successional processes thus resulted in a material landscape pattern that together with the conceptual landscape pattern inherent in such categories as baldío constituted the parameters for further landscape transformation. The recategorization of moribund as well as fallow native fields and orchards as wasteland, obscured the landscape modifications of native labor that would have hindered dispossession and made possible the recovery of native population and reversal of old-field succession.

A positive feedback loop between material and conceptual processes thus resulted in an inexorably unidirectional transformation into a depopulated landscape of livestock estancias. On the basis of that positive feedback loop between depopulation and recategorization of agricultural land as wasteland, the conceptual parameters manifested in the land-grant documents and maps became self-ratifying categories, materially precipitating the very landscape they erroneously described by visually validating their own conceptual parameters and erasing precolonial ones. Native communities continued to disappear during the spread of estancias up until the end of the first century of colonization. These lowlands consequently remained the near exclusive domain of vast cattle herds throughout the colonial period and into the early postcolonial period. Categorized as "wastelands" during the sixteenth century process that replaced people with cattle, these lowlands had become recategorized as "wilderness" by the early postcolonial period. To Sartorius and other nineteenth-century westerners, wilderness meant not only uninhabited but also untamed, wild, unproductive, and undeveloped—a category deriving from the Old English *wilddeoren*, a place where beasts (*deoren*, deer) ran wild (Olwig 1996, 382). Like baldío in the colonial period, such categories as wilderness were integral to the landscape transformation of the postcolonial period.

Notes

1. This and all subsequent Spanish-English translations in this chapter are by the author.

2. Table 5.2 lists the sources, organized by settlement, that provide the data for reconstructing population change.

Table 5.2. Sources of data on native population decline.

Settlement	Sources
Actopan	AGN-T, vol. 2688, exp. 40, f. 435; JGI, xxv-8, ff. 5v-6; Paso y Troncoso 1905, 5:241; Zavala and Castelo 1939-n.d., 4:408-9; 5:241; Paso y Troncoso 1939-1940, 14:81; Cook and Simpson 1948, 118; Velasco 1971, 113.
Alcocahua	AGN-T, vol. 2678, exp. 12, ff. 1-13v; AGN-M, vol. 10, ff. 61v-62, 244-45; Paso y Troncoso 1939-1940, 14:82.
Atezca/Atesca	AGN-T, vol. 2680, exp. 5, f. 98; Zavala and Castelo 1939-n.d., 2: 295; 4:302; Cook and Simpson 1948; Simpson 1950, 160-61; González de Cossio 1952, 277-78; Scholes and Adams 1955, 37; Acuña 1985, 120; Himmerich y Valencia 1991, 188, 225; Gerhard 1993, 373-75.
Boca del Río	Mota y Escobar 1939-1940, 215.
Cerro Gordo	NLC-Ayer, ms. 1121, f. 169v; AGN-M, vol. 17, ff. 116v-17; Zavala and Castelo 1939-n.d., 2:295.
Chicuasen	Paso y Troncoso 1905, 5:241; Zavala and Castelo 1939-n.d., 5:241; Paso y Troncoso 1939-1940, 14:81; Cook and Simpson 1948, 132; Velasco 1971, 113.

Table 5.2, continued.

Settlement	Sources
Cotaxtla	JGI, xxv-8, ff. 5v-6; Aguilar 1938, 97; Mota y Escobar 1939-1940, 210, 289-90; Zavala and Castelo 1939-n.d., 4:288; Paso y Troncoso 1939-1940, 9:5; 11:32-33; 13:36; 14:82; Cook and Simpson 1948; Simpson 1950, 160-61; González de Cossio 1952, 581-82; García Martínez 1969, 137-40, 157-60; Himmerich y Valencia 1991, 145-48; Gerhard 1993, 341-42, 364.
Espiche	JGI, xxv-8, ff. 5v-6; AGN-T, vol. 32, exp. 4, f. 91; vol. 2782, exp. 16, f. 3v; Paso y Troncoso 1905, 5:194; Paso y Troncoso 1939-1940, 13:38; 14:82; BAGN 1940, 209; Gerhard 1993, 360.
Huatusco/ Santiago Huatusco	BAGN 1936, 215; Mota y Escobar 1939-1940, 209-10, 289; BAGN 1940, 206; Cook and Simpson 1948; Simpson 1950, 160-61; Acuña 1985, 295; Himmerich y Valencia 1991, 130; Gerhard 1993, 83-84.
Jalcomulco	Zavala and Castelo 1939-n.d. 1:25-26; 4:302-4; Cook and Simpson 1948; Simpson 1950, 160-61; González de Cossio 1952, 277-78; Scholes and Adams 1955, 37; Acuña 1985, 120; Himmerich y Valencia 1991, 188, 225; Acuña 1985, 120-21; Gerhard 1993, 373-75.
Jamapa	AGN-T, vol. 2764, exp. 18, ff. 238, 245, 257v; AGN-M, vol. 12, ff. 87-87v; vol. 13, ff. 81v-82; Paso y Troncoso 1939-1940 14:82.
Medellín	AGN-M, vol. 15, ff. 191-92; AGN-T, vol. 2764, exp. 15, ff. 189v, 194; JGI, xxv-8, ff. 2v-3; Paso y Troncoso 1905, 5:191, 193-94; Cuevas 1914, 3; Paso y Troncoso 1939-1940, 1:84; 14:82; 15:83; Oviedo 1959, 4:188-89, 244; Gómara 1964, 326; Cervantes de Salazar 1985, 811; Cortés 1988, 199.
Mictanguautla	AGN-M, vol. 10, ff. 61-61v; AGN-T, vol. 2680, exp. 20, f. 253; vol. 2782, exp. 16, f. 3v; Paso y Troncoso 1892-1893, 2:331; Paso y Troncoso 1905, 5:194; García Pimental 1904, 12; Paso y Troncoso 1939-1940, 13:38; 14:82; Gerhard 1993, 360.
Oceloapan	AGN-M, vol. 8, ff. 190-90v; vol. 11, ff. 19-19v; Lyon 1971, 2:209.
Pangolutla/ Plan del Río	NLC-Ayer, ms. 1121, ff. 124v-25; AGN-M, vol. 11, ff. 38v-39; vol. 14, ff. 125-26; vol. 17, ff. 116v-17; Zavala and Castelo 1939-n.d., 1:25-26; 2:295; Paso y Troncoso 1939-1940, 9:22; Cook and Simpson 1948; Simpson 1950, 160-61; González de Cossio 1952, 277; Scholes and Adams 1955, 37; Ciudad Real 1976, 2:272; Gerhard 1993, 373-75.
Rinconada/ Iscalpa	AGN-M, vol. 8, f. 129; JGI, xxv-8, ff. 5v-6; Hakluyt 1904, 9:355; Paso y Troncoso 1905, 5:190; Gage 1928, 43; Paso y Troncoso 1939-1940, 9:5; 11:33; 13:38; 14:82; Cook and Simpson 1948; Simpson 1950, 160-61; González de Cossio 1952, 580-81, 585-86; García Martínez 1969, 137-40, 157-60; Ciudad Real 1976, 2:272; Himmerich y Valencia 1991, 145-48; Gerhard 1993, 341-42, 364.
San Francisco/ Cardel	AGN-M, vol. 5, f. 46v; vol. 6, ff. 227-27v; vol. 8, ff. 129-29v; ANX-Protocolo, vol. 1600-1608, ff. 413v-20v.
Santa María Tlatela	AGN-M, vol. 33, ff. 112v-18v; Paso y Troncoso 1939-1940, 9:32; González de Cossio 1952, 276; Himmerich y Valencia 1991, 189; Gerhard 1993, 363, 366.

Table 5.2, continued.

Settlement	Sources
Veracruz/ San Juan de Ulúa	NLC-Ayer, ms. 1121, ff. 104v-5, 124v-25; AGN-M, vol. 9, f. 97; vol. 10, ff. 266v-67; vol. 11, f. 153; vol. 12, f. 144; vol. 15, ff. 228v-29; vol. 16, f. 192v; vol. 17, f. 48v; vol. 18, ff. 136v-37, 142v-43v, 186v, 200v-1, 218-18v, 302v-3v; vol. 19, ff. 12, 103-3v, 115v-16, 123-23v; vol. 20, ff. 3v, 40-40v, 154-55, 165, 197v-98; vol. 21, ff. 31-31v, 34-34v, 305v-6, 316v, 343v-44, 362v-63v; vol. 22, ff. 25v, 35v-36, 75-75v, 125v-28v, 130v-31, 133-33v, 144v-45v, 160v, 216v-17; vol. 23, ff. 11-12, 46v-47, 49-49v, 52v-53, 54-54v, 65-65v, 79-80, 88v-89v, 93v-97v, 99-99v, 102-2v, 121v-22, 124v-25, 137v-38v, 147v-48v, 154-54v, 201-2v, 208v-9, 214-15v, 279v-80v, 364-64v; vol. 24, ff. 1-6v, 12v-13; 19-19v, 22-28v, 32-33v, 35v-36v, 39v-40, 44v-45v, 47v, 55v-56, 60-61v, 65v-66, 67-67v, 101v-2v, 113-13v, 144v-45, 172-72v; vol. 25, ff. 64-6v, 143-43v; vol. 26, ff. 52v-53, 64-65v, 72v-73, 108v-9; vol. 33, ff. 161v-62v, 276v-77; vol. 35, ff. 56v-57v, 127v-28, 190-91; vol. 36, ff. 144v-45v; Alegre 1841-1842, 1:52; García Icazbalceta 1858-1866, 1:495; Hakluyt 1904, 9:361; Paso y Troncoso 1905, 5:200; Díez de la Calle 1932, 157-58; Mota y Escobar 1939-1940, 215; Paso y Troncoso 1939-1940, 13:1-3, 198-200, 280-83; Vázquez de Espinosa 1948, 121; Oviedo 1959, 4:244; Velasco 1971, 110; Ciudad Real 1976, 1:118; 2:274.
Vera Cruz/ La Antigua Veracruz	NLC-Ayer, ms. 1121, ff. 124v-25; JGI, xxv-8, f. 7-7v; Alegre 1841-1842, 1:151; García Icazbalceta 1858-1866, 1:495; Pérez de Rivas 1896, 2:197-99; Hakluyt 1904, 9:355, 361; Paso y Troncoso 1905, 5:191-93; Latorre 1920, 108, 112; Gage 1928, 37-38; Mota y Escobar 1939-1940, 217; Paso y Troncoso 1939-1940, 13:1-3, 198-200, 280-83; 14:82; Vázquez de Espinosa 1948, 122; Oviedo 1959, 4:244; Velasco 1971, 109; Ciudad Real 1976, 1:117; 2:273.
Xamicolulco	JGI, xxv-8, ff. 5v-6.
Zempoala	AGN-T, vol. 32, exp. 4, f. 104; AGN-M, vol. 2, ff. 173v-74, 250v-53; vol. 6, ff. 218v-19; vol. 9, ff. 33-33v; vol. 15, ff. 43v-45, 169-69v; JGI, xxv-8, ff. 5v-6; Aguilar 1938, 97; Paso y Troncoso 1905, 5:193; Mota y Escobar 1939-1940, 218, 220; Paso y Troncoso 1939-1940, 1:141; 4:76-78; 14:82; BAGN 1940, 204; Oviedo 1959, 4:239; Simpson 1960, 89-93; Gómara 1964, 204-5, 377-78; Motolinía 1971, 10-11, 70, 294; Torquemada 1975-1983, 2:82-83; Díaz 1986, 244, 531.

3. After Viceroy Mendoza's currency standardization in 1538, both the peso de oro común and the peso de oro de minas were divided into eight *tomines*, or ninety-six *granos*. The peso de oro común was worth eight silver *reales*, equal to 272 *maravedís*. The peso de oro de minas was worth thirteen silver reales minus two maravedís, equal to 440 maravedís (Borah and Cook 1958, 9-10). Unless specified otherwise, documentary references to pesos probably refer to the peso de oro común, which was the peso of common circulation.

4. Most tribute paid in kind was maize; conversion to pesos follows Borah and Cook (1958, 17): 1540-1550, 0.25 pesos/fanega; 1550-1560, 0.375 pesos/fanega; 1560-1570,

0.5 pesos/fanega. The fanega denoted both quantity of maize, or other grains, and area of cultivation. One fanega de maíz equaled forty-six kilograms or 55.5 liters (Barnes et al. 1981, 73; Prem 1988, 295). One fanega de sembradura de maíz equaled 1/12 of a caballería, or 3.58 hectares (Carrera Stampa 1949, 20; Prem 1988, 295). One *braza* equaled two varas, and 1,000 square-brazas yielded on the order of 6.5 fanegas of maize, some 1,000 kilograms per hectare (Cook and Borah 1960, 19). Through simple regression, available data also allow conversion of the *ropa menuda* tribute for Cotaxtla into pesos: 1544, 9 pesos/*carga*; 1550, 14.5 pesos/carga; 1557, 20.5 pesos/carga; 1569, 30 pesos/carga (Borah and Cook 1958, 23-26, table 3). Tribute of ropa menuda refers to skirts or shirts, sold in lots of twenty known as cargas.

5. The following grants contain the vegetation data summarized in figure 5.10: AGN-M, vol. 6, ff. 199-99v, 207v-8; vol. 8, ff. 190-90v; vol. 9, ff. 5-5v, 30v-31, 33-33v, 108v-9, 115v-16; vol. 10, ff. 45v-46, 61-61v, 65v-66, 68v-69, 182-82v, 244-45, 266v-67; vol. 11, ff. 38v-40; vol. 12, ff. 5-6, 20v-21, 45v-46, 87-87v, 96-96v, 118-18v; vol. 13, f. 29v,-40v, 81v-82, 87-87v, 113-13v, 132v-33; vol. 14, ff. 80v-81v, 161v-62v, 359v-60v; vol. 15, ff. 25v-26v, 86-87, 169-69v, 191-92; vol. 17, ff. 25-25v; vol. 19, ff. 25, 30v-31, 48-49, 81-81v, 130-131; vol. 20, ff. 20-20v, 21v-23v, 36-36v, 112v-13, 114-14v, 117-18v, 119-19v, 141-42, 144-45, 198-99; vol. 21, ff. 6v-8, 47-48v, 55-55v, 103v-04, 110v-11; vol. 25, ff. 64-64v; vol. 29, ff. 128v-29; vol. 31, ff. 192-92v; vol. 33, ff. 112v-18v. AGN-T, vol. 32, exp. 4; vol. 2678, exp. 12, ff. 1-13v; vol. 2680, exp. 20, fc. 254; vol. 2688, exp. 40, f. 444; vol. 2702, exp. 12, ff. 8-9, 386-97v; vol. 2702, exp. 13, ff. 398-406v; vol. 2702, exp. 14, ff. 6, 407-16v; vol. 2764, exp. 15, fc. 188, fc. 193; vol. 2777, exp. 3, ff. 1-9v; vol. 2782, exp. 16; vol. 3331, exp. 1, ff. 1-9v.

6. The coyol espino (*Acrocomia mexicana*) succeeds disturbed woodlands; the coyol (*Scheelea liebmannii*) also thrives with disturbance, particularly periodic burning; both species yield edible fruits and thus encourage human protection (Santamaría 1959; Pennington and Sarukhan 1968).

7. Ceiba (*Ceiba pentandra*).

8. Xícaro (*Crescentia cujete*). Glyptodonts looked like giant armadillos.

6

The Postcolonial Landscape

From the Grito de Dolores in 1810 to victory over the Spaniards in 1821, a series of armed struggles for sovereignty ushered in postcolonial Mexico. Yet colonial transformations of material/conceptual landscape elements and patterns have persisted into the postcolonial period, far outlasting the end of European sovereign power. Postcolonization has, of course, greatly modified colonial landscapes, and this single chapter can but sketch the complex social/biophysical processes involved. The primary purpose is to consider how those processes elaborated in the chapters on colonial transformations have continued into the postcolonial period and with what consequences for development and conservation. The focus thus remains on landscape transformations involving livestock, agriculture, settlement, and vegetation.

Nineteenth-Century Immigration Schemes

To Sartorius—scientist, entrepreneur, and promoter of German settlement in newly independent Mexico—the early postcolonial lowlands for the most part constituted a wilderness in need of western development. The seeming overgrowth of thorny woodlands, sparse settlement, and dominance of extensive ranching over intensive agriculture defined that wilderness. He certainly recognized some of the vestiges of intensive agriculture left by dense precolonial populations. In fact, he reported more about them than had all of the colonial grant inspectors put together. Paradoxically, however, those vestiges of precolonial agriculture only strengthened his belief that development must proceed on the basis of western models and European immigrants (Mentz 1990, 22-45).

Sartorius somehow reconciled clear evidence that the precolonial Americas had not been pristine with the colonizer's model of the world, despite the myth of emptiness being essential to that model. On the one hand, he believed that ranching wasted the potential of the lowlands because the vestiges of precolonial terracing demonstrated that the soil and climate would support cultivation of tropical commodities such as coffee and sugar cane. On the other hand, he believed that Europeans rather than the descendants of the natives who had created the productive precolonial landscape would have to carry out the postcolonial development project. In order to reconcile that logical contradiction, he ascribed the precolonial vestiges to an antiquity so ancient as to lose all relation to native peoples. In fact, he somehow inferred that the people who had cultivated "every foot of land . . . as diligently . . . as the banks of the Nile or the Euphrates in Solomon's time" had "been extirpated before the Spaniards invaded the country" (Sartorius 1961, 10). He believed that some unknown people—seemingly, he implied, biblical migrants from the Old World—had created the terracing and cities. Native peoples had done nothing but destroy that wonderfully productive landscape. They themselves had then been destroyed by the Spaniards.

Such efforts to reconcile the myth of emptiness with evidence of highly productive precolonial landscapes permeates the writings of nineteenth-century westerners such as Sartorius and von Humboldt.

> When we consider that [natives] had an almost exact knowledge of the duration of the year . . . , we are tempted to believe that this progress is not the effect of the intellectual development of the Americans themselves, but that they were indebted for it to their communication with some very cultivated nations of central Asia (Humboldt 1966, 1:158-59).

> An impartial consideration and observation of the Indians during many years forced me to the conclusion: that, according to their bodily organization, they are incapable of so high a degree of intellectual development as the Caucasian race. . . . The religious systems of the Incas and Aztecs, their knowledge of astronomy, works of art, and mechanical labours for the purposes of every-day life, are the result of their powers of understanding, of the undeniable imitative talents of the whole race. . . . As yet we know not whether influences from the east may not have sown the first seeds of civilization (Sartorius 1961, 64).

Such taken-for-granted biases combined with others, such as the nineteenth-century liberal faith in laissez-faire economics, to equate postcolonial development with further westernization through European immigration and investment. Natives and mestizos were "undisturbed by any care for the future," imitative rather than innovative, and therefore incapable of rational land use without European leadership (Sartorius 1961, 64-66, 83). Development could not rely on natives, who represented the precolonial period. Nor could development count on mestizos, who represented the colonial contamination of the European by the native. Rather, postcolonial development must entirely assimilate both the precolonial native and the colonial mestizo by accelerating the process of westernization. European immigrant farmers would introduce western technologies and inculcate modernism among the natives and mestizos.

Yet none of the nineteenth-century schemes to promote European immigration achieved significant momentum, unlike the U.S. and Canadian experiences. Sartorius's own project failed because Germans favored Texas and points north over Veracruz. The Veracruz government also promoted immigrant colonization projects, involving Italian and French farmers, but none of those schemes have left much of a legacy in terms of ethnicity or otherwise (Stevens 1967; Skerritt 1993a). Resettlement of the Veracruz lowlands would have to await the Revolution of the early twentieth century. Only then would population increase to precolonial levels. Only then would large numbers of farmers begin to reoccupy the putative wilderness. And those farmers would be mestizos from the highlands rather than Europeans or natives.

Twentieth-Century Resettlement

Resettlement involved many processes. Among them, the agrarian reform that followed the social revolution of the 1910s allowed farmers to wrest space from the cattle barons. DDT overcame yellow fever. And hydrological engineering projects favored agricultural commodities over food.

A series of maps of municipal population density captures the broad patterns of the resettlement process (figure 6.1, figure 6.2). The national decadal census, the *Censo General de Población y Vivienda*, provides the population density estimates.[1] Such data generally suffer from changes in definitions of variables, ethnicity being notoriously difficult to track. Some particular censuses, such as that of 1980, are known to be unreliable. Such data also suffer from changes in census tract boundaries, and municipio boundaries in the study region have indeed shifted and names changed. Moreover, the municipal boundaries derived from the digital census database are much less precise than those of figure 4.7, not that a definitive map of municipios exists in any case (Cambrezy and Lascuráin 1992, 155-56). Nonetheless, even accepting a large margin of error, the sequence of maps serves to delineate some dramatic changes in the regional pattern of population density.

The 1910 map reflects the climax of hacienda dominance near the end of the dictatorship of Porfirio Díaz. Families had established haciendas as entailed estates, such as the Mayorazgo de la Higuera, during the colonial period. Several centuries of inheritance fractured and multiplied the haciendas, but at the same time hacendados incrementally appropriated more and more land (Hamon and Niblo 1975). Nineteenth-century liberals, zealous about privatization, alienated church lands and dismantled the colonial legislation that protected what little access to resources surviving native communities had retained. Many haciendas grew larger by appropriating ejidos, the Spanish institution of common lands

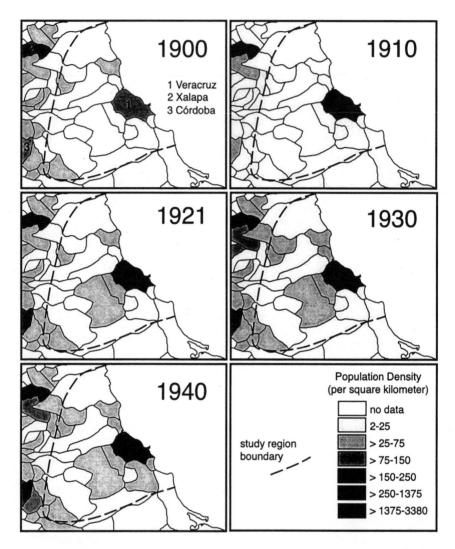

Figure 6.1. Population density by municipality according to the estimates of the decadal national census, 1900-1940.

intended to be used communally or rented to individuals but never alienated from the community (Butzer 1988, 44). More important even than enlarging property size, appropriating ejidos ensured hacendados access to a dependent, flexible labor supply. Deprived of access to the land to sustain themselves, people became tied to haciendas through debt peonage. Mexico's population in

1910 was more than thirteen million, some seventy percent of it rural. One percent of the population owned ninety-seven percent of the agricultural land, ninety-seven percent of rural families owned no land at all, and over half of all rural Mexicans lived and worked within the orbits of haciendas (Hamon and Niblo 1975, 16-17; Meyer and Sherman 1987, 457-60; *Estadísticas Históricas* 1990, 33; Ruiz 1992, 305-7). Poverty, hunger, and misery were endemic.

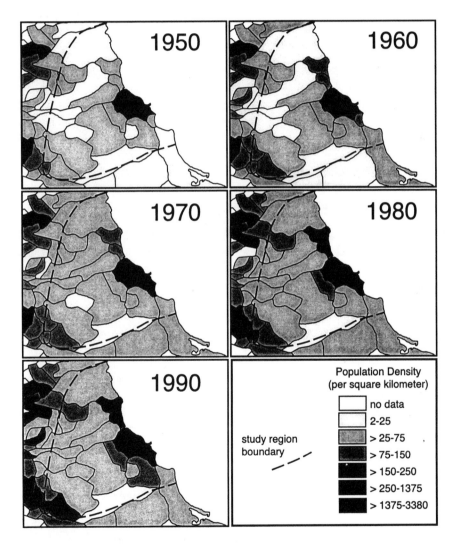

Figure 6.2. Population density by municipality according to the estimates of the decadal national census, 1950-1990.

The lack of cadastral maps for Veracruz precludes precise assessment of the degree of hacienda domination in 1910, but some three dozen haciendas controlled most of the study region in the same way that large landed estates controlled most of rural Mexico just before the close of the Porfiriato (Trens 1947, 444-56; Cambrezy and Lascuráin 1992, 9). Some of the hacendados had intensified their ranches, adopting more productive and palatable African grasses, replacing criollo stock with specialized breeds, and taking advantage of the railroad that had connected Veracruz and Mexico City in 1872 to sell beef and milk rather than hides and tallow (Skerritt Gardner 1989, 29-33). Some had increased sugar cane production. But those operations did not require that much more labor than those of the colonial period, and despite population increase over the nineteenth century, substantial in relative terms, the 1910 population of the same seventeen municipios used in the livestock analysis was only 62,589 (Skerritt Gardner 1989, 108-14).[2] Some seventy-eight percent lived in the municipio of Veracruz, in and immediately around the port. The other municipios had low population densities, the majority of the inhabitants being tenants tied to haciendas, the minority being hacendados, small property owners known as *rancheros*, and villagers living in small service centers strung along the transportation axes.

Many who joined the Revolution of 1910 wanted access to land, and the Constitution of 1917 promised agrarian reform. Article 27 mandated that ejido lands that hacendados had appropriated would be returned to communities. Moreover, any idle lands could be awarded to communities or individuals. The government would award ejidos to communities that would, in turn, award individual plots to the *ejidatarios* who made up the community or, much more rarely, work the land in common. Each *ejidatario* family thus held a usufruct share of the ejido but could not sell or otherwise alienate the land from the community.

The relative cessation of armed conflict after 1917 allowed the central government to assume nominal control, and a few communities received ejidos. A program of DDT spraying eradicated the mosquito vector of yellow fever, the 1920-21 epidemic being the last to strike Veracruz (Ojeda Falcón 1982). The resettlement evident in the 1921 map reflects the early stages of those processes. By 1921, the population of the seventeen municipios had risen to 138,229, with forty-two percent living in the urbanized municipio of Veracruz. The regional population had more than doubled since 1910, most of the immigrants attracted to rural municipios.

After 1924, armed conflict receded even further into the background as the Partido Nacional Revolucionario (PNR), now the Partido Revolucionario Institucional (PRI), ensured peaceful transitions of power from one president to the next.[3] Far from the promised revolution in land tenure, however, most PNR administrations merely dribbled out ejidos to communities; the concentration of land that had characterized the Porfiriato continued. Not until the term of President Lázaro Cárdenas, from 1934 to 1940, did a surge in ejido endowments occur. Cárdenas awarded some twenty million hectares during his six-year term, double the area awarded during the previous sixteen years, even taking the official figures at face value (Meyer and Sherman 1987, 599). By 1940, some 1.5 million ejidatarios controlled nearly half of Mexico's agricultural land, albeit often small, steep, dry, and stony plots (Cockcroft 1990, 135-39; Ruiz 1992, 398-400).

The decadal maps reflect the resettlement associated with ejido endowments, mitigation of yellow fever and malaria, elaboration of the transportation infrastructure, and the oil boom. The lack of cadastral maps frustrates any precise assessment of the current land tenure pattern and its formation through agrarian reform.[4] Violent encounters between the Guardia Blanca of the hacendados and the Liga de Comunidades Agrarias dominated social struggle before ejido endowments become significant during the Cárdenas administration (Fowler-Salamini 1978; Skerritt Gardner 1989, 170-89; Cambrezy and Lascuráin 1992, 135-47).[5] Since the 1930s, ejidos have occupied an increasing proportion of the agricultural land, about thirty-six percent of the total area of the seventeen municipios according to the *VII Censo Ejidal* of 1991. Large and small private properties occupy the rest. By 1990, the total population of the seventeen municipios was 776,066, some sixty-one percent living in the predominantly urban municipios of Veracruz and Boca del Río. Some quarter of a million people spread over the rest of the region, focusing on the coastal plain. Population over much of the region has thus risen to late precolonial levels. People have resettled a landscape after four centuries of domination by livestock.

That resettlement has been nearly exclusively mestizo. Since 1940 the census has recorded data on language and thereby facilitates an assessment of ethnicity. Excluding the notorious 1980 census, only three of the seventeen municipios ever recorded one percent or more Nahuatl or Totonac speakers: Apazapan in 1940 (1.3%), Boca del Río in 1950 (1%), and Paso del Macho in 1940 (1.1%). Native population instead concentrates in the municipios along the escarpment to the west.

Besides including few natives, the resettlement process also did not create a landscape dominated by food crops such as maize and beans—the Mexican staples. On the contrary, exotic biota dominate, fields of maize occupying mere interstices in a landscape of cattle ranches, sugar cane fields, and mango orchards. Those animals and plants, domesticated in Asia and brought to the Americas by Europeans, reflect the goal of postcolonial governments to westernize Mexico. The successive strategies have entailed import substitution, foreign investment and loans, and free trade (Cockcroft 1990, 150-54, 165-78; Ruiz 1992, 411-66). Those strategies have varied the mix of protective tariffs, subsidies and tax relief for industry, investment in energy and transport infrastructure, violent repression of dissent, and control of labor supply and cost. Yet all the plans have promoted the westernization of agriculture, the export of agricultural commodities, and the conversion of rural labor into urban, industrial capital. Agricultural modernization has promised to release rural labor for work in urban

industry, produce cheap food for the urbanizing workforce, produce cheap industrial inputs, and generate foreign exchange to pay for industrial capital
goods. In the study region, institutions such as the Banco Nacional de Crédito
Ejidal (BNCE) and, especially, the Comisión Nacional de Irrigación (CNI) and
its successors, the Secretaría de Recursos Hidráulicos (SRH) after 1947 and the
Secretaría de Agricultura y Recursos Hidráulicos (SARH) after 1976, have been
the primary state instruments promoting that transformation.[6]

Hydraulic Engineering

For the Veracruz lowlands, westernization would hinge on a radical hydrological transformation, initiated by the Cárdenas administration under the auspices
of the CNI (Siemens 1998, 197-203). The engineers saw themselves in a heroic
battle against the limitations of climate, topography, hydrology, and so-called
traditional culture. One agronomist even referred to the valley of the Actopan
River as "frankly hostile" (Skerritt Gardner 1993b, 17). Reports preserved in the
SRH archive exemplify the discourse.

> [They] give us many loaded words, flung as epithets: "traditional" above all
> others, "extensive" (which is almost as bad), and "irrational," or even "vi-
> cious." There is much "disorder"; the plants and animals are mostly *criollo*, the
> grasses are only "natural." On every hand is *subaprovechamiento*, a failure to
> take full advantage (Siemens 1998, 213).

In that discourse, development would require that ranching give way to intensive, irrigated agriculture just as presumably unsophisticated, extensive native
land use had given way to ranching during the colonial period. Varo and Virgil
had also believed in that teleological progression from savage to pastoral to agricultural, and now SRH hydraulic engineering would bring that telos to the
tropical lowlands (Glacken 1967, 141-42; Merchant 1996, 138-40). The "nasty
tropical swamps" were too wet and "poorly" drained, the encompassing coastal
plain and piedmont too dry for much of the year. The engineers would homogenize the hydrology through irrigation and drainage.

Over the course of several decades, the late 1930s through the early 1970s,
the engineers implemented at least some of their blueprints. They created two
irrigation districts. The La Antigua Irrigation District encompassed the lower
drainage of the La Antigua River, and the Actopan Irrigation District did the
same for the Actopan River (figure 6.3). By the 1950s, the two districts covered
a substantial stretch of coastal plain, some 24,000 hectares (SRH 1967, 89-91,
93-95). Dams across streams forced water into concrete-lined canals that carried
the flow along the contours, assisted by tunnels and siphons at obstructions. Hy-
drometric stations measured the flow and sediment load. Gates controlled the

Figure 6.3. Irrigation canal in the Actopan District. Photograph by the author, July 1991.

flow, shunting water from one subsystem to the next, from one field to the next, eventually into the field canals between the rows of sugar cane stalks and mango trees (figure 6.4). Drains carried any excess water away from the bottom lands and back into the streams. A local bureaucracy managed the system, collecting irrigation fees and enforcing maintenance agreements. Besides such canal irrigation projects, deep-well pump irrigation has made inroads on the piedmont, especially for mango and papaya orchards.

The hydraulic projects have diverse users. Between the two irrigation districts, 2,800 ejidatarios control about 14,500 hectares, or sixty percent of the area (SRH 1967, 89-91, 93-95). Their average plot size is 5.2 hectares, although most is farmed as large, collective sugar cane fields. The other 390 users, small and large private landowners, have an average property size of 24.4 hectares. But the largest landowners are far from average—Miguel Alemán, for example. He became governor of Veracruz in 1936, president of Mexico in 1946, and was one of the strongest proponents of hydraulic engineering projects based on the model of the Tennessee Valley (Skerritt Gardner 1989, 259-60; Siemens 1998, 203-7). His estate in the La Antigua Irrigation District, not far from Santa Anna's hacienda of Mango de Clavo was an immense, irrigated mango orchard. Only a cadastral reconstruction, an immense research undertaking given the lack of precise maps, would allow understanding of the processes that have created the twentieth-century agrarian landscape, with its division among ejidos, small private farms, and remnants of the haciendas.

Figure 6.4. Irrigation canals frame cane fields and pyramids at Zempoala. Photograph by the author, July 1991.

Ejidatarios clearly have paid for much of the hydraulic system, gaining access to the necessary capital through production contracts with regional sugar mills. Beyond direct conversion of ejido labor into agroindustrial capital, such as the requirement that irrigation users keep canal walls free of the rampant vegetation growth, users in 1965 paid 100 pesos to irrigate a hectare of sugar cane (SRH 1967, 91). The production contracts serve as collateral to secure BNCE loans to purchase such inputs as water and fertilizer. Colonial mills long produced small amounts of cane liquor, molasses, and cakes of coarse sugar for local consumption. Just before the Revolution some of those mills started to mechanize in order to produce granular sugar for the national market (García de la Rivera 1985). After the Revolution, the mills of El Modelo and La Gloria fully mechanized and began to produce refined granular sugar for the international market (figure 6.5). The two mills control some cane fields but rely on contracts with ejidatarios for much of their raw material.

Despite that reoccupation of the lowlands by agriculturalists, ranching has persisted. In fact, more head now graze the region than during the Porfiriato. Between 1902 and 1991, the number of SLU for the seventeen municipios has soared from 34,204 to 234,142, the average density from 0.071 to 0.486 SLU per hectare (figure 6.6). All municipios except Boca del Río, which has become a densely built-up suburb of Veracruz, have increased in SLU density. The highest density municipios ring the port of Veracruz, which at nearly half a million inhabitants has become a large market for meat and dairy products as well as a

Figure 6.5. The La Gloria sugar mill, just across the Actopan River from Zempoala. Photograph by the author, July 1991.

major trans-shipment facility. Even in those municipios where sugar ejidos dominate, particularly La Antigua and Ursulo Galván, 1991 SLU densities far exceed those of 1902. The loss of pasture to urbanization and agriculture since 1902 implies that the 1991 SLU densities for actual pastures are even higher than the municipal-level data suggest and that ranching has continued to intensify. Ranchers have adopted hybrid fodder crops such as Merkeron, crosses between Zebu and European dairy cattle, and techniques such as artificial insemination, dip tanks, and the excavation of drainage ditches across the backswamps. The colonial pattern of local transhumance persists to some degree, but modifications such as drainage ditches allow more flexibility in the timing of the movement of cattle between wetlands and hill lands (Cisneros Solano et al. 1993, 223; Del Angel P. 1994, 210-13). In both wetlands and piedmont, cultivated pasture of African grasses now predominates. Pastures of Guinea grass, its dense root system adapted to a long dry season, dominate on the piedmont among the deciduous shrublands, woodlands, and areas with vegetation cover so sparse they elude classification on land-cover maps (INEGI 1984). On the coastal plain, pastures of Pará grass do well in the more humid conditions, with African star grass dominating along waterways.[7]

Like the colonial ranchers, neither the ejidatarios nor the SRH engineers seem to have noticed the remains of precolonial agriculture in the wetlands or on the piedmont. The assumption has been that just as colonial ranching had presumably improved on precolonial land use, agroindustrial production of commodities such as sugar is an intensification of land use over ranching and ipso

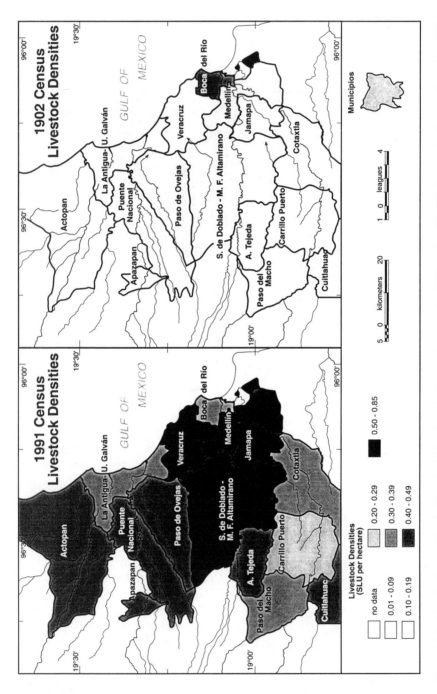

Figure 6.6. Livestock densities in Standard Livestock Units per hectare for 1991 and 1902 (*VII Censo Agrícola y Ganadero 1991; Estadística Ganadera 1903*).

facto a rational improvement. In a logical maneuver similar to that of Sartorius, the nationalistic indigenist rhetoric, or *indigenismo*, has reconciled retention of the pristine myth with glorification of the precolonial past by celebrating urban architecture, Aztec military heroes, and the long-gone Classic Maya—always measured against western benchmarks (Zea 1975; Pozas and Pozas 1971; Cockcroft 1990, 147-48). Thus the Maya became the Greeks of the New World while living natives and their land-use practices became categorically "traditional," too conservative to actively participate in economic development models that focus on the diffusion and adoption of western institutions and technologies. The diverse landraces of maize and other crops actively created and maintained by native peoples become crops that the ancients left behind, museum specimens frozen in time. The vestiges of precolonial agriculture, just beyond the pale of touristic ruins such as Zempoala, remain largely unseen, unsung, and irrelevant.

Alternatives

In both obscuring the intensive agriculture of the precolonial landscape and constituting an extensive land use, the ranching of the colonial period together with development concepts diffused from the West became the parameters for the vision of postcolonial land-use planners. The resulting agroindustrial landscape further obscures the precolonial vestiges that suggest native, sustainable alternatives to western, orthodox development. Only recently have the vestigial wetland and terraced fields become apparent (Siemens 1983; Sluyter and Siemens 1992; Siemens 1998). And only even more recently have such native agroecologies become elements in an effort to achieve so-called sustainable development.

Sustainable Development

The concept of sustainable development has emerged not out of recognition that orthodox development exacerbates the very social inequities that it claims to redress, but out of recognition that it causes unprecedented environmental degradations of global extent that threaten "developed" and "developing" peoples alike (Sachs 1992; Wilbanks 1994; Peet and Watts 1993; Porter and Sheppard 1998). Diverse reactions to the failures of orthodox development have created a widespread zeal for sustainable development despite the lack of thorough conceptualization and the sorts of coherent, easily digestible models that characterize and unify orthodox development. As one major point of contention in those diverse reactions, some believe in the possibility of sustainable development that does not include radical political-economic restructuring while others argue that processes inherent to capitalism preclude the management of resources even for sustained yield let alone for social and environmental well-being (O'Connor 1994). Nonetheless, the broad embrace of sustainable development, no matter how malleable the concept and quite probably because of that characteristic, represents a radical departure from the disregard for environmental parameters so characteristic of orthodox development. Enthusiasm for sustainable development undoubtedly will wane without convincing theorization of just how it might actually erase the global divide in well-being while conserving environmental qualities such as biodiversity. At this point, an emerging science of sustainability can no more than promise the necessary intellectual coherence for understanding how "to meet the needs of a much larger but stabilizing human population, to sustain the life support systems of the planet, and to substantially reduce hunger and poverty" (NRC 1999, 31).

As the birthplace of the Green Revolution, Mexico exemplifies the most egregious failures of orthodox development and the need for sustainable alternatives (Sanderson 1986; Toledo 1989; Wright 1990; McGlade 1997). According to the 2000 decadal census, Some twenty-seven million Mexicans, nearly a third of the population, live in extreme poverty and suffer from chronic hunger and malnourishment (Althaus 2000). Mexicans have invested so much in industrialized agriculture in such places as Veracruz but import maize, nearly a quarter of all that they consumed in the early 1990s (McGlade 1997, 330). The Green Revolution promised so much, but its mania for high labor productivity and commodification causes hyper-urbanization and associated poverty. Its pesticides and herbicides cause pollution. And its intolerance for heterogeneity destroys forests, streams, and biodiversity. Mexico urgently requires sustainable alternatives to orthodox development, alternatives through which people will at a minimum gain the most basic dietary elements of well-being while conserving environmental quality.

Native Ecologies

In particular, the failures of orthodox development have emphasized the need for alternatives to one of its foundational strategies, namely the obsessive diffusion of knowledge, technology, and institutions from the West to the non-West. The knowledges of native peoples constitute the most direct alternatives to westernization. In contrast to a generalized, global knowledge, native knowledges have rooted for many generations in particular places (Altieri 1987; Browder 1989; Gliessman 1990; Carruthers 1997; Berkes 1999). The ecological knowledges and practices of the very cultures that Europeans colonized—native ecologies— have thus come to seem more like the necessary alternatives to an unsustainable westernization than obstacles that orthodox development characterizes as "too traditional" to participate in creating the future.

Research on contemporary native ecologies, so-called ethnoecology, demonstrates that they achieve high productivity and sustainability through mimicking the complex forms and processes of environments undisturbed by humans (Wilken 1987; Altieri 1987; Clay 1988; Gliessman 1990; Jackson 1994). In terms of agroecologies alone, typical characteristics of such mimesis include polyculture, biodiversity, native plants, intercropping, recycling, minimal tillage, biological pest and weed control, and continuous innovation. Such low-tech, high-skill agriculture results in high yields per unit area, energy efficiency, and environmental conservation (Netting 1993). The recent emergence of a "new" ecology, one that emphasizes the histories and spatial heterogeneities of ecosystems, has led to the emergence of applied models such as ecosystem management and adaptive management that aspire to replicate the dynamism, particularism, and holism of native ecologies (Botkin 1990; Aley et al. 1999). Those models contrast with the efforts of the last several generations of ecologists, who labored under the teleological myths of the West to incorporate poorly supported hypotheses and overly simplistic successional and equilibrium models into the complex realities of development and conservation efforts. With hindsight, then, the intricate fit between local parameters and native ecologies has come to seem more appropriate than the attempts of the central planners to impose homogeneity and equilibrium (Doolittle 1984, 1989; Zimmerer and Young 1998).

Complementary historical research, so-called historical ecology, demonstrates the long-term sustainability of such native ecologies (Denevan 1970). Historical ecologists struggle to produce functional understandings of defunct native ecologies in anything like the detail possible for ethnoecologists. But historical research has demonstrated the sustainability, over millennia in some cases, of native ecologies (Sluyter 1994). Because both "native" and "sustainable" connote a substantial time span, historical ecology rather than ethnoecology must address the sustainability of native ecologies. The concept of nativity implies a multigenerational relationship between a group of people and a place; that of sustainability implies the long-term viability of that human-environment relationship. (Both also connote a particular area, one extensive enough to sustain but small enough to know intimately.) Moreover, only historical ecology can recover native knowledge lost during centuries of colonialism.

On the basis of such research, the belief that native ecologies can serve as models for environmental conservation and sustainable development efforts, considered idiosyncratic just a generation ago, has become mainstream (Chambers 1994; Warren 1999). Institutionally, the process of valuing native ecologies rather than attempting to eliminate them as supposedly premodern vestiges accelerated with the same publication that popularized the term sustainable development: the Brundtland Report, commissioned by the United Nations (UN) and published in 1987 as *Our Common Future* (WCED 1987, 114-16; Carruthers 1997, 260-62). Within half a decade, the 1992 UNEP Conference on Environment and Development had codified TEK as acceptable, even desirable, in the *Rio Declaration* and *Agenda 21* (UN 1992, 1993).

> Indigenous people and their communities have an historical relationship with their lands and are generally descendants of the original inhabitants of such lands. . . . They have developed over many generations a holistic traditional scientific knowledge of their lands, natural resources and environment. . . . In

view of the interrelationship between the natural environment and its sustainable development and the cultural, social, economic and physical well-being of indigenous people, national and international efforts to implement environmentally sound and sustainable development should recognize, accommodate, promote and strengthen the role of indigenous people and their communities (UN 1993, 227).

Other international agreements originating in that same conference, the so-called Earth Summit, have reiterated the importance of native ecologies—Article 8-j of the Convention on Biological Diversity, for example. And in parallel with that institutionalization, of course, the acronyms have proliferated: TK, traditional knowledge; IK, indigenous knowledge; ITK, indigenous technical knowledge; IKS, indigenous knowledge systems; and CBNRM, community-based natural resource management, a participatory development and conservation model closely related to TEK.

If Mexico exemplifies the failures of orthodox development, it also exemplifies centuries of denigration of native ecologies, as Sauer noted half a century ago, and their recent revaluation in parallel with the growing political power of native peoples. As a conservative estimate, between ten and fourteen percent of Mexicans are natives, and they make up more than thirty percent of the population in a quarter of all municipios (Carruthers 1997, 260). In the last several decades, natives have increasingly asserted themselves against rampant westernization. Something of a climax occurred in January 1994 when the Ejército Zapatista Liberación Nacional (EZLN) rose in arms against the North American Free Trade Agreement (NAFTA) and the amendment of Article 27 that allowed the privatization of ejido lands.[8] The Zapatistas fight against the myopic orthodox development vision that continues to escalate the very problems its ideologues claim to be solving, and that continues to destroy native peoples, their places, and the generations of local knowledges that weave them together.

Redeploying Precolonial Agroecologies

As elsewhere, then, in Mexico support for native peoples has grown and converged with support for sustainable development. In the example most relevant to Veracruz, the Instituto Nacional de Investigaciones sobre Recursos Bióticos (INIREB), headquartered in Xalapa, has redeployed precolonial intensive wetland agriculture—a native, by definition, agroecology—as a primary component of a plan for sustainable development (Gómez-Pompa et al. 1982).[9] Intensive wetland agriculture promises to alleviate the situation of many ejidatarios and the owners of small private farms by providing an alternative to the Green Revolution's appetite for relatively flat, well-drained land while many farmers have access only to rocky slopes and wetlands. If the many wetlands of Veracruz and the other Gulf Coast states could become productive components of integrated farms that produce high yields—high per unit area, not necessarily high per hour of labor—of food crops, then rural people would be able to significantly increase their level of well-being and not be forced to migrate to a desperate existence in the burgeoning cities. Integrated farms would thus emerge from the wetlands that westernization has marginalized. And they would do so not by draining wetlands but by modifying them in a way that sustains their hydrology and biodiversity.

The discovery, beginning in the late 1960s, of the vestiges of precolonial intensive wetland agriculture along the Gulf Coast lowlands from Campeche to Veracruz provided the direct stimulus for INIREB's redeployment of that agroecosystem. Nearly indiscernible at ground level, the vestiges become readily apparent from the air. The microtopography of sedimented canals and eroded, but still slightly higher and drier, planting platforms creates lineations of dark green hydrophytes separated by lighter toned vegetation. Yet the origin of that vegetation patterning long remained far from apparent. Many archaeologists must have seen the patterning while flying into such ruins as Tikal. SRH engineers and agronomists studied topography with large-scale aerial photographs that record the patterning. Such lineations in wetlands, however, seemingly unrelated to glamorous Maya ruins, seemingly in unproductive "swampland," did not elicit any interest among either archaeologists or agronomists. Nor did the people, native and otherwise, who fish and hunt in the wetlands understand the origins of the microtopography and vegetation patterning they encountered at ground level. Then, in 1968, Alfred H. Siemens observed wetland patterning from a small plane over Campeche and recognized the significance (Siemens 1998, 1-11). His research focused on twentieth-century resettlement, but he was familiar with similar patterning in South American wetlands that James Parsons and William Denevan were investigating and had already identified as vestiges of precolonial agriculture. Excavations soon confirmed that the Campeche patterning also represents the vestiges of precolonial intensive wetland agriculture (Siemens and Puleston 1972). During the 1970s, systematic aerial reconnaissance supplemented by several fortuitous sightings revealed many field complexes in wetlands along both flanks of the Yucatan peninsula and in Veracruz (Siemens 1983a; Sluyter 1994). To archaeologists, those vestiges of intensive agriculture suggest that precolonial lowland peoples had not subsisted exclusively on extensive, so-called slash-and-burn agriculture and that population densities had been much higher than previously believed. To historical ecologists, the vestiges suggest a way of sustaining the rapidly growing lowland population, the very phenomenon Siemens had been studying in Campeche in the 1960s. Those twentieth-century lowland colonists might be able, as had their precolonial predecessors, to grow food in wetlands without destroying those wetlands, a radical alternative to the prevailing processes of deforestation, drainage, and agroindustrialization.

Yet while such discoveries might have stimulated INIREB to redeploy intensive wetland agriculture in the lowlands, the chinampas of the Basin of Mexico provided the model for construction and function. Given the lack of extant lowland fields, historical ecologists have struggled to understand their construction and function. Clearly they were a way of manipulating soil moisture in places otherwise too wet to crop, at least for part of the year. But whether the planting platforms were raised above the original surface or represent remnants of that surface left between the canals, whether dams controlled water levels or not, whether planting surfaces seasonally flooded or not, what crops had been grown, how nutrients had been cycled, how much construction and function varied in time and space, and nearly every other issue remains, to some degree, under investigation. In contrast, understanding of the construction and function of the chinampas of the Basin of Mexico, while imperfect, far exceeds understanding of the lowland vestiges. The chinampas constitute the main extant example of precolonial intensive wetland agriculture, albeit much reduced from their sixteenth-century extent. Historical ecology and ethnoecology have together yielded a model of chinampa construction and function as well as suggesting their sustainability over several millennia (Sluyter 1994). Canals separate planting platforms built up out of alternating layers of lake mud and vegetation (figure 6.7). Willow trees line the edges of the platforms to stabilize them. Platforms range around ten meters in width and one hundred meters in length. The water in the canals dampens temperature fluctuations, thus mitigating frost damage, subirrigates the crops by infiltrating the platforms, and harbors fish. Mud from the canal bottoms provides fertilizer. Overall, the chinampas have a rectilinear plan, with ranks of rectangular fields separated by canals on which boats carry produce to market. Such features combine in a labor intensive

Figure 6.7. Chinampas at Xochimilco. Photograph by the author, June 1988.

system to produce sustainably high yields per unit area. The chinampas, therefore, became INIREB's model for the redeployment of lowland intensive wetland agriculture.

During the 1970s and early 1980s, INIREB worked with chinampa farmers from the Basin of Mexico, known as *chinamperos*, to build fields based on the chinampa model in Veracruz and Tabasco (Gómez-Pompa et al. 1982). Near Zempoala, INIREB built an experimental field complex at its La Mancha Biological Research Station in order to study biodiversity, nutrient cycling, yields, labor intensity, and other issues. The most ambitious project, however, was the *camellones* Chontales of Tabasco—part experiment, part demonstration, and part CBNRM. Backers included the Tabasco and federal governments, the Inter-American Foundation (IAF), the Instituto Nacional Indigenista (INI), and the community of Chontal natives who would farm the fields.[10] The project was so ambitious in scale that instead of manually building up fields out of alternating layers of mud and plants, INIREB employed large mechanical dredges to build sixty-five platforms, called camellones, each about thirty meters across and one hundred to three hundred meters long. The Chontal people themselves did not participate in the construction, only in the subsequent farming.

Initially, the camellones Chontales did not meet expectations. Mac Chapin of Cultural Survival, an organization that advocates for the rights of native peoples, has done the most to publicize the failings. In 1987, on behalf of the IAF, he surveyed several of the INIREB projects, including the camellones Chontales. He published his conclusions in *Grassroots Development* and *The DESFIL Newsletter*, the first a publication of the IAF and the second a publication of the Development Strategies for Fragile Lands Project (Chapin 1988a, 1988b). Chapin claimed that the chinampa model had so "seduced" INIREB, blinding its director, Arturo Gómez-Pompa, and others to the flawed assumptions of their project (Chapin 1988a; 1991). The series of miscalculations seemed to support that conclusion. The use of dredges had inverted the soil profile, burying fertile lake mud underneath infertile clay and necessitating application of large amounts of imported organic matter and fertilizer to achieve acceptable yields. The dredges had also made the canal bottoms so irregular that the Chontal could not use their dragnets to fish. The crops, mainly vegetables grown on the Basin of Mexico chinampas, were exotic to the Chontal and oriented to market rather than subsistence. The great diversity of lowland insects only added to the project's failings by requiring application of large amounts of insecticide.

The chinampa model, then, while native to Mesoamerica, diffused from the highlands to the lowlands with discouraging initial results. Chapin's overall conclusion, that such diffusion amounts to the imposition of yet another exogenous model, certainly seems warranted since wetland field vestiges do not even occur in Tabasco. One reason might be that the Tabasco wetlands generally have a much greater annual fluctuation in water level than those of Campeche and Veracruz. Regardless, none of the known lowland field vestiges more than superficially resemble the chinampas. The chinampas have large rectangular platforms, occur in lakes, and their surfaces do not flood annually. The lowland fields have much smaller platforms, interconnected in labyrinthine, curvilinear patterns, occur in backswamps, and their surfaces probably flooded every wet season, bringing an increment of nutrients and drowning pests and weeds. Even discounting that the dredges resulted in camellones Chontales that are but super-ficial implementations of the chinampa model, that model has no precedent in the wetlands of Tabasco or even in those of Veracruz and Campeche.

Notably, despite the initial failings, the camellones Chontales began to pro-duce more positive results once the Chontal actually took control (Gómez-Pompa 1990). Before the project, the Chontal village of three hundred families was crushed between the wetland and cattle ranches (Chapin 1988a, 12-14). Only some thirty families had any farmland at all, the largest plots being about half a hectare. Many more families now have adequate farmland. They have de-emphasized the vegetable market production INIREB promoted in favor of maize, beans, and bananas for household consumption. They combine that farm-ing with wage labor in the nearby city of Villahermosa. The fields certainly do not function as chinampas, but they have significantly improved the level of well-being without obliterating the wetland environment.

Such involvement by locals has been successful elsewhere as well. Quechua and Aymara farmers have revamped more than a hundred hectares of long aban-doned, intensive wetland fields at Lake Titicaca (Erickson and Candler 1989; Erickson 1992). Historical ecological research provided an initial model for field construction and function, but the local farmers have implemented and incre-mentally adjusted that model. The project has accomplished both of its goals: an experimental test of construction and cultivation techniques hypothesized on the basis of excavations, and the production of bumper potato crops. In Veracruz, even while INIREB was diffusing the chinampa model to the lowlands, locals had been reinventing fields more appropriate to the backswamp context, initially motivated but subsequently discouraged by changes in Mexican economic pol-icy (Siemens 1990b). As noted in chapter 2, some farmers near Zempoala culti-vate the margin of a wetland. Toward the end of the dry season, they plant maize in seedbeds in the still humid wetland soil. As the rains begin in May, before the seedbeds flood, the farmers transplant the maize seedlings to piedmont fields. That strategy advances the crop's growth far enough by the canícula, the August dry period which typically lasts one to two weeks, to mitigate its worst effects.

Chapin's critique of the camellones Chontales elicited many responses that emphasized the profound differences between those who envision development as further westernization and those who envision development that includes, even emphasizes, non-western knowledges. Of the many and varied responses—recorded as letters and a running debate in *Grassroots Development* and *The DESFIL Newsletter* in 1989 and 1990—an agronomist best represents the ortho-dox perspective.

I enjoyed Mac Chapin's very forthright article. My only concern was the editorializing in the subtitle—"Can an agricultural technology devised by the Aztecs rescue today's small farmers from the excesses of the Green Revolution?"— might more accurately have read, "Can agronomy protect village people against the romantic ideology of the agroecologists?" Certainly no self-respecting agronomist would promote the transfer of technology to farmers without adequate testing under both experimental and field conditions.

The agronomist clearly missed the essence of Chapin's critique: centrally planned projects, whether based on western or native ecologies, conceived and tested by agronomists and then transferred to local peoples, typically fail to increase well-being let alone do so in sustainable ways, either socially or environmentally. Historical and ethnoecologists, much more reflectively and self-critically, recognized that INIREB had indeed abstracted a native agroecology from its appropriate context—"seduced," as Chapin observed, by the sustainability and productivity of the chinampas. Native ecologies in and of themselves cannot provide a sustainable alternative to orthodox development. But while native "agricultural methods are not necessarily successfully transferable to different times, environments, and cultures . . . ; the same is true, of course, of modern [, western] methods" (Denevan 1995, 37). Native ecologies can, however, provide alternatives that when redeployed in dynamic ways allow for learning and change by the people who use those systems. As Siemens pointed out in his letter, the most seductive model of all has been that of agroindustrialization, which continues to receive vast amounts of funding despite failing to live up to its promises. That observation seems particularly apt regarding projects that are literally and figuratively cast in concrete, the users unable to make ongoing adjustments to dynamic local conditions, as in the case of the Actopan and La Antigua Irrigation Districts but not in the case of the camellones Chontales.

Notes

1. The digital database is called SIMBAD (Sistema de Información Municipal de Bases de Datos), available at www.inegi.gob.mx/basededatos/espanol/simbad.html. SIMBAD provided the municipio boundary files as well as the population data from the *XI Censo General de Población y Vivienda* of 1990. All other data derived from microfilm copies of the decadal census.

2. The seventeen municipios are Actopan, Adalberto Tejeda, Apazapan, Boca del Río, Carrillo Puerto, Cotaxtla, Cuitlahuac, Jamapa, La Antigua, Manlio Fabio Altamirano, Medellín, Paso de Ovejas, Paso del Macho, Puente Nacional, Soledad de Doblado, Ursulo Galván, Veracruz.

3. Partido Nacional Revolucionario (Revolutionary National Party), Partido Revolucionario Institucional (Institutional Revolutionary Party).

4. Incidentally, the lack of cadastral maps also frustrates localization of the sixteenth-century land grants by working backward from current property boundaries (Cambrezy and Lascuráin 1992, 4-5, 133-34).

5. Guardia Blanca (White Guards), Liga de Comunidades Agrarias (League of Agrarian Communities). Another violent group that operated in Veracruz to preserve the concentration of land ownership and dominance of ranching over farming was the so-called Mano Negra, or Black Hand (Skerritt Gardner 1989, 239).

6. Banco Nacional de Crédito Ejidal (National Bank of Ejidal Credit), Comisión Nacional de Irrigación (National Commission of Irrigation), Secretaría de Recursos Hidráulicos (Secretariat of Hydraulic Resources), Secretaría de Agricultura y Recursos Hidráulicos (Secretariat of Agriculture and Hydraulic Resources).

7. Guinea grass (*Panicum maximum*), Pará grass (*Brachiaria mutica*), African star grass (*Cynodon nlemfluensis* and *C. plectostachyus*).

8. Ejército Zapatista Liberación Nacional (Zapatista National Liberation Army).

9. Instituto Nacional de Investigaciones sobre Recursos Bióticos (National Institute for Research on Biotic Resources).

10. Instituto Nacional Indigenista (National Indigenist Institute), a federal agency similar in function to the U.S. Bureau of Indian Affairs.

7

Colonialism, Landscape, and the Future of Geography

This chapter returns to broader theoretical issues. First, the case study provides a test of the suitability of the colonial triangle as a basis for developing a comprehensive geographical theory of colonialism and landscape in relation to conservation and development applications. Second, a closer consideration of the congenital relationship between geography and colonialism suggests why such an effort, despite its academic and practical significance, has not been a disciplinary priority and why it should be.

The Colonial Triangle: Evaluation and Extrapolation

The case study generally confirms the utility of the conceptual framework established in chapter 1 (figure 1.7). That colonial triangle encompasses several major aspects of the colonization process for the Veracruz lowlands. Epidemic disease, expansion of ranching, desettlement, and other processes relate changes in the three elements: landscape, natives, and non-natives. Those processes entailed much more than unilateral impositions—of exotic biota or categories, for example—with the outcome predetermined by the "intrinsic natures" of natives and non-natives. Rather, those processes entailed dynamic interactions among the changing elements, relationships that were reciprocal and, potentially at least, equal in both directions. The colonial triangle facilitates the integration of the diverse social/biophysical processes involved into a unified understanding of material/conceptual landscape transformation at the regional scale of analysis (figure 7.1). The conceptual transformation cannot be understood without

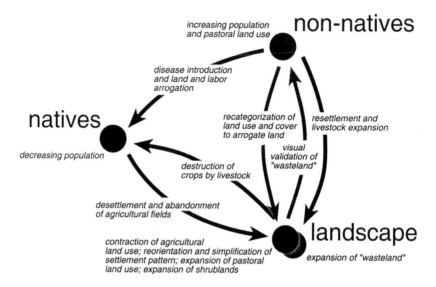

Figure 7.1. Major aspects of the colonization process for the Veracruz lowlands, emphasizing the sixteenth century.

understanding the material transformation and vice versa; likewise, social and biophysical processes so interweave that they can only be understood together.

That transformation so obscured the productive precolonial landscape that orthodox development has ignored native ecologies that might provide more conservationist, sustainable alternatives to continued westernization. Only recently has western science begun to achieve even a basic understanding of defunct native agroecosystems such as intensive wetland agriculture. The lesson learned from attempts to redeploy them is that western expertise must interface with native expertise in a dynamic, open-ended, flexible process rather than through the imposition of a static model intended to be a final solution. Local idiosyncrasies can thereby draw on a global resource as opposed to having a global imperative subsume local idiosyncrasies. Such initiatives hold out the promise of beginning to achieve alternatives to the utopianism of universal solutions as well as to that of radical particularism.

The case study certainly does not address all aspects of the colonization process. No brief case study can address all processes, and the role of the church, for example, receives almost no attention relative to the role of secular institutions such as mercedes. In the case of some processes that do receive attention, lack of data hobbles fuller elaboration. Figure 7.1 for that reason does not warrant an arrow from the native to the non-native element. The archives only hint at a few instances of native agency, such as defying congregación by moving back to Zempoala, but not enough to demonstrate let alone understand such processes. Moreover, the focus on the relationship between natives and non-natives overshadows the internal dynamics of each element. That issue becomes more problematic with time: first as the non-native population becomes more diverse, including more women and African slaves, for example; second as the distinction between native and non-native becomes more equivocal in terms of both ethnicity and residency. By the postcolonial period the colonial triangle no longer suffices, hence its absence from chapter 6. More research might fill some of those gaps; others will forever lack suitable data.

Beyond generating more data, however, further research must refine the colonial triangle—extrapolating and adapting it to other case studies. The type and degree of such alterations will only become evident through a process of scholarly critique on the basis of application to regional case studies throughout the Americas. That effort must go well beyond any single scholar to become a disciplinary priority. Defining a suite of complementary case studies for the Americas alone will require collaboration. Developing the data sources and analytic methods necessary to operationalize the conceptual structure for each of those case studies will require intensive, perhaps multidisciplinary, focus on each case study. And developing integrative methods and means of representation to integrate the resulting models at the hemispheric scale will require involved methodological expertise that can translate among the complexities of the case studies.

Selecting a coherent group of complementary case studies requires inclusion of the range of cultural and environmental contexts. Each case should differ in terms of the dominance of particular processes because of different social relations, economies, environments, periods of colonization, and so on. Such a group of case studies would permit the identification of types of regional material/conceptual formations, each having undergone distinctive transformative processes and each being involved in particular ongoing social/environmental challenges. To illustrate, settler and extractive colonization would have entailed distinct material/conceptual interactions among natives, non-natives, and landscapes. Settler colonization is associated with a landscape transformation that removes natives and accumulates space for non-natives, while extractive colonization is associated with a landscape transformation that exploits native labor or non-native forced labor. In terms of racial categorizations alone, in relation to such material transformations of landscape and labor, the natives of North America impeded space accumulation and became a "dying race with a naturally weak constitution" while African Americans labored on plantations and became a "fecund race endowed with a primal virility and sense of rhythm" (Wolfe 1997, 419). Strikingly, Australian Aborigines, while as dark skinned as African Americans, also impeded European space accumulation and became as much a "dying race" as Native Americans. Another commonality of settler colonization has been that, in both Australia and North America, one of the environmental consequences of native desettlement has been a radical change in fire regimes, with continuing effects on vegetation composition. The U.S. Northeast, for example, experienced an alteration of fire regimes due to native depopulation in mixed oak forests, cessation of native-set fires to manage vegetation and game, and consequent diffusion of a European fire suppression paradigm (Pyne 1997, 30; Sluyter et al. 1998). The associated shift in fire frequency and intensity seems to be related materially to the now ongoing replacement of oaks by later successional species such as red maple as well as conceptually to opposition to the implementation of the prescribed burning that might reverse that trend.

Relevant data to operationalize the colonial triangle must also be available for each case study. In part, data availability is as much a matter of method as of existence, as demonstrated by the analysis of land grants. While relatively mature methods are available to analyze the quadrangular land surveys associated with parts of North America, particularly to determine the vegetation at the time of survey, spatially analyzing the mercedes of New Spain first required development of appropriate methods. Similar innovations will no doubt be necessary for other case studies since operationalizing the colonial triangle will require new types of data and analysis. Moreover, dynamical methods to represent complex material-conceptual feedbacks at the regional scale of analysis require development. And, ultimately, integration of regional case studies at the hemispheric scale will also require development of appropriate methods of analysis and representation that can dynamically encompass the material and the conceptual, the social and the biophysical.

Application beyond the Americas would require even broader collaboration. Research on the other major realms of European colonialism has produced indications of the emergence of a similar conceptual framework. Urban landscapes have formed a focus, but highly nuanced research on the relationships comprising the colonial triangle are becoming increasingly common in a wider range of contexts (Duncan 1990, 1993; Leach and Mearns 1996; Meyers 1998). Given very different colonization processes in Africa and Asia, characterizing that work in terms of the colonial triangle remains problematic. Similarities between the Americas, Africa, and Asia do suggest some promise for doing so, however. For example, dramatic depopulations due to introduced epidemic diseases were certainly not as pervasive in Asia and Africa as in the Americas, but depopulation due to enslavement and forced emigration was regionally consequential.

The theoretical lacuna of colonialism and landscape is as compelling as it is vast, yet filling it remains an outstanding disciplinary obligation. Pulitzer Prize-winning determinisms now encroach on its edges—not with cultural, environmental, and racial determinism all in the same package, of course, but all underpinned by the same Eurocentric teleology (Meinig 1986; Diamond 1997; Landes 1998; Blaut 1999). And they will continue to dominate the academy, mystify understanding, and stultify policy until geographers motivate themselves to undertake a disciplinary effort to generate compelling alternatives through formulation and testing of a comprehensive theory of colonialism and landscape, whatever its eventual form. To understand why such an effort has not been a disciplinary priority, and why it should become one, requires analysis of geography's emergence as a discipline and its current status as a "dead science."

Geography as Exploration: Colonial Boom, Postcolonial Bust

On an evening in June 1859, the month after Alexander von Humboldt passed away and the year Sartorius published *Mexico About 1850*, some of London's most Victorian of Victorians crowded into the meeting room of the Royal Geographical Society (RGS) (Shaw 1859, 347-58). The Earl of Ripon presided. Captain Richard Burton, already famous for his pilgrimage to Mecca, and Captain John Speke were to lecture on their recent explorations in search of the source of the Nile (McLynn 1990). Burton had led the expedition but Speke now claimed to have discovered the Nile's source by himself, an honor that Burton disputed. Together they had taken the caravan route westward from Zanzibar as far as Lake Tanganyika. On the way back to the coast, as Burton lay ill with malaria, Speke had struck out northward and reached Lake Victoria. He then beat Burton home to London to claim that Lake Victoria was the southernmost source of the Nile. The lectures that June evening would serve as something of a public rapprochement. The Earl of Ripon gave Burton the first and last words, but the RGS nonetheless commissioned Speke to lead the follow-up expedition that would further fill in the map of East Africa. While personal honor might have been uppermost in the minds of the two lecturers, the Earl left no doubt about the bigger stakes involved nor about how importantly such RGS expeditions contributed to "the industry, manufactures, and commerce" of the British Empire by filling in the blanks on its maps (Shaw 1859, 348). If the essence of that contribution were not already clear enough, Sir Roderick Murchison pointed to the two maps that had illustrated the lectures: "There *was* our knowledge (pointing to the old map) a year ago; there *is* our knowledge now (pointing to the new map)" (Shaw 1859, 352; italics as in original).

Burton, Speke, and other explorer geographers—many of them Fellows of the RGS such as Sir John Franklin, Dr. David Livingstone, Sir Henry Morton Stanley, and Sir Ernest Shackleton—so impressed the public and the Crown with their exploits that they gave geography considerable social status and power during colonialism's palmy days and retain good name recognition even today (Stoddart 1986). Over the course of several centuries, as the landscapes of the world had successively become geographic objects of European power and landscape had become an object of increasingly professionalized geographic knowledge, geography and colonialism established their congenital relationship. By the mid-nineteenth century, the founding of geographical societies had institutionalized that relationship in many modernizing states: the Société de Géographie in 1821, the Gesellschaft für Erdkunde in 1827, the RGS itself in 1830, the Società Geografica Italiana in 1867, the Koninklijk Nederlands Aardrijkskundig Genootschap in 1873, and many others. Given the imperialist ambitions of such states, they valued explorer geographers for making contributions to basic knowledge that significantly furthered those ambitions, hence the leading roles of the Hydrographer of the Navy and the Secretary to the Admiralty, respectively Sir Francis Beaufort and Sir John Barrow, in founding the RGS (Stoddart 1986, 20). Newly independent states such as Mexico also realized that power over space and knowledge about space proceed together, founding the Sociedad Mexicana de Geografía y Estadística in 1833.

But the status enjoyed during the colonial period would not endure the emergence of the modern sciences because—most obviously, anyway—as the European world map filled in, geography came to seem less and less a source of significant contributions to basic knowledge and more and more a dead science. By the first decades of the twentieth century, geographers were having increasing difficulty finding regions unknown to westerners and therefore increasing difficulty justifying a discipline with an intellectual core focused on exploration and regional description. Every disciplinary history became at once a celebration of past accomplishment and an epitaph; the timeline marking one heroic discovery after another had come to the end of the line (Baker 1931). As the explorer geographers filled in the last interstices of the global map, they rendered themselves obsolete. In the aftermath of the Second World War, with the crumbling of overseas sovereign power for one colonial empire after another, geography's status crumbled even further. The elimination of the Harvard geography department in 1948 most tellingly marked the slide into public and academic obscurity (Livingstone 1992, 311-12). Arguably geography's postcolonial health actually improved in concert with the boom in university funding during the first two decades of the Cold War: the number of geographers with doctoral degrees went up, along with the number of faculty positions, publications, and majors, along with the size of research budgets, along with membership in professional societies (Stoddart 1986, 51-55). But such absolute institutional measures obscure retrenchment relative to most other disciplines and in any case cannot compensate for the failure of geographers to make the intellectual case that they have continued to produce recognizably unique, coherent, and significant contributions to basic knowledge (Livingstone 1992, 32). That most other elite and some public universities have emulated Harvard's example best demonstrates that intellectual failure. Geography might well have many more creative intellects now than ever before, but while such individuals make significant contributions to knowledge, they are so diverse that they do not define a coherent intellectual core. If, in contrast, those individuals were scattered across the academy, they would be at least as intellectually productive as now, the only real consequence being that the core-less "donut discipline" would become a dead science in institutional as well as intellectual terms.

Science as Phenomenon

Understanding that decline from aristocratic lectures in Victorian London, through the closings of geography departments at elite U.S. universities during the Cold War, to the discipline's current postcolonial status as an intellectually dead and institutionally dying discipline requires understanding science itself as a phenomenon rather than simply accepting science as a way of understanding other phenomena. And understanding change in what counts as significant versus dead science requires application of models developed in science studies, for want of a better designation, models ranging from Thomas Kuhn to Bruno Latour.

Given the broad influence of Kuhn's model, despite the many critics of such generalizations, several generations of geographers should be somewhat familiar with his *Structure of Scientific Revolutions*, and it therefore provides a reasonable entry into understanding how what counts as good science changes (Kuhn 1962; Barnes 1985; Stoddart 1986, 9-16; Livingstone 1992, 13-14). Although Kuhn derives his model from the operation of natural sciences, the deeper implications if not the superficial details are equally applicable to social and nature/society science aspects of geography. The model focuses on paradigms, defined as the foundational terms of reference within which scientists conduct research. The vast majority of scientists are, by definition, mediocre and therefore never question the paradigm within which they work because through socialization and institutional authority the paradigm normalizes its own assumptions. Since scientists know approximately nothing about the totality of phenomena, however, all paradigms necessarily provide no more than partial explanations and consequently rationalize an inescapable remainder of inexplicable observations as "exceptions that prove the rule" or as "bad science." Given that constantly changing residuum of unexplained observations, scientists can never claim the absolute veracity of their own paradigm on the basis of reason and data alone and, in fact, can never have any objective foundation to arbitrate among competing paradigms. According to Kuhn's logic, then, what counts as good science, bad science, and dead science must in part change for social rather then for logical or empirical reasons. An accumulation of observations that the existing paradigm has trouble assimilating might play a partial role in its capitulation to a new paradigm, but such observations cannot by themselves justify the paradigm turnover because no new paradigm will ever be able to explain all observations. Kuhn's model thus counters the teleology inherent in the conventional model of science: the heroic denouement of natural and social laws— eureka after eureka, seminal thinker after seminal thinker, classic treatise after classic treatise—that vanquishes ideological biases and irrational myths through the progress of objective reason, truth, technology, and society. Kuhn's relativistic model, in contrast, implies that social processes authorize different groups to assert their versions of so-called social and natural laws, that authority deter-

mines what counts as good science rather than good science determining authority.

A variety of other models—social constructivist, antifoundational, or postcolonial, all broadly characterizable as postmodern—elaborate on the relativism
of Kuhn's model. Although such models differ substantially from each other in
assumptions, modes of argumentation, and conclusions, all deny that natural or
social processes can reveal themselves as if reflected ever more clearly in a mirror polished ever more assiduously by apolitical scientists (Rorty 1979). Foucault (1970) demonstrates that indivisibility of knowledge/power through case
studies of the emergence of several social sciences and professional fields in
relation to the consolidation of modern state surveillance and control (Philp
1985). In doing so, he reconfigures the concept of paradigm into the much more
general concept of discourse and extrapolates it from constituting the normalized
terms of reference for regulating science to constituting the normalized terms of
reference for regulating society; normal science becomes a subset of normal
society. More effective than absolute power, more subtle than force, more in-
sidious than ideology, so-called hegemonic or totalizing discourses define normality and abnormality through supposedly objective categorizations and
thereby enable diffuse and continuous regulation of challenges to the status
quo—presumed, of course, to be the normal condition (Foucault 1979). Said
(1979) converts that model into a postcolonialist one by extrapolating it beyond
the internal relations of western society to the West's relationship with the Orient, particularly as mediated through the field of orientalist studies. He shows
how the category Orient emerged as part of the process through which the West
colonized the Rests and, in fact, as part of the process through which the West
itself came into being in relation to the Rests (Said 1993). The West became
everything normal in that hegemonic discourse: progressive, rational, scientific.
The Orient became everything abnormal: despotic, irrational, mired in myth.
The so-called Edinburgh School of science studies has done much to consolidate
such social constructivist models and depict science as just one more battlefield
for class, gender, cultural, ethnic, and other social struggles rather than as an
objective arbiter of those struggles (Barnes and Shapin 1979). Questions related
to the advance of objective scientific truth in the face of myth, the focus of conventional histories of science, have thus become passé in science studies, and the
emphasis has shifted to understanding the relationship between the power of
certain social groups and the status of, for example, psychology over parapsy-
chology.

Yet modern science retains its defenders, pitted against the postmodernists
in what have come to be called the Science Wars. While the absolutely objective
model of science no longer convinces many academics (nor for that matter any-
one else), realists argue for at least a less subjective, less relativistic model of
science than the postmodernists offer. If nature does not reveal essential truths
that counter transient myths that societies construct, nature still might serve as
the foundation for at least some certainty about what is true and what is false. In

general terms, the defense brief posits that since phenomena—noumena in Kantian terms—exist irrespective of human perceptions and conceptions, phenomena themselves must restrict what scientists can conclude about them (Leplin 1984; Bhaskar 1978). In other words, reality itself places limits on the degree to which society can construct reality (Livingstone 1995). But a realist argument cannot directly counter relativism because realism concerns ontology while relativism concerns epistemology and does not equate to idealism (Proctor 1998). Relativists, after all, do not necessarily deny the existence of a reality outside of human experience. What could be more real, more material, than the bricks and mortar of the prisons that Foucault (1979) helps us to see as aspects of a socially constructed normality? Rather, relativists have demonstrated that once reality becomes part of subjective human experience, humans cannot use that reality to arbitrate objectively among understandings of reality because doing so would itself presuppose an objective understanding of reality. To many that philosophical punch line sounds rational enough, even fairly obvious in hindsight, but also fairly esoteric and irrelevant to how science operates and interfaces with society more broadly. The real punch line, however, is political and anything but esoteric or irrelevant: despite the fact that no epistemological basis can ever exist for claims to absolute objective understanding, such claims have justified global westernization and increasing state power over more and more aspects of everyday life.

To some, the fractious Science Wars suggest the need to sign a truce on intermediate ground, somewhere between the bunkers of the extreme modernists and the trenches of the extreme postmodernists, perhaps in what remains of one of several shell-cratered villages that survive between the frontlines: critical realism or postpositivism, maybe pragmatism, or even ecumenical pluralism (Turner 1997; Proctor 1998). After all, a position that society completely constructs nature, that nature constructs nothing, that social factors explain both truths and myths, that no correspondence exists between the conceptual and the material, between words and things, and that people can therefore impose any random categorization on any phenomenon seems just as fruitless as a position that science objectively mirrors nature. If postmodernists insist on the difficulty of objectively understanding any phenomenon, modern science constitutes a sustained effort to struggle with exactly that difficulty. If neither a naturalized model of science nor a socialized model of science seems entirely plausible, everyone suffers daily from the inflexibility of nature and the arbitrariness of social constructions. If facts cannot speak for themselves in a scientific voice from nowhere, science remains at least as legitimate a voice as any other. If different cultures ask different questions and believe different answers, those questions and answers remain very far from infinite in number. If truth is subjective, representation is in crisis, and the facts are unable to speak for themselves, then truth is inter-subjective, representation is inevitable, and facts mean little without theory. If knowing cannot be reduced to being, then being cannot be reduced to knowing. If science is an organized effort to clone mediocre minds, it also inspires the determination to go beyond the dictatorship of the lowest common denominator. If the moderns, whether pro-modern or anti-modern, still believe in the solid ground of nature while the postmoderns believe in nothing but shifting political quicksand, we do face pressing social and environmental challenges that threaten to overrun the Science Wars unless the combatants achieve a compromise.

Yet Bruno Latour (1993, 1999) discounts the utility of compromise on intermediate ground, even if possible given the epistemological incompatibility of modernism and postmodernism, proposing instead a *non*-modern model of science that would allow escape from the conundrum of polarizations such as modernist-postmodernist, objectivist-subjectivist, absolutist-relativist, or naturalized-socialized. While he does not directly address geography in any detail, he does address the nature-society dichotomy that forms the research focus for many geographers (Turner 1997). In fact, that aspect of his model and somewhat similar formulations by others (Haraway 1991, 1997) have increasingly drawn geographers to Latour's work (Swyngedouw 1999).

In *We Have Never Been Modern*, Latour (1993) argues that westerners have dichotomized nature and society into two separate poles, a trait intrinsic to modernism and a process he calls purification, i.e., of the nature and society poles (figure 7.2). On the one hand, we believe that non-westerners are premodern, habitually get nature and society mixed up, and are therefore locked in the grip of myths that naturalize social processes and socialize natural processes. On the other hand, we believe that we keep nature and society separate, thereby achieving objective understandings of both nature and society, thereby emancipating society from nature's limits, and thereby emancipating society's members from each other.

At the same time, argues Latour, all societies unavoidably create phenomena that are both social and natural, what Haraway (1991) has dubbed cyborgs and what Latour more broadly terms quasi-objects. Such quasi-objects include domesticated plants or entire landscapes, phenomena that encompass politics, molecules, religions, genes, climates, and much more. Latour refers to the creation of these quasi-objects as mediation, i.e., between the nature and society poles. For the West these quasi-objects have become vast in scale, phenomena of planetary consequence such as global warming and the Green Revolution. They thereby impact both westerners and non-westerners, whose own quasi-objects never attain such vast scales. The better we have become at purifying the nature and society poles, at believing and acting as if they truly were separate (even if we can conceptualize that they are not), the more we have proliferated vast quasi-objects that mediate between those poles.

Moreover, as part of the process of purification, we have fragmented knowledge into the social and the natural sciences, thereby rendering our understandings of nature and of society so incommensurable that we do not even know how to understand the mediation processes that proliferate quasi-objects.

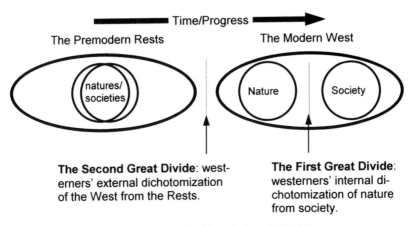

Figure 7.2. View from the West (modified from Latour 1993, 99).

We certainly recognize quasi-objects but have long given them little significance, and they have therefore grown insidiously. Responsibility for developing the technologies that proliferate quasi-objects falls to many reductionistic disciplines: material science, microbiology, and so on. Responsibility for monitoring and understanding quasi-objects falls to no discipline. Only such sporadic collections of odd scholars as those who gathered for the *Man's Role in Changing the Face of the Earth* conference in the mid-1950s, attributed much significance to the harbingers of the vast quasi-objects we have come to know and fear half a century later (Thomas 1956).

The irony, and hence the title of Latour's book, is that we have never truly been modern at all, if we define being modern as the ability to dichotomize nature and society, achieve objective understandings of both, and thereby allow the modern West to escape the myths of the premodern Rests and the limits of nature. We have, in fact, begun to doubt the modernist ideology that time will consume and make irrelevant the premodern past. We have begun to suspect that the diffusion of westernization might be less like heroic progress toward emancipation from nature's limits and more like tragic declension toward staggering social/environmental disasters. Environmental limits have not faded with modernization. In fact, as is becoming increasingly apparent, the very technologies we have relied on to emancipate society from nature have created social/natural phenomena that now threaten us more than any natural hazard ever did—from hybrid crops reliant on fossil water and oil to global warming and sea-level rise. As quasi-objects have attained vast proportions and their negative consequences become undeniable, many more people than the few at the *Man's Role* conference have begun to proclaim the significance of such social/natural phenomena.

The Science Wars, argues Latour, are therefore symptomatic of the post-modernists' realization that modernism has created the very problems it hoped to solve. Postmodernist critiques reflect growing awareness of the modern dilemma but themselves cannot cure it. In fact, both modernists and postmodernists continue to purify nature and society, the one emphasizing the nature pole and the other the society pole. The postmodernists, in other words, are really (post)modernist. For that reason, an intermediate position—perhaps a reaffirmation of that old compromise dialectic in which the harder parts of nature determine the softer parts of society, and the harder parts of society determine the softer parts of nature—cannot address the fundamental issue. Rather, Latour proposes a non-modern alternative, one which collapses the nature-society dichotomy by focusing on the quasi-objects themselves, and not as mixtures of purified nature and society but as active mediators that create what we then categorize as social or natural. Quasi-objects, then, are equally quasi-subjects.

Like most big ideas, especially new ones, Latour's model is abstract enough to frustrate but also general enough to engage a broad spectrum of intellectuals, familiar enough to seem trite but also novel enough to compel engagement, and above all different enough from both the modernists and the postmodernists to offer escape from their irresolvable polarization. Latour does tend to work at a highly abstract level, and his model certainly seems to echo the familiar epistemological debate between reductionists and holists, between an emphasis on understanding phenomena through research on the properties of their parts and their simple interactions versus an emphasis on understanding phenomena as emerging from a history of complex interactions that cannot have been predicted on the basis of reductionism. Yet while Latour does emphasize understanding emergent phenomena, thereby supporting the familiar case for holism, his case studies connect epistemological abstraction to scientific practice, the emergence of science, and the emergence of the West itself. An analysis of fieldwork called "Circulating Reference: Sampling the Soil in the Amazon Forest" holds particular relevance for geographers (Latour 1999, 24-79). The resulting general applicability of the model, its novel alternative to the modernism-postmodernism conundrum, and its focus on the relationship between nature and society all encourage its application to understanding how the discipline of geography has changed in relation to the processes through which modernity emerged, going from a major role in its emergence to lacking the type of distinctive intellectual core that defines any modern science as making contributions that are unique, coherent, and significant.

How Geography Lost Its Core

Latour's model clarifies why geographers faced an increasingly impossible task in justifying the significance of their discipline during the emergence of the modern academic sciences. On the surface, the struggle over academic turf was an institutional one. In concert with modernization—industrialization, urbanization, rapid population increase, and a growing middle class—the number of students, faculty, and universities all began to increase in the late nineteenth century. Each discipline had to struggle for a share of the curriculum, the textbooks, the faculty positions, and the infrastructure—and has continued that struggle ever since (Stoddart 1986, 37-38). Yet institutional power in academia strongly relates to a discipline's intellectual stature (Landes 1998, 4).

> Some of the discipline's current leaders speak of the "vacuum" at the core of geography, of its formlessness, of its conceptual sickliness, while spectators from other subjects remind us of its lack of intellectual repute (Livingstone 1992, 32).

Latour's model provides some crucial insights into how geography's intellectual core became incompatible with the model of a normal intellectual core for the modern sciences.

Geography started on an equal intellectual footing with other nascent disciplines. Exploration was, in fact, essential to the emergence of the Enlightenment and the systematic disciplines, with the observations and specimens that Columbus, Raleigh, Champlain, Cook, Bougainville, and many others brought back vastly increasing the information available to stimulate new ideas (Glacken 1967, 502-3). Like all the other scientific societies founded in nineteenth-century England, beginning with the Royal Astronomical Society in 1820, the RGS employed the model of the Royal Society, which since its founding in 1660 had been the overarching scientific institution (Stoddart 1986, 18-19, 42-48). Explorers shared RGS fellowship with notable scientists, including William Whewell (who coined the term scientist), Alexander von Humboldt, and the originators of evolutionary theory, Charles Darwin and Alfred Wallace. But between founding in 1830 and 1900, the proportion of RGS Fellows who were also fellows of the Royal Society fell from twenty-seven percent to a mere one percent (Stoddart 1986, 66). If the aphorism that geography is the mother of the systematic sciences be true, then her prodigal children soon abandoned her.

Certainly the filling in of the West's world map hindered academic geographers' struggle to establish a modern scientific discipline out of a tradition of exploration and regional description, but the imperative in any case was to go beyond the explorer geographers, to become scientific, to explain the areal differentiation of the Earth's surface into distinct cultural/natural landscapes. Humboldt rather than Burton therefore had to become the paragon of the academic geographers. As part of that reformation, the RGS had by the end of the nineteenth century begun to insist that expeditions follow Humboldt's lead and make systematic observations, collect specimens, and discover general patterns where the explorer geographers had seen only a grab-bag of imperialist opportunity. Scott's expedition, for example, expired on the way out from the South Pole while transporting twenty kilos of rock samples (Stoddart 1986, 151). Burton's dictum—that "geography is good, but gold is better" (Stoddart 1986, 155)—became anathema.

But not only was the age of exploration fading away in the late nineteenth century, so too was the age of Humboldt. As the sciences became increasingly purified, to follow Latour's terminology, into the social and natural sciences as well as further fragmented within those broad categories, "Renaissance man" came to seem like a backhanded compliment—a jack of all sciences but a master of none, a dilettante. The rocks and butterflies that RGS expeditions brought back were becoming the objects of systematic disciplines such as geology and zoology. Darwin's biography provides a synecdoche for that nineteenth-century transition from exploration to modern science. His global circumnavigation aboard the *Beagle*, a copy of Humboldt's *Personal Narrative of Travels to the Equinoctial Regions of the New Continent* his guide to systematic observation, earned him election to fellowship in the RGS in 1838 (Livingstone 1992, 179). The observations collected on that voyage formed the basis for publication of *On the Origin of Species by Means of Natural Selection* in 1859. The ensuing acceleration of the secular quest for natural and social laws forced the demise of the Victorian penchant for comprehensive cataloging of a natural diversity presumed to have derived from providential design (Stoddart 1986, 160-80).

Academic geography, then, would have to follow Darwin's lead, even while deifying Humboldt as the last great comprehensive scientist. The growing number of academic geographers did so by drawing on evolutionary theory in order to elaborate environmental determinism. That nature-society theory held great appeal because of a long and impressive pedigree that includes the Hippocratic corpus, Ptolemy, St. Thomas, Bodin, and Montesquieu (Glacken 1967). Environmental determinism also, like all deterministic theories, integrates well with the teleological frameworks of providential design and western superiority; both determinisms and teleologies obviate any concern with process (Blaut 1999). Environmental determinism must thus have seemed the perfect theory to facilitate transition from exploration and cataloguing of the Earth's diverse landscapes to scientific explanation of their areal differentiation. From opposite sides of the Atlantic, William Morris Davis and Halford Mackinder drew on evolutionary theory to preserve geography's claim on the realm of nature-society relationships at the scale of landscape and region: a "Lamarckian-derived attempt to couch geography's traditional concerns in the language of evolution during a time of professionalizing specialisms" (Livingstone 1992, 190-91, 209-12). Prominent geographers of the next generation continued that effort by promoting environmental determinism as a grand theory that explained the areal differentiation of the Earth into diverse landscapes as the result of consistent patterns of evolutionary adaptation of society to nature (Semple 1911; Huntington 1917; Taylor 1919).

Yet environmental determinism ultimately failed to provide the intellectual core geography required to assume a place as a modern science and, in fact, became anathema to the modern sciences. A modernist would argue that environmental determinism failed because too many contradictory observations accumulated, revealing it as bad science, as ideology, as falsehood rooted in racism and imperialism (Livingstone 1992, 290-97). But the same sorts of contradictory observations accumulated for the theories that anchored the cores of other disciplines, from geology to anthropology to astronomy, and they have thrived by claiming an increment of scientific progress with every paradigm turnover. According to the modernist model of science, then, geographers should also have thrived as they replaced environmental determinism with a more objective theory of the relationship between society and nature. A postmodernist, in contrast, would argue that environmental determinism failed because the discourse of liberalism supplanted the discourse of imperialism and that liberalism required a more elastic relationship between nature and society than did imperialism. Liberalism required that the premodern Rests, irrespective of their environments, could progress to become the modern producers and consumers required by a postcolonial global economy. According to a postmodernist model of science, then, just as much as the modernist model, geographers should have thrived as they replaced environmental determinism with a different theory of the relationship between society and nature. Yet, despite such modifications as the relatively unmemorable possibilist and probabilist qualifications, environmental determinism remains academic geography's first and only major attempt at a universal, grand theory of the relationship between nature and society that explains the global patterning of landscapes. Inexplicably, at least in terms of the modernist and postmodernist models of science, geography did not emerge as a science of nature-society relations and neither did any other discipline.

Unlike the modernist and postmodernist models of science, Latour's nonmodern model does clarify why geographers were not able to anchor their intellectual core with environmental determinism, with some less deterministic nature-society theory such as possibilism or probabilism, nor with any other sort of nature-society theory. Environmental determinism failed not only because it theorized the relationship between nature and society in a specious way but because it presumed to theorize that relationship in any way at all. Environmental determinism naturalizes social processes, and any theory that naturalizes social processes must by definition be antithetical to the social sciences and irrelevant to the natural sciences—as well illustrated by the derision of social scientists and disinterest of natural scientists towards sociobiology. Yet any other type of nature-society theory would have failed just as thoroughly because it diametrically opposes the modern imperative to purify nature and society, and therefore any discipline that builds its core around nature-society theory diametrically opposes the character of modern scientific disciplines. Those geographers like Davis and Mackinder who insisted that geography be explanatory at the same time as bridging the nature-society dichotomy therefore insisted on a disciplinary model that became incompatible with the modern model of a normal disciplinary core.

To survive the modernizing sciences' increasing purification of nature and society, the academic geographers who followed Davis and Mackinder had to repudiate environmental determinism in particular and any nature-society theory in general, although influential geographers such as Isaiah Bowman "retained a lifelong commitment to the Davisian programme modulating only the shrillest tones of its determinism" (Livingstone 1992, 312). On both sides of the Atlantic, geographers retreated from explanatory theory into descriptive regionalization, defining regions on various criteria such as climate or culture, interpreting regions as more than the sum of the parts that the systematic disciplines studied, and thereby continuing to bridge the widening chasm between the natural and the social (Johnston 1983, 42-47). Those geographers who, like Hartshorne, retreated into that descriptive core therefore retreated into a core just as incompatible with normal science as environmental determinism, one that earned the label of mere description, of an "easy subject." As geographers began to appear more and more as dilettantes, as spatial bookkeepers to the systematic disciplines, many realigned themselves more strongly with either the social or the natural sciences. Thus geographical subfields emerged that could claim to be explanatory sciences, but the vast territory where nature and society come into being together remained not only *terra incognita* but became *terra inconcessus*—forbidden territory.

The fragmentation of the acquisition of knowledge has only accelerated since then, as inexorable institutional, methodological, and epistemological pressures manifest the modern imperative to purify nature and society. Institutionally, groups and individuals gain power over funding and publishing much more easily through splitting than through lumping, through founding new disciplines and journals than through consolidating existing ones. Thus geography has internally fragmented into subdisciplines that would rather look outward to other disciplines than look inward to forge a disciplinary core, most especially not toward a core in terra inconcessus (Kates 1987; Trimble 1992). Methodologically, as disciplines have developed increasingly specialized and demanding research methods, no individual can master all those of even a single discipline, let alone the several that Humboldt could, and geography has become internally fragmented by the vastly different modes of analysis, types of data, and techniques used across its subfields. Epistemologically, despite a general recognition that on purely intellectual grounds reductionistic and holistic science are complementary, reductionists dominate because they focus on low-level phenomena and thereby can make relatively restricted predictions that can be deductively tested, generate status for those who do so, and result in marketable technologies. Because of the greater difficulty of understanding complex, historical, ramifying interactions among a great number of diverse phenomena, holism has become associated with induction, idealism, claims about emergent phenomena that are impossible to test, and little potential to produce marketable technology. The use of genomics to produce transgenic organisms versus the attempt to understand the broader social/environmental consequences of those organisms (or even to understand organisms as organisms rather than as the sum of their genes), provides an example of that contrast between reductionistic and holistic knowledge—and how that knowledge simultaneously constitutes and is constituted by social power. The same reductionistic pressures epistemologically fragment geography among the diverse and seemingly incommensurable theories, politics, jargons, and literatures of the humanities, social sciences, and biophysical sciences—towards which our subfields turn for new ideas and validation much more assiduously than they turn towards each other. As literatures grow exponentially, specialization and reductionism become imperatives, any mutual agreement on an intellectual core becomes strained, and competition overwhelms collaboration as each subfield attempts to justify itself by demonstrating the intellectual and political bankruptcy of the others (Turner 1997, 199).

Common colonial stigmata certainly mark the body from which spring the many subdisciplinary heads. Many geographers cling to the spatial theme, for example, emphasizing the importance of spatial processes, spatially explicit models, spatial scale, spatial statistics, GIS, maps, atlases, landscape, and so on—all of which derive from the close linkage between exploration, cartography, and landscape description established by the explorer geographers. Exploration and discovery tropes also remain meaningful to many geographers, as witnessed by the American Association of Geographers's 1997 publication of *Rediscovering Geography: New Relevance for Science and Society*. But phenomena, not modes of analysis or representation define the intellectual cores of other disciplines, which then adopt and develop methods as they seem useful for understanding their phenomena. A whole range of other disciplines are necessarily just as spatial as geography, for example, from geology and archaeology to astronomy and atmospheric science. In other words, given that disciplines are defined by phenomena rather than by method, geography seems best defined by the eclecticism of the phenomena that geographers study, arrayed from highly purified nature to highly purified society, and therefore by the lack of a modern intellectual core that focuses on a particular social *or* natural phenomenon.

The Future of Geography

Surely the proliferation of so many vast, threatening quasi-objects has recently increased westerners' recognition of the significance of the mediation processes that create those quasi-objects, somewhat countering the modern imperative to purify; and therefore *We Have Never Been Modern*, despite not even mentioning geography, contains insights for rescuing our anachronistic, premodern discipline from obscurity. Latour, in fact, actually hints at two possibilities, perhaps two complementary aspects of the same possibility, through which geography might begin to make coherent, recognizably unique, significant contributions to knowledge. Each of the possibilities is associated with one of the two great dichotomies intrinsic to modernism that emerged as the West defined itself relative to the Rests during the colonial period. The first dichotomy, that which purifies nature and society, that which Latour calls the First Great Divide, is internal to the West. The second dichotomy, that which purifies the modern and the premodern, that which Latour calls the Second Great Divide, is external to and divides the West and the Rests. The two Great Divides are interdependent, having emerged together and reinforced one another. On one side of the Second Great Divide, according to westerners, the West purifies nature and society; on the other side, the Rests habitually get nature and society mixed up. The more westerners have purified nature and society, the more they have purified the West from the Rests, and the more they have insisted that they simply need to catch up, develop, modernize, and become diligent purifiers like ourselves.

Now the First Great Divide seems to be crumbling. As we have become all too aware, the more we have acted as if we really do separate nature and society, the more we have actually done the opposite by proliferating vast natural/social quasi-objects that threaten both the West and the Rests. We have begun to realize that we never actually did separate nature and society, neither emancipating society from nature nor ourselves from each other. Thus economists, in the face of failing modernization theory, have attempted to reincorporate nature into economics, the initial naïve attempts consisting of neo-environmental determinism (Landes 1998; Sachs et al. 2001).

As the First Great Divide has crumbled, so too has the Second. We are now beginning to suspect that the West's superiority over the Rests is our own enormous myth, one that can never provide a basis for transcending itself, for meeting the social and environmental challenges that have emerged together with that myth. As the very technologies we relied on to emancipate society from nature not only have not done so but have created quasi-objects that threaten society, we have begun to realize that rather than obstacles that are "too traditional" to participate in creating the future, the knowledges and practices of the very peoples that the West colonized might provide workable alternatives to an unsustainable modernization.

The First Great Divide/Possibility: A Science of Nature and Society

The first possibility for revitalizing our intellectual core relates most closely to the crumbling of the First Great Divide, the one internal to the West, the one that purifies nature and society. Because of the obvious relevance to geography, geographers who have drawn on Latour have focused on this first dichotomy to the exclusion of the second (Swyngedouw 1999). Geographers have had some success in convincing other disciplines that we are central to the effort to understand quasi-objects such as global warming because by bridging the institutional, methodological, and epistemological chasm between the social and the natural sciences we can claim the expertise to take on the interdisciplinary leadership role necessary to a science of nature and society (NRC 1999). In doing so, we have reasserted our interest in the topics raised by the *Man's Role* conference at a time when the phenomena that so concerned Sauer have escalated into so-cial/natural threats of such magnitude that they have come to command broad political, public, and scientific concern (Thomas 1956; Turner et al. 1990). We have been involved in the establishment of relevant interdisciplinary institutions such as research centers, journals, and funding programs. And we have been involved in the development of GIS as a method to integrate diverse types of natural and social data. That effort to lead a science of nature and society bodes well for asserting the significance of geography except for two issues, one con-cerning an interdisciplinary science of nature and society in general and the other concerning geography's specific role in leading such a science.

Latour suggests that purification is so intrinsic to the West that even inter-disciplinary efforts currently treat quasi-objects as mixtures of purely natural and purely social phenomena, as passive intermediates rather than as active me-diators. In other words, westerners tend to define a quasi-object such as global warming in terms of how many of its parts are natural and how many are social. We then assign responsibility for studying those parts to various natural and social science disciplines and try to splice the resulting analyses together with systems diagrams that show feedbacks and other interactions. For example, our attempt to understand global warming splices together the most commensurable models from the social and natural sciences, typically derived on the society side from economics and on the nature side from climatology. Following Latour's logic, because of that tendency to purify, our interdisciplinary efforts achieve the counterproductive result of continuing to proliferate rather than rein in the quasi-objects. Instead of treating quasi-objects as passive intermediates between nature and society, Latour argues, we need to treat them as much as quasi-subjects as quasi-objects, as active mediators that create what we then categorize as social and natural. Quasi-objects, in other words, do not result from a mixture of the social and the natural, nor even do they manifest a dialectical relationship be-tween the social and the natural; they manifest social/biophysical mediation processes as phenomenon that we purify into social and natural categories. Whether or not an interdisciplinary effort will succeed in redefining the way we conceptualize quasi-objects—treating them as mediators rather than intermedi-ates and thereby making a broader range of disciplines commensurable in order to better understand social/biophysical mediation processes—remains to be seen.

Regarding geography's specific role in leading such interdisciplinary ef-forts, whether or not any particular discipline can convince the others that its intellectual core concerns interdisciplinary leadership also remains to be seen. If geography can make that case, it would go from being a premodern anachronism to being a vital non-modern science that leads the way to better understanding of social/biophysical mediation processes. But can geography really mediate be-tween the social and natural sciences, or is geography itself actually more of a passive intellectual intermediate than an active intellectual mediator? After all, no more than a few geographers encompass the necessary social/biophysical breadth to intellectually mediate a transdisciplinary science of nature and society, no more than those few intellectuals of incredible breadth who can be found in many other disciplines. Most geographers study either social or natural phenomena—or, at least, in concert with the rest of modern science, convince themselves that they can purify their social or natural phenomena of choice. Most geographers actually act like most other scientists, focusing on very specific phenomenon, using a narrow range of methods, working within normal science, and publishing in a narrow range of specialized journals using highly specialized jargon. What does seem certain is that any discipline that does try to define itself as interdisciplinary must become an oxymoron—a dilettantish "interdisciplinary discipline"—in terms of the modern model of a normal disciplinary core. The transdisciplinary talent necessary to establish what would be a non-modern nature/society science will therefore have to emerge from within interdisciplinary centers established to focus on particular types of quasi-objects/subjects. The best of the applied expertise to emerge, some doubtlessly with intellectual roots in geography, will then be able to build a broader, basic science of nature/society.

The Second Great Divide/Possibility: Colonialism and Landscape

But if that first possibility for intellectual redemption remains a work in progress, the second possibility, the one related most closely to the crumbling of the Second Great Divide, remains even less realized. At the scale of landscapes, that divide is strongly associated with the pristine myth and more general myth of emptiness, a key assumption in the teleological belief that the premodern Rests simply need to develop and pass through the Second Great Divide to join the modern West. In Latour's terms, at the hemispheric scale, purification created American landscapes that were categorized as mainly natural and European landscapes that were categorized as mainly cultural, while in reality social/natural landscapes were active mediators (quasi-objects/subjects) engaged in a colonization process that simultaneously transformed landscapes and obscured that transformation. Yet the issue of how to study and represent the social/biophysical processes involved in such material/conceptual transformation remains just as vexing for landscape as for phenomena such as global warming. Geographers do not in the case of this second possibility need to bridge the First Great Divide in general, but they will need to bridge that nature-society dichotomy in relation to a specific phenomenon: colonial landscape transformation. And that effort will face all the difficulties that have epistemologically, institutionally, and methodologically fragmented science in general and geography in particular because a nature/society theory of colonialism and landscape threatens both the First and the Second Great Divides.

As with the first possibility, this second one also might establish geography's intellectual and applied significance but, unlike the first, does not require convincing other disciplines that leadership in bridging the First Great Divide should fall to geography. All disciplines that focus on quasi-objects, in fact, will need to bridge the nature-society dichotomy in relation to particular phenomena at particular scales. Some, like the economists, will no doubt initially fall back on neo-environmental determinism. Geographers nonetheless have a clear claim on the study of the phenomenon of colonial landscape transformation, complements of the explorer geographers.

We Shall Not Cease from Exploration

A quote from a renowned academic geographer, published some five centuries after the explorer geographers initiated the opening of the two Great Divides, succinctly draws together the above points.

> One of the great themes of American History emerges from the epochal story of Americans confronting and coming to terms with a huge wild country. Quite unlike the Old World, where people had occupied the land for as long as history could recall, and where adjustment to environment came so gradually as to be almost imperceptible, Americans' encounter with their land was abrupt and often violent, consuming much of the nation's energies, and powerfully gripping its collective imagination. . . . It took less than four hundred years to subdue more than three million square miles of territory. . . . So it is no accident that the greatest works of American literature—such novels as Moby Dick and Huckleberry Finn—tell stories not so much of the confrontation of Man with Man, or even Man with God—but rather of the confrontation of Man with a rich and varied and powerful Nature (Lewis 1992, 43, 65-66).

If you agreed with both the substance of that quote—including the merging of the supernatural and of unmentioned native societies into nature—then you are modern. If you also agreed with the sentiment that glorifies the colonization of a continent as a heroic epic of taming unexploited resources, then you are not only modern, you are pro-modern. If you agreed with the substance but rankled at the sentiment, instead seeing the continental colonization as a heinous crime that destroyed a primeval paradise in which native societies lived in harmony with nature, then you are just as modern; but instead of being pro-modern, you are anti-modern, your sympathies being with the premoderns. If you think that both the substance and sentiment of the quote are an amusing example of western naïveté because nature itself is socially constructed, then you are postmodern.

But if you want to forgo judgment on such assessments of the European colonization of what became the United States and, instead, seek to understand them as a phenomenon—how they became possible through social/biophysical processes of landscape transformation—then you are neither pro-modern, anti-modern, nor postmodern. You are instead non-modern and ready to get on with the research it will take to understand the emergence of the two Great Divides and overcome their debilitating effects. You are ready to take up study of the phenomenon that gave geographers great social status during the heyday of the colonial era but to explore those landscapes in an effort to as much as possible see them on their own terms, to paraphrase Wes Jackson and Wendell Berry, rather than impose western visions. As T. S. Eliot put it "We shall not cease from exploration/And the end of all our exploring/Will be to arrive where we started/And know the place for the first time."

Bibliography

Archives Used and Their Abbreviations

Archivo General de la Nación, Mexico City	AGN
Fomento Caminos section	AGN-Fomento Caminos
Hospital de Jesús section	AGN-Hospital de Jesús
Indiferente de Guerra section	AGN-Indiferente de Guerra
Indios section	AGN-Indios
Mercedes section	AGN-M
Reales Cédulas Duplicados	AGN-Reales Cédulas Duplicados
Ríos y Acequias section	AGN-Ríos y Acequias
Tierras section	AGN-T
Vínculos section	AGN-Vínculos
Archivo Notarial de Xalapa, Xalapa, Veracruz	
Protocolo section	ANX-Protocolo
Benson Latin American Library, Austin, Texas	
Joaquin García Icazbalceta Collection	JGI
Library of Congress, Washington, D.C.	
Kraus Collection	LOC-Kraus
Newberry Library, Chicago, Illinois	
Ayer Collection	NLC-Ayer

References

Acosta, Jose de. 1590. *Historia Natural y Moral de las Indias*. Seville: Casa de I. de Leon.

Acuña, René, ed. 1985. *Relaciones Geográficas del Siglo XVI, Tlaxcala*. Vol. 2. Mexico City: Universidad Nacional Autónoma de México.

Adams, R. E. W. 1977. *Prehistoric Mesoamerica*. Boston: Little, Brown & Co.

Adas, Michael. 1989. *Machines as the Measure of Men: Science, Technology, and Ideologies of Western Dominance*. Ithaca: Cornell University Press.

Aguilar, Francisco de. 1938. *Historia de la Nueva España*. Mexico City: Ediciones Botas.

Aguirre Beltrán, Gonzalo. 1972. *La Población Negra de México*. Mexico City: Fondo de Cultura Económica.

Ajofrín, Francisco de. 1958-1959. *Diario del Viaje que por Orden de la Sagrada Congregación de Propoganda Fide Hizo a la América Septentrional en el Siglo XVIII*. Madrid: Real Academia de la Historia.

Alcina Franch, José. 1973. Juan de Torquemada, 1564-1624. In *Guide to Ethnohistorical Sources, Part 2, The Handbook of Middle American Indians*, vol. 13, edited by Howard F. Cline, 256-75. Austin: University of Texas Press.

Alcorn, J. B. 1984. *Huastec Maya Ethnobotany*. Austin: University of Texas Press.

Alegre, Francisco Javier. 1841-1842. *Historia de la Compañía de Jesús en Nueva España*. 3 vols. Mexico City Carlos María de Bustamante.

Aley, J., W. R. Burch, B. Conover, and D. Field. 1999. *Ecosystem Management: Adaptive Strategies for Natural Resources Organizations in the Twenty-First Century*. London: Taylor and Francis.

Althaus, Dudley. 2000. A New Sun Poverty. *The Houston Chronicle*, 26 November, Special-4.

Altieri, M. A., ed. 1987. *Agroecology: The Scientific Basis of Alternative Agriculture*. Boulder: Westview Press.

Alva Ixtlilxóchitl, Fernando de. 1985. *Obras Históricas*. 2 vols. Mexico City: Universidad Nacional Autónoma de México.

Alvarado Tezozomoc, Hernando. 1944. *Crónica Mexicana*. Mexico City: Editorial Leyenda.

Anderson, Roger C. 1982. An Evolutionary Model Summarizing the Roles of Fire, Climate, and Grazing Animals in the Origin and Maintenance of Grasslands: An End Paper. In *Grasses and Grasslands: Systematics and Ecology*, edited by James R. Estes, Ronald J. Tyrl, and Jere N. Brunken, 297-308. Norman: University of Oklahoma Press.

Arreola, Daniel D. 1980. Landscapes of Nineteenth-Century Veracruz. *Landscape* 24:27-31.

———. 1982. Nineteenth-Century Townscapes of Eastern Mexico. *The Geographical Review* 72:1-19.

Aschmann, Homer. 1974. Environment and Ecology in the "Northern Tonto" Claim Area. In *Apache Indian V, American Indian Ethnohistory Series*, 167-232. New York: Garland.

Atran, Scott, Douglas Medin, Norbert Ross, Elizabeth Lynch, John Coley, and Edilberto Ucan Ek. 1999. Folkecology and Commons Management in the Maya Lowlands. *Proceedings of the National Academy of Sciences of the United States of America* 96:7598-603.

BAGN (*Boletín del Archivo General de la Nación*). 1936. Tributos de los Indios de la Nueva España, 1536. *Boletín del Archivo General de la Nación* 7:185-226.

———. 1940. Tributos de Pueblos de Indios (Virreinato de Nueva España), 1560. *Boletín del Archivo General de la Nación* 11:199-243.

Baker, J. N. L. 1931. *A History of Geographical Discovery and Exploration*. London: Harrap.

Ballesteros Gaibrois, Manuel. 1973. Antonio de Herrera, 1549-1625. In *Guide to Ethnohistorical Sources, Part 2, The Handbook of Middle American Indians*, vol. 13, edited by Howard F. Cline, 240-55. Austin: University of Texas Press.

Baran, Paul. 1973. *The Political Economy of Growth*. Harmondsworth: Penguin.

Barlow, R. H. 1949. *The Extent of the Empire of the Culhua Mexica, Ibero-Americana*, no. 28. Berkeley: University of California Press.

Barnes, Barry. 1985. Thomas Kuhn. In *The Return of Grand Theory in the Human Sciences*, edited by Quentin Skinner, 83-100. Cambridge: University of Cambridge Press.

Barnes, Barry, and Steven Shapin, eds. 1979. *Natural Order: Historical Studies of Scientific Culture*. London: Sage.

Barnes, Thomas C., Thomas H. Naylor, and Charles W. Polzer. 1981. *Northern New Spain: A Research Guide*. Tucson: University of Arizona Press.

Bell, Morag, Robin Butlin, and Michael Heffernan, eds. 1995. *Geography and Imperialism, 1820-1940*. Manchester: Manchester University Press.

Berdan, F. F., and J. de Durant-Forest, eds. 1980. *Matricula de Tributos (Codice de Moctezuma)*. Graz: Akademische Druck und Verlagsanstalt.

Berkes, Fikret. 1999. *Sacred Ecology: Traditional Ecological Knowledge and Resource Management*. Philadelphia: Taylor and Francis.

Bermúdez Gorrochotegui, Gilberto. 1987. *El Mayorazgo de la Higuera*. Xalapa: Universidad Veracruzana.

Bernal, Ignacio, and Eusebio Dávalos Hurtado, eds. 1953. *Huastecos, Totonacos y sus Vecinos, Revista Mexicana de Estudios Antropológicos*. Vol. 13.

Berry, Wendell. 1996. *The Unsettling of America: Culture and Agriculture*. San Francisco: Sierra Club Books.

Bhaskar, Roy. 1978. *A Realist Theory of Science*. Sussex: Harvester.

Binford, Michael W. 1983. Paleolimnology of the Petén Lake District, Guatemala. *Hydrobiologia* 103:199-203.

Bishko, C. J. 1952. The Peninsular Background of Latin American Cattle Ranching. *The Hispanic American Historical Review* 32:491-515.

Blaikie, Piers M., and Harold Brookfield. 1987. *Land Degradation and Society*. London: Methuen.

Blaut, James M. 1993. *The Colonizer's Model of the World: Geographical Diffusionism and Eurocentric History*. New York: Guilford Press.

———. 1999. Environmental Determinism and Eurocentrism. *Geographical Review* 89:391-408.

Blazquez Dominguez, Carmen. 1988. *Veracruz: Una Historia Compartida*. Mexico City: Gobierno del Estado de Veracruz, Instituto Veracruzano de Cultura, and Instituto Mora.

Booker, Jackie R. 1993. *Veracruz Merchants, 1770-1829: A Mercantile Elite in Late Bourbon and Early Independent Mexico*. Boulder: Westview Press.

Borah, Woodrow. 1941. The Collection of Tithes in the Bishopric of Oaxaca During the Sixteenth Century. *Hispanic American Historical Review* 21:387-409.

Borah, Woodrow, and Sherburne F. Cook. 1958. *Price Trends of Some Basic Commodities in Central Mexico, 1531-1570, Ibero-Americana*, no. 40. Berkeley: University of California Press.

———. 1960 *The Population of Central Mexico in 1548, Ibero-Americana*, no. 43. Berkeley: University of California Press.

———. 1963. *The Aboriginal Population of Central Mexico on the Eve of the Spanish Conquest, Ibero-Americana*, no. 45. Berkeley: University of California Press.

Botkin, Daniel B. 1990. *Discordant Harmonies: A New Ecology for the Twenty-First Century*. Oxford: Oxford University Press.

Bowden, Martyn J. 1992. The Invention of American Tradition. *Journal of Historical Geography* 18:3-26.

Bowman, I. 1931. *The Pioneer Fringe*. New York: American Geographical Society.

Boyd-Bowman, P. 1964. *Índice Geobiográfico de Cuarenta Mil Pobladores Españoles de América en el Siglo XVI, Tomo I, 1493-1519*. Bogota: Instituto Caro y Cuervo.

———. 1968. *Índice Geobiográfico de Cuarenta Mil Pobladores Españoles de América en el Siglo XVI, Tomo II, 1520-1539*. Mexico City: Editorial Jus.

———. 1976. Patterns of Spanish Emigration to the Indies until 1600. *Hispanic American Historical Review* 56:580-604.

Brand, D. D. 1961. The Early History of the Range Cattle Industry in Northern Mexico. *Agricultural History* 35 (3):132-39.

Brooks, Francis J. 1993. Revising the Conquest of Mexico: Smallpox, Sources, and Populations. *Journal of Interdisciplinary History* 24:1-29.

Browder, John O., ed. 1989. *Fragile Lands of Latin America: Strategies for Sustainable Development*. Boulder: Westview Press.

Brown, R. B. 1985. A Summary of Late-Quaternary Pollen Records from Mexico West of the Isthmus of Tehuantepec. In *Pollen Records of Late-Quaternary North American Sediments*, edited by V. M. Bryant Jr. and R. G. Holloway, 71-93. Dallas: American Association of Stratigraphic Palynologists Foundation.

Brüggemann, Jürgen K. 1989. Los Sitios Arqueológicos de la Cuenca Inferior del Actopan: Estudio de un Caso para la Aplicación del Cálculo de Aproximación a la Prospección Arqueológica. In *Homenaje a Román Piña Chán*, edited by Roberto García Moll and Angel García Cook, 187-203. Mexico City: Instituto Nacional de Antropología e Historia.

———. 1991. Análisis Urbano de la Antigua Ciudad con Base en los Objetos Inmuebles. In *Zempoala: El Estudio de una Ciudad Prehispánica*, edited by Jürgen K Brüggemann, 85-108. Mexico City: Instituto Nacional de Antropología e Historia.

Bryant, Raymond L. 1992. Political Ecology: An Emerging Research Agenda in Third-World Studies. *Political Geography* 11:12-36.

Burrus, Ernest J. 1973. Religious Chroniclers and Historians: A Summary with Annotated Bibliography. In *Guide to Ethnohistorical Sources, Part 2, The Handbook of Middle American Indians*, vol. 13, edited by Howard F. Cline, 138-85. Austin: University of Texas Press.

Butzer, Karl W. 1988. Cattle and Sheep from Old to New Spain: Historical Antecedents. *Annals of the Association of American Geographers* 78:29-56.

———. 1989. Cultural Ecology. In *Geography in America*, edited by Gary L. Gaile and Cort J. Willmott, 192-208. Columbus, Ohio: Merrill.

———. 1991. Spanish Colonization of the New World: Cultural Continuity and Change in Mexico. *Erdkunde* 45:205-19.

———. 1992. From Columbus to Acosta: Science, Geography, and the New World. *Annals of the Association of American Geographers* 82:543-65.

Butzer, Karl W., and Elisabeth K. Butzer. 1993. The Sixteenth-Century Environment of the Central Mexican Bajío: Archival Reconstruction from Colonial Land Grants and the Question of Spanish Ecological Impact. In *Culture, Form, and Place: Essays in*

Cultural and Historical Geography, edited by Kent Mathewson, 89-124. Baton Rouge, La.: Geoscience Publications.

————. 1995. Transfer of the Mediterranean Livestock Economy to New Spain: Adaptation and Ecological Consequences. In *Global Land Use Change: A Perspective from the Columbian Encounter*, edited by B. L. Turner II, Antonio Gómez Sal, Fernando González Bernáldez, and Francesco de Castri, 151-93. Madrid: Consejo Superior de Investigaciones Científicas.

Cambrezy, Luc, and Bernal Lascuráin. 1992. *Crónicas de un Territorio Fracionado: de la Hacienda al Ejido (Centro de Veracruz)*. Mexico City: Ediciones Larousse.

Carrera Stampa, Manuel. 1949. The Evolution of Weights and Measures in New Spain. *Hispanic American Historical Review* 29:2-24.

Carroll, Patrick J. 1991. *Blacks in Colonial Veracruz: Race, Ethnicity, and Regional Development*. Austin: University of Texas Press.

Carruthers, David V. 1997. Agroecology in Mexico: Linking Environmental and Indigenous Struggles. *Society and Natural Resources* 10:259-72.

Casas, Bartolomé de las. 1951. *Historia de las Indias*. 3 vols. Mexico City: Fondo de Cultura Económica.

————. 1953. *Brevísima Relación de la Destrución de las Indias*. Buenos Aires: Mar Oceano.

————. 1967. *Apologética Historia Sumaria*. 2 vols. Mexico City: Universidad Nacional Autónoma de México.

Casimir, Gladys. 1990. Proyecto Loma Iguana, La Antigua, Veracruz. In *Consejo de Arqueología, Boletín, 1989*, 12-15. Mexico City: Instituto Nacional de Antropología e Historia.

————. 1991. Proyecto Loma Iguana, La Antigua, Veracruz. In *Consejo de Arqueología, Boletín, 1990*, 50-52. Mexico City: Instituto Nacional de Antropología e Historia.

Catlin, George. 1973. *Letters and Notes on the Manners, Customs and Conditions of the North American Indians*. 2 vols. New York: Dover.

Cervantes de Salazar, Francisco. 1985. *Crónica de la Nueva España*. Mexico City: Porrúa.

Chambers, Robert. 1994. The Origins and Practice of Participatory Rural Appraisal. *World Development* 22:953-69.

Chapin, Mac. 1988a. The Seduction of Models: Chinampa Agriculture in Mexico. *Grassroots Development* 12 (1):8-17.

————. 1988b. The Seduction of Models: Chinampa Agriculture. *The DESFIL Newsletter* 2 (1):3, 22-24.

————. 1991. Travels with Eucario: In Search of Ecodevelopment. *Orion* 10 (2):49-58.

Chardon, Roland. 1980. The Linear League in North America. *Annals of the Association of American Geographers* 70:129-53.

Chávez Orozco, Luis, and Enrique Florescano. 1965. *Agricultura e Industria Textil de Veracruz, Siglo XIX*. Xalapa: Universidad Veracruzana.

Cházaro Basáñez, Miguel de J. 1977. El Huizache, *Acacia pennatula* (Schlech. & Cham.) Benth.: Una Invasora del Centro de Veracruz. *Biótica* 2 (3):1-18.

Chesworth, John. 1992. *Ruminant Nutrition*. London: MacMillan.

Chevalier, François. 1952. *La Formation des Grands Domaines au Mexique: Terre et Société aux XVI-XVII Siècles*. Paris: Institut d'Ethnologie.

————. 1963. *Land and Society in Colonial Mexico: The Great Hacienda*. Translated by Alvin Eustis. Berkeley: University of California Press.

Church, R. J. Harrison. 1951. *Modern Colonization*. London: Hutchinson's University Library.

Cisneros Solano, V., D. Martínez Pérez, S. Díaz Cárdenas, J. A. Torres Rivera, C. Guadarrama Zugasti, and A. Cruz León. 1993. *Caracterización de la Agricultura de la Zona Central de Veracruz*. Chapingo: Universidad Autónoma Chapingo.

Ciudad Real, Antonio de, ed. 1976. *Tratado Curioso y Docto de las Grandezas de la Nueva España: Relación Breve y Verdadera de Algunas Cosas de las Muchas que Sucedieron al Padre Fray Alonso Ponce en las Provincias de la Nueva España Siendo Comisario General de Aquellas Partes*. 2 vols. Mexico City: Universidad Nacional Autónoma de México.

Claassen, M. M., and R. H. Shaw. 1970. Water Deficit Effects on Corn. II. Grain Components. *Agronomy Journal* 62:652-55.

Clay, Jason W. 1988. *Indigenous Peoples and Tropical Forests: Models of Land Use and Management from Latin America*. Cambridge, Mass.: Cultural Survival.

Clayton, Daniel. 2000. The Creation of Imperial Space in the Pacific Northwest. *Journal of Historical Geography* 26:327-50.

Cline, Howard F. 1961. The Patiño Maps of 1580 and Related Documents: Analysis of 16th Century Cartographic Sources for the Gulf Coast of Mexico. *El México Antiguo* 9:633-83.

———. 1972. The Relaciones Geográficas of the Spanish Indies, 1577-1648. In *Guide to Ethnohistorical Sources, Part 1, The Handbook of Middle American Indians*, vol. 12, edited by Howard F. Cline, 183-242. Austin: University of Texas Press.

Cockcroft, James D. 1990. *Mexico: Class Formation, Capital Accumulation, and the State*. New York: Monthly Review Press.

Cook, David Noble, and W. George Lovell. 1991. Unraveling the Web of Disease. In *"Secret Judgments of God": Old World Disease in Colonial Spanish America*, edited by David Noble Cook and W. George Lovell, 213-42. Norman: University of Oklahoma Press.

Cook, Sherburne F., and Lesley Byrd Simpson. 1948. *The Population of Central Mexico in the Sixteenth Century, Ibero-Americana*, no. 31. Berkeley: University of California Press.

Cook, Sherburne F., and Woodrow Borah. 1960. *The Indian Population of Central Mexico, 1531-1610, Ibero-Americana*, no. 44. Berkeley: University of California Press.

———. 1970-1974. *Essays in Population History: Mexico and the Caribbean*. 2 vols. Berkeley: University of California Press.

Cooper Clark, James, ed. 1938. *Codex Mendoza*. London: Waterlow & Sons.

Cormack, Lesley B. 1997. *Charting an Empire: Geography at the English Universities, 1580-1620*. Chicago: University of Chicago Press.

Corominas, Joan. 1973. *Breve Diccionario Etimológico de la Lengua Castellana*. Madrid: Gredos.

Cortés, Hernán. 1988. *Cartas de Relación*. Mexico City: Editorial Porrúa.

———. 1915. *Cartas y Otros Documentos de Hernán Cortés*. Seville: F. Díaz.

———. 1963. *Cartas y Documentos*. Mexico City: Editorial Porrúa.

Cortés Hernández, Jaime. 1991. El Sistema Hidráulico en la Zempoala Prehispánica. In *Zempoala: El Estudio de una Ciudad Prehispánica*, edited by Jürgen K Brüggemann, 269-92. Mexico City: Instituto Nacional de Antropología e Historia.

Cosgrove, Denis. 1993. *The Palladian Landscape: Geographical Change and Its Cultural Representations in Sixteenth-Century Italy.* University Park: The Pennsylvania State University Press.

Cronon, William. 1983. *Changes in the Land: Indians, Colonists and the Ecology of New England.* New York: Hill & Wang.

Crosby, Alfred W. 1972. *The Columbian Exchange: Biological and Cultural Consequences of 1492.* Westport, Conn.: Greenwood Press.

———. 1986. *Ecological Imperialism: The Biological Expansion of Europe, 900-1900.* Cambridge: Cambridge University Press.

Cuevas, P. Mariano. 1914. *Documentos Inéditos del Siglo XVI para la Historia de México.* Mexico City: Museo Nacional de Arqueología, Historia e Etnología.

Daneels, Annick. 1990. Prospección y Levantamiento Topográfico en el Centro de Veracruz. In *Consejo de Arqueología, Boletín, 1989,* 33-35. Mexico City: Instituto Nacional de Antropología e Historia.

———. 1991. Patrón de Asentamiento Prehispánico en la Cuenca de Veracruz. In *Consejo de Arqueología, Boletín, 1990,* 79-82. Mexico City: Instituto Nacional de Antropología e Historia.

———. 1992. Patrón de Asentamiento Prehispánico en la Cuenca de Veracruz, México. In *Consejo de Arqueología, Boletín, 1991,* 71-74. Mexico City: Instituto Nacional de Antropología e Historia.

Darby, H. C. 1973. Domesday Book: The First Land Utilization Survey. In *Man Made the Land: Essays in English Historical Geography,* edited by Alan R. H. Baker and J. B. Harley, 37-45. Newton Abbot: David and Charles.

Davidson, David M. 1966. Negro Slave Control and Resistance in Colonial Mexico, 1519-1650. *Hispanic American Historical Review* 46:236-53.

Davis, J. E., and J. M. Norman. 1988. Effects of Shelter on Plant Water Use. *Agriculture, Ecosystems and Environment* 22/23:393-402.

Deevey, E. S. Jr., D. S. Rice, P. M. Rice, H. H. Vaughan, M. Brenner, and M. S. Flannery. 1979. Maya Urbanism: Impact on a Tropical Karst Environment. *Science* 206:298-306.

Del Angel P., Ana Lid. 1994. Formación de la Estructura Productiva Ganadera en al Llanura Costera de Veracruz Central. In *Las Llanuras Costeras de Veracruz: La Lenta Construcción de Regiones,* edited by Odile Hoffmann and Emilia Velázquez, 193-218. Xalapa: Universidad Veracruzana.

Denevan, William M. 1970. Aboriginal Drained-Field Cultivation in the Americas. *Science* 169:647-54.

———. 1980. Tipología de Configuraciones Agrícolas Prehispánicas. *América Indígena* 40:619-52.

———. 1992a. The Pristine Myth: The Landscape of the Americas in 1492. *Annals of the Association of American Geographers* 82:369-85.

———, ed. 1992b. *The Native Population of the Americas in 1492.* Madison: University of Wisconsin Press.

———. 1995. Prehistoric Agricultural Methods as Models for Sustainability. *Advances in Plant Pathology* 11:21-43.

Denevan, W. M., and B. L. Turner II. 1974. Forms, Functions and Associations of Raised-Field Agriculture in the Old World Tropics. *Journal of Tropical Geography* 39:24-33.

Deur, Douglas. 1997. Was the Northwest Coast Agricultural?: Ecological, Archaeological, and Ethnographic Evidence. Paper presented at the Annual Meeting of the American Association for the Advancement of Science, Seattle, Wash., February 15.

Diamond, Jared M. 1997. *Guns, Germs, and Steel: The Fates of Human Societies.* New York: W. W. Norton.

Díaz del Castillo, Bernal. 1986. *Historia Verdadera de la Conquista de la Nueva España.* Mexico City: Editorial Porrúa.

Díez de la Calle, Juan. 1932. *Memorial y Noticias Sacros y Reales de las Indias Occidentales.* Mexico City: Bibliófilos Mexicanos.

D'Olwer, Luis Nicolau, and Howard F. Cline. 1973. *Sahagún and His Works.* In *Guide to Ethnohistorical Sources, Part 2, The Handbook of Middle American Indians,* vol. 13, edited by Howard F. Cline, 186-239. Austin: University of Texas Press.

Doolittle, William E. 1984. Agricultural Change as an Incremental Process. *Annals of the Association of American Geographers* 74:112-37.

———. 1987. La Marismas to Pánuco to Texas: The Transfer of Open Range Cattle Ranching from Iberia through Northeastern Mexico. *Conference of Latin Americanist Geographers Yearbook* 13:3-11.

———. 1989. Arroyos and the Development of Agriculture in Northern Mexico. In *Fragile Lands of Latin America: Strategies for Sustainable Development,* edited by John O. Browder, 251-69. Boulder: Westview Press.

———. 1990. *Canal Irrigation in Prehistoric Mexico: The Sequence of Technological Change.* Austin: University of Texas Press.

Doolittle, William E., and Charles D. Frederick. 1991. Phytoliths as Indicators of Prehistoric Maize (*Zea mays* subsp. *mays,* Poaceae) Cultivation. *Plant Systematics and Evolution* 177:175-84.

Dorantes de Carranza, B. 1987. *Sumaria Relación de las Cosas de la Nueva España con Noticia Individual de los Conquistadores y Primeros Pobladores Españoles.* Mexico City: Editorial Porrúa.

Driever, Steven L. 1991. The Debate Over the New Road to Mexico During the Viceroyalty of Luis de Velasco, el Hijo (1590-5). Paper presented at the Annual Meeting of the Association of American Geographers, Miami, Fla., April 13-17.

———. 1995. The Veracruz-Mexico City Routes in the Sixteenth Century and the Study of Pre-Industrial Transport in Historical Geography. *Geografía y Desarrollo* 12 (September):5-18.

Duncan, James S. 1980. The Superorganic in American Cultural Geography. *Annals of the Association of American Geographers* 70:181-98.

———. 1990. *The City as Text: The Politics of Landscape Interpretation in the Kandyan Kingdom.* Cambridge: Cambridge University Press.

———. 1993. Landscapes of the Self/Landscapes of the Other(s): Cultural Geography 1991-92. *Progress in Human Geography* 17:367-77.

———. 1994. The Politics of Landscape and Nature, 1992-93. *Progress in Human Geography* 18:361-70.

———. 1995. Landscape Geography, 1993-94. *Progress in Human Geography* 19:414-22.

Durán, Diego. 1967. Historia de las Indias de Nueva España e Islas de la Tierra Firme. 2 vols. Mexico City: Editorial Porrúa.

Edwards, P. J., and N. M. Tainton. 1990. Managed Grasslands in South Africa. In *Ecosystems of the World 17A, Managed Grasslands*, edited by A. I. Breymeyer, 99-128. Amsterdam: Elsevier.

Eidt, Robert C. 1977. Detection and Examination of Anthrosols by Phosphate Analysis. *Science* 197:1327-33.

Erickson, Clark. 1992. Applied Archaeology and Rural Development: Archaeology's Potential Contribution to the Future. *Journal of the Steward Anthropology Society* 20:1-16.

Erickson, Clark, and Kay L. Candler. 1989. Raised Fields and Sustainable Agriculture in the Lake Titicaca Basin of Peru. In *Fragile Lands of Latin America: Strategies for Sustainable Development*, edited by John O. Browder, 230-48. Boulder: Westview Press.

Escobar, Arturo. 1995. *Encountering Development: The Making and Unmaking of the Third World*. Princeton: Princeton University Press.

———. 1998. Whose Knowledge, Whose Nature?: Biodiversity, Conservation, and the Political Ecology of Social Movements. *Journal of Political Ecology* 5:53-82.

Estadística Ganadera de la República. 1903. Mexico City: Secretaría de Fomento, Colonización, e Industria.

Estadísticas Históricas de México. 1990. 2 vols. Mexico City: Instituto Nacional de Estadística, Geografía e Informática.

Esteva, José María. 1843. Apuntes Arqueologicos. *El Museo Mexicano* 2:465-67.

Fernández Alés, R., A. Martín, and J. Merino. 1995. Landscape Change in the Last 500 Years in the Guadalquivir River Valley, Spain, with Special Reference to Doñana National Park. In *Global Land Use Change: A Perspective from the Columbian Encounter*, edited by B. L. Turner II, A. Gómez Sal, F. González Bernáldez, and F. de Castri, 361-76. Madrid: Consejo Superior de Investigaciones Científicas.

Fernández de Recas, Guillermo S. 1965. *Mayorazgos de la Nueva España*. Mexico City: Universidad Nacional Autónoma de México.

Fewkes, Jesse Walter. 1907. Certain Antiquities of Eastern Mexico. *Twenty-Fifth Annual Report of the Bureau of American Ethnology to the Secretary of the Smithsonian Institution, 1903-04*, 221-296. Washington, D.C.: Smithsonian Institution.

———. 1919. *Antiquities of the Gulf Coast of Mexico. Smithsonian Miscellaneous Collection*. Vol. 70, no. 2. Washington, D.C.: Smithsonian Institution.

Finck, Hugo. 1871. Account of Antiquities in the State of Vera Cruz, Mexico. *Smithsonian Annual Report for 1870*, 373-76.

Fisher, R. W. 1989. The Influence of Farming Systems and Practices on the Evolution of the Cotton-Boll Weevil Agroecosystem in the Americas: A Review. *Agriculture, Ecosystems and Environment* 25:315-28.

Florescano, Enrique. 1980. *Análisis Histórico de las Sequías en México*. Mexico City: Secretaría de Agricultura y Recursos Hidráulicos.

———. 1987. The Hacienda in New Spain. In *Colonial Spanish America*, edited by Leslie Bethell, 250-85. Cambridge: Cambridge University Press.

Florescano, Enrique, and Elsa Malvido, eds. 1982. *Ensayos Sobre la Historia de las Epidemias en México*. Mexico City: Instituto Mexicano del Seguro Social.

Fonseca, Fabian de, and Carlos de Urrutia. 1852. *Historia General de Real Hacienda*. Vol. 5. Mexico City: Vicente García Torres.

Forman, R. T. T., and M. Gordon. 1986. *Landscape Ecology*. New York: Wiley.

Foucault, Michel. 1970. *The Order of Things: An Archaeology of the Human Sciences.* New York: Random House.

———. 1979. *Discipline and Punish: The Birth of the Prison.* New York: Random House.

Fowler-Salamini, Heather. 1978. *Agrarian Radicalism in Veracruz, 1920-38.* Lincoln: University of Nebraska Press.

Frank, Andre Gunder. 1979. *Mexican Agriculture 1521-1630: Transformation of the Mode of Production.* Cambridge: Cambridge University Press.

Friedlander, Judith. 1969. Malaria and Demography in the Lowlands of Mexico: An Ethno-Historical Approach. In *Forms of Symbolic Action, Proceedings of the 1969 Annual Spring Meeting of the American Ethnological Society,* edited by Robert F. Spencer, 217-33. Seattle: American Ethnological Society and University of Washington Press.

Gage, Thomas. 1928. *A New Survey of the West Indies, 1648.* London: George Routledge.

Galindo y Villa, Jesús. 1912. *Las Ruinas de Cempoala y del Templo del Tajín (Estado de Veracruz).* No publication details specified.

Galván, Mariano. 1851 *Ordenanzas de Tierras y Aguas.* Mexico City: Mariano Galván.

García, Enriqueta. 1970. Los Climas del Estado de Veracruz. *Anales del Instituto de Biología, Serie Botánica* 41:3-42.

García de la Rivera, Livia. 1985. Breve Historia del Ingenio "El Modelo." *Historia Mexicana.* 35:299-307.

García Icazbalceta, Joaquin. 1858-1866. *Colección de Documentos para la Historia de México.* 2 vols. Mexico City: J. M. Andrade.

García Martínez, Bernardo. 1969. *El Marquesado del Valle: Tres Siglos de Régimen Señorial en Nueva España.* Mexico City: El Colegio de México.

García Payón, José. 1949a. Zempoala: Compendio de su Estudio Arqueologico. *Uni-Ver* 1:449-76.

———. 1949b. La Zona Arqueológica de Oceloapan. *Uni-Ver* 1:492-504.

———. 1950. Restos de una Cultura Prehistórica Encontrados de la Región de Zempoala, Ver. *Uni-Ver* 2:99-130.

———. 1963. *Bibliografía Arqueológica de Veracruz.* Mexico City: Universidad Veracruzana.

———. 1966. *Prehistoria de Mesoamérica: Excavaciones en Trapiche y Chalahuite, Veracruz, México, 1942, 1951 y 1959.* Xalapa: Universidad Veracruzana.

———. 1971. Archaeology of Central Veracruz. In *Archaeology of Northern Mesoamerica, Part 2, The Handbook of Middle American Indians,* vol. 11, edited by G. F. Ekholm and I. Bernal, 505-42. Austin: University of Texas Press.

García Pimentel, Luis, ed. 1904. *Relación de los Obispados de Tlaxcala, Michoacan, Oaxaca, y Otros Lugares en el Siglo XVI.* Mexico City: García Pimentel.

Gatenby, Ruth M. 1991. *Sheep.* London: MacMillan.

Gemelli Careri, J. F. 1745. A Voyage 'Round the World. In *A Collection of Voyages and Travels,* vol. 4, edited by Awnsham Churchill and John Churchill, 5-670. London: Churchill.

Gerhard, Peter. 1977. Congregaciones de Indios en la Nueva España antes de 1570. *Historia Mexicana* 26:347-95.

———. 1993. *A Guide to the Historical Geography of New Spain.* Norman: University of Oklahoma Press.

Gibson, Charles. 1964. *The Aztecs Under Spanish Rule: A History of the Indians of the Valley of Mexico, 1519-1820.* Stanford: Stanford University Press.

———. 1966. *Spain in America.* New York: Harper & Row.

———. 1967. *Tlaxcala in the Sixteenth Century.* Stanford: Stanford University Press.

———. 1968. *The Spanish Tradition in America.* Columbia: University of South Carolina Press.

Gibson, Charles, and John B. Glass. 1975. A Census of Middle American Prose Manuscripts in the Native Historical Tradition. In *Guide to Ethnohistorical Sources, Part 4, The Handbook of Middle American Indians,* vol. 15, edited by Howard F. Cline, 322-400. Austin: University of Texas Press.

Glacken, Clarence J. 1967. *Traces on the Rhodian Shore: Nature and Culture in Western Thought from Ancient Times to the End of the Eighteenth Century.* Berkeley: University of California Press.

Gliessman, S. R., ed. 1990. *Agroecology: Researching the Ecological Basis for Sustainable Agriculture.* New York: Springer-Verlag.

Godlewska, A., and Neil Smith, eds. 1994. *Geography and Empire.* Oxford: Blackwell.

Gold, Robert L. 1965. The Settlement of the Pensacola Indians in New Spain, 1763-1770. *Hispanic American Historical Review* 45:567-76.

———. 1970. Conflict in San Carlos: Indian Immigrants in Eighteenth-Century New Spain. *Ethnohistory* 17:1-10.

Gómara, Francisco López de. 1964. *Cortés: The Life of the Conqueror by His Secretary.* Translated by Lesley Byrd Simpson. Berkeley: University of California Press.

———. 1987. *La Conquista de Mexico.* Madrid: Historia 16.

Gómez-Pompa, Arturo. 1973. Ecology of the Vegetation of Veracruz. In *Vegetation and Vegetational History of Northern Latin America,* edited by Alan Graham, 73-148. Amsterdam: Elsevier.

———. 1990. Seduction by the Chinampas. *The DESFIL Newsletter* 3 (4):3, 6-8.

Gómez-Pompa, Arturo, H. L. Morales, E. Jiménez Avilla, and J. Jiménez Avilla. 1982. Experiences in Traditional Hydraulic Agriculture. In *Maya subsistence: Studies in memory of Dennis E. Puleston,* edited by K. V. Flannery, 327-42. New York: Academic Press.

González, Juan José. 1943. *Documentos Coloniales de la Nueva Veracruz.* Veracruz: Ciudad de Veracruz.

González de Cossio, Francisco. 1952. *El Libro de las Tasaciones de Pueblos de la Nueva España, Siglo XVI.* Mexico City: Archivo General de la Nación.

———. 1957. *Historia de la Tenencia y Explotación de Campo desde la Epoca Precortesiana hasta las Leyes del 6 de Enero de 1915.* Mexico City: Instituto de Estudios Históricos de la Revolución Mexicana.

González Jácome, Alba. 1988. *Población, Ambiente y Economía en Veracruz Central Durante la Colonia.* Mexico City: Universidad Iberoamericana.

Goulding, M. 1980. *The Fishes and the Forest: Explorations in Amazonian Natural History.* Berkeley: University of California Press.

Gregory, Derek. 1994. *Geographical Imaginations.* Cambridge, Mass.: Blackwell.

Hackett, C. W., ed. 1923. *Historical Documents Relating to New Mexico, Nueva Viscaya, and Approaches Thereto, to 1773.* 3 vols. Washington, D.C.: Carnegie Institution of Washington.

Hakluyt, Richard, ed. 1904. *The Principal Navigations, Voyages, Traffiques, and Discoveries of the English Nation.* 12 vols. Glasgow: James MacLehose and Sons.

Hamon, James L., and Stephen R. Niblo. 1975. *Precursors de la Revolución Agraria en México*. Mexico City: SEP/Setentas.

Hannah, Matthew G. 1993. Space and Social Control in the Administration of the Oglala Lakota ("Sioux"), 1871-1879. *Journal of Historical Geography* 19:412-32.

Haraway, Donna. 1991. *Simians, Cyborgs, and Women: The Reinvention of Nature*. New York: Chapman and Hall.

———. 1997. *Modest_Witness@Second_Millennium. Female_Man`_Meets_Onco-Mouse*™. London: Routledge.

Harley, J. Brian. 1992. Rereading the Maps of the Columbian Encounter. *Annals of the Association of American Geographers* 82:522-42.

Harris, David R. 1966. Recent Plant Invasions in the Arid And Semi-Arid Southwest of the United States. *Annals of the Association of American Geographers* 56:408-22.

Harris, R. Cole. 1991. Power, Modernity, and Historical Geography. *Annals of the Association of American Geographers* 81:671-83.

———. 1994. Voices of Disaster: Smallpox Around the Strait of Georgia in 1782. *Ethnohistory* 41:591-626.

———. 1997. *The Resettlement of British Columbia: Essays on Colonialism and Geographical Change*. Vancouver: University of British Columbia Press.

Hecht, Susanna B., and Alexander Cockburn. 1989. *The Fate of the Forest: Developers, Destroyers and Defenders of the Amazon*. London: Verso.

Henige, David. 1998. *Numbers from Nowhere: The American Indian Contact Population Debate*. Norman: University of Oklahoma Press.

Herrera, Antonio de. 1944-1947. *Historia General de los Hechos de los Castellanos en las Islas, y Tierra-Firme de el Mar Oceano*. 10 vols. Buenos Aires: Editorial Guarantied.

Himmerich y Valencia, R. 1991. *The Encomenderos of New Spain, 1521-1555*. Austin: University of Texas Press.

Holmes, W. 1987. Beef Production from Marginal Grasslands. In *Ecosystems of the World 17B, Managed Grasslands*, edited by R. W. Snaydon, 91-100. Amsterdam: Elsevier.

Hulme, Peter. 1992. *Colonial Encounters: Europe and the Native Caribbean, 1492-1797*. New York: Routledge.

Humboldt, Alexander von. 1966. *Political Essay on the Kingdom of New Spain*. 4 vols. New York: AMS Press.

Huntington, Ellsworth. 1917. Graphic Representation of the Effect of Climate on Man. *Geographical Review* 4:401-3.

Icaza, F. A. de., ed. 1923. *Diccionario Autobiográfico de Conquistadores y Pobladores de Nueva España*. 2 vols. Madrid: Adelantado de Segovia.

INEGI (Instituto Nacional de Estadística, Geografía e Informática). 1984. *Carta Uso del Suelo y Vegetación*, sheets E14-3, E14-6, and E15-1-4. Thematic map, 1:250,000. México City: Instituto Nacional de Estadística, Geografía e Informática.

Jackson, Wes. 1994. *Becoming Native to this Place*. Lexington: University Press of Kentucky.

Janzen, Daniel H., and Martin, Paul S. 1982. Neotropical Anachronisms: The Fruits the Gophotheres Ate. *Science* 215:19-27.

Jennings, Bruce H. 1988. *Foundations of International Agricultural Research: Science and Politics in Mexican Agriculture*. Boulder: Westview Press.

Johnston, R. J. 1983. *Geography and Geographers: Anglo-American Human Geography Since 1945*. London: Edward Arnold.

Jordan, T. G. 1993. *North American Cattle-Ranching Frontiers: Origins, Diffusion, and Differentiation*. Albuquerque: University of New Mexico Press.

Kates, Robert W. 1987. The Human Environment: The Road Not Taken, the Road Still Beckoning. *Annals of the Association of American Geographers* 77:525-34.

Keller, Albert G. 1908. *Colonization: A Study of the Founding of New Societies*. Boston: Ginn & Co.

Kelly, Isabel, and Angel Palerm. 1952. *The Tajín Totonac, Part 1: History, Subsistence, Shelter and Technology*. Washington, D.C.: Smithsonian Institution.

King, Anthony D. 1999. (Post)colonial Geographies: Material and Symbolic. *Historical Geography* 27:99-118.

Kiple, Kenneth F., and Brian T. Higgins. 1992. Yellow Fever and the Africanization of the Caribbean. In *Disease and Demography in the Americas*, edited by John W. Verano and Douglas H. Ubelaker, 237-48. Washington, D.C.: Smithsonian Institution.

Klor de Alva, J. Jorge. 1995. The Postcolonization of the (Latin) American Experience: A Reconstruction of "Colonialism," "Postcolonialism," and "Mestizaje." In *After Colonialism: Imperial Histories and Postcolonial Displacements*, edited by Gyan Prakash, 241-75. Princeton: Princeton University Press.

Krickeberg, Walter. 1933. *Los Totonac*. Mexico City: Secretaría de Educación Pública.

Kuhn, Thomas S. 1962. *The Structure of Scientific Revolutions*. Chicago: University of Chicago Press.

La Ganadería en el Estado de Veracruz. 1965. Xalapa: Universidad Veracruzana.

Lambert, Dean P. 1992. *Changes in a Tropical Dry Forest Shifting Cultivation System, Guerrero, Mexico*. Unpublished Ph.D. dissertation, University of Texas at Austin.

Landes, David. 1998. *The Wealth and Poverty of Nations: Why Some Are So Rich and Some So Poor*. New York: W. W. Norton.

Latorre, Germán. 1920. *Relaciones Geográficas de Indias*. Seville: Centro Oficial de Estudios Americanistas de Sevilla.

Latour, Bruno. 1993. *We Have Never Been Modern*. Cambridge, Mass.: Harvard University Press.

———. 1999. *Pandora's Hope: Essays on the Reality of Science Studies*. Cambridge, Mass.: Harvard University Press.

Lauer, Wilhelm. 1978. Okologische Klimatypen am Ostabfall der Mexikanischen Meseta. *Erdkunde* 32:101-10.

Leach, M., and Mearns, R. 1996. *The Lie of the Land: Challenging Received Wisdom on the African Environment*. Portsmouth: Heinemann.

León Pérez, Ignacio. 1991. Proyecto de Rescate Arqueológico en la Región de Medellín, Veracruz. In *Consejo de Arqueología, Boletín, 1990*, 159-62. Mexico City: Instituto Nacional de Antropología e Historia.

León-Portilla, Miguel. 1959. *Visión de los Vencidos*. Mexico City: Universidad Nacional Autónoma de México.

Leplin, Jarrett. 1984. *Scientific Realism*. Berkeley: University of California Press.

Lewis, Oscar. 1966. The Culture of Poverty. *Scientific American* 215 (4):19-25.

Lewis, Peirce. 1992. America's Natural Landscapes. In *Making America: The Society and Culture of the United States*, edited by Luther S. Luedtke, 41-67. Chapel Hill: University of North Carolina Press.

Licate, Jack A. 1981. *Creation of a Mexican Landscape: Territorial Organization and Settlement in the Eastern Puebla Basin, 1520-1605*. Chicago: Department of Geography, University of Chicago.

Lightfoot, Dale R. 1993. The Cultural Ecology of Pueblo Pebble-Mulch Gardens. *Human Ecology* 21:115-43.

Livingstone, David N. 1992. *The Geographical Tradition: Episodes in the History of a Contested Enterprise*. Oxford: Blackwell.

———. 1995. The Polity of Nature: Representation, Virtue, Strategy. *Ecumene* 2:353-77.

Lockhart, James. 1969. Encomienda and Hacienda: The Evolution of the Great Estate in the Spanish Indies. *Hispanic American Historical Review* 49:411-29.

———. 1992. *The Nahuas After the Conquest: A Social and Cultural History of the Indians of Central Mexico, Sixteenth Through Eighteenth Centuries*. Stanford: Stanford University Press.

Lockhart, James, and Enrique Otte. 1976. *Letters and People of the Spanish Indies, Sixteenth Century*. Cambridge: Cambridge University Press.

Los Municipios de Veracruz. 1988. Mexico City: Secretaría de Gobernación y Gobierno del Estado de Veracruz-Llave.

Lovell, W. George. 1992. "Heavy Shadows and Black Night": Disease and Depopulation in Colonial Spanish America. *Annals of the Association of American Geographers* 82:426-43.

Lowe, Lisa. 1991. *Critical Terrains: French and British Orientalisms*. Ithaca: Cornell University Press.

Lowenthal, David. 1990. Awareness of Human Impacts: Changing Attitudes and Emphases. In *The Earth as Transformed by Human Action: Global and Regional Changes in the Biosphere Over the Past 300 Years*, edited by B. L. Turner II, William C. Clark, Robert W. Kates, John F. Richards, Jessica T. Mathews, and William B. Meyer, 121-35. Cambridge: Cambridge University Press.

Lowenthal, David, and Martyn J. Bowden, eds. 1976. *Geographies of the Mind: Essays in Historical Geosophy in Honor of John Kirtland Wright*. New York: Oxford University Press.

Lyon, G. F. 1971. *Journal of a Residence and Tour in the Republic of Mexico in the Year 1826*. 2 vols. London: Kennikat Press.

Mallon, Florencia E. 1994. The Promise and Dilemma of Subaltern Studies: Perspectives from Latin American History. *American Historical Review* 99:1491-515.

Martínez, Rodrigo. 1992. Los Libros de Gobierno de Antonio de Mendoza y Luis de Velasco. In *Las Formas y Las Políticas del Dominio Agrario, Homenaje a François Chevalier*, edited by Ricardo Avila Palafox, Carlos Martínez Assad, and Jean Meyer, 123-35. Guadalajara: Editorial Universidad de Guadalajara.

Martyr de Algeria, Pedro. 1964. *Decades del Nuevo Undo*. 2 vols. Mexico City: Porrúa.

Mason, Charles T., and Patricia B. Mason. 1987. *A Handbook of Mexican Roadside Flora*. Tucson: University of Arizona Press.

Matesanz, J. 1965. Introducción de la Ganadería en Nueva España, 1521-1525. *Historia Mexicana* 14:533-66.

Mathewson, Kent. 1998. Cultural Landscapes and Ecology, 1995-96: Of Oecumenics and Nature(s). *Progress in Human Geography* 22:115-28.

———. 1999. Cultural Landscape and Ecology II: Regions, Retrospects, Revivals. *Progress in Human Geography* 23:267-81.

Mayer, Brands. 1847. *Mexico, As it Was and As it Is*. Philadelphia: G. B. Fiebre.

McBride, George M. 1923. *The Land Systems of Mexico.* New York: American Geographical Society.

McCann, Joseph M. 1999a. Before 1492: The Making of the Pre-Columbian Landscape. Part I: The Environment. *Ecological Restoration* 17 (1 and 2):15-30.

―――. 1999b. Before 1492: The Making of the Pre-Columbian Landscape. Part II: The Vegetation, and Implications for Restoration for 2000 and Beyond. *Ecological Restoration* 17 (3):3-15.

McGlade, Michael S. 1997. The Potential of Irrigated Lands to Reduce Food Dependency in Mexico. *Society and Natural Resources* 10:329-40.

McLynn, Frank J. 1990. *Burton: Snow Upon the Desert.* London: John Murray.

Meadows, Donella H., Dennis L. Meadows, Jørgen Randers, and William W. Behrens III. 1972. *The Limits to Growth.* New York: Universe Books.

Medellín Zenil, Alfonso. 1952. *Exploraciones en Quauhtochco.* Xalapa: Gobierno del Estado de Veracruz.

―――. 1953. Desarrollo de la Cultura Prehispánica Central Veracruzana. *Anales del Instituto Nacional de Antropología e Historia* 7:101-109.

―――. 1955. *Exploraciones en la Isla de Sacrificios.* Xalapa: Gobierno del Estado de Veracruz.

―――. 1960. *Cerámicas del Totonacapan: Exploraciones en el Centro de Veracruz.* Xalapa: Universidad Veracruzana.

Meinig, D. W. 1969. A Macrogeography of Western Imperialism: Some Morphologies of Moving Frontiers of Political Control. In *Settlement and Encounter: Geographical Studies Presented to Sir Grenfell Price,* edited by Fay Gale and Graham H. Lawton, 213-40. London: Oxford University Press.

―――. 1986. *The Shaping of America: A Geographical Perspective on 500 Years of History, Volume 1, Atlantic America, 1492-1800.* New Haven: Yale University Press.

―――. 1993. *The Shaping of America: A Geographical Perspective on 500 Years of History, Volume 2, Continental America, 1800-1867.* New Haven: Yale University Press.

Melgarejo Vivanco, José Luis. 1943. *Totonacapan.* Xalapa: Talleres Gráficos del Gobierno del Estado.

―――. 1949. *Historia de Veracruz.* Vol. 1. Xalapa: Gobierno del Estado de Veracruz.

―――. 1975. *Breve Historia de Veracruz.* Xalapa: Gobierno del Estado de Veracruz.

―――. 1976. *Antigua Historia de México.* Vol. 3. Mexico City: Secretaría de Educación Pública, Mexico.

―――. 1980. *Antigua Ecología Indígena en Veracruz.* Xalapa: Gobierno del Estado de Veracruz.

―――. n.d. *Historia de la Ganadería en Veracruz.* Mexico City: Ediciones del Gobierno de Veracruz.

Melville, Elinor G. K. 1983. *The Pastoral Economy and Environmental Degradation in Highland Central Mexico, 1530-1600.* Unpublished Ph.D. dissertation, University of Michigan.

―――. 1990. Environmental and Social Change in the Valle de Mezquital, Mexico, 1521-1600. *Comparative Studies in Society and History* 32:24-53.

―――. 1994. *A Plague of Sheep: Environmental Consequences of the Conquest of Mexico.* Cambridge: Cambridge University Press.

Mentz, Brígida von. 1990. Estudio Preliminar. In *México Hacia 1850*, edited and translated by Brígida von Mentz, 11-45. Mexico City: Consejo Nacional para la Cultura y las Artes.

Merchant, Carolyn. 1989. *Ecological Revolutions: Nature, Gender, and Science in New England*. Chapel Hill: University of North Carolina Press.

———. 1996. Reinventing Eden: Western Culture as a Recovery Narrative. In *Uncommon Ground: Rethinking the Human Place in Nature*, edited by William Cronon, 132-159. New York: W. W. Norton.

Metcalfe, S. E. 1987. Historical Data and Climate Change in Mexico: A Review. *Geographical Journal* 153:211-22.

Meyer, Melissa L., and Kerwin L. Klein. 1998. Native American Studies and the End of Ethnohistory. In *Studying Native America: Problems and Prospects*, edited by Russell Thornton, 182-216. Madison: University of Wisconsin Press.

Meyer, Michael C., and William L. Sherman. 1987. *The Course of Mexican History*. New York: Oxford University Press.

Meyer, William B., Derek Gregory, B. L. Turner II, and Patricia F. McDowell. 1992. The Local-Global Continuum. In *Geography's Inner Worlds: Pervasive Themes in Contemporary American Geography*, edited by Ronald F. Abler, Melvin G. Marcus, and Judy M. Olson, 255-79. New Brunswick, N.J.: Rutgers University Press.

Millares Carlo, A., and J. I. Mantecón, eds. 1945. *Indice y Extractos de los Protocolos del Archivo de Notarías de México, D. F. (Siglo XVI)*. 2 vols. Mexico City: El Colegio de México.

Miranda, José. 1965. *La Función Económica del Encomendero en los Origenes del Regimen Colonial*. Mexico City: Universidad Nacional Autónoma de México.

Mitchell, Don. 1996. *The Lie of the Land: Migrant Workers and the California Landscape*. Minneapolis: University of Minnesota Press.

Mörner, Magnus. 1973. The Spanish American Hacienda: A Survey of Recent Research and Debate. *Hispanic American Historical Review* 53:183-216.

Morrisey, Richard J. 1957. Colonial Agriculture in New Spain. *Agricultural History* 31:24-29.

Mota y Escobar, Alonso de la. 1939-1940. Memoriales del Obispo de Tlaxcala. *Anales del Instituto Nacional de Antropología e Historia* 1:191-306.

———. 1987. *Fray Alonso de la Mota y Escobar: Memoriales del Obispo de Tlaxcala: Un Recorrido por el Centro de México a Principios del Siglo XVII*. Mexico City: Secretaría de Educación Pública.

Motolinía (Toribio de Bernadette). 1971. *Memoriales o Libro de las Cosas de la Nueva España y de los Naturales de Ella*. Mexico City: Universidad Nacional Autónoma de México.

Muir, John. 1894. *The Mountains of California*. New York: The Century Company.

Myers, Garth A. 1998. Intellectual of Empire: Eric Dutton and Hegemony in British Africa. *Annals of the Association of American Geographers* 88:1-27.

Naipaul, V. S. 1995. *A Way in the World*. New York: Vintage International.

Nash, Gary B. 1974. *Red, White, and Black: The Peoples of Early America*. Englewood Cliffs, N.J.: Prentice-Hall.

Navarrete Hernández, Mario. 1988. Asentamientos Culturales Primitivos en Veracruz Central. In *Orígenes del Hombre Americano*, edited by Alba González Jácome, 231-36. Mexico City: Secretaría de Educación Pública.

Netting, Robert McC. 1993. *Smallholders, Householders: Farm Families and the Ecology of Intensive, Sustainable Agriculture.* Stanford: Stanford University Press.

Neumann, A. L., and Roscoe R. Snapp. 1969. *Beef Cattle.* New York: John Wiley.

Niembro Rocas, Aníbal. 1986. *Arboles y Arbustos Utiles de México.* Mexico City: Limusa.

Nietschmann, B. 1972. Hunting and Fishing Focus Among the Miskito Indians, Eastern Nicaragua. *Human Ecology* 1:41-67.

NRC (National Research Council). 1987. *Predicting Feed Intake of Food-Producing Animals.* Washington, D.C.: National Academy Press.

———. 1999. *Our Common Journey: A Transition Toward Sustainability.* Washington, D.C.: National Academy Press.

Nuttal, Zelia. 1910. The Island of Sacrificios. *American Anthropologist* 12:257-95.

Ober, Frederick A. 1887. *Travels in Mexico and Life Among the Mexicans.* Boston: Estes and Lauriat.

Ocaranza, Fernando. 1982. Las Grandes Epidemias del Siglo XVI, en la Nueva España. In *Ensayos Sobre la Historia de las Epidemias en México,* edited by Enrique Florescano and Elsa Malvido, 201-4. Mexico City: Instituto Mexicano del Seguro Social.

O'Connor, Martin, ed. 1994. *Is Capitalism Sustainable: Political Economy and the Politics of Ecology.* New York: Guilford.

O'Gorman, Edmundo. 1941. *Catálogo de Pobladores de Nueva España, Registro de Informes de la Real Audiencia, Ultimo Tercio del Siglo XVI-Principios del Siglo XVII.* Mexico City: Archivo General de la Nación.

———. 1958. *La Invención de América: El Universalismo de la Cultura de Occidente.* Mexico City: Fundo de Cultura Económica.

———. 1961. *The Invention of America: An Inquiry into the Historical Nature of the New World and the Meaning of its History.* Bloomington: Indiana University Press.

Ojeda Falcón, Ramón. 1982. Apuntes sobre el Ultimo Brote de Fiebre Amarilla Ocurrido en el Puerto de Veracruz (1920-21). In *Ensayos Sobre las Epidemias en México,* vol. 2, edited by Enrique Florescano and Elsa Malvido, 725-39. Mexico City: Instituto Mexicano del Seguro Social.

Olwig, Kenneth R. 1996. Reinventing Common Nature: Yosemite and Mount Rushmore—A Meandering Tale of a Double Nature. In *Uncommon Ground: Rethinking the Human Place in Nature,* edited by William Cronon, 379-408. New York: W. W. Norton.

Ouweneel, Arij. 1996. *Shadows Over Anahuac: An Ecological Interpretation of Crisis and Development in Central Mexico, 1730-1800.* Albuquerque: University of New Mexico Press.

Oviedo, Gonzalo Fernández de. 1959. *Historia General y Natural de las Indias.* 5 vols. Madrid: Atlas.

Palerm, Angel. 1955. The Agricultural Basis of Urban Civilization in Mesoamerica. *Social Science Monographs* 1:28-42.

———. 1961. Distribución del Regadío Prehispánico en el Area Central de Mesoamérica. *Revista Interamericana de Ciencias Sociales* 1:242-66.

———. 1973. *Obras Hidráulicas Prehispánicas en el Sistema Lacustre del Valle de México.* Mexico City: Instituto Nacional de Antropología e Historia.

Palerm, Angel, and Eric R. Wolf. 1957. Ecological Potential and Cultural Development in Mesoamerica. In *Studies in Human Ecology,* edited by L. Krader and Angel Palerm, 1-37. Washington, D.C.: Anthropological Society of Washington and General Secretariat of the Organization of American States.

Parsons, James J. 1970. The "Africanization" of the New World Tropical Grasslands. *Tubinger Geographische Studien* 34:141-53.

Paso y Troncoso, Francisco del, ed. 1892-1893. *Exposición Histórico-Americana de Madríd: Catálogo de la Sección de México.* 2 vols. Madrid: Sucesores de Rivadeneyra.

———. 1905. *Papeles de Nueva España.* 9 vols. Madrid: Sucesores de Rivadeneyra.

———, ed. 1939-1940. *Epistolario de Nueva España.* 16 vols. Mexico City: Porrúa.

Pasquel, Leonardo. 1958. *La Ciudad de Veracruz.* Vol. 1. Xalapa: Editorial Citlaltépetl.

Patrick, L. 1977. A Cultural Geography of the Use of Seasonally Dry, Sloping Terrain: The *Metepantli* Crop Terraces of Central Mexico. Unpublished Ph.D. dissertation, University of Pittsburgh.

———. 1985. *Agave* and *Zea* in Highland Central Mexico: The Ecology and History of the *Metepantli.* In *Prehistoric Intensive Agriculture in the Tropics,* edited by I. S. Farrington, 539-46. Oxford: British Archaeological Reports.

Pearsall, D. M. 1989. *Paleoethnobotany: A Handbook of Procedures.* New York: Academic Press.

Peet, Richard, and Michael Watts. 1993. Development Theory and Environment in an Age of Market Triumphalism. *Economic Geography* 69:227-53.

Pennington, T. D., and José Sarukhan. 1968. *Manual para la Identificación de Campo de los Principales Arboles Tropicales de México.* Mexico City: Instituto Nacional de Investigaciones Forestales and Organización de las Naciones Unidas para la Agricultura y la Alimentación.

Pérez de Rivas, Andrés. 1896. *Crónica y Historia Religiosa de la Provincia de la Compañía de Jesús de México.* 2 vols. Mexico City: Sagrado Corazon de Jesús.

Perry, Richard J. 1996. *From Time Immemorial: Indigenous Peoples and State Systems.* Austin: University of Texas Press.

Pezzat, Delia A. 1980. *Catálogo de Ramo de Congregaciones.* Mexico City: Archivo General de la Nación.

Philp, Mark. 1985. Michel Foucault. In *The Return of Grand Theory in the Human Sciences,* edited by Quentin Skinner, 65-81. Cambridge: University of Cambridge Press.

Pickett, S. T. A., and M. L. Cadenasso. 1995. Landscape Ecology: Spatial Heterogeneity in Ecological Systems. *Science* 269:331-34.

Piñón Flores, M. Irais. 1984. La Tenencia de la Tierra en la Región de Tlazazalca-Zacapu-Huaniqueo. In *Michoacan en el Siglo XVI,* edited by Carlos S. Paredes M., M. Irais Piñón Flores, Armando M. Escobar O., and María Trinidad Pulido Solís, 105-89. Morelia: Fimax

Piperno, Dolores R. 1988. *Phytolith Analysis: An Archaeological and Geological Perspective.* New York: Academic Press

Pollock, Norman. 1980. Colonies, Explorers, Pioneers and Settlers. In *Studies in Overseas Settlement and Population,* edited by Anthony Lemon and Norman Pollock, 3-30. London: Longman.

Porter, Philip W., and Eric S. Sheppard. 1998. *A World of Difference: Society, Nature, Development.* New York: Guilford.

Powell, J. M. 1982. Archibald Grenfell Price 1892-1977. *Geographers: Bibliographical Studies* 6:87-92.

Pozas, Ricardo, and Isabel H. de Pozas. 1971. *Los Indios en las Clases Sociales de México*. Mexico City: Siglo XXI.

Pratt, M. L. 1992. *Imperial Eyes: Travel Writing and Transculturation*. London: Routledge.

Prem, Hanns J. 1984. Early Spanish Colonization and Indians in the Valley of Atlixco, Puebla. In *Explorations in Ethnohistory: Indians of Central Mexico in the Sixteenth Century*, edited by H. R. Harvey and Hanns J. Prem, 205-228. Albuquerque: University of New Mexico Press.

———. 1988. *Milpa y Hacienda: Tenencia de la Tierra Indígena y Española en la Cuenca del Alto Atoyac, Puebla, México (1520-1650)*. Translated by María Martínez Peñaloza. Mexico City: Centro de Investigaciones y Estudios Superiores en Antropología Social, Estado de Puebla, and Fondo de Cultura Económica.

———. 1991. Disease Outbreaks in Central Mexico During the Sixteenth Century. In *Secret Judgments of God: Old World Disease in Colonial Spanish America*, edited by Noble David Cook and W. George Lovell, 20-48. Norman: University of Oklahoma Press.

———. 1992. Spanish Colonization and Indian Property in Central Mexico, 1521-1620. *Annals of the Association of American Geographers* 82:444-59.

Price, A. Grenfell. 1963. *The Western Invasions of the Pacific and its Continents: A Study of Moving Frontiers and Changing Landscapes, 1513-1958*. London: Oxford University Press.

Proctor, James D. 1998. The Social Construction of Nature: Relativist Accusations, Pragmatist and Critical Realist Responses. *Annals of the Association of American Geographers* 88:352-76.

Pyne, Stephen. 1997. Frontiers of Fire. In *Ecology and Empire: Environmental History of Settler Societies*, edited by Tom Griffiths and Libby Robin, 19-34. Seattle: University of Washington Press.

Ramirez Cabañas, Joaquin. 1943. *La Ciudad de Veracruz en el Siglo XVI*. Mexico City: Imprenta Universitaria.

Rattray, P. V. 1987. Sheep Production from Managed Grasslands. In *Ecosystems of the World 17B, Managed Grasslands*, edited by R. W. Snaydon, 113-22. Amsterdam: Elsevier.

Recopilación de Leyes de los Reynos de las Indias. 1987. 5 vols. Mexico City: Porrúa.

Redclift, M., and T. Benton. 1994. *Social Theory and the Global Environment*. London: Routledge.

Rees, Peter W. 1975. Origins of Colonial Transportation in Mexico. *Geographical Review* 65:323-34.

Rice, P. M., and D. S. Rice. 1979. Home on the Range: Aboriginal Maya Settlement in the Central Petén Savannas. *Archaeology* 32:16-25.

Roberts, Leslie. 1989. Disease and Death in the New World. *Science* 246:1245-47.

Rojas Rabiela, T. 1988. *Las Siembras de Ayer*. Mexico: Secretaría de Educación Pública.

Rorty, Richard. 1979. *Philosophy and the Mirror of Nature*. Princeton: Princeton University Press.

Rosenberg, Nathan. 1982. Natural Resource Limits and the Future of Economic Progress. In *Progress and Its Discontents*, edited by Gabriel A. Almond, Marvin Chodorow, and Roy H. Pearce, 301-18. Berkeley: University of California Press.

Rouse, J. E. 1977. *The Criollo: Spanish Cattle in the Americas*. Norman: University of Oklahoma Press.

Ruiz, Ramón Eduardo. 1992. *Triumphs and Tragedy: A History of the Mexican People.* New York: W. W. Norton.

Ruíz Gordillo, J. Omar. 1985. Rescate Arqueologico en el Conchal, Veracruz. In *Tres Estudios en Arqueología de Veracruz*, 39-46. Mexico City: Instituto de Antropología e Historia.

———. 1989. *Oceloapan, Apuntes para la Historia de un Sitio Arqueológico en Veracruz.* Mexico City: Instituto de Antropología e Historia.

Russell, Emily W. B. 1997. *People and the Land Through Time: Linking Ecology and History.* New Haven: Yale University Press.

Rzedowski, J. 1983. *Vegetación de México.* Mexico City: Limusa.

Sachs, J. B., A. D. Mellinger, and J. L. Gallup. 2001. The Geography of Poverty and Wealth. *Scientific American* 284 (3):70-75.

Sachs, Wolfgang, ed. 1992. *The Development Dictionary: A Guide to Knowledge as Power.* London: Zed Books.

Sahagún, Bernardino de. 1950-1982. *Florentine Codex: General History of the Things of New Spain.* 13 vols. Translated by Arthur J. O. Anderson and Charles E. Dibble. Santa Fe: School of American Research.

Said, Edward W. 1979. *Orientalism.* New York: Vintage Books.

———. 1993. *Culture and Imperialism.* New York: Alfred A. Knopf.

Sale, Kirkpatrick. 1990. *The Conquest of Paradise: Christopher Columbus and the Columbian Legacy.* New York: Alfred A. Knopf.

Salvucci, Richard J. 1987. *Textiles and Capitalism in Mexico: An Economic History of the Obrajes, 1539-1840.* Princeton: Princeton University Press.

Sanders, William T. 1953. The Anthropogeography of Central Veracruz. In *Huastecos, Totonacos y sus Vecinos, Revista Mexicana de Estudios Antropológicos*, vol. 13, edited by Ignacio Bernal and Eusebio Dávalos Hurtado, 27-78.

———. 1971. Cultural Ecology and Settlement Patterns of the Gulf Coast. In *Archaeology of Northern Mesoamerica, Part 2, The Handbook of Middle American Indians*, vol. 11, edited by G. F. Ekholm and I. Bernal, 543-57. Austin: University of Texas Press.

———. 1992. The Population of the Central Mexican Symbiotic Region, the Basin of Mexico, and the Teotihuacán Valley in the Sixteenth Century. In *The Native Population of the Americas in 1492*, edited by William M. Denevan, 85-150. Madison: University of Wisconsin Press.

Sanders, William T., and Barbara Price. 1968. *Mesoamerica: The Evolution of a Civilization.* New York: Random House.

Sanderson, S. E. 1986. *The Transformation of Mexican Agriculture: International Structures and the Politics of Rural Change.* Princeton: Princeton University Press.

Santamaría, Francisco J. 1959. *Diccionario de Mejicanismos.* Mexico City: Porrúa.

Sartorius, Carl. 1869. Fortificaciones Antiguas. *Sociedad Mexicana Geográfica, Boletín*, series 2, 1:818-27.

———. 1961. *Mexico About 1850.* Stuttgart: F. A. Brockhaus.

Sauer, Carl O. 1935. *Aboriginal Population of Northwestern Mexico, Ibero-Americana*, no. 10. Berkeley: University of California Press.

———. 1938a. Destructive Exploitation in Modern Colonial Expansion. *Comptes Rendu du Congrès International de Géographie* 2 (3c):494-99.

———. 1938b. Theme of Plant and Animal Destruction in Economic History. *Journal of Farm Economics* 20:765-75.

———. 1941. Foreword to Historical Geography. *Annals of the Association of American Geographers* 31:1-24.

———. 1950. Grassland Climax, Fire, and Man. *Journal of Range Management* 3:16-21.

———. 1956. Summary Remarks: Retrospect. In *Man's Role in Changing the Face of the Earth*, vol. 2., edited by William L. Thomas, 1131-35. Chicago: University of Chicago Press.

———. 1958. Man in the Ecology of Tropical America. *Proceedings of the Ninth Pacific Science Congress, 1957* 20:105-10.

———. 1966. *The Early Spanish Main.* Berkeley: University of California Press.

———. 1969. The Morphology of Landscape. In *Land and Life*, edited by John Leighly, 315-50. Berkeley: University of California Press.

Scholes, F. V., and E. B. Adams, eds. 1955. *Relación de las Encomiendas de Indios Hechas en Nueva España a los Conquistadores y Pobladores de Ella, Año de 1564, Documentos para la Historia del México Colonial.* Vol. 1. Mexico City: Editorial Porrúa.

Semple, Ellen C. 1911. *Influences of Geographic Environment on the Basis of Ratzel's System of Anthropo-geography.* New York: Henry Holt.

Shaw, Norton, ed. 1859. Thirteenth Meeting, June 13th, 1859. *Proceedings of the Royal Geographical Society of London.* 3:347-58.

Siemens, Alfred H. 1980. Indicios de Aprovechamiento Agrícola Prehispánico de Tierras Inundables en el Centro de Veracruz. *Biótica* 5:83-92.

———. 1983a. Wetland Agriculture in Pre-Hispanic Mesoamerica. *Geographical Review* 73:166-81.

———. 1983b. Oriented Raised Fields in Central Veracruz. *American Antiquity* 48:85-102.

———. 1983c. Modeling Prehispanic Hydroagriculture on Levee Backslopes in Northern Veracruz, Mexico. In *Drained Field Agriculture in Central and South America*, edited by J. P. Darch, 27-54. Oxford: British Archaeological Reports.

———. 1985. Results of Recent Air Reconnaissance Over the Mexican State of Veracruz. In *Prehistoric Intensive Agriculture in the Tropics*, edited by I. S. Farrington, 127-48. Oxford: British Archaeological Reports.

———. 1989. *Tierra Configurada: Investigaciones de los Vestigios de Agricultura Precolumbiana en Tierras Inundables Costeras desde el Norte de Veracruz hasta Belice.* Mexico City: Consejo Nacional para la Cultura y las Artes.

———. 1990a. *Between the Summit and the Sea: Central Veracruz in the Nineteenth Century.* Vancouver: University of British Columbia Press.

———. 1990b. Reducing the Risk: Some Indications Regarding Pre-Hispanic Wetland Agricultural Intensification From Contemporary Use of a Wetland/Terra Firma Boundary Zone in Central Veracruz. In *Agroecology: Researching the Ecological Basis for Sustainable Agriculture*, edited by S. R. Gliessman, 233-50. New York: Springer-Verlag.

———. 1998. *A Favored Place: San Juan River Wetlands, Central Veracruz, A.D. 500 to the Present.* Austin: University of Texas Press.

Siemens, Alfred H., and Dennis E. Puleston. 1972. Ridged Fields and Associated Features in Southern Campeche: New Perspectives on the Lowland Maya. *American Antiquity* 37:228-39.

Siemens, Alfred H., and Lutz Brinckmann. 1976. El Sur de Veracruz a Finales del Siglo XVIII, un Análisis de la "Relación" de Corral. *Historia Mexicana* 26:263-324.

Siemens, Alfred H., Richard J. Hebda, Mario Navarrete Hernández, Dolores R. Piperno, Julie K. Stein, and M. G. Zolá Báez. 1988. Evidence for a Cultivar and a Chronology from Patterned Wetlands in Central Veracruz, Mexico. *Science* 242:105-107.

Simpson, Lesley Byrd. 1950. *The Encomienda in New Spain: The Beginning of Spanish Mexico*. Berkeley: University of California Press.

———. 1952. *Exploitation of Land in Central Mexico in the Sixteenth Century, Ibero-Americana*, no. 36. Berkeley: University of California Press.

Skerritt Gardner, David. 1989. *Una Historia Agraria en el Centro de Veracruz, 1850-1940*. Xalapa: Universidad Veracruzana.

———. 1993a. Colonización y Modernización del Campo en el Centro de Veracruz (Siglo XIX). *Cuadernos de Historia* 2 (5):39-57.

———. 1993b. *Rancheros Sobre Tierra Fértil*. Xalapa: Universidad Veracruzana.

Sluyter, Andrew. 1993. Long-Distance Staple Transport in Western Mesoamerica: Insights Through Quantitative Modeling. *Ancient Mesoamerica* 4:193-99.

———. 1994. Intensive Wetland Agriculture in Mesoamerica: Space, Time, and Form. *Annals of the Association of American Geographers* 84:557-84.

———. 1996. The Ecological Origins and Consequences of Cattle Ranching in Sixteenth-Century New Spain. *The Geographical Review* 8:161-77.

———. 1997a. On Excavating and Burying Epistemologies. *Annals of the Association of American Geographers* 87:700-702.

———. 1997b. Archival Research on Livestock and Landscape Change in Sixteenth-Century Mexico. *Conference of Latin Americanist Geographers Yearbook* 23:27-39.

———. 1997c. Regional, Holocene Records of the Human Dimension of Global Change: Sea-Level and Land-Use Change in Prehistoric Mexico. *Global and Planetary Change* 14:127-46.

———. 1998. From Archive to Map to Pastoral Landscape: A Spatial Perspective on the Livestock Ecology of Sixteenth-Century New Spain. *Environmental History* 3:508-29.

———. 1999. The Making of the Myth in Postcolonial Development: Material-Conceptual Landscape Transformation in Sixteenth-Century Veracruz. *Annals of the Association of American Geographers* 89:377-401.

Sluyter, Andrew, and Alfred H. Siemens. 1992. Vestiges of Prehispanic, Sloping-Field Terraces on the Piedmont of Central Veracruz, Mexico. *Latin American Antiquity* 3:148-60.

Sluyter, Andrew, Charles M. Ruffner, and James M. Adovasio. 1998. A Cultural-Ecological Model of Long-Term Landscape Transformation for the Allegheny National Forest. Paper presented at the 69th Annual Meeting of the Society for Pennsylvania Archaeology, New Cumberland, Pa., April 24-26.

Smith, N. 1994. Geography, Empire and Social Theory. *Progress in Human Geography* 18:491-500.

Smith, Richard T. 1987. Indigenous Agriculture in the Americas: Origins, Techniques and Contemporary Relevance. In *Latin American Development: Geographical Perspectives*, edited by David Preston, 34-69. New York: Longman Scientific & Technical.

Sparke, Matthew. 1998. A Map that Roared and an Original Atlas: Canada, Cartography, and the Narration of Nation. *Annals of the Association of American Geographers* 88:463-95.

Spengler, J. J., ed. 1961. *Natural Resources and Economic Growth.* Washington, D.C.: Resources for the Future.

Spivak, Gayatri C. 1988. Can the Subaltern Speak? In *Marxism and the Interpretation of Culture,* edited by C. Nelson and L. Grossberg, 271-313. Urbana: University of Illinois Press.

SRH (Secretaría de Recursos Hidráulicos). 1967. *Caracteristicas de los Distritios de Riego, Tomo III: Zonas Centro, Golfo de México y Sur.* Mexico City: Secretaría de Recursos Hidráulicos.

————. 1973a. *Rehabilitación de los Distritos de Riego de Antigua/Actopan.* Topographic map, 1:5,000. Mexico City: Secretaría de Recursos Hidráulicos.

————. 1973b. *Rehabilitación de los Distritos de Riego de Antigua/Actopan.* Topographic maps, 1:20,000. Mexico City: Secretaría de Recursos Hidráulicos.

————. 1973c. *La Antigua/Actopan.* Vertical aerial photographs, 1:8,000. Mexico City: Secretaría de Recursos Hidráulicos.

Stevens, Rayfred L. 1967. European Settlement Ventures in the Tropical Lowlands of Mexico. *Erdkunde* 21:258-77.

Steward, J. H. 1955 *Irrigation Civilizations: A Comparative Study.* Washington, D.C.: Pan American Union.

Stoddart, David R. 1986. *On Geography and its History.* Oxford: Basil Blackwell.

Strabo. 1923. *The Geography of Strabo.* 8 vols. Translated by Horace. L. Jones. New York: Putnam.

Strebel, Hermann. 1883. *Die Ruinen von Cempoallan im Staate Veracruz (Mexico) und Mitteilungen über die Totonaken der Jetztzeit.* Hamburg: no publisher specified.

————. 1889. *Alt-Mexiko.* 2 vols. Hamburg: Verlag von Leopold Voss.

Super, John C. 1988. *Food, Conquest, and Colonization in Sixteenth-Century Spanish America.* Albuquerque: University of New Mexico Press.

Swyngedouw, E. 1999. Modernity and Hybridity: Nature, Regeneracionismo, and the Production of the Spanish Waterscape, 1890–1930. *Annals of the Association of American Geographers* 89:443-65.

Taylor, Griffith T. 1919. Climatic Cycles and Evolution. *Geographical Review* 8:289-328.

Taylor, William B. 1972. *Landlord and Peasant in Colonial Oaxaca.* Stanford: Stanford University Press.

Thomas, William L. Jr., ed. 1956. *Man's Role in Changing the Face of the Earth.* 2 vols. Chicago: University of Chicago Press.

Thornthwaite, C. W. 1964. *Average Climatic Water Balance Data of the Continents, Part IV: North America (Excluding United States).* Centerton, N.J.: National Science Foundation.

Tichy, F. 1976. Orientación de las Pirámides e Iglesias en el Altiplano Mexicano. *Comunicaciones del Proyecto Puebla-Tlaxcala, Suplemento* 4:1-16.

Todorov, Tzvetan. 1987. *The Conquest of America: The Question of the Other.* New York: Harper and Row.

Toledo, Victor M. 1989. *Naturaleza, Producción, Cultura: Ensayos de Ecología Política.* Xalapa: Universidad Veracruzana.

Tolstoy, Paul. 1978. Western Mesoamerica Before A.D. 900. In *Chronologies in New World Archaeology,* edited by R. E. Taylor and Clement W. Meighan, 241-84. New York: Academic Press.

Torquemada, Juan de. 1969. *Monarquía Indiana.* 3 vols. Mexico City: Editorial Porrúa.

———. 1975-1983. *Monarquía Indiana.* 7 vols. Mexico City: Universidad Nacional Autónoma de México.

Trens, Manuel B. 1947. *Historia de Veracruz, Tomo 2, La Dominación Española, 1519-1808.* Xalapa: Gobierno del Estado de Veracruz.

———. 1955. *Historia de la H. Ciudad de Veracruz y de su Ayuntamiento.* Mexico City: Secretaría de Educación Pública.

Trimble, Stanley W. 1992. Preface. In *The American Environment: Interpretations of Past Geographies,* edited by L. M. Dilsaver and Craig E. Colten, xv-xxii. Lanham, Md.: Rowman & Littlefield.

Troll, Carl. 1971. Landscape Ecology (Geoecology) and Biogeocenology: A Terminological Study. *Geoforum* 8:43-46.

Turner, B. L. II. 1997. Spirals, Bridges and Tunnels: Engaging Human-Environment Perspectives in Geography. *Ecumene* 4:196-217.

Turner, B. L. II, and Karl W. Butzer. 1992. The Columbian Encounter and Land-Use Change. *Environment* 34 (8):16-20, 37-44.

Turner, B. L. II, William C. Clark, Robert W. Kates, John F. Richards, Jessica T. Mathews, and William B. Meyer, eds. 1990. *The Earth as Transformed by Human Action: Global and Regional Changes in the Biosphere Over the Past 300 Years.* Cambridge: Cambridge University Press.

Turner, Matthew. 1993. Overstocking the Range: A Critical Analysis of the Environmental Science of Sahelian Pastoralism. *Economic Geography* 69:402-21.

UN (United Nations). 1992. *Rio Declaration and Forest Principles (Final Text).* New York: United Nations.

———. 1993. *Agenda 21: The United Nations Programme of Action from Rio.* New York: United Nations.

Van Young, Eric. 1983. Mexican Rural History Since Chevalier: The Historiography of the Colonial Hacienda. *Latin American Research Review* 18 (3):5-61

Vance, James E. 1970. *The Merchant's World: The Geography of Wholesaling.* Englewood Cliffs: Prentice-Hall.

Vázquez de Espinosa, Antonio. 1948. *Compendio y Descripción de las Indias Occidentales.* Washington, D.C.: Smithsonian Institution.

Velasco, Juan López de. 1971. *Geografía y Descripción Universal de las Indias.* Madrid: Atlas.

Velázquez, Primo Feliciano, trans. 1945. *Codice Chimalpopoca.* Mexico City: Universidad Nacional Autónoma de México.

Warren, D. M. 1999. Indigenous Knowledge for Agricultural Development. In *Traditional and Modern Natural Resource Management in Latin America,* edited by F. J. Pichón, J. E. Uquillas, and J. Frechione, pp. 197-211. Pittsburgh: University of Pittsburgh Press.

Warren, D. M., L. J. Slikkerveerand, D. Brokensha, eds. 1995. *The Cultural Dimension of Development: Indigenous Knowledge Systems.* London: Intermediate Technology Publications.

Warren, J. Benedict. 1973. An Introductory Survey of Secular Writings in the European Tradition on Colonial Middle America, 1503-1818. In *Guide to Ethnohistorical Sources, Part 2, The Handbook of Middle American Indians,* vol. 13, edited by Howard F. Cline, 42-137. Austin: University of Texas Press.

Watts, D. 1987. *The West Indies: Patterns of Development, Culture, and Environmental Change Since 1492.* Cambridge: Cambridge University Press.

WCED (World Commission on Environment and Development). 1987. *Our Common Future*. Oxford: Oxford University Press.

West, Robert C. 1949. *The Mining Community in Northern New Spain: The Parral Mining District, Ibero-Americana*, no. 30. Berkeley: University of California Press.

———. 1970. Population Densities and Agricultural Practices in Pre-Columbian Mexico, with Emphasis on Semi-Terracing. *Proceedings of the XXXVIII International Congress of Americanists, Stuttgart-München, 1968* 2:361-69.

White, David H. 1987. Stocking Rate. In *Ecosystems of the World 17B, Managed Grasslands*, edited by R. W. Snaydon, 227-38. Amsterdam: Elsevier.

Whitmore, Thomas M. 1992. *Disease and Death in Early Colonial Mexico, Simulating Amerindian Depopulation*. Boulder: Westview Press.

Widmer, Rolf S. 1990. *Conquista y Despertar de las Costas de la Mar del Sur (1521-1684)*. Mexico City: Consejo Nacional para la Cultura y las Artes.

Wilbanks, Thomas J. 1994. "Sustainable Development" in Geographic Perspective. *Annals of the Association of American Geographers* 84:541-56.

Wilken, Gene C. 1970. The Ecology of Gathering in a Mexican Farming Region. *Economic Botany* 24:286-95.

———. 1987. *Good Farmers: Traditional Agricultural Resource Management in Mexico and Central America*. Berkeley: University of California Press.

Wilkerson, S. J. K. 1983. So Green and Like a Garden: Intensive Agriculture in Ancient Veracruz. In *Drained Field Agriculture in Central and South America*, edited by J. P. Darch, 55-90. Oxford: British Archaeological Reports.

Willems-Braun, Bruce. 1997. Buried Epistemologies: The Politics of Nature in (Post)colonial British Columbia. *Annals of the Association of American Geographers* 87:3-31.

Wilson, L. L., and J. C. Burns. 1973. Utilization of Forages with Beef Cows. In *Forages: The Science of Grassland Agriculture*, edited by Maurice E. Heath, Darrel S. Metcalfe, and Robert F. Barnes, 677-89. Ames: Iowa State University Press.

Winfield Capitaine, Fernando, ed. 1984. *Esclavos en el Archivo Notarial de Xalapa, Veracruz, 1668-1699*. Xalapa: Universidad Veracruzana.

Wittfogel, K. A. 1972. The Hydraulic Approach to Pre-Spanish Mesoamerica. In *Chronology and Irrigation, Prehistory of the Tehuacán Valley*, vol. 4, edited by F. Johnson, 59-80. Austin: University of Texas Press.

Wobeser, Gisela von. 1989. *La Formación de la Hacienda en la Epoca Colonial*. Mexico City: Universidad Nacional Autónoma de México.

Wolf, Eric R. 1959. *Sons of the Shaking Earth*. Chicago: University of Chicago Press.

———. 1982. *Europe and the People Without History*. Berkeley: University of California Press.

Wolfe, Patrick. 1997. History and Imperialism: A Century of Theory, from Marx to Postcolonialism. *American Historical Review* 102:388-420.

Wright, Angus. 1990. *The Death of Ramón González: The Modern Agricultural Dilemma*. Austin: University of Texas Press.

Wright, John K. 1947. Terrae Incognitae: The Place of the Imagination in Geography. *Annals of the Association of American Geographers* 37:1-15.

Yapa, Lakshman. 1996. Innovation Diffusion and Paradigms of Development. In *Concepts in Human Geography*, edited by Carville Earle, Kent Mathewson, and Martin S. Kenzer, 231-70. Lanham, Md.: Rowman & Littlefield.

Zambardino, Rudolpho A. 1980. Mexico's Population in the Sixteenth Century: Demographic Anomaly or Mathematical Illusion? *Journal of Interdisciplinary History* 11:1-27.

Zavala, Silvio. 1935. *La Encomienda Indiana*. Madrid: Imprenta Helenica.

Zavala, Silvio, and María Castelo, eds. 1939-n.d. *Fuentes para la Historia del Trabajo en Nueva España*. 8 vols. Mexico City: Fondo de Cultura Económica.

Zea, Leopoldo. 1975. *El Positivismo en México: Nacimiento, Apogeo y Decadencia*. Mexico City: Fondo de Cultura Económica.

Zimmerer, Karl S. 1994. Human Geography and the "New Ecology": The Prospect and Promise of Integration. *Annals of the Association of American Geographers* 84:108-25.

———. 1996. *Changing Fortunes: Biodiversity and Peasant Livelihood in the Peruvian Andes*. Berkeley: University of California Press.

Zimmerer, Karl S., and Kenneth R. Young, eds. 1998. *Nature's Geography: New Lessons for Conservation in Developing Countries*. Madison: University of Wisconsin Press.

Zorita, Alonso de. 1963. *The Lords of New Spain: The Brief and Summary Relation of the Lords of New Spain*. Translated by Benjamin Keen. London: Phoenix House.

Index

About the Author

Andrew Sluyter is assistant professor in the ecology and geography programs of the Pennsylvania State University. He has graduate degrees from the University of British Columbia and the University of Texas at Austin. His work has appeared in the *Annals of the Association of American Geographers*, *Geographical Review*, *Environmental History*, *Latin American Antiquity*, and other scholarly journals.